Sociology

Classes in Modern Society

Critics of Society: Radical Thought
in North America

T. B. Bottomore
SOCIOLOGY
A Guide to Problems and Literature

PANTHEON BOOKS

A Division of Random House, New York

For Mary

Preface to Second Edition

In the few years that have passed since the first edition of this book was published much has changed in sociology and in the state of society. A more radical intellectual temper and new radical movements emerged during the 1960s—in the advanced industrial countries, whether their economic and political régimes are capitalist or socialist in character, and in the countries which are making the transition from an agrarian to an industrial economy. As a result, sociologists have become more aware of the elements of conflict and change in social life; their interest in historical and comparative studies has revived; and they have turned their attention once more to large social issues of the kind which preoccupied the founding fathers of the discipline. There is now, unmistakably, a renaissance of the classical tradition in sociology, as it was fashioned by Marx, Max Weber and Durkheim.

At the same time, the field of sociology has become more strictly defined and more professional. I do not mean this in the sense which a reviewer attributed to professional sociology when he described it as 'slick, bureaucratized, establishment-supported, computer-based, and *status quo* oriented sociology', although it is obvious that the subject has frequently been tempted too far in these directions. I mean that sociology now constitutes, in spite of the controversies which still rage within and about it, a distinct and recognized field of study, with its own increasingly refined models, approaches and methods of research; and that its rapid expansion, in numbers of teachers and students, reflects the need for extensive and critical social research carried out by qualified people, and for public administration informed by sociological knowledge, if modern societies are to be capable of dealing successfully and humanely with the complex problems arising from revolutionary advances in technology and of sustaining an elaborate network of social services. Many of the students of sociology are preparing, in fact, for careers in social administration or research. But they, as well as others who have no such professional aim in mind, may also study the subject for the equally good reason that it will extend systematically their comprehension of human life, and so help them to live and struggle in a world in which there are multiplying uncertainties and, on the

9

other side, expanding opportunities for the individual choice of a style of life.

It was in part the desire to depict a wide variety of forms of social life and to show the uses of a historical and comparative method, in part the fact that the original idea for this book came from a suggestion that it would be valuable to expound the concepts and methods of sociology in relation to the culture and institutions of a society belonging to quite a different sphere of civilization from that of Western Europe, which led me to devote a good deal of attention, in the first edition, to some aspects of social structure and social change in India. In the present edition I have devoted rather less space to India, but at the same time I have broadened the scope of the book to deal more comprehensively with the developing countries, taking into consideration not only their internal problems of development and modernization, but also the relations between them and the industrial countries. These relations are the focal point of some of the most important social issues of the present day: the contrast between 'affluent' and 'proletarian' nations, which merges into the problems of racial discrimination and race conflict; the transfer of revolutionary aspirations and movements from the industrial to the developing countries and their changed political significance as a result of this metamorphosis; the emergence of new forms of empire. I discuss some aspects of these questions in a new chapter dealing with the role of force in social life, and in an extended discussion of the problems of developing countries in the chapters devoted to social change.

These new problems, superimposed upon the older issues of class, democracy and socialism in the Western industrial countries, have arisen also in a new context—that of the 'global village' in which the interdependence of societies is much greater than ever before in human history. It is all the more necessary then, that sociologists should hold to the original conception which inspired their discipline; namely, to see men's social life whole and to be continually aware of the system of social relations, ramifying in time and space, within which every human action is set.

T.B.B.

September 1970

Contents

CONTENTS

Part I

THE SCOPE AND METHODS OF SOCIOLOGY

Chapter 1

THE STUDY OF SOCIETY

'Contemplating all the men of the world, who come together in
society to work, struggle and better themselves, cannot but
please you more than any other thing.' Antonio Gramsci, in a
letter from prison to his son Delio.

For thousands of years men have observed and reflected upon the
societies and groups in which they live. Yet sociology is a modern
science, not much more than a century old. Auguste Comte, in his
classification of the sciences, made sociology both logically and
chronologically posterior to the other sciences, as the least general
and most complex of all, while one of the most eminent of modern
anthropologists observed, much later, that 'the science of human
society is as yet in its extreme infancy'.[1]

It is true that we can find, in the writings of philosophers, religious
teachers and legislators of all civilizations and epochs, observations
and ideas which are relevant to modern sociology. Kautilya's
Arthashástra and Aristotle's *Politics* analyse political systems in
ways which are still of interest to the sociologist. Nevertheless, there
is a real sense in which a new science of society, and not merely a
new name,[2] was created in the nineteenth century. It is worthwhile
to consider the circumstances in which this happened, and to
examine the characteristics which distinguish sociology from earlier
social thought.[3]

[1] A. R. Radcliffe-Brown, *Structure and Function in Primitive Society* (1952).

[2] It was Comte who named the new science *Sociology*. At one time he 'regretted
the hybrid character' of the word, derived from the Latin *socius* and the Greek
logos, but later suggested that 'there is a compensation . . . for this etymological
defect, in the fact that it recalls the two historical sources—the one intellectual,
the other social—from which modern civilization has sprung'. *System of Positive
Polity* (trans. J. H. Bridges) Vol. I, p. 326.

[3] The general histories of social thought have emphasized unduly its continuity; and there have been lacking, in particular, studies of the modern social
sciences which would illuminate their origins in the manner of H. Butterfield's
account of the natural sciences in his book *The Origins of Modern Science*
(1950), where the repercussions of a radical change in men's attitude to the

The conditions which gave rise to sociology were both intellectual and social, and I shall consider these two aspects in turn. Naturally, they were interwoven, and an adequate sociological history of sociology, which has not yet been attempted, would have to take account of these interconnections. In this brief introduction I can only mention some of the more important factors.

The chief intellectual antecedents of sociology are not difficult to identify. 'Broadly it may be said that sociology has had a fourfold origin in political philosophy, the philosophy of history, biological theories of evolution, and the movements for social and political reform which found it necessary to undertake surveys of social conditions.'[1] Two of these, the philosophy of history and the social survey, were particularly important at the outset. They were themselves latecomers in the intellectual history of man.

The philosophy of history as a distinct branch of speculation is a creation of the eighteenth century.[2] Among its founders were the Abbé de Saint-Pierre, and Giambattista Vico. The general idea of progress which they helped to formulate profoundly influenced men's conception of history, and is reflected in the writings of Montesquieu and Voltaire in France, of Herder in Germany, and of a group of Scottish philosophers and historians of the latter part of the eighteenth century, Ferguson, Millar, Robertson and others. This new historical attitude is clearly expressed in a passage in Dugald Stewart's 'Memoir of Adam Smith',[3] 'When, in such a period of society as that in which we live, we compare our intellectual acquirements, our opinions, manners and institutions, with those which prevail among rude tribes, it cannot fail to occur to us as an interesting question, by what gradual steps the transition has been made from the first simple efforts of uncultivated nature, to a state of things so wonderfully artificial and complicated.' Stewart goes on to say that information is lacking on many stages of this

physical world are given prominence. However, in some recent works—notably Raymond Aron's *Main Currents in Sociological Thought* and Robert Nisbet's *The Sociological Tradition*—a similar approach has begun to reveal the sources of sociology by relating its appearance to the rise of industrial capitalism and the changed conceptions of social life which this provoked.

[1] M. Ginsberg, *Reason and Unreason in Society* (1947), p. 2.

[2] We must except the work of the fourteenth century Arab philosopher and historian, Ibn Khaldûn. His *Muqadimma* (entitled *An Introduction to History* in the English translation by Franz Rosenthal, Pantheon Books, 1958) is remarkable in expounding a theory of history which anticipates that of the European eighteenth century writers, and even Marx; but also as the work of an exceptional man who had neither predecessors nor followers. See C. Issawi, *An Arab Philosophy of History* (2nd ed. 1955).

[3] Dugald Stewart, *Works*, Vol. 10, pp. 33–4.

progress, and that its place must be taken by speculation based on the 'known principles of human nature'. 'To this species of philosophical investigation, which has no appropriated name in our language, I shall take the liberty of giving the title of *Theoretical* or *Conjectural* History, an expression which coincides pretty nearly in its meaning with that of *Natural History* as employed by Mr Hume, and with what some French writers have called *Histoire Raisonnée.*'

In the early part of the nineteenth century the philosophy of history became an important intellectual influence through the writings of Hegel and of Saint-Simon.[1] From these two thinkers stems the work of Marx and Comte, and thus some of the important strands in modern sociology. We may briefly assess the contributions of the philosophy of history to sociology as having been, on the philosophical side, the notions of development and progress, and on the scientific side, the concepts of historical periods and social types. It was the philosophical historians who were largely responsible for the new conception of society as something more than 'political society' or the state. They were concerned with the whole range of social institutions, and made a careful distinction between the state and what they called 'civil society'. Adam Ferguson's *Essay on the History of Civil Society* (1767) is perhaps the best example of this approach; in its German translation it seems to have provided Hegel with his terminology and influenced his approach in his early writings on society. Ferguson, in this essay and in later writings, discusses the nature of society, population, family and kinship, the distinctions of rank, property, government, custom, morality and law; that is, he treats society as a system of interrelated institutions. Furthermore, he is concerned to classify societies into types, and to distinguish stages in social development. Similar features are to be found in many of the writings of those whom I have called the philosophical historians; they represent a remarkable unanimity and an abrupt change in the direction of men's interest in the study of human society. These features re-appear in the nineteenth century in the work of the early sociologists, Comte, Marx, and Spencer.

A second important element in modern sociology is provided by the social survey, which itself had two sources. One was the growing conviction that the methods of the natural sciences should and could be extended to the study of human affairs; that human phenomena

[1] For accounts of the development of the philosophy of history and studies of some of the writers mentioned above, see R. Flint, *History of the Philosophy of History* (1893) and J. B. Bury, *The Idea of Progress* (1920).

could be classified and measured. The other was the concern with poverty (the 'social problem'), following the recognition that, in industrial societies, poverty was no longer a natural phenomenon, an affliction of nature or of providence, but was the result of human ignorance or of exploitation. Under these two influences, the prestige of natural science and the movements for social reform, the social survey came to occupy an important place in the new science of society. Its progress can best be traced in the industrial societies of Western Europe, in such pioneer works as Sir John Sinclair's *Statistical Account of Scotland* (21 vols. 1791-9), and Sir F. M. Eden's *The State of the Poor* (3 vols. 1797), in Condorcet's attempts to work out a 'mathématique sociale',[1] in Quételet's 'physique sociale';[2] and in later studies such as Le Play, *Les ouvriers Européens* (1855, 2nd enlarged edn., 1877-9), and Booth, *Life and Labour of the People in London* (1891-1903). The social survey has remained one of the principal methods of sociological enquiry.

These intellectual movements, the philosophy of history and the social survey, were not isolated from the social circumstances of the eighteenth and nineteenth centuries in Western Europe. The new interest in history and in social development was aroused by the rapidity and profundity of social change, and by the contrast of cultures which the voyages of discovery brought to men's attention. The philosophy of history was not merely a child of thought; it was born also of two revolutions, the industrial revolution in England, and the political revolution in France. Similarly, the social survey did not emerge only from the ambition of applying the methods of natural science to the human world, but from a new conception of social evils, itself influenced by the material possibilities of an industrial society. A social survey, of poverty or any other social problem, only makes sense if it is believed that something can be done to remove or mitigate such evils. It was, I think, the existence of widespread poverty in the midst of great and growing productive powers which was responsible for the change of outlook whereby poverty ceased to be a natural problem (or a natural condition) and became a social problem, open to study and amelioration. This was, at the least, an important element in the conviction that exact knowledge might be applied in social reform; and later, that as man had established an ever more complete control over his physical environment so he might come to control his social environment.

[1] See G. G. Granger, *La mathématique sociale du Marquis de Condorcet* (Paris, 1956).

[2] A. Quételet, *Sur l'homme et le développement de ses facultés ou essai de physique sociale* (1835).

So far I have considered the liberal and radical elements in socio-logical thought, which emerged directly from the Enlightenment and the French Revolution. In some recent writing, however, much greater prominence is given to the ideas which were contributed to sociology by the thinkers of the conservative and romantic reaction, especially de Bonald and de Maistre, through their influence upon Saint-Simon, Comte and de Tocqueville. Robert Nisbet, for example, refers to the reorientation of social thought which gave rise to sociology as '. . . a reaction of traditionalism against analytical reason', and he sums up his view as follows: 'The paradox of socio-logy . . . lies in the fact that although it falls, in its objectives and in the political and scientific values of its principal figures, in the mainstream of modernism, its essential concepts and its implicit perspectives place it much closer, generally speaking, to philosophical conservatism. Community, authority, tradition, the sacred: these are primary conservative preoccupations in the age . . .'. According to Nisbet, they also constitute the important 'unit-ideas' of sociology.[1] A similar argument has been propounded by Marcuse, who contrasts the conservatism of Comte's sociological positivism with the radicalism of 'critical reason' which he takes to be the essential feature of Hegel's social theory, achieving its full expression in Marxist thought.[2]

The influence of the conservative thinkers upon sociology is not in doubt. Saint-Simon's distinction between 'critical' and 'organic' periods in history, and his advocacy of a new moral doctrine to bind men together in the post-revolutionary industrial society, reflect this influence, and at the same time prepare the way for Comte's concern with the re-establishment of 'social order'. But Saint-Simon was also the source of other ideas, concerning class and property, which gave rise to a different style of thought in the socialism of the Saint-Simonians and later of Karl Marx. There is a dual tradition in sociological thought, and the diverse elements which went to make it need to be carefully distinguished.

The pre-history of sociology as I have sketched it can be assigned to a period of about one hundred years, roughly from 1750 to 1850; or, let us say, from the publication of Montesquieu's *De l'esprit des lois* up to the work of Comte and the early writings of Spencer and Marx. The formative period of sociology as a distinct science occupies the second half of the nineteenth century and the early

[1] Robert A. Nisbet, *The Sociological Tradition* (London, 1967), Chapter 1.
[2] Herbert Marcuse, *Reason and Revolution: Hegel and the Rise of Social Theory* (New York, 1941), and subsequently in *One Dimensional Man: Studies in the Ideology of Advanced Industrial Society* (New York, 1964).

part of the twentieth century.[1] We can see from this brief survey of its origins some of the characteristics which early sociology assumed. In the first place it was *encyclopaedic:* it was concerned with the whole social life of man and with the whole of human history. Secondly, under the influence of the philosophy of history, reinforced later by the biological theory of evolution, it was *evolutionary*, seeking to identify and account for the principal stages in social evolution. Thirdly, it was conceived generally as a *positive science*, similar in character to the natural sciences. In the eighteenth century the social sciences were conceived broadly upon the model of physics. Sociology, in the nineteenth century, was modelled upon biology, as is evident from the widely diffused conception of society as an organism, and from the attempts to formulate general laws of social evolution. Fourthly, in spite of its claim to be a general science, sociology dealt particularly with the social problems arising from the political and economic revolutions of the eighteenth century; it was above all *a science of the new industrial society.* Finally, it had an *ideological* as well as a scientific character; conservative and radical ideas entered into its formation, gave rise to conflicting theories, and provoked controversies which continue to the present day.

The wide claims made by the early sociological thinkers naturally aroused opposition, especially from those who were working in narrower and more specialized fields; among them historians, economists, and political scientists. It is doubtful whether, even at the present day, sociology has altogether succeeded in living down its early pretentiousness. But we should distinguish among the different claims which were made, and also make a distinction between the claims as to the scope of the subject and the claims as to its discoveries. No-one believes any longer that Comte or Spencer discovered the laws of social evolution (though some people still believe that Marx did). But it does not follow from this that Comte and Spencer (or, for unbelievers, Marx) were entirely mistaken about the scope of sociology, or that they made no important contributions to its advancement. It seems clear that there is a need for a social science which is concerned with society as a whole, or with total social structure. To say this, however, is to raise the

[1] An adequate history of this period has yet to be written. There are useful discussions of some aspects of the development of ideas (but not of research) in H. Stuart Hughes, *Consciousness and Society: The Reorientation of European Social Thought 1890–1930* (London, 1959); and in Raymond Aron, *German Sociology* (London, 1957), and *Main Currents in Sociological Thought*, Vol. II (London, 1967).

problem of how such a synoptic science can be pursued, and how it is to be related to the other social sciences.

The opposition to sociology in its early phase came largely from the feeling that it aimed, not at co-ordinating, but at absorbing, the other social sciences. In the work of later sociologists such ambitions are explicitly disclaimed. Hobhouse, for example, conceived sociology as 'a science which has the whole social life of man as its sphere', and not as another specialism, but he viewed its relation with the other social sciences as one of mutual exchange and mutual stimulation. '. . . General Sociology is neither a separate science complete in itself before specialism begins, nor it it a mere synthesis of the social sciences consisting in a mechanical juxtaposition of their results. It is rather a vitalizing principle that runs through all social investigation, nourishing and nourished by it in turn, stimulating inquiry, correlating results, exhibiting the life of the whole in the parts and returning from the study of the parts to a fuller comprehension of the whole.'[1]

Similarly Durkheim, although he was especially concerned to emphasize the autonomy of sociology and to specify the particular range of phenomena with which it should deal, did not suppose that sociology could be an encyclopaedic science, or that it could be pursued in isolation from the other social sciences. He envisaged, in much the same way as Hobhouse, a diffusion of the sociological approach, and thus a transformation of the special social sciences from within. Only at a later stage did he think that it might be possible to construct a general sociology, comprising more general laws based upon the laws established in the particular fields of the special sciences.[2] In his editorial preface to the first volume of the *Année Sociologique*, Durkheim explained that 'our efforts will tend especially to promote studies dealing with very limited subjects, and belonging to special branches of sociology. For since general sociology can only be the synthesis of these special sciences, since it can consist only in a comparison of their most general results, it is only possible to the extent that these sciences are developed'.[3]

It can hardly be claimed that even the more modest aims which Hobhouse and Durkheim formulated have been achieved in a manner compelling general recognition. Of the two thinkers Durkheim was

[1] L. T. Hobhouse, Editorial Introduction, *The Sociological Review* (London) I (1), 1908.
[2] See especially Emile Durkheim, 'Sociologie et sciences sociales', *Revue Philosophique*, LV, 1903, and 'On the relation of Sociology to the social sciences and to philosophy', *Sociological Papers* (London), I, 1904.
[3] *Année Sociologique*, I, 1898, p. iv.

more successful in introducing the sociological approach into other social sciences. Many French scholars, in diverse disciplines, were influenced and stimulated by Durkheim's work; in law (Davy, Lévy-Bruhl and Duguit), in economics (F. Simiand), in anthropology (Mauss), in history (Marc Bloch, Granet), in linguistics (Cahen, Meillet)—to mention only the most prominent. Durkheim's ideas were conveyed not only through his own writings but also, and perhaps even more effectively, through the *Année Sociologique* which he founded in 1898. His conception of sociology was, so to speak, incarnated in the organization of the *Année Sociologigue*, each issue of which contained one or two original monographs, and a number of surveys from a sociological viewpoint of the year's writing in several distinct fields of social enquiry. Durkheim justified this arrangement by saying: 'Sociologists have, we believe, a pressing need to be regularly informed of researches made in the special sciences, the history of law, customs and religion, social statistics, the economic sciences, etc., for it is here that are to be found the materials from which sociology must be constructed'.[1]

In Germany, as Raymond Aron has noted,[2] sociology was at first rejected on account of its encyclopaedic character. Here, as elsewhere, an attempt was made to define and limit the field of sociology, in this case by the construction of an abstract science of the 'forms' of social life, largely under the influence of Georg Simmel, who formulated his conception of a science of society in the following terms: 'To separate, by scientific abstraction, these two factors of form and content which are in reality inseparably united; to detach by analysis the forms of interaction or sociation from their contents (through which alone these forms become social forms); and to bring them together systematically under a consistent scientific viewpoint—this seems to me the basis for the only, as well as the entire, possibility of a special science of society as such.'[3] But alongside these endeavours there was a continuing interest in historical interpretation and in the sociology of culture, stimulated especially by Marxism. These various interests were brought together in the writings of Max Weber, in whose work, as in that of Durkheim, we can see the same concern to promote a sociological approach

[1] *Année Sociologique*, I, 1898. The *Année Sociologique* was restarted, for the second time, after 1945 and retains its character as a valuable interdisciplinary journal.
[2] Raymond Aron, *German Sociology* (London, 1957), p. 1.
[3] In his essay 'The Problem of Sociology', translated in Kurt H. Wolff (ed.), *Georg Simmel, 1858–1918* (Columbus, Ohio, 1959). See also Lewis A. Coser (ed.), *Georg Simmel* (Englewood Cliffs, N.J., 1965), and my discussion of formal sociology on pp. 60–61 below.

within existing disciplines; in history, law, economics, politics, comparative religion.

Thus the classical sociologists aimed to establish the scope and methods of the new discipline, to show its worth by the investigation and explanation of major social phenomena, and to associate it closely with other social sciences. Later sociology departed, in certain respects, from these aims. During the 1940s and 1950s there developed, on one side, a preoccupation with the construction of elaborate conceptual schemes, exemplified most fully in the work of Talcott Parsons and his followers;[1] and on the other side, a fascination with the techniques of sociological enquiry, applied to small-scale, and sometimes trivial, problems. At the same time sociologists began to show a preference, in their research, for 'residual' subjects which did not fall clearly within the sphere of other social sciences, and which could be regarded, therefore, as strictly sociological in rather a narrow sense. A survey of American sociology in 1953–54 revealed that the two main areas of sociological work, in terms of the number of research projects in progress, were urban and community studies, and marriage and the family.[2] There was a similar trend in other countries.

These tendencies were encouraged, to some extent, by a desire to establish the autonomy, the 'professional' standing, and the scientific character of sociology as an academic discipline. Their actual result, however, in spite of some real advances (for example, in the study of social mobility), was rather to sow doubts about the value of the contribution which sociology might make either to social thought, or to the solution of practical social problems. Not a few sociologists gave the impression of 'lecturing on navigation while the ship is going down', to use W. H. Auden's phrase, which Robert Lynd quoted in his critical assessment of the social sciences, *Knowledge for What?*, published in 1939. In this book Lynd outlined an array of problems and a programme of research which were obviously relevant to the contemporary economic and political crisis in the Western industrial countries, as well as being close in spirit to the work of the classical sociologists, but his ideas were largely ignored for the next twenty years.

[1] For Parsons's original exposition of his conceptual scheme, which he called the 'theory of action', see *The Structure of Social Action* (New York, 1937). There is a concise later formulation of the theory in *Societies; Evolutionary and Comparative Perspectives* (Englewood Cliffs, N.J., 1966). I have criticized Parsons's scheme in an essay, 'Out of This World', in the *New York Review of Books*, XIII, 8, November 6, 1969.

[2] H. Zetterberg (ed.), *Sociology in the United States of America* (UNESCO, 1956), p. 18.

23

Within the last decade, however, sociology has taken a new direction, largely inspired at the outset by the work of C. Wright Mills. In his writings on social class and power in the USA, particularly in *White Collar* (1951) and *The Power Elite* (1956), Mills showed the value of historically orientated studies of fundamental structural elements in a complex industrial society; and in *The Sociological Imagination* (1959) he drew upon his own experience, as well as upon the sociological tradition of Marx and Weber in Europe, of Veblen and Lynd in America, to criticize prevailing trends in sociology and to advocate more adventurous, more imaginative studies of the momentous social and political problems of the postwar world. Since then, the kind of sociology which Mills espoused has enjoyed a revival, aided by a general upsurge of social criticism. Sociologists have begun to look again at the larger aspects of social structure and its changes; to examine the basic characteristics of industrial societies, to study the social implications of rapid advances in science and technology, to investigate the origins and consequences of social movements and revolutions, to consider the processes of industrialization and economic growth. In so doing they have adopted a more questioning and controversial attitude toward social events, much more in the spirit of the early sociologists; they are no longer satisfied with the received interpretations of modern societies, or with the mere description and classification of social phenomena just as they appear in a moment of time. One indication of this new outlook is the renewed interest in problems concerning the historical development of societies. Another, closely connected with the first, is the revival of Marxism, in undogmatic and much revised forms, as a general theory of society.

These recent developments have led to a much wider diffusion of the sociological approach in other social sciences. In political science there has long been an important area of sociological research, deriving from the work of Max Weber, Michels and Pareto, as well as from Marxist writing, but this has been greatly extended by more intensive studies of political parties, elites, pressure groups, voting behaviour, and bureaucracy, and more recently by studies of social movements (particularly the new radical movements of the 1960s) and of political changes in the developing countries.[1] In economics, which has its own highly developed

---

[1] The extent of sociological work in this field up to the mid-1950s can be seen in the following trend reports published in *Current Sociology*: Vol. III (4), 1954–5, 'Electoral Behaviour' by G. Dupeux; Vol. VI (2), 1957, 'Political Sociology' by R. Bendix and S. M. Lipset; Vol. XIII (2), 1964, 'Political Sociology in Eastern Europe' by J. Wiatr. For a brief discussion of more recent work see pp. 73-6 below.

theoretical system, the influence of sociology was much less marked after the eclipse of the German historical school of economics towards the end of the nineteenth century, except for Max Weber's great unfinished study of economy and society and the work of such eccentric scholars as Thorstein Veblen; but this situation has begun to change as sociological studies of the structure of industrial societies, of work and leisure, of industrial relations, of the administration of industrial enterprises, of occupations and education, make increasingly important contributions to the discussion of economic problems. In addition, the extension of economic planning, the concern with economic growth, the widespread recognition of the new problems which technological progress and growing prosperity themselves create, all bring into greater prominence the social aspects of economic activity and the consequent need for sociological research.

These instances are meant only to illustrate the nature of the sociological approach to the study of society, and to assist in defining more clearly the place of sociology among the social sciences.[1] Sociology was, with social anthropology, the first science to concern itself explicitly with social life as a totality, with the whole intricate network of social institutions and groups which constitute a society, instead of singling out a particular aspect of society for study. The basic conception, or directing idea, of sociology is, therefore, that of *social structure*: the systematic interrelation of forms of behaviour or action in particular societies. From this follows the sociologist's interest in those aspects of social life which had previously been studied only in a desultory manner, or which had been the object of philosophical reflection rather than empirical inquiry: the family and kinship, religion and morals, social stratification, urban life. As I noted earlier, the preoccupation with some of these 'residual' subjects may be carried to excess, but the study of such phenomena is an important part of sociology, and properly considered it is inseparable from the study of economic and political institutions.

In these matters social anthropologists have had certain advantages, due in part to the character of the societies which they have usually studied. Dealing with small-scale tribal societies they have been able to view them as totalities, and to investigate every aspect of behaviour, from the economic to the sexual, without fear of encroaching upon the domain of other specialized disciplines. At the same time, however, under the influence of new conceptions of anthropological method which became prevalent a generation

---

[1] The relations between sociology and other social sciences will be discussed more fully in Chapter 4.

ago,[1] they have tended to ignore the historical development of societies, and to reject comparative studies in order to concentrate upon giving a very full account of the social life of particular communities. Sociologists, on the other hand, carrying out their studies alongside already established disciplines—economics, political science, law, the history of religion—have made one of their main contributions by showing the connections between particular institutions or areas of social life and other elements in the social structure (for example, between religion and economic life, between property, class and politics), and by emphasizing the need for comparative studies which would reveal the constancy or variability of these connections across different types of society and different historical periods. More recently, sociology and social anthropology have drawn closer together. One important influence has been the rise of new nations from former colonial empires, and the efforts of these economically underdeveloped countries to bring about rapid economic growth, which pose a host of new problems, the study of which requires both knowledge of the traditional forms of society and a historical and comparative view of the social process of industrialization.

These changes in the world situation have brought into prominence another aspect of the study of human society. The great nineteenth century sociologists have often been criticized for their encyclopaedic and over-ambitious conceptions of the new science. But their view of the subject had one great advantage: it demanded a very wide knowledge of many different types of society and historical periods. Even though sociology was formed in Western Europe, in large measure as a response to the advent of industrial capitalist society, these early scholars did not confine their interest to the European societies. They regarded the whole range of human societies as constituting the subject matter of their science.[2] By contrast, recent sociology has been characterized by a much narrower field of interest. For the past two or three decades most sociologists have been deeply committed to studying very small segments of

[1] The functionalist method, which is associated particularly with the work of Malinowski and Radcliffe-Brown. See below, pp. 57–9.

[2] It is true that they were inclined to attribute a special importance to the Western societies, as having attained a stage of civilization which other societies would eventually reach after going through similar stages of development. In this way Comte justified the limitation of his main investigations to the 'elite or *avant garde* of humanity' (i.e. the European nations). The view was not entirely unfounded inasmuch as Western science and technology, and for that matter Western social doctrines such as Marxism, have been the principal factors in transforming the modern world.

their own national societies, and during this time the subject took on a distinctly ethnocentric, and even parochial, character. There were a number of reasons for this situation. The great accumulation of knowledge has undoubtedly made much more difficult the kind of wide-ranging scholarship which was displayed in the work of Max Weber and Durkheim, although a recent study such as Barrington Moore's *Social Origins of Dictatorship and Democracy* demonstrates that work of similar scope can still be successfully undertaken. Again, the greater involvement of sociologists in policy making has meant that they have tended to concentrate upon relatively small-scale practical problems within their own societies. The most important influence, however, was probably a change in the direction of intellectual interest, which showed itself in the adoption of a functionalist approach (involving the study of particular societies, or sub-systems within a society, from the aspect of their persistence and immutability), and the consequent abandonment of historical and comparative studies. This change itself was undoubtedly connected with the changed social situation in the Western democracies, which seemed to have attained a condition of relative stability, in their form as developed industrial societies, after the economic and political crises of the 1930s which culminated in the second world war.

The very recent revival of historical and comparative studies, which I commented upon earlier in this chapter, has been affected profoundly by the rise of the newly independent nations of the Third World. Just as the historian is obliged to take a new view of history as 'world history' in the light of the rise of Asian and African nations,[1] so also the sociologist has now to conceive his subject matter in a wider context. The formation of new political communities, economic development, urbanization, the transformation of the class structure, in the developing countries, show many similarities with earlier processes of change in Western societies, but they have also many distinctive features which must be taken into account in any comprehensive theory of social structure and social change. The expansion of sociological studies in the developing countries themselves, in response to their need for an overall view of the radical changes through which they are passing, provides a mass of new material and new ideas which can enter into a reconsideration of some of the fundamental problems of sociology.

The differences between 'encyclopaedists' and 'specialists' in sociology are not likely to be resolved quickly or easily. Human

[1] See, for a good discussion of this question, G. Barraclough, *An Introduction to Contemporary History* (London, 1964).

society is, as Comte declared, an extremely complex phenomenon, and the systematic study of it is evidently impossible without specialization. Yet the central ideas from which sociology developed require that each society should be conceived as a totality, itself embraced in the larger totality of an area of civilization and of a continuing historical process. The initial specialization of the social sciences depended upon easily observable and distinguishable features of society; the distinctions, for example, between political, economic, familial and religious institutions. The formation of sociology challenged this division and specialization, but it has nonetheless been reproduced within sociology itself. It may be that these traditional distinctions, in terms of the 'elements of social structure', are the most useful ones, but we should bear in mind two other considerations. First, as Gerth and Mills have observed, the autonomy of the separate institutions is often limited: 'In "less developed" societies than the mid-nineteenth century West, as well as in more developed societies, any one of the functions we have isolated may *not* have autonomous institutions serving it. Just what institutional orders exist in a more or less autonomous way is a matter to be investigated in any given society.'[1] Secondly, it is apparent that the increasing scientific concern with solving theoretical problems, and the interdisciplinary research which this often involves, is tending to bring about a new division of the subject matter, in terms of types of society, of microscopic and macroscopic phenomena, and so on. For purposes of description and exposition it is still convenient to deal with social phenomena under the traditional headings, but we should not assume that the scientific division of labour will always follow these lines, or that the presently existing specialization of research will prove ultimately to be the most fruitful one.

[1] Hans Gerth and C. Wright Mills, *Character and Social Structure* (London, 1954), p. 27.

Chapter 2

SOCIOLOGICAL THEORY

There is not, at the present time, any general body of sociological theory which has been validated or widely accepted. The early sociologists believed that they had discovered a number of fundamental 'social laws', principally laws of social evolution, which constituted a body of theory capable of guiding both thought and action. Modern sociologists have been, on the whole, more modest in their claims. They have been chiefly concerned to elucidate the character of the sociological approach (i.e. with methodology rather than theory), and to work out more precise concepts and more adequate classifications. In the latter activity they have formulated mainly that kind of limited generalization which is involved by the activity of classification itself. R. B. Braithwaite[1] makes a distinction between sciences at different stages of development, and says: 'If a science is in a highly developed stage, as in physics, the laws which have been established will form a hierarchy in which many special laws appear as logical consequences of a small number of highly general laws expressed in a very sophisticated manner; if the science is in an early stage of development—what is sometimes called its "natural-history" stage—the laws may be merely the generalizations involved in classifying things into various classes.'[2]

As to the so-called laws of social evolution, it has become doubtful whether they should be regarded as laws at all. K. R. Popper, in his discussion of 'historicism' observes: 'The evolution of life on earth, or of human society, is a unique historical process. Such a process, we may assume, proceeds in accordance with all kinds of

[1] *Scientific Explanation* (London, 1953).
[2] Cf. S. F. Nadel, *The Theory of Social Structure* (London, 1957), p. 1 '. . . only the most advanced sciences have reached this level of explanatory theory-building. But "theory" can also be understood in another, less ambitious, sense, namely as a body of propositions (still interconnected) which serve to *map out* the problem area . . . the propositions serve to classify phenomena, to analyse them into relevant units or indicate their interconnections and to define "rules of procedure" and "schemes of interpretation". "Theory" here equals conceptual scheme or logical framework, and it is in this sense that the present enquiry can be said to aim at a "theory".'

causal laws, for example, the laws of mechanics, of chemistry, of heredity and segregation, of natural selection, etc. Its description, however, is not a law, but only a singular historical statement. Universal laws make assertions concerning some unvarying order . . . i.e. concerning all processes of a certain kind. . . . But we cannot hope to test a universal hypothesis nor to find a natural law acceptable to science if we are for ever confined to the observation of one unique process.'[1] This does not mean that the evolutionary scheme has no value. In biology it led ultimately to the science of genetics and the formulation of universal laws of heredity. In sociology, the concept of evolution produced a good deal of confusion (between evolution, development and progress),[2] and was frequently a basis for philosophical rather than scientific thinking.[3] But it led also to some useful attempts at social classification, and to fruitful analyses of the processes of social change; results which the critics of historicism usually overlook. For the rejection of laws of social evolution does not mean that social change cannot be explained in terms of universal laws. Popper himself makes a distinction between 'laws' and 'trends', and suggests that universal laws of the type 'Whenever there are conditions of the kind c there will be a trend of the kind t', can be formulated.[4] It would not be difficult to reformulate many propositions of the classical sociologists, including Marx, in such terms. Let us take as an example Max Weber's statement of the relationship between the Protestant ethic and capitalism, which is already close to this formulation. We could say: Whenever there exist economic circumstances a, b, c (to be specified) and a calvinist-type social ethic (emphasizing the value of secular activity and the duty of abstinence), there will be a trend towards rationalized economic production aiming at maximum output with minimum cost. Supposing this to be, in a more precise formulation, a true universal law, we should be able, in any particular instance, to answer the question: how is this trend to be brought about?[5]

[1] K. R. Popper, *The Poverty of Historicism* (London, 1957), pp. 108–9. Durkheim, in his criticism of Comte expressed a similar idea; he remarked that Comte's 'law of three stages' was not only *not* a law, but was not even a reasonable hypothesis (since it could not be tested).

[2] See M. Ginsberg, *Essays in Sociology and Social Philosophy* (London, 1957), Vol. 1, 'On the concept of evolution in sociology'.

[3] For further discussion see Chapter 17 below.

[4] *Op. cit.*, p. 129.

[5] It is an important question for the economically under-developed countries. There is an attempt to specify the conditions for such a trend, using sociological as well as economic concepts, in W. Arthur Lewis, *The Theory of Economic Growth* (London, 1955).

It has been assumed, so far, that the social sciences are generalizing sciences which aim, like the natural sciences, at the establishment of a theoretical system, but which are as yet at a low stage of development. This is the view which has been taken by many, probably most, sociologists and social anthropologists, among the most eminent and explicit being Durkheim and Radcliffe-Brown.[1] It has been opposed by those philosophers and social theorists who have tried to make a rigorous distinction between the natural sciences on the one hand, and the historical and cultural sciences on the other, asserting that while the former aim at 'causal explanation' the latter aim at the 'interpretation' or 'understanding' of meaning. A major influence in shaping this second conception of the social sciences is the work of Wilhelm Dilthey, and especially his *Einleitung in die Geisteswissenschaften* (1883).[2] Dilthey's influence was particularly strong in German sociology, as can be seen from Max Weber's essays on the methods of the social sciences.[3] In England, Collingwood put forward views similar to those of Dilthey but had little direct influence on the social sciences. However, a number of English writers have claimed the social sciences as historical disciplines.[4] In Italy, Croce's historical philosophy was for a long time the dominant influence in social studies. The more Hegelian

[1] Cf. E. Durkheim, *The Rules of Sociological Method*, where it is argued that the business of the sociologist is to establish causal connections and causal laws; and A. R. Radcliffe-Brown, *A Natural Science of Society*, p. 3. 'The theses to be maintained here are that a theoretical science of human society is possible; that there can only be one such science. . . .'

[2] Dilthey's works have not been translated into English. There is, however, a good exposition and discussion of his views in two books by H. A. Hodges, *Wilhelm Dilthey; An Introduction* (London, 1944) and *The Philosophy of Wilhelm Dilthey* (London, 1952).

[3] Max Weber, *Methodology of the Social Sciences* (English translation, 1949) especially the essays, 'Critical Studies in the logic of the cultural sciences'. But Weber also believed that causal explanation was possible and necessary in sociology: '. . . it cannot be too strongly emphasized that any understanding of, or insight into, the [human] action in question must be carefully verified by the customary methods of causal inference . . .'.

[4] E. E. Evans-Pritchard in his *Social Anthropology* (London, 1951) says, 'In my view [social anthropology] is much more like certain branches of historical scholarship—social history and the history of institutions and of ideas as contrasted with narrative and political history—than it is like any of the natural sciences'. Sir A. M. Carr-Saunders, in a lecture on this theme (*Natural Science and Social Science*, Liverpool, 1958) argues that: 'Social science aims at interpreting social facts, that is the actions of men in relation to things, and to one another. These facts are entangled in a network so intricate that an attempt to discover invariable sequences must meet with failure. Such sequences, however, if discoverable, would not yield an interpretation of social facts in the light of our knowledge of people, and that is the interpretation which social science seeks.' (p. 11.)

31

of Marxist writers have also proposed a philosophical theory of history in opposition to sociology as a generalizing science.[1]

Over the past century this has been one of the fundamental controversies in the social sciences and especially in sociology. It is too large a question to be examined thoroughly here. It will be convenient to examine some aspects of the problem in discussing sociological methods in the next chapter, since a part of the dispute turns upon the question whether the methods of the natural sciences can appropriately be used in studying social phenomena. But there are some general points which may be rapidly reviewed.

One powerful argument against the scientific character of the social sciences has been that they have not in fact produced anything resembling a natural law. This might be answered (and often is) by referring to the youthfulness of the social sciences, and implying that they will eventually reach a higher theoretical level. But the answer is not entirely convincing; critics would say that the plea of immaturity has been made for a long time, without much sign of growth. Yet the criticism is exaggerated. In sociology, despite the complexity of the subject matter, causal connections and functional correlations have been established with a reasonable degree of probability. Durkheim's study of suicide and Max Weber's analysis of the relations between Protestantism and capitalism establish such connections, and there are other examples which we shall examine later. Moreover, those who dispute the scientific character of sociology are themselves open to criticism. If, as they hold, sociology is concerned with historical interpretation, or with interpreting the social actions of individuals on the basis of introspective knowledge of our own states of mind, the scientific sociologist may ask, in turn, what generally acceptable results have been produced by these methods, and whether in fact they go beyond the insights of poets and novelists.

In any case, those who believe that sociology is a scientific discipline are not obliged to claim that the formulation of laws constitutes its entire value. A part of sociology consists of exact description within an orderly framework of categories which involve only simple theorizing. Descriptive sociology is valuable in two ways. First, in the case of contemporary studies it provides information

He concludes the lecture by asserting a close affinity between social science and history; and 'since no one doubts that the place of history is among the humanities, the place of social science must be there also' (p. 15).

[1] One of the most influential writings of this tendency is G. Lukács, *Geschichte und Klassenbewusstsein* (1923). A more recent book which critically examines sociology from this point of view is H. Marcuse, *Reason and Revolution: Hegel and the Rise of Social Theory* (New York, 1941).

which is indispensable for the solution of practical problems and for the formulation of, and choice among, rational social policies. Secondly, where historical description, or the description of little known societies, is concerned it makes an important contribution to humane studies. For if a humane education consists in becoming sympathetically acquainted with a wide variety of human situations, strivings, ideals, and types of personality, then sociological studies are an essential element in such an education. Along with history, literary studies and, I would say, the historical aspects of the natural sciences, but in a more striking way than most of these, sociology makes us aware of the wealth and diversity of human life. It is, or should be, the centrepiece of modern humane studies, and a bridge between the sciences and the humanities.

Between those who regard sociology as a historical discipline and those who consider it a 'natural science of society', there seems to be a third view which, while emphasizing the scientific character of sociology, insists that the study of society requires a different theoretical model and different methods from those of the natural sciences. This point is, in certain respects, trivial. Every science must have an appropriate scheme of explanation and appropriate methods, but there may still be a fundamental unity of scientific method.[1] A more important point is that there may be a radical difference between social laws and natural laws. Many writers have drawn attention to the reflexive character of social laws, in discussing the 'self-fulfilling prophecy' and the 'self-destroying prophecy'.[2] The wider issue involved is whether, and in what sense, men can change the laws of social science. Alan Gewirth has examined the problem in a recent essay[3] and concludes that, 'in their *conditional* aspect, social laws can be changed by men in a sense in which natural ones cannot', for men can 'create new correlations of social variables by making new decisions which function as antecedent conditions from which new consequences follow'. The matter can be briefly (and inadequately) summarized as follows: in the natural sciences it is possible to conceive an ultimate closed theoretical system, while in the social sciences this is inconceivable because in human affairs genuine novelty can result from conscious volition. A similar point has been made by H. Marcuse in his study of the development of social theory. He condemns sociology, especially Comte's sociology, on account of its search for invariant laws and its con-

---

[1] This is discussed further in Chapter 3.

[2] See R. K. Merton, *Social Theory and Social Structure* (*op. cit.*).

[3] Alan Gewirth, 'Can men change laws of social science?', *Philosophy of Science*, XXI (3), July 1954.

ception of a unified science, because this eliminates man's freedom and rationality.[1]

These diverse views might lead to various conceptions of sociology: as historical interpretation, or as a 'critical philosophy' (Marcuse), as ultimately reducible to psychology plus historical knowledge, or as a generalizing science whose laws have a very limited range. Some of these points will be considered further in the next chapter. First, however, I propose to examine sociological theory as it has actually developed up to the present time, under three headings: *types of generalization, basic concepts and schemes of classification*, and *explanatory theories*.

Types of generalization

It is perhaps surprising, in view of the claims sometimes made for the scientific maturity of sociology, that there have been so few attempts to set out in a systematic way, and to evaluate, the different types of generalization to be found in sociological work. One such attempt is the brief discussion in M. Ginsberg's essay on 'The problems and methods of sociology'.[2] Ginsberg finds six types of generalization in social science:

1. Empirical correlations between concrete social phenomena (e.g. urban life and divorce rates).

2. Generalizations formulating the conditions under which institutions or other social formations arise (e.g. various accounts of the origins of capitalism).

3. Generalizations asserting that changes in given institutions are regularly associated with changes in other institutions (e.g. association between changes in class structure and other social changes, in Marx's theory).

4. Generalizations asserting rhythmical recurrences or phase-sequences of various kinds (e.g. attempts to distinguish the 'stages' of economic development, Bücher, Schmoller and others).

5. Generalizations describing the main trends in the evolution of humanity as a whole (e.g. Comte's law of the three stages, the Marxist theory of development from primitive society to communist society, Hobhouse's theory of social development).

6. Laws stating the implications of assumptions regarding human behaviour (e.g. some laws in economic theory).

It will be seen that these types of generalization are very different in range and level; and that they differ also in the extent to which

[1] H. Marcuse, *op. cit.*, pp. 340–59.
[2] *Reason and Unreason in Society* (London, 1947).

they can be regarded as validated. Those of the first type are empirical generalizations; many of them can be considered well established, but they have not been incorporated in a more general system of laws in such a way as to form part of a scientific theory. The generalizations of types (2) and (3) can be regarded as formulations of universal laws relating to trends, of the kind discussed earlier (p. 30). On the other hand, the generalizations of types (4) and (5) are not really theoretical generalizations; they are compounds of descriptive-historical statements and interpretations. Comte's law of the three stages and Hobhouse's theory of social development *describe* the growth of knowledge, the Marxist theory of social development *describes* the growth of technology and productive powers. All of them also *interpret* historical changes in terms of the phenomena which they emphasize. Finally, the generalizations of type (6) seem to occur only in economic theory. In sociology it is these very assumptions about human behaviour which are investigated.

Sociologists have shown relatively little interest in constructing broader generalizations from the empirical correlations which they have established. Yet it may well be possible to do this, as some examples will show. Durkheim, in a well-known study,[1] established a relationship between certain suicide rates and the degree of integration of individuals in a social group. Durkheim's methods and results have been criticized in some respects, but they have also been found useful and partly confirmed by later studies.[2] There are other social phenomena for which rates can be calculated (homicide and other types of crime, mental illness), and which might also be related in various ways to the degree of group integration. Thus, it may be possible to construct a more general law concerning social integration of which suicide rates would be one instance.

Another example may be taken from the study of social conflict. Simmel, in an essay on conflict,[3] formulated on the basis of general knowledge a number of propositions concerning conflict within and between social groups. These propositions have been expanded, revised and reformulated, and related to empirical research, in a recent study by Lewis Coser, *The Functions of Social Conflict*.[4]

[1] *Suicide* (1897, English translation, 1952).
[2] See, in particular, the essays by Jack D. Douglas, 'The Sociological Analysis of Social Meanings of Suicide', and A. Giddens, 'A Typology of Suicide', in *European Journal of Sociology*, VII (2), 1966.
[3] Recently published in an English translation by Kurt H. Wolff, along with another essay, in E. C. Hughes (ed.), *Conflict and The Web of Group Affiliations* (Glencoe, 1955).
[4] Glencoe, 1956.

Coser ends his study with some theoretical reflections upon the functions of conflict. It seems equally possible to use these propositions in causal explanation. Some attempts along these lines are summarized and examined in an essay by Jessie Bernard on 'The sociological study of conflict'.[1] Here again we can see the possibility of constructing general laws about the incidence and extent of conflict, and on the basis of such laws making statements about trends, or even definite predictions of the occurrence of conflict. Even at the present time it is, I think, possible to make rather simple predictions concerning the effects of particular changes upon the degree of conflict within a group; e.g. that if the group becomes engaged in external conflict, the intra-group conflict will usually diminish. Some experimental testing of hypotheses concerning intra-group conflict has been undertaken in studies of small groups.[2]

It may be argued, from what has been said above, that sociological theorizing should be increasingly devoted to the construction of broader generalizations from the empirical correlations which have been established. These generalizations could then be tested by further research. In this way sociology might come nearer to the cumulative theory construction which characterizes some other sciences, at least in those periods which T. S. Kuhn, in *The Structure of Scientific Revolutions* (2nd edn., Chicago, 1970) calls 'normal science'. Even so, the general 'progress' of sociology would still differ significantly from that of the physical sciences; in Kuhn's terms there have been no real 'scientific revolutions' in sociology, because there has not been, at any stage, a universally accepted paradigm which was subsequently overthrown.

Concepts and schemes of classification

It is in the fields of conceptualization and classification that sociology has so far been most productive. New concepts serve two purposes. In the first place, they distinguish, and draw attention to, classes of phenomena which had not hitherto been considered as forming separate classes. Secondly, the concepts serve as shorthand descriptions of the phenomena and as instruments for further analysis. In the course of this book the principal concepts will be introduced and discussed, but it may be useful to mention some of the more important ones at this stage. Such terms as *social structure, social*

---

[1] In *The Nature of Conflict* (UNESCO, 1957), pp. 33–117; see especially, pp. 64–73 'Mathematical studies in the sociology of conflict'. See also, Jessie Bernard, 'The theory of games of strategy as a modern sociology of conflict', *American Journal of Sociology*, LIX (5), 1954, pp. 411–24.

[2] See below, p. 102.

institution, role, function, kinship, primary group, social class, status, mobility, bureaucracy, ideology, community, association, are regularly and frequently used by all sociologists (and increasingly by other social scientists) and form part of the necessary equipment by means of which they organize their thinking, do research, and communicate the results of research. A large part of the teaching of sociology, in the early stages, consists in showing students how to use such terms appropriately.

It is true, however, that the concepts of sociology are still unsatisfactory. In the first place, it may be suggested that while many useful terms have been defined, we have not yet discovered those central concepts which would be most fruitful in the elaboration of systematic theory.[1] Secondly, it remains the case that many concepts are employed in different senses by different sociologists. Thirdly, the various concepts are not firmly linked by any web of description or explanation. It seems, indeed, that misunderstanding of the use of concepts is a primary source of difficulty. In some recent attempts to improve the 'conceptual framework' of sociology, and notably in that of Talcott Parsons and his collaborators, the whole emphasis is placed upon definition of concepts rather than upon the use of concepts in explanation.[2] This is a retrograde step by comparison with the work of Durkheim and Max Weber, both of whom introduced and defined concepts in the course of working out explanatory theories. Weber's exposition of his 'ideal type' method deals more clearly with this matter than any later writing, and had his ideas been followed up sociology would have been spared much confused and aimless discussion. In essentials his argument is that all definitions are in part arbitrary, and that the value of a definition (i.e. of a concept) is only to be determined by its fruitfulness in research and theorizing.

In the field of social classification much useful work has been done, although it has not yet resulted in any generally accepted schemes of classification. We may consider first the various attempts to classify societies, beginning with those of Comte, Spencer, Marx and Hobhouse. In these attempts different criteria are employed to distinguish one type of society from another; Marx employs an economic criterion, Spencer uses the criteria of size and complexity, while Comte and Hobhouse use principally the criterion of levels

[1] Cf. Radcliffe-Brown, *A Natural Science of Society:* while claiming that a theoretical science of human society is possible he goes on to say that 'such a science does not yet exist except in its elementary beginnings' and also that 'we have not yet thought of the important concepts for social science'.

[2] I have discussed this aspect of Parsons's work more fully in my essay, 'Out of This World', in *The New York Review of Books,* XIII (8), November 6, 1969.

of intellectual development. The actual classifications do not differ so widely, however, and all the writers I have mentioned attach importance to the economic structure as an element determining the type of social structure.[1] It seems doubtful today whether any really useful classification can be developed on the basis of a single criterion; and it may be that no single classification will serve all purposes. It is clear, for instance, that the classifications proposed by the early sociologists derived their meaning from the theories of social evolution with which they were connected. In view of present-day concern with industrial societies and processes of economic growth, and at the same time with the relative autonomy of economic and political institutions, it might be well to attempt a new classification of societies on the basis of their economic structure and to elaborate this by a sub-classification on the basis of political systems. Such an attempt might be helped by efforts to refine some of the crude classifications which are widely used by sociologists and anthropologists; e.g. the distinction between primitive and civilized societies, or that between developed and under-developed countries. Much more work has been devoted, in recent years, to such problems of classification, particularly in connection with the distinction between 'industrial' and 'developing' societies.[2]

In the classification of social groups there are many familiar distinctions; face-to-face and impersonal groups, primary and secondary groups, groups and quasi-groups, groups distinguished in terms of size (Simmel), etc. Many of these distinctions are illuminating and useful in sociological analysis; for example, that made between face-to-face groups and large impersonal associations, or Simmel's subtle analysis of the connections between the size of

[1] Hobhouse used an economic criterion exclusively in his attempt at a sub-classification of primitive societies: Hobhouse, Wheeler and Ginsberg, *The Material Culture and Social Institutions of the Simpler Peoples* (London, 1915). Comte and Spencer both proposed, besides their other classification, a distinction between 'militant' and 'industrial' societies which rests upon economic differences.

[2] See Raymond Aron, *18 Lectures on Industrial Society* (London, 1967), and *The Industrial Society* (London, 1967); Paul Halmos (ed.), *The Development of Industrial Societies*, Sociological Review Monograph No. 8 (Keele, October 1964). On the Marxist classification see S. Avineri, *Karl Marx on Colonialism and Modernization* (New York, 1970); Eric Hobsbawm's introduction to Karl Marx, *Pre-Capitalist Economic Formations* (London, 1964); and K. Wittfogel, *Oriental Despotism* (New Haven, 1957). A highly critical survey of sociological conceptions of developing countries is given by A. Gunder Frank in his essay, 'Sociology of Development and Underdevelopment of Sociology', *Catalyst* No. 3 (Buffalo, 1967). The types of society are discussed in a more general way by G. Gurvitch, *La vocation actuelle de la sociologie* (2nd edn., Paris, 1957), Vol. I, Chapter 7, 'Les types de société globale'.

groups, their structure, and the relationships among their members.[1] But these do not yet amount to a satisfactory typology of groups. In some recent writing there has been some attempt to advance beyond these elementary distinctions. Thus G. Gurvitch, in his *Vocation actuelle de la sociologie*, has proposed a complex set of criteria for classifying social groups; these criteria include some which were employed by earlier sociologists, such as size, duration, recruitment of members, etc., but also some new characteristics.[2] Although the scheme is set out in a very abstract fashion, Gurvitch shows, by an analysis of social class which is intended to exemplify its use, that it may be fruitful.

Finally, we should consider the attempts to classify social relationships. These have taken many different forms. There are, first, the various accounts of the major types of social bond. Hobhouse made a distinction between three broad 'types of social union', based respectively upon *kinship, authority* and *citizenship*. Durkheim distinguished two principal types of 'social solidarity', *mechanical* and *organic*. Tönnies also distinguished two types of social bond, which he termed *community* (*Gemeinschaft*) and *society* (*Gesellschaft*). Similarly, Sir Henry Maine made a distinction between societies based upon *status* and those based upon *contract*. These accounts of the types of social relationship which underly social union are not entirely divergent; there is clearly some affinity between the accounts given by Durkheim, Tönnies and Maine. Hobhouse's distinction is more narrowly political and is thus more similar in its aim to the distinction which Max Weber made between *traditional, charismatic* and *bureaucratic* types of authority; but the two schemes of classification are otherwise very different—the type of political system which Hobhouse terms 'citizenship', Weber terms 'bureaucracy', and these terms reflect a fundamental divergence in the focus of interest and in philosophical outlook.

If we look at the more general classifications, and especially that of Tönnies, it seems reasonable to suppose that they might be employed in differentiating between social groups, as well as between societies. Tönnies' distinction has in fact been widely used in this way; and it has also been revised and expanded by a number of writers who have sought a more adequate classification of the basic types of social relation. Thus Schmalenbach[3] distinguished three

[1] G. Simmel, 'The number of members as determining the sociological form of the group', *American Journal of Sociology*, VIII, 1902.

[2] For further discussion see Chapter 6.

[3] H. Schmalenbach, 'Die soziologische Kategorie des Bundes', *Dioskuren*, I, 1922.

major types, community, federation and society; and Gurvitch[1] has proposed a similar classification into communion, community and mass.

In this field of classification of social relations there are, secondly, the attempts to distinguish basic social relationships as such. The forerunner here is Simmel whose analyses of conflict, competition, authority, subordination, etc., influenced all later German sociologists. Simmel's distinctions were systematized by von Wiese[2] who attempted to classify all social relationships in terms of their tendency towards association, or dissociation, towards diminishing or increasing the social distance between individuals.

Finally, there are the classifications in terms of social action, which play a large part in contemporary sociology. Max Weber was the originator of this way of classifying social relationships,[3] and the distinction which he made between traditional action, affective action, action which is *wertrational* (in which a line of conduct is determined by absolute values), and action which is *zweckrational* (in which both ends and means are rationally calculated), has been the basis of most later work. Talcott Parsons has been foremost in expounding and developing Weber's typology.[4] The concept of social action has been claimed by some recent sociologists as the key concept in sociology,[5] but it has not yet proved very fruitful in the analysis of actual social systems. In Max Weber's own work the typology of social action was only one part of a much wider effort to classify social structures and institutions. Weber was a historian as well as a sociologist, or perhaps we may say a historical sociologist, who was extremely gifted in seizing upon the distinctive

[1] G. Gurvitch, *La vocation actuelle de la sociologie*, 2nd ed., Ch. 3.

[2] L. von Wiese, *Allgemeine Soziologie*, and 'Beziehungslehre' in *Handwörterbuch der Soziologie* (1931); for an English version of von Wiese's sociology see H. Becker, *Systematic Sociology* (1932).

[3] See M. Weber, *The Theory of Economic and Social Organization* (trans. Henderson and Parsons).

[4] Talcott Parsons, *The Structure of Social Action* (1937) which analyses the concept of social action in the work of Pareto, Durkheim, and especially Max Weber; and *The Social System* (1952) which expounds a 'general theory of action systems', relating types of action to types of social structure. Parsons has given a concise exposition of his theory of action in *Societies: Evolutionary and Comparative Perspectives* (Englewood Cliffs, N.J., 1966), Ch. 1. Weber's concept of action is discussed from other aspects in Raymond Aron, *German Sociology* (London, 1957), and in Julien Freund, *The Sociology of Max Weber* (New York, 1969).

[5] Cf. R. K. Merton, *Social Theory and Social Structure* (2nd edn., 1957); and W. J. H. Sprott, *Science and Social Action*, especially Ch. I where there is a very clear analysis of the concept of action and an exposition of the general theory based upon it.

features of particular historical periods, and types of society. It is this sense of history, and the feeling for historically existing societies, which is most obviously lacking in the work of those who have been concerned to develop theories of social action.

This brief survey indicates that while many useful distinctions have been made, an adequate classification of societies, social groups and social relationships has still not appeared. It should be added that the interest shown by sociologists in these problems has evidently waned until quite recently; the last major discussion of the different forms of classification is that by R. Steinmetz, published in the *Année Sociologique* for 1898–9. This loss of interest in the classification of societies, groups and relationships is connected with the neglect of explanatory theories in favour of conceptual clarification and functional analysis. However, a new starting point for classifying social phenomena has been found recently, as I have indicated, in the concern with the character of industrial societies and the changes in the economically underdeveloped societies; for in the first case we have to differentiate industrial societies from other types of society, both present and past, and in the second case, if we are to explain, and possibly control, events we need to distinguish between different types of underdeveloped society and different lines of change.

Explanatory theories

It may be well to begin with some remarks on scientific explanation. On the whole, recent writers on methodology have followed J. S. Mill's account of explanation: 'An individual fact is said to be explained by pointing out its cause, that is, by stating the law or laws of causation, of which its production is an instance. . . . And in a similar manner, a law or uniformity in nature is said to be explained, when another law or laws are pointed out, of which that law itself is but a case, and from which it could be deduced.'[1] L. S. Stebbing in *A Modern Introduction to Logic* (3rd edn., 1942) Ch. 20, and R. B. Braithwaite in *Scientific Explanation* (1953) Ch. I, say much the same thing. K. R. Popper in *The Logic of Scientific Discovery* (English translation, 1960), and in *The Poverty of Historicism* (1957) has proposed a modification of Mill's account in respect of 'individual facts'. He argues that 'a causal explanation of a certain *specific event* means deducing a statement describing this event from two kinds of premises: from some *universal laws*, and from some singular or specific statement which we may call the specific initial conditions'. This allows a distinction to be made

[1] J. S. Mill, *A System of Logic* (10th edn. 1879), Book III, Ch. 12.

between two types of causal explanation, scientific and historical; in scientific explanation attention is concentrated upon the relation between a particular fact and a universal law, whereas in historical explanation it is concentrated upon the relation between a particular fact and specific initial conditions.

Scientific explanation is causal in the above sense. But if we conceive explanation more generally as an answer to the question 'Why?', then we can see that it may take either of two forms: *causal* explanation which is of the kind 'Because of . . .' and *teleological* explanation which is of the kind 'In order that . . .'[1] The latter kind may be further differentiated, as it is by R. S. Peters who, in the course of a detailed examination of various explanations advanced in psychological theories, distinguishes between causal explanations, explanations in terms of purpose, and explanations in terms of end-states.[2] We have seen that many of the classical sociologists took the view that sociology, as a generalizing science, must aim at establishing causal connections and causal laws. On the other hand, the kind of explanation of human behaviour that first occurs to us is the teleological, in terms of purposes; and it is from this point of view that the advocates of 'interpretation' conduct their argument against a 'natural science of society'.

Between these two, the 'social-causal' and the 'individual-purposive', types of explanation we may locate those explanations which refer to end-states of society. The functionalist theory purports to explain social phenomena in terms of the part which they play in maintaining the existence of a society. This observation should at once be qualified by saying that one version of the functionalist theory, that of Malinowski, proposed to explain social phenomena by referring them to individual biological needs and 'derived cultural needs'. In practice, Malinowski oscillated between description and psychological explanations,[3] and the functionalist theory as he propounded it no longer has any adherents. As a sociological theory, functionalism originated with Durkheim, and the classical work of functionalist explanation is Durkheim's *The Elementary Forms of the Religious Life*. It should be noted, however, that Durkheim proposed two incompatible kinds of explanation, *causal* and *functional*, that he never resolved the question as to which of the two was most appropriate in sociology, or considered how they were

[1] R. B. Braithwaite, *op. cit.*

[2] R. S. Peters, *The Concept of Motivation* (London, 1958).

[3] For an acute criticism along these lines see Max Gluckman, *An Analysis of the Sociological Theories of B. Malinowski* (Rhodes-Livingstone Papers, No. 16, 1949).

related, and that for the most part he seemed, indeed, unaware that there was any question to resolve. It is true that in his earlier writings he observed that functional explanation alone was inadequate; the fact that a social phenomenon had a function did not account for its existence, which had to be explained in terms of efficient causes. But in later writings, he simply explained social phenomena by their functions, without qualification. Radcliffe-Brown largely followed him in this course, advocating causal explanation and a 'natural science of society', but also using the concept of social function, reformulated in a way which he believed, erroneously, eliminated its teleological implications: 'the *function* of any recurrent activity, such as the punishment of a crime, or a funeral ceremony, is the part it plays in the social life as a whole and therefore the contribution it makes to the maintenance of the structural continuity' (of a society).[1] More explicitly than Durkheim, Radcliffe-Brown distinguished different kinds of problems: the systematic investigation of social life involved, he thought, three sets of problems: (i) what kinds of social structure are there? (ii) how do social structures function? (iii) how do new types of social structure come into existence? But he did not show, any more than did Durkheim, that the answers to such questions could be brought within a single, rigorous theoretical system.

After Radcliffe-Brown's work, explanation in British social anthropology (and to some extent in social anthropology generally) came to consist in elucidating the functions of recurrent activities, or institutions, in a social system; and somewhat later, the same kind of explanation became prevalent in sociology through the influence of Talcott Parsons, R. K. Merton and others. But it may be questioned whether functionalism is a theory at all. First, it can be argued that the postulation of end-states may *never* be explanatory and that it is certainly *not always* explanatory. What we are given is description or re-description.[2] It may be noted here that in the biological sciences, where the notion of function has mainly been used, there has been a consistent development from functional description to causal explanation. Secondly, because the concept of function is based upon an analogy between social life and organic life, it may be argued that the analogy is not sufficiently close for functionalism, so far as it provides explanations at all, to provide valid explanations of social phenomena. The analogy presents several difficulties: societies change their structure while organisms

---

[1] 'On the concept of function in social science', *Structure and Function in Primitive Society* (London, 1952), pp. 178–87.
[2] See R. S. Peters, *op. cit.*, pp. 22 *sqq.*

do not; it is impossible to determine the health or sickness of societies in the way that this can be done for organisms, and consequently it is impossible to speak precisely about the 'normal' and 'pathological' functioning of the 'organs', or about 'function' and 'dysfunction' (in fact, all such ways of speaking about societies involve value judgments); it is difficult to determine the function of a social activity or institution with the same precision as the function of organs is determined in biology by the examination of numerous instances (and in the organic world there is, moreover, a one-to-one correspondence between organ and function which does not seem to hold in the social world). It follows from these difficulties: (i) that even if some functional explanations of social phenomena were valid, the range of explanation would be severely limited since the important phenomena of structural change could not be so explained; (ii) that we cannot in fact decide in many cases the contribution which a social activity makes to the maintenance of the social system, except in evaluative terms; and (iii) that we cannot easily assign a specific function to a particular social activity. On the last point E. A. Gellner has observed that there may exist in human societies 'functionless appendices', and that, in general, comparative study (including historical study) is necessary if we are even to attempt to verify a statement about the real function of an activity in any given society.[1]

In fact, functionalism as a theory in the sense which Durkheim and Radcliffe-Brown gave to it has been largely abandoned; and those who remain in some degree functionalists now recognize its limitations and justify it increasingly as being one among several useful approaches or methods in the study of society. It will be considered in this form in the next chapter. On the other hand, in the context of explanatory theories, the concept of function is now used frequently in its more acceptable mathematical sense, in which it is sought to show that specific social activities are functionally related, i.e. that x varies as y.

In the sociological work of the past two or three decades there has been much less concern with the construction of all-embracing theories than there was during the age of Weber and Durkheim. The work of Talcott Parsons may appear to be an exception, but Parsons has been largely concerned, in fact, with elucidating the conceptual structure in the thought of the classical sociologists, and with elaborating new concepts within the framework of his notion of 'social action'. He has not developed any comprehensive explanatory

[1] E. A. Gellner, 'Time and Theory in Social Anthropology', *Mind*, LXVII (266), April 1958, pp. 182–202.

theory, and his work has not given rise to a school of sociology characterized by new kinds of explanation of social events. Leaving aside these conceptual and methodological explorations, which are to be found in much recent Marxist writing as well as in Parsons, it may be said that by far the greater part of recent sociological work has been descriptive, 'interpretative', or confined to testing very limited 'commonsense' hypotheses. A few sociologists have given some attention to what R. K. Merton has called 'theories of the middle range'.[1] Merton defines these as 'theories intermediate to the minor working hypotheses evolved in abundance during the day-by-day routines of research, and the all-inclusive speculations comprising a master conceptual scheme from which it is hoped to derive a very large number of empirically observed uniformities of social behaviour'. He gives as examples of middle-range theories, concerned with a limited range of data, which might be developed at the present time, theories of class dynamics, of conflicting group pressures, of the flow of power and the exercise of interpersonal influence. We shall examine in later chapters, some theories of this kind, and I have already suggested a number of other areas in which such theories might be developed; e.g. theories of social conflict, and of group integration. There are also indications that a socio-logical theory of industrialization, or economic growth, is being worked out.[2]

It is a hopeful sign that attention is again being paid to theories which keep close to the empirical data, and thus to some kind of verification. But sociological theory still suffers from an excessive specialization which has separated theory and research, and from some misconceptions about the nature of scientific theory. Social anthropology has benefited greatly from the institutionalization of field-work, which results in the anthropologist being obliged to test his concepts, hypotheses or theories in research which he carries out for himself. In sociology, on the other hand, it has been all too easy for an individual to choose between theory and research, and for theorists to spin their intricate webs in the expectation or hope that these will some day (and by someone else) be attached to the empirical world. But there has been a more radical defect in both

[1] R. K. Merton, *Social Theory and Social Structure* (2nd edn., 1957), Introduction.

[2] I shall examine this theory more fully in Chapter 17. For a preliminary account see my essay 'Recent Theories of Development', *European Journal of Sociology*, III (1962), and the critical survey of recent work by A. Gunder Frank, 'Sociology of Development and Underdevelopment of Sociology', *Catalyst* (Buffalo, 1967).

social anthropology and sociology, which consists in the failure to take seriously the preliminary stage of formulating a theoretical problem. In this respect, there is still much to be learned from Marx, Durkheim and Max Weber, all of whom understood very well that a science of society must begin, as does every science, by posing questions. Durkheim's major works, in particular—within the limits set by the means of investigation available to him, and by his specific theoretical orientation—are exemplary models of scientific enquiry and exposition; in each case the theoretical problem is first clearly stated, then the existing explanations are reviewed and criticized, and finally Durkheim presents his own solution, with the supporting evidence. His studies are supplemented in several cases with a discussion of the practical implications of his theoretical conclusions and discoveries. It would be difficult to find, in later sociology, many studies which formulate equally significant problems or proceed with equal scientific rigour.

This chapter may fittingly conclude with some general reflections upon the formulation of theoretical problems in sociology. Such problems may be derived from various sources. I have already noted that sociology itself emerged as a response to the social and intellectual concerns aroused by the economic and political revolutions which created modern capitalist society. The broadest theoretical questions were posed in terms of the origins and development of this new social system, the character of the new social groups (above all, social classes) which appeared in it, and the changes which it brought about in traditional social institutions and in men's social consciousness. Similarly, at the present time, theoretical questions may be derived from philosophical or speculative thought about social trends in the advanced industrial societies: about mass society and alienation; about the prospects for democracy or socialism, in relation to the actual historical development of collectivist societies; about the nature and aims of radical social movements, and the significance of the utopian political ideas which they often express. Or, on the other hand, such questions may arise from problems in the development or 'modernization' of underdeveloped countries.

A second source of theoretical problems, related to the foregoing, is provided by previously elaborated theories, which may be rejected or revised in the light of new discoveries and intepretations. Thus, Marx's theory of the development of production and the formation of social classes, Durkheim's theory of the division of labour and social solidarity, and Max Weber's theory of bureaucracy as an element in a comprehensive movement toward the total rationalization of social life, have all given rise to theoretical controversies which should lead eventually to the formulation of new theories.

Finally, theoretical questions may be derived from practical problems, especially when these are connected with broader issues of social policy. For example, the concern about poverty, in Britain and other industrial societies in the later nineteenth century, led to a number of fact-finding inquiries, which revealed both the extent of poverty and some of its principal causes, namely prolonged ill-health and unemployment. These inquiries were one factor stimulating an interest in the causes of unemployment, and this interest in turn was linked with more general theories of the trade cycle, of the operation of capitalist economic systems, and of social classes.

It is not the case, therefore, that we cannot see how to formulate the theoretical problems of sociology, but rather that most sociologists, since the age of the classical thinkers, have failed to give sufficient importance to this kind of theoretical work, have conceived their theories on too narrow a scale, or have been inhibited by doubts about the proper method of sociological inquiry and argument.

Chapter 3

SOCIOLOGICAL METHODS[1]

The French mathematician, Henri Poincaré, once referred to sociology as 'the science with the most methods and the fewest results'. This is an unduly harsh judgment. It is true that the work of sociologists over the past century has produced few, if any, high level generalizations which might form the elements of a body of scientific theory. Nevertheless, as was pointed out in the previous chapter, a good deal has been achieved at a lower level of scientific generalization, in providing a body of concepts, in classifying social types, and in establishing some elementary correlations between social phenomena. Perhaps the principal contribution to date, however, has been that of descriptive sociology (and anthropology). Many societies, institutional forms, and social groups have been exhaustively and precisely described, in a manner which makes possible the establishment of further correlations, and provides a basis both for classification and for interpretations of various kinds.

The truth in Poincaré's observation is that there has been much dispute over the proper methods of sociology, and an inclination on the part of each sociological theorist (like each metaphysician) to propose a new approach to the subject.

It will be useful to begin by outlining the controversy between those who think of sociology in terms of natural science and those who think of it as being quite different from any natural science and perhaps more like history or philosophy. What are the differences between 'nature' and 'society' which would require radically different methods of enquiry? They were first clearly stated by Dilthey,[2]

[1] This chapter deals with methods in the sense of scientific method, or the logic of sociology; not with the techniques of research. On the latter subject see such works as C. A. Moser, *Survey Methods in Social Investigation* (London, 1958); L. Festinger and D. Katz (eds.), *Research Methods in the Behavioral Sciences* (New York, 1953); H. H. Hyman, *et al.*, *Interviewing in Social Research* (Chicago, 1954); Johan Galtung, *Theory and Methods of Social Research* (London, 1967). Galtung's book is particularly interesting in that it attempts to connect research methods with theory construction.

[2] W. Dilthey, *op. cit.* For an account in English of Dilthey's views see the books by H. A. Hodges mentioned above.

and were then widely discussed by German historians and philosophers, especially Windelband and Rickert.[1] There are two major differences between the natural world and the social or cultural world. First, the natural world can only be observed and explained from the outside, while the world of human activity can be observed and comprehended from the inside, and is only intelligible because we ourselves belong to this world and have to do with the products of minds similar to our own. Secondly, the relations between phenomena of the natural world are mechanical relations of causality, whereas the relations between phenomena of the human world are relations of value and purpose. It follows from this, in Dilthey's view, that the 'human studies' should be concerned, not with the establishment of causal connections or the formulation of universal laws, but with the construction of typologies of personality and culture which would serve as the framework for understanding human strivings and purposes in different historical situations. I cannot here examine, in all its complexity, Dilthey's account of the methods of the 'human studies'. His approach has been re-stated recently, in an extreme form, in the arguments of F. A. Hayek against 'scientism',[2] and it is implicit in the views of Evans-Pritchard and Carr-Saunders which were quoted earlier. Dilthey's ideas are relevant to the distinction between causal explanation, explanation in terms of purpose, and explanation in terms of end-states which we have already examined, and much 'functional explanation' in social anthropology seems consonant with his conception of method. For example, Malinowski related the function of institutions to biological needs as modified by conscious purpose. The later functionalists, though remaining on the level of sociological explanation, without recourse to psychology or biology, have for the most part interpreted social institutions in terms of the values and purposes of individuals in the communities they have studied.

This *Methodenstreit* between positivists and anti-positivists, which began in Germany in the latter part of the nineteenth century and is reflected very clearly in Max Weber's methodological writings,[3] has been vigorously resumed during the last decade, in a number of different forms. In England, several writers have attempted to

[1] Some aspects of this debate are discussed in R. G. Collingwood, *The Idea of History* (Oxford, 1946), pp. 165–82.

[2] F. A. Hayek, 'Scientism and the study of society' in *The Counter-Revolution of Science*.

[3] Max Weber, *The Methodology of the Social Sciences* (Glencoe, 1949). This volume contains only a part of Weber's methodological writings, which were collected in *Gesammelte Aufsätze zur Wissenschaftslehre* (Tübingen, 1922).

reformulate a sharp distinction between the methods of the social sciences and those of the natural sciences. P. Winch, in *The Idea of a Social Science* (rev. edn., London, 1963), starts from Wittgenstein's philosophy and the notion that language expresses a way of life in order to argue that since sociology is concerned with the study of ways of life its method is close to, or indistinguishable from, that of linguistic philosophy. Another, less restrictive, philosophical view of the social sciences is provided by A. R. Louch, who argues persuasively in his *Explanation and Human Action* (Oxford, 1966) that the sciences which deal with human action are 'moral sciences', which require, not measurement and experiment, but appraisal, reflection, and detailed accounts of action in particular contexts. One of the best short statements of an anti-positivist view has been given by Isaiah Berlin in an essay on Vico: 'Vico . . . uncovered a species of knowing not previously clearly discriminated, the embryo that later grew into the ambitious and luxuriant plant of German historicist *Verstehen*—empathetic insight, intuitive sympathy, historical *Einfühlung*, and the like. . . . This is the sort of knowledge which participants in an activity claim to possess as against mere observers; the knowledge of the actors, as against that of the audience, of the "inside" story as opposed to that obtained from some "outside" vantage point; knowledge by "direct acquaintance" with my "inner" states or by sympathetic insight into those of others, which may be obtained by a high degree of imaginative power; the knowledge that is involved when a work of the imagination or of social diagnosis, or a work of criticism or scholarship or history is described not as correct or incorrect, skilful or inept, a success or a failure, but as profound or shallow, realistic or unrealistic, perceptive or stupid, alive or dead.'[1]

In France and Germany the revival of this methodological controversy has taken place largely in the context of Marxist thought. Jean-Paul Sartre, in his *Critique de la raison dialectique*, draws upon Marxism and existentialism in order to establish the value of a dialectical method—opposed to positivism—which consists in the interpretation of individual action (man's *project*) in relation to social groups, and of group action in relation to a whole society, itself conceived as part of a historical totality.[2] The debate in Germany has occurred principally among the Marxist thinkers of

---

[1] Isaiah Berlin, 'A Note on Vico's Concept of Knowledge', *New York Review of Books*, XII (8), April 24, 1969.

[2] A part of Sartre's book is available in English under the title *Search for a Method*. See also the useful commentary by Wilfrid Desan, *The Marxism of Jean-Paul Sartre* (New York, 1965).

the Frankfurt school, inspired largely by the late Theodor Adorno and continued by Jürgen Habermas.[1] It has taken up again the issues raised in the earlier German controversies around the works of Dilthey, Rickert and Max Weber, but with a particular emphasis on the place of values in social science, and on the opposition between a 'critical theory' of society (derived from Hegel and Marx) and a positivist, 'value-free' sociology.

Those who defend the 'unity of scientific method' have not, on the whole, replied adequately to the kind of criticism advanced by Dilthey and by later writers. Radcliffe-Brown, one of the most fervent advocates of a 'natural science of society' refers freely to sociological 'laws' and 'explanations' without ever enquiring into their logical character. K. R. Popper, in his *Poverty of Historicism*, sets out in the first chapter ('The anti-naturalistic doctrine of historicism') some of the objections against the application of the methods of physics to the social sciences, including the distinction between causal explanation in physics and the understanding of purpose and meaning in sociology, but when he comes later to criticize the anti-naturalistic doctrines he confines his criticism to certain aspects ('holism' and 'historicism') and makes no reference to Dilthey's fundamental distinction.

It should be added here that Dilthey did not aim to create an abyss between the natural sciences and the human studies. They are related, and up to a point they use the same methods of investigation. But the human studies also use *other* methods and they arrive at different results. These ideas were later re-considered by Max Weber, but Weber gave much greater importance to causal explanation. His position is summed up in the view that sociological explanation must be both causally adequate and adequate in terms of meaning. This is illustrated in his study of the relation between Protestantism and capitalism; he gives a historical causal explanation (with an implicit reference to universal laws which he later examined) of the development of Western capitalism, and at the same time presents the explanation in such a way that we can 'understand' the affinity between the Protestant ethic and the business creed of the capitalist entrepreneur.

Dilthey and Weber formed their methodological conceptions on the basis of their own work in the field of 'human studies', in history and sociology respectively. Much recent discussion of methodology

[1] See, in particular, Theodor Adorno, *et al.*, *Der Positivismusstreit in der deutschen Soziologie* (Neuwied, 1969); Albrecht Wellmer, *Kritische Gesellschaftstheorie und Positivismus* (Frankfurt, 1969); Jürgen Habermas, *Erkenntnis und Interesse* (Frankfurt, 1968).

has not, unfortunately, been grounded in actual study.[1] But suppose we ask what methodological conclusions can be drawn from the great volume of sociological enquiry of the last twenty or thirty years? I do not think a definitive answer can yet be given. The controversies which I have briefly sketched above are still unresolved. Sociologists have succeeded in establishing many empirical generalizations, but they have produced no significant sociological laws. In social anthropology, there have been some illuminating studies which seem to conform with Dilthey's conception of the interpretation of human values and purposes; and anthropologists have on the whole been much less interested than sociologists in formulating general laws. But it seems that such advances as have been made in sociology have been due to the increasing use of the ordinary methods of science. Most of the significant work of the past few decades has followed the procedure of investigating theoretical problems by formulating a hypothesis (which states a causal connection or a correlation), and testing the hypothesis by the collection and analysis of relevant data. At the same time the techniques of data collection and analysis which are employed have become increasingly refined and exact. Sociology differs from most of the natural sciences in dealing with phenomena which it is often difficult, and sometimes impossible, to measure or calculate, or to subsume under relations of causality; but this does not involve a total divergence in the methods of enquiry. It involves considering the limits upon sociological enquiry and assessing more realistically what it can achieve. Before dealing with this question I shall examine some more specific canons of method which seem to have directed sociological work. Five important methods or approaches can be distinguished, which we may term the historical, the comparative, the functionalist, the formal or systematic, and the structuralist.

Historical sociology

The historical approach has taken two principal forms. The first is that of the early sociologists, influenced by the philosophy of history and afterwards by the biological theory of evolution. This approach involves a certain order of priorities in the problems for

[1] This is the case, for example, with the expositions of 'methodological individualism', which arose out of K. R. Popper's writings on the logic of the social sciences. For a useful account of the questions raised by this approach see Joseph Agassi, 'Methodological Individualism', *British Journal of Sociology*, XI (3), September 1966. Similar criticisms, on the grounds of remoteness from actual social research, can be brought against much of the recent discussion of the Marxist method; for instance, against Sartre's *Critique de la raison dialectique*.

research and theory; it concentrates upon problems of the origins, development and transformation of social institutions, societies, and civilizations. It is concerned with the whole span of human history, and with all the major institutions of society, as in the work of Comte, Spencer and Hobhouse, or with the whole development of a particular social institution, as in E. Westermarck's *History of Human Marriage*, or F. Oppenheimer's *The State*. It was argued earlier that there is no 'law of evolution' and that these evolutionist works are in fact historical descriptions and interpretations. A severe critic has remarked that 'the evolutionist comparative method had achieved a kind of massive futility in the vast tomes of Frazer and Westermarck. . . .'[1] It is unlikely that sociologists will, in the future, be much concerned with such evolutionary schemes. The work of the evolutionists was bound up with the eighteenth and nineteenth century controversies over social progress; it was done under the influence of that 'animating and controlling idea', as Bury called it. Ginsberg, in an early essay,[2] replied to some detailed criticisms of the evolutionist approach, but he justified the concept of evolution in sociology by its relevance to our concern with the direction of human development. Such pre-occupations have, I think, largely passed away. The present interest in problems of social development is almost entirely focused upon industrialization and economic growth; it is concerned, therefore, with a particular historical phenomenon and also recognizes that there are diverse starting points and lines of development, as well as different possible outcomes. In any case, it is difficult to see that much would be added to our understanding of social changes in the modern world by the attempt to bring them within a comprehensive scheme of the whole social development of mankind. It should also be frankly recognized that there are many divergent evolutionary schemes, and that in some cases they have acquired a dogmatic character which obstructs thought and research. An obvious example is orthodox Marxism; the 'guiding thread' which Marx followed in an original study of modern capitalism has been transformed into a doctrine of social evolution, tediously re-iterated and carefully secluded from the kind of misfortune envisaged by Spencer, 'a deduction killed by a fact'.

This is not to disparage the genuine achievements of the early evolutionists. They classified in illuminating ways a mass of ethno-

---

[1] E. R. Leach, 'The epistemological background of Malinowski's empiricism', in R. Firth (ed.), *Man and Culture: An Evaluation of the Work of Malinowski* (London, 1957), p. 121.

[2] M. Ginsberg, 'On the concept of evolution in sociology' (1932) reprinted in *Essays in Sociology and Social Philosophy*, Vol. I (London, 1957).

graphic and historical materials, and outlined possible typologies of human society. They made important contributions to our knowledge of social changes. On the basis of their work we can distinguish some of the factors which produce change in social structures, and perhaps formulate, in place of a general account of social evolution, a number of laws and conditions relevant to particular kinds of change.

In another form the historical approach is characteristic of the work of Max Weber, and of a number of later sociologists influenced by him. Criticizing the Marxists of his time, Weber argued that 'the so-called materialist conception of history, as a *Weltanschauung* or as a formula for the causal explanation of historical reality, has certainly to be rejected. But the advancement of the economic *interpretation* of history is one of the most important aims of our journal'.[1] Here Weber contends for 'interpretation' against causal explanation as an all-sufficing method, and opposes the Marxist pretension to explain the whole course of social evolution. His own historical approach is exemplified especially in his studies of the origins of capitalism, the development of modern bureaucracy, and the economic influence of the world religions. The main methodological features of these studies are that particular historical changes of social structures and types of society are investigated (and these are compared in certain respects with other types of change and of society); and that both causal explanation and historical interpretation find a place. It is also implicit in Weber's work that the general sociological propositions refer only to trends, while their application to particular societies and situations involves historical study in detail, and even then finds a limit imposed by human creativity, the results of which neither the sociologist nor the historian can predict.

In recent sociology, this historical approach has directed the work of C. Wright Mills[2] and Raymond Aron,[3] both of whom have also devoted essays to Weber's methodology.[4] The growing interest in social change in industrial societies, and in the industralization of underdeveloped societies, is now encouraging a wider acceptance of Weber's method, in the formulation of problems, in the ideal-type

---

[1] Editorial article in *Archiv für Sozialwissenschaft und Sozialpolitik* (1904).

[2] See especially *White Collar* (1951).

[3] See 'Conflict and War from the viewpoint of historical sociology' in *The Nature of Conflict* (UNESCO, 1957), *War and Industrial Society* (Oxford, 1958), and *18 Lectures on Industrial Society*.

[4] Gerth and Mills, *From Max Weber*, Introduction; Aron, *German Sociology*, Ch. 3, and *Main Currents in Sociological Thought*, Vol. II.

definition of concepts, and in the aim to provide causal explanations and historical interpretations.

The comparative method

The comparative method was for long considered the method *par excellence* of sociology. It was first used by the evolutionist sociologists, but its use does not involve a necessary commitment to an evolutionary approach.[1] Durkheim, in *The Rules of Sociological Method*, first set out clearly the significance of the method. After claiming that sociological explanation 'consists entirely in the establishment of causal connections' he observes that the only way to demonstrate that one phenomenon is the cause of another is to examine cases in which the two phenomena are simultaneously present or absent, and thus to establish whether one does depend upon the other. In many of the natural sciences the establishment of causal connections is facilitated by experiment, but since experiment is impossible in sociology we are obliged, says Durkheim, to use the method of indirect experiment, i.e. the comparative method. Even if there is some doubt as to whether causal connections can be rigorously demonstrated in the social field, it may at least be claimed that systematic comparisons are illuminating in so far as they show that certain social phenomena are frequently associated with each other, or frequently occur in a regular order of succession.

But as Radcliffe-Brown observed, 'the comparative method alone gives you nothing. Nothing will grow out of the ground unless you put seeds into it. The comparative method is one way of testing hypotheses'.[2] The difficulties when using the comparative method seem to be due in part to the absence of hypotheses, or of clearly formulated hypotheses, at the outset, and in part to the problem of defining the unit of comparison. Thus, for example, Comte's use of the comparative method to establish his 'law of three stages' is based, not upon a scientific hypothesis but upon a philosophical view of the development of humanity as a whole. A similar criticism may be brought against much of the work of Hobhouse. In *Morals in Evolution*, for example, Hobhouse is not so much concerned with comparing social institutions in different types of society in order to test limited hypotheses as with tracing the general development of the different social institutions in terms of a philosophical conception of progress.

In defining the unit of comparison, other difficulties arise. There

[1] See M. Ginsberg's discussion of the comparative method: 'The problems and methods of sociology' in *Reason and Unreason in Society* (*op. cit.*).

[2] *A Natural Science of Society* (*op. cit.*).

are formidable problems in comparing whole societies with each other, and a common procedure has been to compare a particular social institution, or the relationship between two institutions, in different societies. Critics of the comparative method have pointed out that what appear superficially to be similar institutions may in fact be very different in the societies being considered, and secondly, that an institution detached from the context of the whole society in which it functions may easily be misunderstood.[1] These objections indicate real difficulties. They can perhaps be overcome by limiting the range of comparisons to societies which are broadly similar, i.e. societies of the same type, as determined by a prior classification. The classification itself, of course, involves comparison but only of a very broad and general kind. The detailed comparisons involved in testing hypotheses could then be undertaken with some assurance that the units of comparison were not totally dissimilar or radically misinterpreted. In fact, it seems that the comparative method has been most fruitfully used in this way. A number of studies, some old, and some recent, illustrate this. Hobhouse, Wheeler and Ginsberg made a systematic comparative study of some major institutions in primitive societies.[2] Their method was to distinguish, within the broad category of primitive societies, different types of economic system, and then to examine how far variations in the institutions of government and social stratification were correlated with the economic differences. More recently, a number of studies of social stratification and social mobility in industrial societies have been sponsored by the International Sociological Association.[3] These studies, although conducted independently, were broadly planned to facilitate comparisons and deliberately employed similar methods and categories of analysis. In neither of these instances is there much attempt to test clearly formulated hypotheses, but the studies are in fact connected with implicit hypotheses, and indeed with more general theories, of social development in the one case and of social class in the other. Some other recent studies concerned with the characteristics of industrial societies have aimed more deliberately at testing hypotheses by

[1] The major criticism on these lines was made by Malinowski. In his article 'Culture' in the *Encyclopaedia of the Social Sciences* Malinowski advanced an extremist view according to which the best possible object of study is a particular society as a whole.

[2] L. T. Hobhouse, G. C. Wheeler and M. Ginsberg, *The Material Culture and Social Institutions of the Simpler Peoples* (London, 1915).

[3] The first results were reported in *Transactions of the Second World Congress of Sociology* (London, 1954), Vol. I and *Transactions of the Third World Congress of Sociology* (London, 1956), Vol. III.

comparative enquiry; among them S. M. Lipset and R. Bendix, *Social Mobility in Industrial Society* (1959), and S. M. Lipset's studies of voting behaviour and of the social pre-requisites for democratic government in his *Political Man* (1960). There have also been some attempts to compare the processes of industrialization in different modern or present-day societies; for example, in Barrington Moore's *Social Origins of Dictatorship and Democracy* (*op. cit.*), and in Irving L. Horowitz's *Three Worlds of Development* (New York, 1966).

For more rigorous comparative studies we have to turn to those more restricted investigations which have been concerned with variations within particular societies. The best example, here, is Durkheim's study of suicide,[1] which aims to discover the social causes of suicide by relating the rates of suicide in different social groups to characteristics of the groups. Much recent sociological research has concentrated on testing limited hypotheses by small-scale comparisons, e.g. connections between urban living and divorce or delinquency rates, between family size and social mobility, between social class and educational attainment, etc. Such studies have resulted in the kind of empirical correlation and generalization which was discussed in the previous chapter.

The nineteenth century advocates of the comparative method, however, regarded it as a method of general application. E. A. Freeman claimed that 'the establishment of the comparative method of study has been the greatest intellectual achievement of our time'.[2] He cited especially its results in the study of language, and went on to show how it might be applied in the study of social institutions. After a period in which the comparative method has been extensively used in small-scale studies in particular societies, with greatly improved techniques of investigation, there is now a renewed interest, as I have indicated, in making comparisons between societies. Such cross-national comparisons are in fact necessary in many cases to test the conclusions of the small-scale studies.

Functionalism

The functionalist approach, in sociology and social anthropology, appeared initially as a reaction against the methods and claims of the evolutionists. It was a criticism of naïve and superficial uses of the comparative method, and of the methods of 'conjectural history', which employed unverified and unsystematic data on contemporary

[1] E. Durkheim, *Suicide* (English trans., London, 1952).
[2] *Comparative Politics* (1873).

primitive societies for reconstructing the early stages of human social life. It was also a criticism of the intention or claim of the evolutionists to give a scientific account of the whole social history of mankind.

The notion of 'social function' had, of course, been formulated in the nineteenth century; most explicitly by Herbert Spencer. It is based upon an age-old analogy between a society and an organism, but it could be presented in a more scientific guise after the development of modern biology. Spencer, however, like most of those influenced by biological conceptions, was most concerned to work out a theory of social evolution, and his analyses of social structure and social function in the *Principles of Sociology*, though of some interest, are brief and unconvincing.[1] It was Durkheim, as Radcliffe-Brown insists,[2] who first gave a rigorous formulation of the concept of social function in *The Division of Labour in Society* and in *The Rules of Sociological Method*.

Durkheim defined the function of a social institution as the correspondence between it and the needs of the social organism. It has been shown earlier, in considering functionalism as a theory, what difficulties arise from this analogy between society and an organism, and from attempts such as Durkheim's to distinguish between the 'normal' and the 'pathological' functioning of institutions. As a method, functionalism cannot be entirely detached from its theoretical imperfections; yet it has some features which we may consider independently. The extreme form of the functionalist approach, as propagated by Malinowski, was influential in persuading many social anthropologists to devote themselves to the detailed and meticulous description of actual social behaviour in particular societies, and to forsake and condemn both the historical approach and the comparative method. Similar results followed the later adoption of the functionalist approach in sociology, although here, because of the difference in scale of the societies studied, it often meant limiting enquiry to village and community studies. This redirection of interest brought some obvious gains, especially in the study of primitive societies, by its emphasis on field work involving exact observation and recording of social behaviour.

But, again, in the work of Malinowski, the functionalist approach involved the dogmatic assertion of the functional integration of

---

[1] The most elaborate, and also most fantastic, presentation of the analogy between society and an organism, influenced by Spencer's ideas, is A. Schäffle, *Bau und Leben des sozialen Körpers* (1875–78).

[2] A. R. Radcliffe-Brown 'On the concept of function in social science'. This essay provides the best short account of the functionalist approach.

every society rather than the tentative formulation of a hypothesis about the inter-relation of institutions. Thus every social activity had a function by virtue of its existence, and every activity was so completely integrated with all the others that no single phenomenon was intelligible outside the whole social context. This also meant that it was difficult, if not impossible, to give an explanation of social change in a society except in terms of external influences.

In the course of time the functionalist approach has been modified, so as to become less dogmatic and less exclusive. R. K. Merton presents it as *one* possible approach to the study of social behaviour, and attempts to make it more useful by introducing a number of qualifications.[1] One of these, the distinction between function and dysfunction (which is intended to allow for endogenous social change and to rebut the charge that functionalism expresses a conservative political ideology) is, however, no more acceptable than Durkheim's distinction between 'normal' and 'pathological' functioning, from which it derives, since it claims to discriminate scientifically between activities which, in most cases, are matters of moral evaluation. Merton's other important distinction, between manifest and latent functions, is an elaboration of Durkheim's principle that the functions of social institutions are by no means obvious, and are not always what they seem to be. It directs us to more careful, and also more imaginative, study of the actual working of social institutions, as against the received interpretations of their working. It also indicates that any institution may have several functions, any one of which may be of crucial importance in a particular society. This point is made in another way in Merton's criticism of Durkheim's theory of religion. Durkheim claimed to have discovered *the* social function of religion; the expression and reinforcement of social solidarity. This may be so in some societies, but religion has also frequently been a source of discord and social conflict. It follows that historical and comparative enquiry is necessary to discover the range of functions of a social institution—and also that we have to do here with a phenomenon which is very different from 'function' in the biological sense, and which we might do better to call the 'working' of an institution or the 'way in which it is connected with other specific social institutions or activities'. What is most valuable in the functionalist approach is the greater emphasis and clarity given to the simple idea that in every particular society the different social activities are interconnected. It still remains to discover, however, in each case, *which* activities are closely related, and *how* they are related.

[1] R. K. Merton, *Social Theory and Social Structure* (2nd edn., 1957), Ch. 1.

Formal sociology

Formal or systematic sociology also represented a reaction against the evolutionary and encyclopaedic science of the early sociologists. Its originator was Georg Simmel, and it remained very largely a German approach to sociology. The controversy about the status of the social sciences in relation to the natural sciences, and the philosophical school of phenomenology were important influences upon its development,[1] but its immediate source was the concern to define the field of sociology in relation to the existing social sciences. Simmel's conception of sociology, although it was much discussed in his own time, was not attentively studied by later sociologists until a decade or so ago.[2] It is expounded chiefly in the first essay, 'The problem of sociology',[3] in his *Soziologie* (1908), where Simmel argues, first, that sociology is a new *method*, a new way of looking at facts which are already treated by the other social sciences, this new approach consisting in considering the 'forms' of sociation or interaction as distinguished from the historical content;[4] and secondly, that sociology is therefore also concerned with forms of interaction which have not been studied at all by the traditional social sciences, forms which appear not in major institutions such as the state, the economic system, and so on, but in minor and fleeting relationships between individuals. Nevertheless, Simmel claims, the latter are important in the mass and exhibit society *statu nascendi*. So far as Simmel's work was continued by later thinkers it became divided between these two aspects. Von Wiese elaborated the method, and attempted to construct a general sociology on the basis of relational concepts such as 'social distance', 'approach' and 'withdrawal'. Others, and most recently G. C. Homans, devoted

---

[1] Dilthey regarded Simmel's sociology with favour because it rejected any attempt to explain the whole cultural life of mankind and aimed, at the most, to establish a typology of social relationships.

[2] The most comprehensive survey is in the centenary volume edited by K. H. Wolff, *Georg Simmel, 1858–1918* (Columbus, Ohio, 1959). See also the volume of essays by Lewis Coser (ed.), *Georg Simmel* (Englewood Cliffs, 1967).

[3] English translation in K. H. Wolff, *op. cit.*

[4] Simmel justifies this distinction as follows: 'Superiority, subordination, competition, division of labour, formation of parties . . . and innumerable similar features are found in the state as well as in a religious community, in a band of conspirators as in an economic association, in an art school as in a family. However diverse the interests which give rise to these sociations, the forms in which the interests are realized are identical. On the other hand, an identical interest may be embodied in very different sociations. Economic interest is realized both in competition and in the planned organization of producers . . . The interests upon which the relations between the sexes are based are satisfied by an almost endless variety of family forms . . .' (*op. cit.*

themselves to the study of 'elementary forms of social behaviour' (or small groups), but frequently diverged from Simmel's intention by reducing their accounts of the relationships to psychological terms.

Simmel's sociology had a wider range than is suggested by the later studies in which his influence is apparent. In his *Soziologie* he was concerned with 'minor' forms of interaction, but in the *Philosophie des Geldes* he examined some major social relationships, especially in the modern capitalist societies. It also deserves notice, in reconsidering Simmel's conception of sociology, that among the relatively few propositions which can be produced as evidence that sociology is a generalizing science, a high proportion are due to Simmel, e.g. the propositions on conflict and on the effects of changes in the size of social groups.

Structuralism

In the past decade a new method has been proposed, for social anthropology and sociology, under the name of 'structuralism'. Its principal exponent is Claude Lévi-Strauss,[1] and its main influence, so far, has been upon social anthropologists,[2] although it is still far from clear what that influence may be in the long term. Edmund Leach, in his introduction to a symposium on structuralism, claims only that Lévi-Strauss offers 'new insights' in the analysis of myth: 'He has provided us with a new set of hypotheses about familiar materials. We can look again at what we thought was understood and begin to gain entirely new insights.'[3] As yet, there seems to have been no systematic attempt to use the structuralist method in sociology, and it is not easy to see exactly what kind of problem orientation or type of inquiry the method would involve. In other ways, however, structuralism has begun to have a certain influence; particularly in renewing the discussion of the concept of 'social structure'. Lévi-Strauss himself made an early contribution in his essay on social structure in A. L. Kroeber's *Anthropology Today*,[4]

[1] See, in particular, his *Structural Anthropology* (London, 1963), *The Savage Mind* (London, 1966), and *The Raw and the Cooked* (London, 1969).

[2] In a more general way, however, structuralism has already become an important method; notably in linguistics, through the work of Noam Chomsky and others, and in literary criticism through the writings of such critics as Roland Barthes. There is a useful brief survey of structuralism in various fields in Jean Piaget, *Le structuralisme* (Paris, 1968). See also the essays collected in Michael Lane (ed.), *Structuralism: A Reader* (London, 1970).

[3] Edmund Leach (ed.), *The Structural Study of Myth and Totemism* (London, 1967).

[4] Reprinted in *Structural Anthropology*.

which provoked an interesting controversy with G. Gurvitch;[1] and more recently the varied uses of the notion of structure in the social sciences have been examined very thoroughly by Raymond Boudon in his book *A quoi sert la notion de 'structure'?* (Paris, 1968). Perhaps the most significant feature of structuralism is that it aims to discover universal elements in human society, and that in Lévi-Strauss' own work the elements which are sought appear to be basic characteristics of the human mind itself, which are seen as determining the possible varieties of social structure. Thus, in this form at least, structuralism seems to involve a psychological reductionism. More generally, since it looks for universal elements it stands opposed to a historical approach to social structure; and Lévi-Strauss has emphasized this aspect in his discussion of 'analytical' and 'dialectical' reason (with reference to Sartre's version of Marxism) in the concluding chapter of *The Savage Mind*.

Of the sociological approaches which I have briefly reviewed two—the evolutionist and the functionalist—appear to have outlived their usefulness. The evolutionists contributed instructive schemes of classification and some suggestive interpretations of human social history; above all, they formulated and analysed problems of social change. But their interpretations are not scientific theories of social evolution; nor have their general conceptions of evolution produced, or seemed likely to produce, any scientific theory of the factors or mechanisms of social development. Along these lines no further advance is to be expected. The functionalists performed a service in directing attention to the actual working of social institutions (including their interrelations) in particular societies, but the biological analogy upon which their approach is based is theoretically unsatisfactory and at the same time projects a misleading image of social cohesion.

Formal sociology and comparative sociology both provide appropriate methods for the systematic study of human society. They have in common that they formulate scientific generalizations and they are also complementary, in the sense that the former may be regarded as a micro-sociology, concerned with the informal, everyday interrelations among individuals, while the latter is concerned with the formal social institutions. In another sense, they may be considered as alternative approaches, but this would require a more ample discussion than is possible here.[2] The historical approach in

---

[1] See G. Gurvitch, *La vocation actuelle de la sociologie* (2nd edn., Paris, 1900), and Lévi-Strauss' reply in *Structural Anthropology*.

[2] No historian of sociology has yet examined the opposition between Simmel and Durkheim which would be the necessary starting point for such a study.

the form which Max Weber gave to it, also makes possible generalizations about processes of social change and historical trends.

How far, in the case of these approaches, are we justified in speaking of the 'scientific procedure' of sociology? The discipline is scientific, it seems to me, in its method and in its intentions. The important features of method are: (i) that it is concerned with facts (not with value judgments upon them); (ii) that it brings empirical evidence in support of the statements made; (iii) that it is objective (in the sense that no one is prevented from basing his statements upon consideration of the evidence). In its scientific intention, sociology aims at (i) exact description, by the analysis of the properties and relations of social phenomena, and (ii) explanation, by the formulation of general statements.[1] It may be readily admitted that sociology as a scientific pursuit encounters great difficulties in all these respects; but the wide-ranging discussions of the difficulties only confirm that the discipline exists because it strives to be a science—factual, empirical, objective, descriptive and explanatory.

We may conclude here by considering briefly what the sociological methods of enquiry can accomplish and what are their limitations. First, the sociologist can assemble empirical data which make possible a more rational judgment upon practical issues than can be got from traditional ideas. Secondly, he can sometimes make reasonable predictions even when he is not able to give an explanation of the phenomena. Thirdly, he can explain some social phenomena, i.e. subsume statements about them under more general statements. It is in the last case that sociological methods have their most serious limitations, because of the complexity or interrelatedness of social happenings and because of human creativity. It follows that sociological generalizations only describe trends or tendencies. Like all scientific generalizations they are corrigible by the discovery of new instances, but they are *also* corrigible by the *creation* of new instances which results from human freedom. And when they are used to account for specific instances they need to be supplemented by detailed historical inquiry which may reveal unique features in the situation.

The ultimate test of the various methodological approaches which I have considered in this chapter is whether they provide an adequate general scheme of ideas and procedures which enables us to understand more fully, or to investigate more realistically, particular social events or processes at different levels of complexity.

---

[1] See Quentin Gibson, *The Logic of Social Enquiry* (London, 1960), Introduction, from which the above account is taken with slight modifications.

The controversies between adherents of different methods are valuable in their own right, however, in so far as they oblige us to look more closely at the difficulties inherent in our subject matter, and induce us to adopt a more critical and tentative approach in our own inquiries.

Chapter 4

THE SOCIAL SCIENCES, HISTORY AND PHILOSOPHY

Sociology, though it no longer claims to be the all-inclusive science of society (still less a *scientia scientiarum*), does claim to be synoptic. We have, therefore, to consider in somewhat more detail than we did in the first chapter, how it is or should be related to the other social sciences and to other disciplines concerned with the social life of man. In the following pages I shall first discuss its relations with two other general sciences, social anthropology and psychology, then its relations with two of the special social sciences, economics and political science, and finally its relations with history and philosophy.

Social anthropology

It is often said that although sociology and social anthropology had quite different origins (the one in the philosophy of history, political thought, and the social survey, the other in physical anthropology and ultimately in biology) they are now practically indistinguishable. This statement expresses an aspiration rather than a fact. If one examines the concepts, methods of investigation and analysis, and directions of interest of the two disciplines, it soon becomes apparent that they are still widely separated. Nevertheless, looking at the history of their relations, it can be seen that after an early period of close connection, where individual work could not easily be assigned to one or the other (e.g. Tylor, Spencer, Westermarck), there was a period of extreme divergence when the functional approach was generally adopted in anthropology while sociology (at least in the European countries) continued to be historically oriented and concerned with problems of social development; and that finally, in recent years, there has been a new convergence of the two disciplines. The broad differences between sociology and social anthropology that emerged during the period of divergence can easily be related to differences in the object of study. Social anthropologists, once field work had become a fundamental requirement, were involved in studying small societies, of a very different character from their own societies, relatively unchanging, and lacking historical records. The methods followed from these facts; such societies could be observed as functioning wholes, they could be described and analysed in ethically neutral terms since the anthropologist as an outsider was in no way involved in their values and strivings,[1] and since they changed little and had no records of past changes, a historical approach was unnecessary and more or less impossible. This situation has now radically altered; many if not most primitive societies are changing under the influence of Western ideas and technology, larger groupings are beginning to predominate over tribal societies, and social and political movements are developing which involve the social anthropologist in the same kind of value problems which the sociologist has had to face in studying his own society, or societies of the same civilization.[2] In brief, we can see that the object of study now is societies in the process of economic growth and social change, and thus an object for both the sociologist and the social anthropologist, who work increasingly in Africa and Asia upon the same kinds of problems. It should be added that as primitive societies, regarded as the preserve of the social anthropologist, have more or less disappeared, so to some extent the special prerogatives of the sociologist in studying advanced societies have been challenged. There is an increasing number of anthropological studies in advanced societies; studies of the 'little community', of kinship groups, etc. Sociology and social anthropology are still divided by differences of terminology, approach and method (and the excursions into the other's territory are sometimes methodologically unsound) but there is both convergence and a desire to further it.

We should also note that, among contemporary societies, there is a third very important category of those which are neither primitive nor industrially advanced. In such societies, of which India may be taken as an example, the distinction between sociology and social anthropology has little meaning. Sociological research in India, whether it is concerned with the caste system, village communities, or the process of industrialization and its effects, is and should be carried out by sociologists and social anthropologists. There is a

[1] However, this was often a qualified neutrality. Many of the societies studied were under colonial rule, and the anthropologist might well find himself obliged to take sides, with or against the colonial rulers.

[2] For example, both sociologists and anthropologists have to face the fact of revolutionary movements in the Third World. A radical view of these issues is vigorously expounded by Kathleen Gough, 'World Revolution and the Science of Man', in T. Roszak (ed.), *The Dissenting Academy* (New York, 1967).

real opportunity in this case for the traditional division between these disciplines to be overcome. It is true that the present training of sociologists and anthropologists works against this, to some extent, since their training is usually obtained in one of the Western countries in which the division persists; but the growth of the social sciences in the developing countries, and the diminishing dependence upon foreign educational resources will give an opportunity for a real integration of the methods and concepts of the two disciplines in terms of the problems and research tasks relevant to these societies.

Psychology

The problem of the relation between psychology and sociology, and of the status of social psychology in relation to both, is difficult and unsettled. There are two extreme views. J. S. Mill believed that a general social science could not be considered firmly established until its inductively established generalizations could be shown to be also logically deducible from the laws of mind. 'Human beings in society have no properties but those which are derived from, and may be resolved into, the laws of the nature of individual man'.[1] Durkheim, on the other hand, made a radical distinction between the phenomena studied by psychology and sociology respectively. Sociology was to study *social facts*, defined as being external to individual minds and exercising a coercive action upon them; the explanation of social facts could only be in terms of other social facts, not in terms of psychological facts. 'Society is not a simple aggregate of individuals; the system formed by their association represents a specific reality possessing its own characteristics. . . . In short, there is the same discontinuity between psychology and sociology as there is between biology and the physico-chemical sciences. Consequently, whenever a social phenomenon is directly explained by a psychological phenomenon one can be sure the explanation is invalid.'[2]

The opposed views of Mill and Durkheim still have their partisans today, but most sociologists seem to have adopted various intermediate positions. Some, like Ginsberg, would hold that many sociological generalizations can be more firmly established by being related to general psychological laws, but that there may also be sociological laws *sui generis*.[3] Similarly, S. F. Nadel argued that some problems posed by social enquiry might be 'illuminated by a move to lower levels of analysis—psychology, physiology and

---

[1] J. S. Mill, *System of Logic*, Book VI, Ch. 7.
[2] E. Durkheim, *The Rules of Sociological Method*, Ch. 5.
[3] M. Ginsberg, *Sociology* (London, 1934), Ch. 1.

biology'.[1] Under Dilthey's influence, many German sociologists, including Max Weber, came to hold the view that even where strictly sociological explanation is possible, the sociologist gains an additional satisfaction or conviction in being able to 'understand' the meaning of social actions which he explains in causal terms. Such understanding was conceived in terms of 'common sense psychology', but neither Dilthey nor Weber was hostile to the development of a scientific psychology in the broad sense, and Weber was sympathetic to some of Freud's ideas. Freud's psychology, although it emphasized the role of individual and biological factors in social life, nevertheless recognized that the innate impulses were transformed in various ways before they became manifest in social behaviour; and in the work of the post-Freudian school— especially Karen Horney and Erich Fromm—the influence of society in moulding individual behaviour is given still greater prominence. Fromm's concept of the 'social character' is intended precisely to relate individual psychological characteristics to the characteristics of a particular social group or social system.[2]

In spite of this wide recognition that sociological and psychological explanation may complement each other, the two disciplines are not, in practice, closely associated, and the place of social psychology, which ought to be specially close to sociology, is still disputed. It is easy to say that social psychology is that part of general psychology which has a particular relevance to social phenomena, or which deals with the psychological aspects of social life. In fact, all psychology may be considered 'social' in some degree, since all psychic phenomena occur in a social context which affects them to some extent; and it becomes difficult to mark out even roughly the boundaries of social psychology. This means that social psychologists have usually felt a closer association with general psychology than with sociology, have been bound to a particular method (emphasizing experiment, quantitative studies, etc.) and have often ignored the structural features of the social milieu in which their investigations are conducted. This divergence between sociology and social psychology can be illustrated from many fields. In the study of conflict and war there have been mutually exclusive sociological and psychological explanations.[3] In

[1] S. F. Nadel, *The Foundations of Social Anthropology* (London, 1951), Ch. 8.

[2] Erich Fromm, *The Fear of Freedom* (London, 1942), Appendix 'Character and Social Process'.

[3] See M. Ginsberg, 'The causes of war' in *Reason and Unreason in Society* (*op. cit.*), pp. 177–95. The differences between the sociological and psychological approaches, and some attempts to overcome them, can be studied in *The Nature of Conflict* (UNESCO, 1957).

studies of social stratification, the psychological approach seems to have produced a particular account of class and status in subjective terms, which is contrasted with the sociological account in terms of objective factors, rather than systematic investigation of the psychological aspects of a significant element in the social structure. The 'psychology of politics' hardly deserves to be mentioned, so remote does much of the writing appear to be from the most obvious facts of political structure and behaviour. In almost every field of enquiry it could be shown that psychology and sociology constitute for the most part two separate universes of discourse.

There have, of course, been many declarations in favour of closer association between the two disciplines, and, more usefully, a small number of attempts to bring them together. One of the most valuable is the work of Gerth and Mills.[1] The authors say, 'The social psychologist attempts to describe and explain the conduct and motivations of men and women in various types of societies. He asks how the external conduct and inner life of one individual interplay with those of others. He seeks to describe the types of persons usually found in different types of societies, and then to explain them by tracing their inter-relations with their societies.' The field of study of social psychology is thus the interplay between individual character and social structure, and as Gerth and Mills say, it can be approached either from the side of biology or from the side of sociology. In the recent past the trouble has been that those coming from either side remained largely ignorant of what was being done on the other side, and were enclosed in their own world of academically approved terminology and method. Gerth and Mills attempt to bridge the gap by using the concept of 'role' as the key term both in their definition of the person and in their definition of institutions:

'Social role represents the meeting point of the individual organism and the social structure, and it is used as the central concept in a scheme which makes possible an analysis of character and social structure in the same terms.'

This is quite similar to Fromm's view which I mentioned above; and Gerth and Mills, like Fromm, take up again the fundamental problem of the relation between the individual and society, which was earlier examined by Ginsberg in an illuminating study dealing with the respective influence of instinct and reason in social life, with theories of the 'group mind', and with problems of public opinion

[1] Hans Gerth and C. Wright Mills, *Character and Social Structure* (London, 1954).

and organized group behaviour.[1] Later social psychology has for the most part abandoned this line of study in favour of statistical and experimental enquires which are far too much concerned with the individual or with simple aggregates of individuals; and it has therefore lost contact with sociology.

Finally, we should reconsider one objection to the possibility of a close association between sociology and psychology. Durkheim wished to exclude psychological explanation from sociology, though he often resorted to it implicitly. More recently, Radcliffe-Brown argued that sociology and psychology study two entirely different systems, one a social system, the other a mental system; and claimed that these two levels of explanation could not be combined.[2] This seems an extreme view, and one unlikely to be sound at a time when much of the fruitful research even in natural science is taking place on the frontiers of different sciences. Yet we should acknowledge the genuine difficulties. Sociology and psychology do offer alternative accounts of behaviour, and if they are to be brought closer together it will be necessary to work out more rigorously than has yet been done (in studies of attitudes or of socialization) the conceptual and theoretical links between them.

Economics

Alfred Marshall, in an inaugural lecture delivered in Cambridge in 1885, referring to Comte's idea of a general social science, observed: 'No doubt if that existed Economics would gladly find shelter under its wing. But it does not exist; it shows no signs of coming into existence. There is no use in waiting idly for it; we must do what we can with our present resources.'[3] Would this judgment still be true today? I do not think so. Sociology exists; sociologists have both critically examined the limitations of economic theory and made contributions to the study of economic phenomena. On the other side, economists themselves seem to have become weary of the frequency with which the phrase 'other things being equal' recurs in economic analysis, and many of them have attempted to go beyond description (which forms a large part of most economic textbooks) or deduction from a small number of simple presuppositions about human behaviour.

The recent sociological criticisms and contributions can be grouped under several headings. There are, first, the critical studies which attempt to show that economics cannot be an entirely autono-

---

[1] M. Ginsberg, *The Psychology of Society* (London, 1921).

[2] A. R. Radcliffe-Brown, *A Natural Science of Society*.

[3] A. C. Pigou (ed.), *Memorials of Alfred Marshall* (London, 1925), pp. 163–4.

mous science. Such, for example, is the approach of A Löwe in his book *Economics and Sociology*[1] which examines the 'significance and limits of pure economics', and discovers two sociological principles which underly (as logical conditions) the classical laws of the market; the 'economic man', and competition or mobility of the factors of production. Löwe goes on to suggest fruitful areas of co-operation between economics and sociology. A similar approach was formulated earlier by F. Simiand, in *La méthode positive en science économique*.[2] Simiand was a collaborator of Durkheim in the *Année Sociologique* and consciously adopted a sociological approach to economic problems. His argument, in the essays which make up this book, is that the 'first principles' of economics are hypotheses which need to be tested, rather than being taken as the starting point for deductive reasoning leading to conclusions no more certain than the original hypotheses. The only way of testing the hypotheses, in Simiand's view, is by sociological enquiry. Max Weber's *Wirtschaft und Gesellschaft*[3] is the classical attempt to bring some of the concepts of economic theory within the framework of general sociology. A recent work by Talcott Parsons and N. J. Smelser,[4] attempts, on Weberian lines but in a more ambitious way, to show economic theory as a part of general sociological theory. In this category we may also include the writings which have attempted to formulate principles of sociological economics.[5]

We can distinguish, secondly, the numerous sociological studies which have directly concerned themselves with problems of economic theory. Simiand, in *Le salaire, l'évolution sociale et la monnaie*, (Paris, 1932, 3 vols.), examined empirically the relation between wage and price levels and advanced a sociological theory of wages. A more recent book in the same field is Barbara Wootton's *The Social Foundations of Wage Policy* (London, 1955), which first analyses the inadequacies of the classical economic theory of wages and then presents a sociological analysis of the determinants of wage and salary differentials, based upon the data for Britain. A very interesting later part of the book examines the actual procedures and arguments in wage negotiations in modern Britain. There are many similar sociological studies of different aspects of economic theory, perhaps the most interesting being those concerned with the theory

[1] London, 1935.   [2] Paris, 1912.
[3] Tübingen 1921–2 [English trans. of Part I under the title *The Theory of Economic and Social Organization* (New York, 1947)].
[4] Talcott Parsons and N. J. Smelser, *Economy and Society: A Study in the Integration of Economic and Social Theory* (Glencoe, 1957).
[5] Especially, D. M. Goodfellow, *Principles of Economic Sociology* (London, 1939), and M. J. Herskovits, *Economic Anthropology* (New York, 1952).

of the firm. Here we have Thorstein Veblen's classical study, *The Theory of Business Enterprise* (New York, 1904) and many later studies of the business corporation, including A. A. Berle and G. C. Means, *The Modern Corporation and Private Property* (New York, 1934), and J. K. Galbraith's recent book, *The New Industrial State*.

Thirdly, there are the sociological works concerned with the general features of economic systems. It is here that the sociological literature is most plentiful, and that sociologists have explored aspects of economic behaviour neglected or treated in a cursory fashion by economists. Among the general studies which treat economic systems as wholes, and which have been produced both by sociologists and by sociologically minded economists are Marx's *Capital*, much of the work of the German historical school, as for example W. Sombart's *Der moderne Kapitalismus*, and K. Bücher's *Die Entstehung der Volkswirtschaft*, Max Weber's writings on capitalism, the work of J. A. Hobson, especially *The Evolution of Modern Capitalism* and *Imperialism: A Study*, and numerous writings of Henri Sée. There have been many recent studies in the same field, most of them concerned with the later development of capitalism: J. Schumpeter, *Capitalism, Socialism and Democracy;* J. Strachey, *Contemporary Capitalism;* J. K. Galbraith, *American Capitalism* and *The Affluent Society;* and Raymond Aron, *18 Lectures on Industrial Society*, are perhaps the principal examples. But there have also been a number of works on other types of economic system, including primitive types.[1]

In addition to these general studies of economic systems, sociologists have contributed to the study of particular aspects of economic organization; e.g. the property system, the division of labour and occupations, and industrial organization. Some of these contributions will be considered in a later chapter devoted to the economic institutions of society.

It can be argued that sociology and economics, which were very closely related at their origins, e.g. in the work of Quesnay and Adam Smith, but which then diverged, except in the work of the German historical economists, have come closer together again in recent years. This has been due not only to the development of sociology and its direct contributions to economic studies, but also to changes within economics itself. There are two particular aspects of modern economics which should be mentioned in this connection. The first is the shift in interest from the market mechanism to the

---

[1] On primitive economic systems see especially R. Firth, *Primitive Polynesian Economy* (London, 1939), M. J. Herskovits, *op. cit.*, M. Mauss, *The Gift* (English trans., 1954) and R. Thurnwald, *Economics of Primitive Communities* (1932).

total national product and national income, which has led economists to an examination of the social factors influencing economic
growth.[1] This change of emphasis is apparent in much recent work on
problems of economic development in underdeveloped regions, where
the economist has either to collaborate with the sociologist or to
become a sociologist himself. The second aspect is the application
of the theory of games to economic phenomena. This has led to
more realistic studies of the behaviour of firms, and more importantly
to the construction of models of one kind of social action which
might be generalized to apply to a variety of types of action. If this
were to be achieved it would mean that specifically economic, and
more general sociological, problems would be capable of analysis
in terms of a single conceptual scheme. In this way certain parts
at any rate of economic and sociogical theory might be unified.

Such achievements are no doubt still far off, but there have
already been some interesting attempts to use economic models
in sociology,[2] and on the other side to make use of sociological
accounts of economic behaviour in economic theory, particularly in
dealing with questions of economic growth.

Political science

Traditional political science has had three main aspects: *descriptive*
(accounts of the formal organization of central and local government,
and historical studies of the development of such organization);
practical (the study of current problems of organization, procedure,
etc.); and *philosophical* (the mingling of descriptive and evaluative
statements in what is called, in a broad sense, political theory). In
most political science of this kind there has been little attempt at
generalization beyond that which is involved in an elementary
classification of the types of political régime, largely in terms of
their formal characteristics.

[1] See the review of the literature in Lyle W. Shannon, 'Social factors in
economic growth', *Current Sociology*, VI (3), 1957. This change has also brought
about a revaluation of Marxist economics; see, in particular, David Horowitz
(ed.), *Marx and Modern Economics* (New York, 1968), where the sociological
element in Marx's work, which underlies its value as a macro-economic theory
of growth, is contrasted with the abstraction from the institutional framework
which characterizes orthodox theory.

[2] For example, games theory and exchange models. On the former, see the
article by Jessie Bernard in *The Nature of Conflict* (UNESCO, 1957); on the latter,
Peter M. Blau, *Exchange and Power in Social Life* (1964). See also the attempt
by Talcott Parsons to use economic concepts in the analysis of political power,
within the framework of his general theory of social action, in *Sociological
Theory and Modern Society* (New York, 1967), Ch. 10, 'On the Concept of
Political Power'.

The influence of sociology in the field of political studies has been to direct attention toward *political behaviour* as an element in a social system, rather than the formal aspects of political systems considered in isolation, and to encourage attempts at scientific generalization and explanation. This influence began to be felt at an early stage in the development of sociology, largely through the work of the Marxists, since in Marx's theory political institutions and behaviour are closely linked with the economic system and with social classes, and have to be analysed in this general social context. It was Marxist thought which provoked, at the end of the nineteenth century, the political sociology of Michels, Max Weber and Pareto, and thus led directly to the modern studies of political parties, elites, voting behaviour, bureaucracy and political ideologies.

Another, quite different, sociological influence is to be seen in the development of behaviourism in American political science. This may be dated roughly from Charles Merriam's Presidential Address to the American Political Science Association in 1925, in which he said: 'Some day we may take another angle of approach than the formal . . . and begin to look at political behaviour.' Thereafter, a behaviourist approach developed rapidly at the University of Chicago, and although it was aided in the 1930s by an influx of European scholars who brought their own sociological orientation, derived from Michels and Weber, it took quite a different direction from that in Europe, being largely unaffected by Marxist ideas and having as its principal aim the creation of a strictly 'scientific' (and to some extent, quantitative) discipline.[1]

In recent years the sociological influence upon political science has become even more marked. First, there has been a direct borrowing of explanatory schemes and models; for example, of functionalism, as in G. A. Almond and J. S. Coleman, *The Politics of the Developing Areas* (Princeton, 1960), or of the idea of a 'social system,' as in David Easton's work, particularly *A Systems Analysis of Political Life* (New York, 1965). There has also been a renewal of Marxist sociological ideas, inspired on one side by the revolutions in developing countries,[2] and on the other side by the new social movements which have emerged in the advanced industrial countries.[3]

[1] The behaviourist approach is reviewed comprehensively and critically in Bernard Crick, *The American Science of Politics* (London, 1959).

[2] See, for example, Peter Worsley, *The Third World* (2nd edn., London, 1967).

[3] There has not yet been a comprehensive sociological study of these movements, but some useful analyses will be found in such works as Daniel Bell (ed.), *The Radical Right* (New York, 1964); Raymond Aron, *La révolution introuvable* (Paris, 1968; English trans., *The Elusive Revolution*); Alain Touraine,

Studies of the political development of 'new nations', because of the nature of the problems which are raised, have brought together the work of political scientists and sociologists (and frequently of anthropologists as well). The forces at work, and the changes which take place, in a peasant society, in a society made up of tribal units, or in a society organized in a caste system, belong more to the sphere of knowledge of the sociologist and anthropologist than to that of most political scientists; and to study political processes in such societies requires extensive borrowing from these other disciplines.[1]

Finally, there has been a continuation and extension of work in fields which I have already mentioned: on political parties and pressure groups, on the relation between class and politics, on elites, and on the processes of government and administration. A particular feature of these studies is that they are carried out increasingly on a comparative basis, with the aim of arriving at some general statements about political organizations and political action, at least within the limits of specific type of society (e.g. Western industrial society).[2]

The orientation of theory and research in political science over the past decade has made it increasingly difficult to distinguish the subject from political sociology. The behaviourist approach which was characteristic of American political science has been severely criticized and in part abandoned, but other general schemes of thought have been adopted from sociology—including those derived from Marxism—and the objects of research are increasingly sociological in kind. Some differences perhaps remain. Political scientists still devote a good deal of attention to the formal structure of government, which sociologists sometimes unwisely neglect. Political theory is still seen by many as being closely associated with philosophical ideas and problems, but here the case of sociology is hardly different, as I shall argue later; though its philosophical connections have not, perhaps, been so fully recognized. In general, we may say that the trend in political science, unlike that in economics, has been

Le mouvement de mai ou le communisme utopique (Paris, 1968); S. M. Lipset (ed.), *Student Politics* (New York, 1967); Norman Birnbaum, *The Crisis of Industrial Society* (New York, 1969).

[1] As examples of recent studies see Colin Leys (ed.), *Politics and Change in Developing Countries* (London, 1969); Samuel P. Huntington, *Political Order in Changing Societies* (New Haven, 1968).

[2] See, for example, Maurice Duverger, *Political Parties* (English trans., London, 1954). There are now regular international conferences on Comparative Political Sociology; the papers of the most recent conference deal in part with new political movements and have been published under the title *Party Systems, Party Organizations and the Politics of New Masses* (Berlin, 1968).

toward a merger with sociology in many of the most significant fields of research.

History

In an earlier chapter some account was given of that view of the social or cultural sciences which regards them as being of the same general character as history, or even as being a kind of historical study. This seems to me mistaken. Sociology and history may overlap in one area, but diverge widely in another. I should like here to examine briefly some aspects of their relationship.

The first and simplest point is that the historian frequently provides the material which the sociologist uses. The comparative method often requires, and historical sociology always requires, data which only the historian can supply. It is true that the sociologist must sometimes be his own historian, amassing information which had not previously seemed worth collecting, but he cannot always be so—time does not allow.

But, secondly, the historian also uses sociology. Until recently it was perhaps from philosophy that the historian took his clues to important problems, as well as many of his concepts and general ideas; these are now drawn increasingly from sociology. Indeed, we can see that modern historiography and modern sociology have both been influenced, and in similar ways, by the philosophy of history. The latter established the conception of historical periods, and thus bequeathed to historiography theoretical ideas and concerns which were entirely absent from the work of the earlier narrative historians, the chroniclers and annalists. It bequeathed to modern sociology the notion of historical types of society, and thus the first elements of a classification of societies. In much contemporary historiography and sociology it seems to me that the same basic framework of reference, to types of society, is employed. In the historical field, the connection is most evident where economic and social history (especially the latter) are concerned. It is worthy of note, for instance, that the editors of one of the leading journals of social history, the *International Review of Social History*, defined the scope of the review in its first number in the following terms: 'Social history is taken to mean the history of estates, classes, social groupings regardless of name, seen both as separate and as mutually dependent units.'[1] In only slightly different terms this could also define the scope of historical sociology. At the present time there is, in several countries, evidence of co-operation and even trespassing into each other's territory, by sociologists and social historians. In France, the review

[1] *International Review of Social History*, Assen, 1956, Vol. I, Part I, p. 4.

Annales, founded and edited for many years by the late Lucien Febvre, has for long béen a meeting place for historians, sociologists and other social scientists; and the traditions represented by the work of Febvre, Marc Bloch and others are still influential. In England, much recent work indicates the convergence of sociology and social and economic history: for example, historians' accounts of the social structure of nineteenth century towns, or of the characteristics of the medieval peasantry or the eighteenth century nobility, and sociologists' studies of the social history of a variety of professions.[1]

In what ways, then do historiography and sociology differ? It used to be said that the historian describes unique events, while the sociologist produces generalizations. This is not true. The work of any serious historian abounds in generalizations, while many sociologists have been concerned with describing and analysing unique events or sequences of events. Perhaps we should say that whereas the historian usually sets out to examine a particular sequence of events, the sociologist usually begins with a generalization which he proposes to test by the examination of a number of similar sequences of events. In short, the intention is different. But even this qualified distinction is not wholly true. It depends very much upon the kind of historiography (e.g. it is most true of diplomatic history) and the kind of sociology (where it is most true of comparative studies). Making a still weaker distinction, we might say with H. R. Trevor-Roper, that the historian is concerned with the interplay between personality and massive social forces,[2] and that the sociologist is largely concerned with these social forces themselves.

The more the distinction is refined to take account of the actual work of historians and sociologists, the clearer it becomes that historiography and sociology cannot be radically separated. They deal with the same subject matter, men living in societies, sometimes from different points of view, sometimes from the same point of view. It is of the greatest importance for the development of the social sciences that the two subjects should be closely related, and that each should borrow extensively from the other, as they are increasingly inclined to do.[3]

[1] See the examples given in the essay by Asa Briggs, 'History and Society', in Norman McKenzie (ed.), *A Guide to the Social Sciences* (London, 1966).

[2] H. R. Trevor-Roper, *Historical Essays* (1957), Introduction.

[3] Their relations can also be illustrated well from the controversies about some large-scale problems of historical interpretation. For example, the debate about the origins of modern capitalism which began with Max Weber's revision of the Marxist account has been continued by historians and sociologists from

Philosophy

Sociology originated largely in a philosophical ambition; to account for the course of human history, to explain the social crisis of the European nineteenth century, and to provide a social doctrine which would guide social policy. In its recent development sociology has for the most part abandoned such aims; and some would say that it has abandoned them too completely. However this may be, there remain connections between sociology and philosophy in at least three respects.

First, there can be, and is, a philosophy of sociology in the sense of philosophy of science; that is, an examination of the methods, concepts, and arguments used in sociology. And this philosophical scrutiny is more common and more needful in sociology than in, for example, the natural sciences, because of the peculiar difficulties experienced with sociological concepts and reasoning.

Secondly, there is a close relationship between sociology and moral and social philosophy. The subject matter of sociology is human social behaviour, which is directed by values as well as by impulses and interests. Thus the sociologist studies values and human valuations, as facts. But he should also have some acquaintance with the discussion of values, in their own context, in moral and social philosophy. Still more important is it that the sociologist (and of course other social scientists) should be capable of distinguishing between questions of fact and value questions, and between the kinds of discussion and analysis appropriate to each. Yet it is frequently found, in the social sciences, that these distinct questions and kinds of discourse are confused; value problems are claimed to be settled by assertions as to matters of fact, while the discussion of factual questions is often complicated or rendered sterile by the commitment of the discussants to particular values or general philosophical views. Only by some training in social philosophy can the sociologist become competent to distinguish the different issues, and at the same time to see their relationships to each other.

Thirdly, it may be held that sociology leads on directly to philo-

Tawney up to the present time. See, on the general issues involved, Norman Birnbaum, 'Conflicting Interpretations of the Rise of Capitalism: Marx and Weber', *British Journal of Sociology*, IV (2), June 1953; Trevor Aston (ed.), *Crisis in Europe, 1560–1660* (London, 1965). Another example is to be found in the discussions of the significance of the frontier in American history, initiated by the work of F. J. Turner. This issue is re-examined by historians and sociologists in Richard Hofstadter and S. M. Lipset (eds.), *Turner and the Sociology of the Frontier* (New York, 1968).

sophical thought. This was, for instance, the view of Durkheim; in an essay on 'Sociologie religieuse et théorie de la connaissance',[1] he wrote 'I believe that sociology, more than any other science, has a contribution to make to the renewal of philosophical questions ... sociological reflection is bound to prolong itself by a natural progress in the form of philosophical reflection.' In Durkheim's own study of religion this prolongation can be seen in the transition from a discussion of the social influences upon the categories of thought, to epistemological discussion. Other sociologists have taken a similar view and have been concerned with similar problems. Karl Mannheim, for instance, thought that his sociology of knowledge had implications for epistemology, and indeed he stated the implications in detail.[2] Both Durkheim and Mannheim seemed to claim that sociology can make a direct contribution to philosophy, in the sense of settling philosophical questions. But this is an error; thus, epistemology is the basis of a sociology of knowledge, not vice versa. All that is intended here is to suggest that sociology raises, to a greater extent than other social sciences, philosophical problems, and consequently that the sociologist who is at all concerned with the larger aspects of his subject is led on to consider philosophical issues which are always in the background of sociological reflection. It is not, in my view, at all harmful to sociological theory or research that the sociologist should interest himself in such problems and should seek to acquire a philosophical education which will equip him to deal with them, for much of the weakness of sociological theory is due to philosophical naiveté, and much of its triviality comes from disregard of the larger issues involved in any study of man.

In the same context it should be said that while sociology naturally leads on to philosophical reflection, much of it that is most important also begins there. The point which I made earlier about the value of the connection between political science and political philosophy applies over a wider field; sociological research may easily become trivial if it ignores the larger problems of social life which are formulated in philosophical world views and in social doctrines. The vigour and the stimulating character of early Marxism in the field of social research was due in large measure to the fact that Marxism was not only a sociological theory but a philosophical world view and a revolutionary doctrine. To take another example, Beatrice Webb explained more than once how her social research had benefited from her active participation in a social movement and her

[1] *Revue de Métaphysique et de Morale*, XVII, 1909.
[2] Karl Mannheim, *Ideology and Utopia* (London, 1952), Part V, p. 256 *sqq.*

commitment to a social doctrine. It has been, in my view, one of the strengths of much European sociology that it has conceived a science of society as being insufficient by itself, and as needing to be closely connected with a philosophy of society, from which it would begin its formulation of problems and to which it would return for the elucidation of new problems resulting from scientific investigation.

It should be apparent from this brief discussion of the relations between sociology and some other disciplines concerned with the social life of man, how vain it would be to conceive sociology as an all-embracing science, and how difficult it is even to conceive it as contributing a synoptic view of human society. The sociologist must accept his limitations. He can outline a broad conception of social structure by reference to which the special social sciences may direct their investigations towards the solution of important problems. He can draw attention to, and elucidate, relationships between social phenomena which specialization would ignore (e.g. between religious beliefs and economic behaviour, between social stratification and political events, between law and other forms of social control). By the use of the comparative and historical methods he can work towards the construction of a system of general laws. He can bring out the significance and problematic character of the connection between the individual as an organism and as a social being, which the other social sciences tend to ignore, and he can clarify the distinction and relation between the scientific and the philosophical study of values. All this is indispensable as a general framework for specialist studies, and it is increasingly appreciated by the specialists. But except for those who concern themselves entirely with the logical problems of general sociology, sociologists must themselves become specialists. The greater their competence in particular fields of enquiry—in law, religion, economics, politics, etc.—the greater will be the influence of the sociological approach and the profundity and accuracy of their own researches. The unity of the social sciences which now seems much closer as a result of increasing collaboration and cross-fertilization, is best conceived as a unity of method and of conceptual schemes, not as a universal history.

Notes on Reading for Part I

I. THE BACKGROUND OF SOCIOLOGY

Bury, J. B. *The Idea of Progress* (London, Macmillan, 1920).
An excellent short account of the philosophy of history and theories of progress from the seventeenth century up to the sociological theories of Comte and Spencer.

Durkheim, E. 'La contribution de Montesquieu à la constitution de la science sociale' reprinted by A. Cuvillier in E. Durkheim, *Montesquieu et Rousseau: précurseurs de la sociologie* (Paris, Rivière, 1958) pp. 25–113.
An examination of Montesquieu's conception of social types and social laws, and his use of the comparative method.

Bryson, Gladys. *Man and Society: The Scottish Inquiry of the Eighteenth Century* (Princeton, Princeton University Press, 1945).
An admirable study of the development of sociological ideas in the work of the Scottish historians and philosophers.

Bramson, L. *The Political Context of Sociology* (Princeton, 1961).

McClellan, David. *The Young Hegelians and Karl Marx* (London, 1969).
An excellent account of one source of Marx's thought, in German philosophy and social theory.

See also the general histories of sociological thought, by Aron and Nisbet, mentioned in the text.

II. SOCIOLOGICAL THEORIES AND METHODS

1. *General*

The following will be found useful on some of the major problems in the logic of sociology.

Mill, John Stuart. *A System of Logic* (10th edn., London, Longman Green & Co., 1879, 2 vols.) Book VI 'On the logic of the moral sciences'.

Nadel, S. F. *The Foundations of Social Anthropology* (London, Cohen and West, 1951).

Popper, K. R. *The Poverty of Historicism* (London, Routledge & Kegan Paul, 1957).

Hodges, H. A. *Wilhelm Dilthey: An Introduction* (London, Routledge & Kegan Paul, 1944).
A short exposition of Dilthey's views on the characteristics of the social and the natural sciences.

Weber, Max. *The Methodology of the Social Sciences* (English trans., 1949).

Hayek, F. A. *The Counter-Revolution of Science* (London, 1952).
An exposition of the method of 'understanding' the meaning of human action (re-named 'methodological individualism') and a

81

critique of nineteenth century sociologists, especially Comte and Marx.

Louch, A. R. *Explanation and Human Action* (Oxford, 1966).

The best recent statement of an anti-positivist view.

Gibson, Quentin. *The Logic of Social Enquiry* (London, Routledge & Kegan Paul, 1960).

Brown, Robert. *Explanation in Social Science* (London, 1963).

A good exposition, illustrated from several social sciences, of diverse types of explanation.

Braybrooke, David (ed.). *Philosophical Problems of the Social Sciences* (New York, 1965).

A useful short introduction.

Natanson, M. (ed.). *The Philosophy of the Social Sciences* (New York, 1963).

2. *Historical sociology*

Carr, E. H. *What is History?* (Penguin Books, 1961).

Hofstadter, Richard. *Social Darwinism in American Thought* (rev. edn., Boston, 1955).

Ginsberg, M. 'On the concept of evolution in sociology' in *Essays in Sociology and Social Philosophy*, Vol. 1 (London, Heinemann, 1957).

Defends the evolutionist approach against some major criticisms.

Burrow, J. W. *Evolution and Society: A Study in Victorian Social Theory* (London, 1966).

Aron, Raymond. *Introduction à la philosophie de l'histoire* (Paris, Gallimard, 1938; English trans. London, 1961).

Examines in Section III the notions of historical and sociological causation.

See also the discussion of Max Weber's method, in Julien Freund, *The Sociology of Max Weber* (London, 1968).

3. *The comparative method*

Durkheim, E. *The Rules of Sociological Method* (English trans. Glencoe, The Free Press, 1938) Ch. VI.

Ginsberg, M. 'The problems and methods of sociology' in *Reason and Unreason in Society* (London, Longman, Green & Co., 1947).

On pp. 39–41 there is a brief discussion of the comparative method. The most substantial and useful discussion of the comparative method in history and sociology is Marc Bloch, 'Toward a comparative history of European societies'; English trans. in F. C. Lane and J. C. Riemersma (eds) *Enterprise and Secular Change* (London, 1953) pp. 494–521. Originally published in *Revue de Synthèse historique* (1928).

4. *Functionalism*

Radcliffe-Brown, A. R. 'On the concept of function in social science', in *Structure and Function in Primitive Society* (London, Cohen & West, 1952) pp. 178–187.

Malinowski, B. *A Scientific Theory of Culture and Other Essays* (Chapel Hill, Univ. of N. Carolina Press, 1944).
Outlines his functionalist approach in the title essay and in a separate paper entitled 'The functional theory'.

Merton, R. K. *Social Theory and Social Structure* (2nd rev. edn., Glencoe, The Free Press, 1957) Ch. I. 'Manifest and latent functions'.

Firth, Raymond. 'Function' in *The Year Book of Anthropology*, 1956.

Demerath, N. J. and Peterson, R. A. (eds). *System, Change and Conflict* (New York, 1967).
A collection of some of the most important articles on functionalism.

III. THE SOCIAL SCIENCES, HISTORY AND PHILOSOPHY

1. *Economics*

Löwe, A. *Economics and Sociology* (London, Allen & Unwin, 1935).
An illuminating analysis of the sociological presuppositions of economic theory.

Goodfellow, D. M. *Principles of Economic Sociology* (London, 1939).

Shannon, Lyle W. 'Social Factors in Economic Growth', *Current Sociology*, VI (3) 1957.
A trend report and bibliography which shows the convergence of economic and sociological enquiry in one important field of study.

Joan Robinson, *Economic Philosophy* (London, Watts, 1962).
A critical view of economic ideas in relation to general social thought.

François Perroux, *Économie et Société* (Paris, P.U.F., 1960)
A good short analysis of economic relations as part of a social system.

2. *Political science*

Bendix, R. and Lipset, S. M. 'Political sociology', *Current Sociology*, VI (2) (1957).

Wiatr, J. 'Political Sociology in Eastern Europe', *Current Sociology*, XIII (2) (1964).
Two trend reports and bibliographies which survey the work in political sociology up to the late 1950s.

Balandier, Georges. *Anthropologie politique* (Paris, 1967).

Bottomore, T. B. *Elites and Society* (London, 1964).

Lipset, S. M. *Political Man* (London, 1960).

Lipset, S. M. (ed.), *Politics and the Social Sciences* (New York, 1969).

3. *Psychology*

Ginsberg, M. *The Psychology of Society* (London, Methuen, 1921).
Becker, H. *For a Science of Social Man: Convergences in Anthropology, Psychology and Sociology* (New York, Macmillan, 1954).
Fromm, Erich. *The Fear of Freedom* (London, 1942).
Mead, G. H. *Mind, Self and Society* (Chicago, Univ. of Chicago Press, 1934).
Wallas, Graham. *Human Nature in Politics* (3rd edn., London, Constable, 1921).
Bastide, Roger. *Sociologie et Psychanalyse* (Paris, Presses Universitaires de France, 1950).
A very thorough discussion of the relations between sociology and Freudian psychology.

4. *History*

Gardiner, P. *The Nature of Historical Explanation* (London, 1955).
Barth, P. *Die Philosophie der Geschichte als Soziologie* (2nd edn., Leipzig, 1915).
Ginsberg, M. 'History and Sociology' in *Essays in Sociology and Social Philosophy* (*op. cit.*), I, pp. 163–179.
Lipset, S. M. *Revolution and Counterrevolution* (New York, 1968), Ch. 1, 'History and Sociology: some Methodological Considerations'.
The reader should also consult the books by H. A. Hodges on Dilthey (mentioned in the text), K. R. Popper, *The Poverty of Historicism* (*op. cit.*) and some of the literature on the Marxist conception of history [in particular, Eric Hobsbawm's introduction to Karl Marx, *Pre-Capitalist Economic Formations* (London, 1964)]. There is a stimulating critique of the Marxist theory in B. Croce, *Historical Materialism and the Economics of Karl Marx* (English trans. London, 1913).

5. *Philosophy*

Durkheim, E. *Sociology and Philosophy* (English trans. London, Cohen and West, 1953).
Ginsberg, M. 'Durkheim's ethical theory' in *Essays on Sociology and Social Philosophy* (*op. cit.*).
Mannheim, Karl. *Ideology and Utopia* (London, 1940).
Myrdal, Gunnar. *Value in Social Theory* (London, Routledge & Kegan Paul, 1958).

See also H. Marcuse, *Reason and Revolution* (New York, Oxford University Press, 1941), and some of the philosophical criticisms of sociology in works mentioned in the text.

Part II

POPULATION AND SOCIAL GROUPINGS

Chapter 5

POPULATION AND SOCIETY

The phenomena of population constitute the domain of a special science, demography, which was one of the earliest of the modern social sciences to emerge. It played an important part, in the eighteenth century, in stimulating the growth of other social sciences, and it has remained closely associated with sociology. For the demographer, as soon as he goes beyond measurement and calculation to study the causes or consequences of population changes, differential fertility and mortality, and similar problems, enters the domain of sociology. The most interesting demographic problems have always involved social factors of the kind with which sociology is concerned.

At the same time, it is evident that for the sociologist the size, distribution and qualities of the population are basic data. Durkheim made population size one of the principal elements in that branch of sociology which he called morphology. Societies can be classified according to their *volume* and *density*. By volume Durkheim meant the number of 'social units' (i.e. individuals) in the society. By density Durkheim meant the 'number of social relationships' in a society; he distinguished between *material density* influenced by the concentration of population, the growth of towns and the development of means of communication, and *moral density*, which is measured by the number of individuals who effectively have relations (not merely economic but cultural relations) with each other. Durkheim thought that increased volume generally brought about increased density, and that the two factors together produced variations in social structure. In *The Division of Labour in Society* (1893) he set out to show that increase of population produces, through the division of labour, a change from a type of society based upon 'mechanical solidarity' to one based upon 'organic solidarity'. Recent sociology has been little concerned with such general relationships between population size and type of social structure, though the problem has been taken up in a different way by D. Riesman in *The Lonely Crowd*.

More usually, in sociology and other social sciences, population size and population changes have been related to particular aspects of social structure or to particular social phenomena. Thus, a number of sociologists have been concerned with the relation between demographic changes and war.[1] There have also been many discussions of the relations between demographic change and economic activity, from Malthus' *Essay on Population*, up to recent studies of the influence of population movements upon economic growth, as in W. Arthur Lewis's *The Theory of Economic Growth*.[2]

It has always been recognized that there is a reciprocal relation between population and social structure; i.e. that the social structure influences population changes as well as being affected by them. Indeed, sociological study in this field has been predominantly concerned with the social influences upon population size. There is now a very large literature on these questions, and it is impossible to do more than summarize the principal results. The actual problems vary, of course, from one type of society to another. In the 1940s and 1950s Western demographers and sociologists were chiefly interested in the social factors influencing the decline in the birth rate, which slowed down the rate of population growth in the inter-war years and at one stage seemed likely to produce stationary or even declining populations. The various social factors have been distinguished and analysed in a large and increasing literature. We may mention here the studies by Alva Myrdal, *Nation and Family* (London, 1945); A. M. Carr-Saunders, *World Population* (Oxford, 1936), D. V. Glass, *Population Policies and Movements in Europe* (Oxford, 1940), and the study made in Britain by the Royal Commission on Population.[3] The Royal Commission's report lists and examines some of the influences which promoted family limitation; the references are to British experience but very similar influences must have been operative elsewhere. It is clear that improved methods of birth control and more general knowledge of such methods were important in making family limitation easy. But the *desire* to limit family size had other causes; among them the resentment felt by women against excessive child bearing and the emancipation of women which allowed their protest to become effective, the declining importance of the family as a productive unit and the increasing economic burden of children (as a result of restrictions upon child

---

1 For a general discussion of different theories of war, including demographic theories, see Quincy Wright, *A Study of War* (Chicago 1942, 2 vols.).

2 There is a general survey of population theories with reference to 'optimum population' and resources in E. F. Penrose, *Population Theories and Their Application* (Stanford, 1934).

3 *Report of the Royal Commission on Population* (London, HMSO, 1949).

labour and the spread of compulsory education), the growth of new wants which competed with the desire for children, the raising of standards of parental care and especially the desire of parents to give their children the best possible start in life. The last influence was itself affected by the opportunities for social mobility in an expanding economy and in a less rigidly stratified society; only by limiting births could each child be given the fullest opportunities to rise in the social hierarchy. Many recent studies have demonstrated the advantages, in this respect, of the child from a small family. One other feature of family limitation is apparent from all studies; it began in the higher strata of society, and only gradually spread to the lower strata. This could be explained partly in terms of differences in knowledge, but the adoption of birth control in the higher strata still needs some other explanation. A recent study[1] suggests that, in Britain, family limitation in the middle classes began with the economic recession of the 1870s which threatened their new standards of comfort. Its gradual extension to other strata could then be explained by imitation of a social model, as well as by the perception of the advantages of a small family in the competitive struggle for economic and social advancement.

More recently the concern with population size has taken quite a different direction, with the emphasis now upon the rapid growth of population, in particular countries and in the world as a whole.[2] In the developing countries, as we shall see, the main concern is with the effects of population increase upon economic growth; while in the industrial countries it is much more with the social effects, with congestion and pollution.[3]

Demographers and sociologists have been concerned with the distribution of the population, as well as with its size. The outstanding phenomenon of recent times, in Western Europe and America, but increasingly throughout the world, is the growing concentration of population in urban areas, as one effect of industrialization. This has encouraged studies of the conditions favourable to the growth of towns, and attempts to construct a typology of towns by comparative enquiry. It has been recognized that the existence of towns

---

[1] J. A. Banks, *Prosperity and Parenthood* (London, 1954).

[2] World population grew from 2,000 million in 1930 to 3,500 million at the end of the 1960s, and may reach 7,000 million by the year 2000.

[3] *See*, for a discussion of the situation in Britain, L. R. Taylor (ed.), *The Optimum Population for Britain* (London, 1970). The essay by D. E. C. Eversley in this volume makes the point that population management is a very inexact science, largely because of unforeseen fluctuations in the birth rate. In Britain the birth rate has been falling again since 1964, and in due course there may emerge pro-population rather than anti-population campaigns.

depends in the first place upon the existence of an economic surplus, and that their growth is affected by the growth of industry, trade and administration. The relations between urban centres and the country-side have varied from one type of society to another. At most times towns have been dependent upon the country, they have not been dominant in the society as a whole, and they have been subject to variations in size and importance. Only in modern industrial societies has urbanism become the predominant way of life. In many societies, too, there has been conflict between town and country; Pirenne in his *Medieval Cities* showed the role played by the European towns, especially in the fourteenth to sixteenth centuries, in dissolving feudal social relationships and challenging the feudal social order. Ibn Khaldûn, in his *Universal History*, contrasted tribal with city life and outlined a theory of conflict between sedentary city dwellers and nomadic tribes to explain the rise and decay of Arab cities.

In another aspect demography has extended into human geography and urban sociology, with the study of social phenomena in relation to the concentration of population. The major characteristics are the existence of distinct zones and sectors in urban areas, dis-tinguished by economic, class, ethnic and other features, differences between urban and rural areas in respect of such phenomena as crime, divorce and suicide, and also more generally in the types of social relationship and in cultural outlook. The notion of zones and sectors in the city was developed largely by R. E. Park, E. W. Burgess and others belonging to what came to be called the 'ecological school' in the USA. R. E. Park distinguished many different regions within the American city: 'There are regions . . . in which there are almost no children . . . regions where the number of children is relatively very high: in the slums, in the middle class residential suburbs . . . There are other areas occupied almost wholly by young unmarried people . . . There are regions where people almost never vote . . . regions where the divorce rate is higher than it is for any state in the Union, and other regions in the same city where there are almost no divorces . . . There are regions in which the suicide rate is excessive; regions in which there is . . . an excessive amount of juvenile delinquency.'[1] Another member of this school, H. W. Zor-baugh, in *The Goldcoast and the Slum* (Chicago, 1929) studied two extreme regions of the city and contrasted their social characteristics. Recent ecological studies of the city have attempted to provide a general classification into regions combining the notion of concentric zones with that of sectors. One example is P. Chombart de Lauwe's

---

[1] R. E. Park, in *The Urban Community* (ed. E. W. Burgess, Chicago, 1926).

study of Paris,[1] in which concentric zones, elementary units (districts) and the distribution of social classes are treated separately and then combined in a general typology.

Urbanism as a way of life has attracted many students. It is evident from a number of indices—divorce rates, suicide rates, etc.— that there are important differences between town dwellers and those who live in rural areas; and the greatest divergence is to be found in the great cities. Sociologists have attempted to explain these differences in terms of the social situation and group affiliations of town dwellers, but also in terms of the culture of cities. Simmel, in a classical study,[2] showed how city life favoured the intellectual development of the individual, and produced a distinct type of person. A more pessimistic account is that of Lewis Mumford, in his *Culture of Cities*, where the pathological features of city life are emphasized; the isolation of the individual, the fragmentation of his social contacts and his personality, the growth of ennui, frustration, and a sense of futility. The principal features of urban life were examined in a more impartial way in L. Wirth's essay 'Urbanism as a way of life'.[3]

The qualitative aspects of population attracted much attention in the nineteenth century, and were studied from two points of view. First, there were the attempts to distinguish between societies in terms of racial or national characteristics, conceived as innate qualities. This approach has generally been abandoned, for little connection has been found between race as defined by physical anthropology and intellectual or temperamental qualities of interest to the psychologist and sociologist. Modern sociological studies of race are concerned with race prejudice and race relations,[4] while

[1] P. Chombart de Lauwe *et al.*, *Paris et l'agglomération Parisienne* (Paris, 1952, 2 vols.).

[2] G. Simmel, 'Die Grosstädte und das Geistesleben' in *Die Grosstadt*, Dresden 1903. In English in P. K. Hatt and A. J. Reiss, *Cities and Society* [Revised reader in urban sociology] (Glencoe, 1957).

[3] *American Journal of Sociology*, XLIV, 1938, pp. 1–24. Reprinted in P. K. Hatt and A. J. Reiss, *op. cit.* *See also* the interesting study by Morton and Lucia White, *The Intellectual Versus the City* (Cambridge, Mass., 1962).

[4] There is an excellent short survey of the sociological aspects of race in R. Firth, *Human Types* (2nd end., London, 1956), Ch. 1 'Racial traits and mental differences'. *See also* the UNESCO series of booklets on 'The race question in modern science' now republished as a book. In the last decade race relations have become a critical subject of study, and have been approached in a new way, largely as a result of the rise of the Black Power movement in the USA and its influence in other parts of the world. Two good accounts of the movement are Floyd B. Barbour (ed.), *The Black Power Revolt* (Boston, 1968), and Stokely Carmichael and Charles V. Hamilton, *Black Power: The Politics of Liberation in*

national character, so far as it is studied at all, is conceived as the outcome of the institutional arrangements of a society, or of the 'culture pattern' reflected in individual upbringing, or most frequently as the product of both together.

Secondly, there were studies of presumed innate differences between individuals or groups within society, which were connected with elite theories (Pareto) or arose from concern about the effects of differential fertility on the quality (physical or intellectual) of the population. In England, the latter concern crystallized in the eugenics movement started by Francis Galton, and continued by Karl Pearson from his position as professor of eugenics in the University of London. All this was connected with a wider intellectual movement of 'social Darwinism' influenced by the unfortunate biological analogies formulated by Herbert Spencer. Eugenics has little connection with modern sociology, but one particular problem has continued to arouse discussion, the assumed relation between differential fertility and the trend of national intelligence. It was supposed that the declining birth rate in the upper strata of society, resulting in their failure to reproduce themselves, might bring about a gradual decline in the general level of intelligence. The problem was carefully reviewed by Sir Cyril Burt in an article published in 1950,[1] and has been investigated in a comprehensive survey conducted by the Scottish Council for Research in Education.[2] Burt's conclusion is that some kind of 'equilibrium' may have been established and that more research will be needed to determine the character of changes in the national level of intelligence and the factors involved. It seems likely that the improvement in general welfare was an important factor in the result shown by the Scottish survey.

We may fairly conclude that social factors are of great importance, and perhaps of pre-eminent importance, in determining the quality of a population. Racial and other biological accounts are quite clearly inadequate. Differential fertility certainly plays a part in determining the general characteristics of a population, but its influence has not been shown to override that of improved standards of nutrition, medical care, housing and education.

America (New York, 1967). On Britain, see the volume of papers from the British Sociological Association Conference, 1969, edited by S. Zubaida, *Race and Racialism* (London, 1970).

[1] Cyril Burt, 'The trend of national intelligence', *British Journal of Sociology*, I (2), June 1950, pp. 154–68.

[2] Scottish Council for Research in Education, *The Trend of Scottish Intelligence* (London, 1949), and *Social Implications of the 1947 Scottish Mental Survey* (London, 1953). This survey showed a rise in the general level of intelligence between 1932 and 1947.

Population in the Developing Countries

In recent years demographers and others have been particularly concerned with the rapid increase of population in developing countries. We may begin by considering the case of India, for which reliable basic information is available through regular censuses, statistical surveys, and a number of independent inquiries.[1]

TABLE I
Estimated Population 1871–1961*

Year	Undivided India† (millions)	India (millions)	% increase over previous decade
1871	255·2	—	—
1881	257·4	—	—
1891	282·1	—	—
1901	285·3	235·5	−0·2
1911	303·0	249·0	5·8
1921	305·7	248·2	−0·4
1931	338·2	275·5	11·0
1941	389·0	314·9	14·1
1951	—	356·9	13·5
1961	—	436·4	22·3

* These figures up to 1941 are taken from Kingsley Davis, *The Population of India and Pakistan*. For 1871–1921 they are estimates obtained by correction of the census data, by methods described in the book. The 1951 figure is taken from the Indian census report, and the 1961 figure from the provisional census report.

† Before the 1947 partition into India and Pakistan.

For the period before the first census only estimates of the population are available, and these show such large variations that they cannot reasonably be used for calculating the rate of population

[1] The first (partial) census of India was taken in 1867–72; the second census was in 1881, and there have been decennial censuses since that time. The census reports contain, in addition to population statistics, much information on the social and economic background; and this information is supplemented by the statistical surveys, first undertaken in 1869 and condensed in the *Imperial Gazetteer of India* (1881), and thereafter published regularly in the *Imperial Gazetteer*. The most comprehensive general survey of population problems in India is Kingsley Davis, *The Population of India and Pakistan* (Princeton, 1951). More recently Gunnar Myrdal in *Asian Drama* (New York, 1968), Vol. II, Part 6 and Vol. III, has examined in detail the population problems and policies of South Asian countries. The data on world population are presented and analysed regularly in the United Nations *Demographic Yearbook*.

growth. They suggest, however, that the sustained growth of the population began after 1800, in which year the estimated population of undivided India, 120 millions, may have been about the same as that of ancient India. After the first census (1867–72) the growth of the population can be traced more accurately.

The population of undivided India steadily increased over the period 1871–1941. There is little remarkable in this, for the same process has been going on in most countries of the world. Moreover, the actual rate of growth over the whole period (about $0 \cdot 6$ per cent per year) was slightly below that for the world as a whole, and much below that of many European countries, of the USA, or of Japan, in the same period. The distinctive features of the situation in India, and in other developing countries, are that the rate of population increase has risen dramatically in the last two decades, and that population growth has been accompanied by a relatively slow rate of industrial development. Most of the population projections made in the 1950s for the countries of South Asia underestimated substantially the rate of growth. Thus, the First Five Year Plan in India assumed a rate of population growth of $12 \cdot 5$ per cent per decade, whereas the increase in the period 1951–61 was 22 per cent. More recent projections assume a compound rate of growth of $2 \cdot 4$ per cent per annum, which would produce an Indian population of 555 million in 1971 and 625 million in 1976.[1] Similar rates of growth are foreseen for other South Asian countries, and even higher rates for some countries of Latin America. The disparity between rates of population growth in developing countries and industrial countries (even though the latter have experienced larger population increases than demographers expected in the 1940s) are bringing about changes in the balance of world population; the industrial countries of Europe and North America, which had about one-third of the world's population in 1950 will have less than a quarter in the year 2000.

The immediate influences upon the size of a given population are fertility, mortality, and migration. In the future, the role of migration is likely to be very small because of the restrictions imposed by the countries of immigration. Population size in the developing countries will be affected almost entirely, therefore, by the relationship between fertility and mortality; and the problem of rapid population growth will arise, as in the past two decades, from the fact that mortality rates are declining much more sharply than are fertility rates. The decline in the mortality rate may be expected to continue as long as

1 See Gunnar Myrdal, *Asian Drama*, Vol. II, pp. 1448–62.

improvements in nutrition and medical care are maintained, but there can be no such confident expectation about the trend of the fertility rate. As yet there is little indication that any powerful social influences are bringing about deliberate family limitation in the developing countries. It was noted earlier, with reference to the industrial countries, that family limitation began in urban areas and in the higher social strata, but there is little differential fertility of this kind in most of the developing countries, and in the countries of Asia and Africa the urban population and the middle class is still such a small part of the population that even if these groups adopted a strict limitation of family size the influence upon population growth would at first be slight.

In the absence of spontaneous checks to population growth, a continuing rapid increase can only be prevented by a national policy designed to limit the number of births. It is only in the last few years, however, that some of the developing countries have attempted seriously to implement such policies, and it is too early to judge their success. There are formidable difficulties; in countries such as India, where the great majority of the population is rural, family limitation is most urgently required in the villages, but the villages lack many other things which appear to have as high a priority as family planning clinics and which may seem more directly beneficial to the village people themselves. There are also difficulties in disseminating knowledge of birth control methods, and on the other side traditional sentiments in favour of large families, sometimes supported by religious beliefs, are still strong.

The connection between population growth and economic development was at one time a subject of controversy. As Gunnar Myrdal observes there was a lively discussion, ten or fifteen years ago, as to whether the countries of South Asia were faced with a problem of excessive population growth, but he continues: 'By now, it is commonly recognized that all countries in the region have entered a critical phase of sharply accelerated population growth, and that the prospects for successful economic development are crucially related to population trends.'[1] It is true that there has been no absolute decline in the levels of living, and that threatened shortages of basic foodstuffs[2] have been averted for the present by the 'green revolution'—the introduction of new strains of wheat and rice which have a very high yield. But the rapid increase of population absorbs most

[1] Gunnar Myrdal, op cit. Vol. II, pp. 1389-90.
[2] A report by experts of the Ford Foundation, published in May 1959, estimated that the population of India would reach 480 millions by 1965 while agricultural production would only be enough to feed at a reasonable level about 360 millions.

of the benefits of economic growth, and prevents any significant rise in levels of living. This is the case in most Asian countries, and in Latin America, where the rate of economic growth has in any case been low; in large parts of Africa, however, which are relatively sparsely populated the increase of population does not pose the same problems. Nevertheless, in all the developing countries rapid population growth, resulting in a high proportion of dependent children, imposes great strains upon the administration of social services and diverts resources from investment in production to the extension of these services. In another ten or twenty years new problems will appear, of providing employment for the large numbers entering the labour force. The revolution in agricultural production itself, while it has removed the immediate danger of food shortages, is creating new difficulties; it requires fairly substantial investment in seeds, irrigation, etc., and so tends to increase the advantages of large landowners and to drive small farmers and peasants off the land into the cities, which already face problems of inadequate employment opportunities and overstrained urban services.

The extent of the problems which may arise as a result of urbanization in a developing country is suggested in a collection of studies on India, edited by Roy Turner, *India's Urban Future*.[1] In the first essay, by Kingsley Davis, 'Urbanization in India: Past and Future' some estimates are given of the future size of major Indian cities. The 'high estimates' for the year 2000—which do not now appear so high in view of the fact that the total population increase has been greater than was expected at that time, and that migration to the cities may also be larger than estimated—were: for Calcutta 66 millions, for Delhi 33 millions, for Bombay 22 millions. It is not difficult to foresee the problems which such vast urban aggregates may produce in a poor country. In the absence of rapid industrial growth, providing both employment and the resources for urban services, there will be created large areas of concentrated poverty and discontent, and these may engender violent political movements which, unless they prove capable of bringing about economic growth and controlling population increase quickly and effectively, are likely to have mainly destructive effects.

The growth of towns creates opportunities as well as problems. The towns are centres of innovation, of economic growth and political change, and the new values and attitudes which develop there may have an important influence upon the rural population. A study by S. C. Dube[2] shows the influence of Hyderabad upon the political

[1] Berkeley and Los Angeles, 1962.
[2] S. C. Dube, *Indian Village* (London, 1955).

structure, caste relations, and social attitudes in a village within
its orbit; and another study, by F. G. Bailey[1], of a village in the
Orissa hills more remote from an urban centre, shows how even there
the influence of the urban economic system leads to a growth of
commerce, while the development of national administration results
in a breakdown of political isolation, with important effects upon
village organization. At the same time, however, rural attitudes affect
the towns, for a large proportion of the town population consists of
recent immigrants from the countryside. As P. C. Lloyd observes of
some African towns: 'Here the individual may escape the restraint
of his family and kin, of traditional elders and tribal values. How
many men choose to do so is another matter; for . . . the African
townsman tends to remain in a very close relationship with his kin
and community of origin.'[2] A study of immigrant workers in Bombay[3]
reveals a similar attachment to the villages of origin. Nearly half
the sample studied visit their village once a year, and almost all
would have liked to pay more frequent visits. Those with families
send them on visits to the village as often as they can. The immigrant
workers live between two cultures, urban and rural, and urban values
are not yet completely predominant, though they are gradually
tending to prevail: in the city women acquire greater freedom,
there are changes in dress and in the value of education, and caste
rules are not so strictly observed. On the other hand, the joint-
family continues to be highly regarded; it still has a function in the
city as a system of mutual aid, and it maintains the link between the
immigrant and his village.

These are phenomena of a period of transition—which may be
very long—in the largely peasant societies of Asia and Africa which
are slowly becoming more industrial and urban. The problems
which they pose concern the role of the new urban groups which
are being formed. What are the ideologies of the new elites, of the
urban middle class and the working class? How do these groups
influence the mass of the rural population through education, the
mass media, administration, economic relations, and political organization? In considering these questions we have also to bear in mind
that new social and political movements have arisen among peasants
themselves. Peasant based revolutions—inspired and led largely, it

[1] F. G. Bailey, *Caste and the Economic Frontier* (Manchester, 1957).
[2] P. C. Lloyd, *Africa in Social Change* (Harmondsworth, 1967), p. 110.
[3] P. N. Prabhu, 'A Study on the Social Effects of Urbanization on Industrial
Workers Migrating from Rural Areas to the City of Bombay', in *The Social
Implications of Industrialization and Urbanization* (UNESCO, Calcutta, 1956),
pp. 49–106.

is true, by urban intellectuals—have already brought about great changes in some developing countries, and new political doctrines have appeared which give pre-eminence to rural rather than urban groups in the process of social transformation.

These issues, which will be examined more fully in a later chapter, do not detract from the importance of the general problems of population increase and urban growth which I have outlined. In most of the developing countries industrialization, in its economic aspect, has been more or less comprehensively planned, but it is only in recent years that similar attention has been given to the question of planning and controlling population growth, which is at least as important and presents in many respects even greater difficulties, while the planning of urban growth has scarcely been tackled at all. The magnitude of these problems should not be underestimated. They are among the most vital and complex of all those which confront many of the developing countries at the present time, regardless of their social and political systems.

Chapter 6

TYPES OF SOCIAL GROUP

The distribution of the population in social groups, and the size, number, and characteristics of such groups, are important features of the structure of a society. 'The description and classification of the principal types of social groups and institutions' in Ginsberg's view, make up the study of social structure.[1] In actual research it is difficult, and probably undesirable, to make a rigid distinction between the study of groups and the study of institutions, since the latter (which may be defined as enduring patterns of behaviour) arise from the activities of groups. But for purposes of exposition it is convenient to deal first with the different groupings which may exist in a population.

We may begin by distinguishing between social groups proper, and the looser associations which have been termed by some writers 'quasi-groups'. A social group may be defined as an aggregate of individuals in which (i) definite relations exist between the individuals comprising it, and (ii) each individual is conscious of the group itself and its symbols. In other words, a social group has at least a rudimentary structure and organization (including rules, rituals, etc.), and a psychological basis in the consciousness of its members. A family, a village, a nation, a trade union, or a political party is a social group in this sense. A quasi-group, on the other hand, is an aggregate which lacks structure or organization, and whose members may be unaware, or less aware, of the existence of the grouping. Social classes, status groups, age and sex groups, crowds, are examples of quasi-groups. But these examples suggest that the frontier between groups and quasi-groups is fluid and variable. Quasi-groups may give rise to organized social groups, as for example, social classes give rise to political parties or the feminine sex group to feminist associations; or they themselves may become

[1] M. Ginsberg, 'The scope and methods of sociology' in *The Study of Society* (ed. F. C. Bartlett *et al.*, London, 1939). Cf. R. Firth, *Human Types* (2nd ed. London, 1956), p. 98, 'The social structure of a community includes the different types of groups which the people form and the institutions in which they take part'.

fully organized groups, as for example age groups which become organized age sets in some primitive societies.

Social groups can be classified in a variety of ways. We may consider first the character of the relation between the members. The best known distinction here is that first proposed by Tönnies between *Gemeinschaft* (community) and *Gesellschaft* (society or association). Community is defined as 'intimate, private, and exclusive living together', and Tönnies gives as examples of groups based on this type of relationship the family or kin group, the neighbourhood (rural village), and the group of friends. Association is defined as 'public life', as something which is consciously and deliberately entered upon; and Tönnies mentions as examples principally those groups which are concerned with economic interests. Two major criteria are used by Tönnies in defining community and association. First, in communities individuals are involved as complete persons who can satisfy all or most of a wide range of purposes in the group, while in associations individuals are not wholly involved but look to the satisfaction of specific and partial ends. Secondly, a community is united by an accord of feeling or sentiment between individuals, whereas an association is united by a rational agreement of interest.[1]

In Tönnies' own work the distinction between community and association was applied both to the social groups within a society, and to societies themselves. In the latter sense it has an affinity with some other distinctions between two broad types of society, which will be discussed in the next chapter. As applied to social groups it resembles the distinction made by C. H. Cooley between 'primary groups' and others.[2] 'By primary groups I mean those characterized by intimate face-to-face association and co-operation. The result of intimate association, psychologically, is a certain fusion of individualities in a common whole, so that one's very self, for many purposes at least, is the common life and purpose of the group . . . it involves the sort of sympathy and mutual identification for which "we" is the natural expression'.[3] Cooley's definition of the primary group, as has been pointed out,[4] implied three conditions; physical proximity of the members, smallness of the group, and the enduring character of the relation. Tönnies, on the other hand, intended his distinction to apply to all social groups, but it is worthy of note that

[1] F. Tönnies, *Community and Association* (1887; English trans. London, 1955).
[2] C. H. Cooley, *Social Organisation* (1909). The term 'secondary group', which Cooley did not employ, has come into general use to refer to the type of group which he contrasted with 'primary group'.
[3] *Op cit.*, p. 23.
[4] Kingsley Davis, *Human Society* (New York, 1948), Ch 11.

his examples of 'community' (family, village, group of friends, medieval town) also imply, in varying degrees, these three conditions.

Thus, we have a number of criteria which can be applied in the classification of social groups: the end for which the group exists, the emotional or intellectual character of the relations between members of the group, the personal or impersonal nature of their relations, the size of the group, and its duration. Some of these factors have received more attention than others. The size of groups has been studied from different points of view. Simmel, in a well known essay,[1] examined the relationship between the number of members and the structure of a group. In another study, he showed how the concentration of population in cities changed the nature of men's social relationships.[2] Other sociologists have discussed the general problem of changes in the scale of social organization. Durkheim, as we saw earlier, explained the division of labour and the emergence of a new form of society based upon organic solidarity by the growth of population. Hobhouse took increase in scale as one of his criteria of social development, but at the same time examined the repercussions of this increase upon other factors in development. It is evident that one major problem of social life has been that of establishing and maintaining social solidarity in large groups, where the intimate relationships of primary groups are impossible.[3]

Recent studies of social groups have taken a number of different directions. There have been several attempts at a more systematic typology of groups. One of the most comprehensive is that of G. Gurvitch who has proposed fifteen criteria of classification: content, size, duration, rhythm, proximity of members, basis of formation (voluntary, etc.) access (open, semi-closed, closed), degree of organization, function, orientation, relation with the inclusive society, relation with other groups, types of social control, type of authority, degree of unity.[4] This scheme of classification incorporates many of the distinctions which we have already discussed; it has still to be seen whether the additional criteria make possible a typology in which the significant differences between groups would be revealed.

[1] G. Simmel, 'The number of members as determining the sociological form of the group', *American Journal of Sociology*, VIII, 1902.

[2] G. Simmel, 'The metropolis and mental life', reprinted in Hatt and Reiss, *op. cit.*

[3] See G. C. Homans, *The Human Group* (1948) Ch. 18. 'Groups and Civilization'; R. C. Angell, *The Integration of American Society* (New York and London, 1941).

[4] Georges Gurvitch, *La vocation actuelle de la sociologie* (2nd edn. 1957), Vol. I, Ch. 5, 'Typologie des groupements particuliers'.

A second approach is best illustrated by G. C. Homans' study of primary groups.[1] Homans gives a number of reasons for studying such groups; among others that 'perhaps we cannot manage a sociological synthesis that will apply to whole communities and nations, but it is just possible we can manage one that will apply to the small group.' Thus, he aims at formulating generalizations which will apply to all small groups, on the basis of re-analysis of data from a number of detailed empirical studies. The emphasis throughout is upon the similarities between groups, and not upon the differences, as it is in the case of attempts at a typology. While the analysis and interpretation of material provided by the original studies are often illuminating, the resulting generalizations are disappointing in respect of their importance or probable validity. It is difficult to take seriously the proposition that 'the more frequently persons interact with one another, when no one of them originates interaction with much greater frequency than the others, the greater is their liking for one another and their feeling of ease in one another's presence.' (p. 243.) The example given of relations between brothers is unfortunate, since it is between siblings that some of the most violent antipathies arise. Miss Ivy Compton-Burnett's portrayal of family life seems to be as near the truth as that of Mr Homans.

Homans' work has, however, revived interest in the study of primary groups, and the interest has been reinforced by other developments such as J. L. Moreno's sociometric studies.[2] One of the attractions of small group studies is the possibility of experiment, and some useful if limited work has been done on these lines.[3]

In his book Homans makes clear that the study of small groups is only one possible approach to the study of society. But in other cases enthusiasm for small group analysis has led to distortion. The work of Cooley already foreshadowed one error; he wrote that primary groups 'are primary in several senses, but chiefly in that they are fundamental in forming the social nature and ideals of the individual', and again that 'they do not change in the same degree as more elaborate relations, but form a comparatively permanent source out of which the latter are ever springing . . . (they) are springs of life, not only for the individual but for social institutions.'

[1] G. C. Homans, *op. cit.*

[2] For a general account see J. L. Moreno, *Who Shall Survive?* (Washington, 1934).

[3] For example, the experiments in group leadership. There is a useful general survey of small group studies, including experimental studies, in M. Argyle, *The Scientific Study of Social Behaviour* (London, 1957), Pt. II, Ch. V, 'Small social groups', pp. 118–60.

Cooley and some recent sociologists seem to imply that it is possible to move directly from the study of small groups to the study of inclusive societies. This is associated with the view that small groups have a determining influence upon social life. Yet all the evidence points to the opposite conclusion. Historically considered, small groups have been shaped by society much more than they have shaped it. The modern Western family, for example, is the product of industrialism. The transformation of the rural village is likewise due to more general changes in the inclusive society.

Another approach to the study of groups is that suggested in R. Redfield's *The Little Community*. Redfield justifies the choice of this area of study in much the same terms as Homans. He writes, 'The little community has been chosen because it is a kind of human whole with which students of man have a great deal of experience, and because it is easier to develop a chain of thought in relation especially to villages and bands than to try to do so also in relation to personalities and civilizations and literatures'. Moreover, 'the small community has been the very predominant form of human living throughout the history of mankind . . . One estimate is that today three-quarters of the human race still live in villages'. Redfield defines the little community by four characteristics: (1) *distinctiveness*—'where the community begins and where it ends is apparent'; (2) *smallness*—'either it itself is the unit of personal observation or else, being somewhat larger and yet homogeneous, it provides in some part of it a unit of personal observation fully representative of the whole'; (3) *homogeneity*—'activities and states of mind are much alike for all persons in corresponding sex and age positions; and the career of one generation repeats that of the preceding'; (4) *self-sufficiency*—'(it) provides for all or most of the activities and needs of the people in it. The little community is a cradle-to-the-grave arrangement'.[1] Having defined the object of his study Redfield goes on to analyse it in terms of the general concepts which have been applied to all types of groups and inclusive societies; ecology, social structure, life cycles, personality, cultural values, social change. His study clarifies, and suggests modifications of, some of these concepts. In the later chapters he examines directly the problem we have raised about the relation between small groups and the larger communities, up to the inclusive society, within which they exist. First, there are different types of relation. The Siriono Indians are a very distinct and self-sufficient group having only

[1] Thus Redfield (in contrast with Homans) is concerned with one fairly definite type of small group, and his descriptions and generalizations are all the more valuable.

slight contact with other Indian bands and avoiding contacts with white men. On the other hand, the relations of the Nuer (described by Evans-Pritchard) with the larger society can be represented by a diagram of concentric circles. The village of Chan Kom (studied by Redfield) has more complex relations with the state of Yucatan and with Mexico as a whole. There is 'a complex aggregation of settlements to which any one village . . . would be related in a number of kinds of relationships and functions'.

Redfield suggests that we need 'a recognition of a series or range of kinds of communities according to their degree of independence from city, manor, national state, or other centre of a different or more developed mode of living'.[1] He goes on finally to propose, with reference to peasant communities or partly urbanized rural communities, a distinction between abstract kinds of living; between folk society and civilization. Here he encounters the preoccupations of earlier sociologists, Maine, Tönnies and Durkheim, whose dichotomies I have already briefly discussed.

The problem of the relationship between social groups and the inclusive society can be put in another form. We may ask how, and to what extent, types of societies can be distinguished in terms of the social groups which exist within them. There is one very familiar distinction, between 'primitive' and 'civilized' societies, in terms of the *number* and *diversity* of the social groups within them. Spencer, and especially Durkheim, made use of this characteristic in their classifications of societies. Primitive societies are no longer regarded by anthropologists as simple, but they are certainly less differentiated. The contrast which Durkheim draws, in *The Division of Labour in Society*, is broadly accurate; and there is much to be said for his association of individualism with increasing social differentiation, ultimately based upon the more extensive division of labour.

Another approach would be to classify societies in terms of the predominant types of social groups. This has been attempted in various ways. One of the best known distinctions is between societies in which primary groups predominate and those in which secondary groups predominate. Since Tönnies' original distinction between 'community' and 'association', many sociologists have employed this criterion, with slight variations in meaning. It is a commonplace of modern sociology to refer to the impersonal, rationalized, and segmentary relationships between individuals in urban industrial societies, and to contrast these with the relationships existing in primitive and non-industrial societies. Yet all such dichotomies

---

[1] This discussion is in Ch. VIII, pp. 113–31.

appear much too simple; for in spite of all the sociological research we still know little, in detail, of the social relations of modern men, and can still be surprised by the importance of kinship and other primary groupings.[1] Perhaps a more useful classification would result from identifying the specific types of group which are characteristic of different societies. This can be illustrated by a comparison between India, as an example of a rural agrarian society, and a western industrial society.

It is not difficult to identify the major types of group in traditional Indian society; they are the village community, the caste group, and the joint family. By contrast, the types of group which are charactistic and important in western industrial societies seem to be the economic organizations, social classes, and the nuclear family. In addition, the inclusive society itself (as a nation-state) has much greater significance. What can be said about Indian society in terms of these characteristic groups? I shall refer later to the joint family (Ch. 10) and the caste groups (Ch. 11). Here it will be useful to say something about the village community, which has often been regarded as the most important feature of the social structure, and which raises many problems in connection with the process of urbanization which I discussed earlier.

The early studies of the Indian village emphasized its self-sufficiency and its stability. Self-sufficiency meant that the village had its own political, as well as economic, institutions. 'The village communities are little republics, having nearly everything they want within themselves, and almost independent of any foreign relations. They seem to last where nothing else lasts.'[2] Sir Henry Maine referred to the Indian village constitution as 'the least destructible institution of society which never willingly surrenders any of its usage to innovations. Conquests and revolutions seem to have swept over it without disturbing or displacing it, and the most beneficent systems of government in India have always been those which have recognized it as the basis of Indian administration . . .'[3] Karl Marx, emphasizing the economic self-sufficiency of the village, found in this a clue to the unchanging character of Indian, and other Asian, societies: 'The simplicity of the organization for production in these self-sufficing communities that constantly reproduce themselves in the same form, and if destroyed by chance, spring up again on the same spot and with the same name—this simplicity supplies the key to the secret of the

[1] See below, Ch. 11.

[2] Sir Charles Metcalfe; *see* Sir J. W. Kaye, *Selections From the Papers of Lord Metcalfe* (London, 1855).

[3] H. S. Maine, *Village Communities in the East and West* (1876).

unchangeableness of Asiatic *societies*, an unchangeableness in such striking contrast with the constant dissolution and refounding of Asiatic *states*, and the neverceasing changes of dynasty. The structure of the economic elements of society remains untouched by the storm clouds of the political sky.'[1]

Indian villages remained in certain respects self-sufficient and autonomous until well into the nineteenth century, when the development of capitalism under British rule began to exert its influence.[2] The more rapid industrialization and urbanization since 1947 have certainly brought about great changes. A number of village studies give some indication of the nature of these changes. S. C. Dube, in a study of *Shamirpet* in Hyderabad,[3] has shown the increasing influence of Hyderabad town upon the village (which is twenty-five miles away) through the development of transport, making for greater mobility, and the attraction of urban educational facilities. Other influences are the government welfare agencies, and the activities of nationwide political parties.[4] The outcome of these more intensive contacts with the larger society is a change in the social and political hierarchy of the village; wealth, education, position in the government service, are among the new sources of prestige and influence. Yet the change is slow, and 'the grip of the traditional system is still firm'. R. Redfield's work on the 'little community' had an obvious relevance to India, and in 1954 a seminar conducted at the University of Chicago by Redfield and Singer took as its theme 'The Indian Village'. The eight papers discussed at the seminar form a most valuable collection of knowledge about contemporary village life.[5] The fact of change is evident. As Redfield and Singer say in their foreword: 'In village India the traditional landmarks lose their outlines—caste, joint family, festivals, and religious beliefs. The school, the political party, the movie, the community plan, begin to reach even remote villages.' At the same time the traditional groups do not disappear, and they reappear, sometimes in a modified form, in urban areas. The joint family survives in Indian towns, and caste associations are formed which provide housing, employment, and other welfare services for their members. Similarly, in the new African

[1] Karl Marx, *Capital*, Vol. 1 (1867), Berlin, Dietz, Volksausgabe, I, pp. 374–76.

[2] These changes are discussed in A. R. Desai, *Social Background of Indian Nationalism* (op. cit.). The self-sufficiency of the village in modern times has probably been exaggerated; for criticism of the idea *see* M. N. Srinivas, 'Village Studies', *Economic Weekly*, 1954, pp. 605–9.

[3] S. C. Dube, *Indian Village* (London, 1955).

[4] In a more recent book, *India's Changing Villages* (London, 1958), Dube shows in greater detail the effects of the government development programmes.

[5] McKim Marriott (ed.), *Village India* (Chicago, 1955).

states, village, kinship and tribal bonds remain strong, and as P. C. Lloyd suggests, 'tribalism' develops as an urban phenomenon (in much the same way as caste) because it is a familiar way of categorizing oneself and receiving support from others in a strange and complex environment.[1] Thus the traditional social groups give way only slowly to those which arise in a modern industrial society—occupational groups, trade unions, classes, political parties, and a variety of voluntary associations—except in those countries where, as in China, a revolution has accomplished a much sharper break with the past.

Even at a more advanced stage of industrialization the constellation of groups in the countries of the Third World may differ considerably from that in the industrial countries of Europe and North America, for the developing countries are seeking to create new forms of society on the basis of their own heritage of thought and institutions. In India, Gandhi's ideas have entered into more recent political doctrines; for example, the proposal by Jaya Prakash Narayan, a former leader of the Praja Socialist Party, that the village community, expressing the two ideals of the voluntary limitation of wants and of unanimity in social and political views, should be preserved and strengthened as a fundamental element in the Indian political system.[2] In Africa, many exponents of 'African socialism' have emphasized the distinctive 'communitarian' character of traditional African society, and have urged that this should be preserved in the process of economic growth, by embarking upon *gradual* industrialization combined with decentralization and the maximum possible participation of workers and peasants in the planning and execution of development projects.[3] There are already, indeed, new types of social groups which have emerged in the developing countries—the Chinese communes, community development projects, the kibbutzim.

The discussion of types of social group should not be limited, therefore, to the contrast between folk and urban, traditional and modern, or agrarian and industrial societies. These distinctions are important because there correspond with them, as I have shown, differences in the type of social group which is predominant; but there are also other distinctions to be made between types of society (which will be examined in the next chapter), there is a greater variety of social groups than these simple dichotomies suggest, and there are possibilities for the creation of new kinds of social group and social relationship which sociological classifications sometimes obscure.

[1] P. C. Lloyd, *op. cit.*, Chapter 12.
[2] J. P. Narayan, *A Plea for Reconstruction of Indian Polity* (New Delhi, 1959).
[3] See the discussion in Peter Worsley, *The Third World*, Chapter 4.

107

Notes on Reading for Part II

I. POPULATION AND SOCIETY

1. *General*

Carr Saunders, A. M. *World Population* (Oxford, Clarendon Press, 1936).
An early study of the growth of world population.

Penrose, E. F. *Population Theories and Their Applications* (Stanford, Stanford University Press, 1934).
Reviews the main theories of population and discusses the relation between population and resources.

Myrdal, Alva. *Nation and Family* (London, Routledge & Kegan Paul, 1945).
A pioneer study of the modern family and Swedish population policy.

Political and Economic Planning. *World Population and Resources* (London, Allen & Unwin, 1955).
A comprehensive survey of the problems, with detailed studies of nineteen countries grouped according to demographic characteristics. Also discusses population policies.

United Nations. *The Determinants and Consequences of Population Trends* (New York, Population Division, Department of Social Affairs, United Nations, 1954).
A summary of numerous studies made by the United Nations, which briefly presents the available information on population in relation to social, cultural and economic factors.

Sauvy, A. *Théorie générale de la population.* (2 vols., Paris, Presses Universitaires de France, 1952 and 1954).
The first volume deals in detail with the relation between population and the economy.

Thompson, W. S. and Lewis, D. T. *Population Problems* (5th edn., New York, McGraw-Hill, 1965).
A standard textbook.

Wrong, Dennis H. *Population and Society* (3rd edn., New York, Random House, 1967).
A useful short introduction.

2. *Population problems in developing countries*

Davis, Kingsley. *The Population of India and Pakistan* (Princeton, Princeton University Press, 1951).
The most comprehensive survey of the population problem, completed before the 1951 census.

Davis, Kingsley. 'The World's Population Crisis', in R. K. Merton and R. A. Nisbet (eds.), *Contemporary Social Problems* (2nd end., New York, 1966).

Deals with the world situation, but with special emphasis on developing countries.

Ghosh, D. *Pressure of Population and Economic Efficiency in India* (Oxford University Press, 1946).

A study of the economic costs of high birth and death rates.

Coale, A. J., and Hoover, E. M. *Population Growth and Economic Development in Low-Income Countries* (Princeton, 1958).

II. URBANISM

1. *General*

*Simmel, G. 'The Metropolis and mental life'.

A perceptive essay on the cultural effects of urban life.

*Wirth, L. 'Urbanism as a way of life'.

A well-known essay which attempts to outline the sociological problems of urbanism and to construct a typology of cities.

*[These two essays are reprinted in the reader in urban sociology by P. K. Hatt and A. J. Reiss, *Cities and Society* (Glencoe, The Free Press, 1957).]

Lynd, R. A. and H. M. *Middletown* (New York, Harcourt, 1929), and *Middletown in Transition* (New York, Harcourt, 1937).

Two pioneer studies of an American town.

Urban studies in France, Great Britain and Scandinavia up to the mid-fifties are reviewed in *Current Sociology* IV (1) 1955, P. Chombart de Lauwe (France); and IV (4) 1955, Ruth Glass and J. Westergaard (Great Britain and Scandinavia).

Pirenne, H. *Medieval Cities* (English trans. Princeton, Princeton University Press, 1925; republished in Doubleday Anchor Books, New York, 1957).

A classical study of the emergence, growth and role of towns in feudal Europe, by a sociologically-minded historian.

Fustel de Coulanges, N. D. *The Ancient City* (First English trans. 1873; republished in Doubleday Anchor Books, New York, 1956).

A pioneering work on the institutions of Greek and Roman cities, with an emphasis upon the role of religion.

2. *Urbanization in developing countries*

Bopegamage, A. *Delhi: A Study in Urban Sociology* (Bombay, University of Bombay, 1957).

Includes data on neighbourhoods, communications and occupations.

Turner, Roy (ed.), *India's Urban Future* (Berkeley and Los Angeles, 1962).

UNESCO. *The Social Implications of Industrialization and Urbanization* (Calcutta, UNESCO Research Centre on the Social Implications of Industralization in Southern Asia, 1956).
Includes studies on Bangkok, Dacca and Djakarta, and two studies on India.

UNESCO. *Social Implications of Industrialization and Urbanization in Africa South of the Sahara* (Paris, 1956).

III. SOCIAL GROUPS

1. *General*

See especially the following books which are discussed in the text:

Homans, G. C. *The Human Group* (New York, Harcourt, Brace, 1950).

Redfield, R. *The Little Community* (Chicago, University of Chicago, Stockholm, Almquist & Wiksell, 1955).

Argyle, M. *The Scientific Study of Behaviour* (London, Methuen, 1957), Pt. II, Ch. V, pp. 118–160, 'Small social groups'.

For studies of specific primary groups see the following, which are good examples of this kind of research:

Thrasher, F. M. *The Gang* (Chicago, University of Chicago Press, 1936).

Whyte, W. F. *Street Corner Society* (Chicago, University of Chicago Press, 1943).

2. *Indian Village Studies*

The early classical studies are:

Baden-Powell, B. H. *The Indian Village Community* (London, Longmans, Green, 1896).

Baden-Powell, B. H. *The Origin and Growth of Village Communities in India* (London, Swan Sonnenschein, 1899).

Maine, H. S. *Village Communities in the East and West* (London, John Murray, 1872).

Recent studies include:

Dube, S. C. *Indian Village* (London, Routledge & Kegan Paul, 1955). A detailed anthropological study of Shamirpet, Hyderabad.

Dube, S. C. *India's Changing Villages* (London, Routledge & Kegan Paul, 1958).

Marriott, McKim (ed.). *Village India: Studies in the Little Community* (Chicago, University of Chicago Press, 1955).

3. *Other studies of villages and rural groups*

Myrdal, Jan. *Report From a Chinese Village* (New York, Pantheon, 1965).

Wolf, Eric. *Peasants* (Englewood Cliffs, Prentice-Hall, 1966).

Part III

SOCIAL INSTITUTIONS

Chapter 7

SOCIAL STRUCTURE, SOCIETIES AND CIVILIZATIONS

'Social structure' is one of the central concepts of sociology, but it has not been employed consistently or unambiguously. Herbert Spencer, who was one of the first writers to use the term, was too much fascinated by his biological analogies (organic structure and evolution) to make clear what he meant by the structure of society.[1] Durkheim also left the term vague.[2] Many later sociologists and social anthropologists have tried to give it a more precise meaning, but their conceptions of social structure diverge widely. Thus Radcliffe-Brown regards as 'a part of the social structure all social relations of person to person. . . . In the study of social structure the concrete reality with which we are concerned is the set of actually existing relations, at a given moment of time, which link together certain human beings'.[3] But he goes on to say that the object which we attempt to describe and analyse is *structural form*, i.e. the general relationships, disregarding slight variations and the particular individuals involved.[4] It is this structural form which most writers have designated social structure. But Radcliffe-Brown's definition is very broad, as Firth has pointed out: 'It makes no distinction between the ephemeral and the more enduring elements in social activity, and it makes it almost impossible to distinguish the idea of the structure of a society from that of the totality of the society itself'.[5]

Other writers have restricted the term to the more permanent and organized relationships in society. Thus, M. Ginsberg regards social structure as the complex of the principal groups and institutions which constitute societies.[6] This conception is also important for the connection which it emphasizes between the abstract social

[1] H. Spencer, *Principles of Sociology* (3rd revised edn. 1885), Vol. I, Part II.
[2] E. Durkheim, *The Rules of Sociological Method*, Ch. IV; *The Division of Labour in Society*, Ch. VI.
[3] A. R. Radcliffe-Brown, 'On Social Structure', *op. cit.*, p. 191–2.
[4] *Ibid.*, p. 192.
[5] R. Firth, *Elements of Social Organization*, p. 30.
[6] M. Ginsberg, *op. cit.* (*see* above p. 92).

relationships and the social groups which give rise to or are involved in them. From this point of view, the study of social structure can be undertaken in terms of institutional arrangements, or of the relations between social groups, or of both together[1]. If we thus restrict the term 'social structure' to mean those more permanent and important relationships and groups, we perhaps need another term to refer to the other activities which go on in society, and which frequently represent variations from the structural forms. R. Firth has proposed the term 'social organization', which he defines as 'the systematic ordering of social relations by acts of choice and decision'. 'In the aspect of social structure is to be found the continuity principle of society; in the aspect of organization is to be found the variation or change principle—by allowing evaluation of situations and entry of individual choice.'[2]

A third approach, which defines social structure in a still more restricted way is that which makes use of the notion of *social role:* it is exemplified by S. F. Nadel, *The Theory of Social Structure*, and H. Gerth and C. W. Mills, *Character and Social Structure*. Nadel argues that, 'We arrive at the structure of a society through abstracting from the concrete population and its behaviour the pattern or network (or 'system') of relationships obtaining between actors in their capacity of playing roles relative to one another'.[3] Similarly, Gerth and Mills say that the concept of role is '. . . the key term in our definition of institution', and 'just as role is the unit with which we build our conception of institution, so institution is the unit with which we build the conception of social structure'.[4] This latter account makes clear, as is implied by Nadel, that the analysis of social structure in terms of social roles is not fundamentally different from an analysis in terms of social institutions; for an institution is a complex or cluster of roles. Nevertheless, there is, I think, some difference of emphasis. There is some advantage in introducing the concept of role since, as Gerth and Mills observe, it forms a major link between character and social structure. It facilitates the necessary co-operation between psychology and sociology in the study of social behaviour. Yet the emphasis upon individual actors enacting roles also has disadvantages. It tends to produce an excessively individualistic conception of social behaviour, in which society is

---

[1] As was noted above, p. 99.

[2] R. Firth, *op. cit.*, pp. 35–40. It may be questioned whether social organization provides *the* change principle. There are large scale structural changes which could not be brought about by the kinds of evaluation and choice which Firth gives as examples. See Ch. 18 below.

[3] *Op. cit.*, p. 12.   [4] *Op. cit.*, pp. 22–3.

viewed as an aggregate of individuals related only through the complex role system of the society as a whole, while the social groups within society are neglected. We shall see later how this occurs in some recent theories of social stratification in terms of role and status, where the existence of distinctive social groups (e.g. social classes) and the relations of competition and conflict between them receive little attention. It is perhaps worthy of note that the concept of role seems to have been accepted most readily by psychologists interested mainly in individual behaviour, and by social anthropologists who study societies in which there is little diversity of social groups.

One further point should be mentioned. A distinction has sometimes been made between social structure as the system of 'ideal' relations between persons and social structure as the system of actual relations. The distinction is most easily made by anthropologists studying small communities who are able to compare informants' accounts of what relations exist and what behaviour occurs, with the relations and behaviour which they themselves observe. Sociologists are not able to do this in studying historical societies, and even in their studies of present day societies they are often obliged by the size and complexity of the societies to concentrate upon the more easily observed 'ideal' system of institutions as it is expressed in law and in moral and religious codes. But the distinction is important, and sociological research should aim more deliberately than it often does at approaching, by suitable methods, the anthropologists' observation of what actually happens in social behaviour.

Of the different conceptions we have discussed,[1] the most useful seems to me that which regards social structure as the complex of the major institutions and groups in society. There is no great difficulty in identifying these institutions and groups. It can be shown that the existence of human society requires certain arrangements or processes; or, as has been said, that there are 'functional prerequisites of society'.[2] The minimum requirements seem to be: (i) a system of communication; (ii) an economic system, dealing with

[1] I have not discussed the view of C. Lévi-Strauss that 'the term "social structure" has nothing to do with empirical reality but with models which are built up after it' ['Social structure', in *Anthropology Today*, (ed. A. L. Kroeber)] since this raises mainly methodological issues. In his later work Lévi-Strauss appears to modify this view insofar as he claims that it is possible to discover an underlying structure of society which depends upon the structure of the human mind. See my discussion above, pp. 61–2.

[2] See D. Aberle, A. Cohen, A. Davies, M. Levy and F. Sutton, 'The functional prerequisites of society', *Ethics*, LX (2), 1950. This classification of necessary elements in social structure need not, of course, be formulated in functionalist language; one can refer quite simply to 'prerequisites of society'.

the production and the allocation of goods; (iii) arrangements (including the family and education) for the socialization of new generations; (iv) a system of authority and of distribution of power; and perhaps (v) a system of ritual, serving to maintain or increase social cohesion, and to give social recognition to significant personal events such as birth, puberty, courtship, marriage and death. The major institutions and groups are those concerned with such basic requirements. From them, others may emerge, such as social stratification, which then influence them in turn. There is little disagreement among sociologists about which are the major institutions, and in the following chapters I shall examine these elements of social structure in detail.

We still have one difficulty to face. Every society has a social structure, although several societies may have similar social structures. But how are we to determine what is a society; or in other words, the extent of a particular social structure? Was Greece a society, or were the city-states distinct societies? Was India, until recently, a single society, or was it an aggregate of societies brought into some kind of unity by a cultural, and especially a religious tradition? It is difficult, in many cases, to determine the boundaries of a society. R. Firth has argued that '. . . unless there is stark physical isolation, no society can be given a definite limit'. But political independence has often been taken as the criterion of a separate society. I. Schapera has used it in this way: he writes, 'By a 'political community' I mean a group of people organized into a single unit managing its affairs independently of external control . . . No community is completely isolated . . . But so long as it is alone decides on matters of local concern, so long as there is no dictation from outside, and so long as its decisions and actions cannot be overruled by any higher authority, it may be said to have political independence'. Even so, difficulties arise, since 'political independence' is relative (there *are* satellites), and we have to decide what degree of independence shall qualify any group as being a separate society. Moreover, we have to deal with many instances of the absorption of societies into larger units; or conversely, with the emergence or re-emergence of separate societies within such larger units. The latter is the case with the feudal societies resulting from the dissolution of the Roman Empire. And we have already seen how observers at certain periods characterized Indian villages as 'little republics'. In spite of these difficulties, the criterion of political independence is valuable, and where we find political independence along with distinct economic, religious and familial institutions we can safely regard the group as constituting a separate society.

116

So far we have been concerned with the spatial separation of societies, but what of their separation in time? Britain is a society, but is Britain in 1970 the same society as in 1870 or 1770? Is India the same society as a hundred or two hundred years ago? Here we readily find a criterion, though its practical application may not always be easy. Wherever there is an important change in social structure in a particular group, we should regard the society after this change as a new and distinct society. We have to decide what constitutes an *important* change; and this is not easy. We might say provisionally that it is a change which transforms all or most of the institutions in the society. Thus capitalist Britain or France are different societies from feudal Britain or France; the USSR is a different society from Tsarist Russia. But our judgment will be influenced to some extent by more general considerations about the classification of societies which we have now to discuss.

Types of Society

One of the first steps in sociology, as in any science, is a systematic classification of the phenomena with which it deals. I have discussed in earlier chapters the classification of social relations and social groups. Here I shall be concerned with the classification of inclusive societies, or social structures.

We may begin by considering the numerous dichotomous classifications which have already been mentioned on several occasions: e.g. Tönnies' 'Gemeinschaft' and 'Gesellschaft', Durkheim's 'mechanical solidarity' and 'organic solidarity', Maine's 'status' and 'contract', Spencer's 'militant' and 'industrial' societies. The first thing to remark is that such classifications appear very inadequate to encompass all the varieties of human society which exist or have existed. If we now look more closely at the classifications we shall find that they resemble each other in important ways. All four writers contrast a type of society in which the group dominates the individual and determines for him an unalterable situation, with a type of society in which the individual is properly speaking an 'individual', whose situation in society is at least partially the outcome of rational calculation and contractual relations with other individuals.[1] There are important differences between these writers on points of detail, in the accounts which they provide of how the change has come about, and in their valuations of the change. But the essential similarity of the classifications is unmistakable. It results from the fact that all four writers were profoundly impressed

[1] The contrast has been repeated recently by K. R. Popper in his distinction between 'tribal' and 'open' societies.

by the characteristics of the new industrial societies in which they lived. Thus they were led to contrast modern industrial societies with all other human societies; this was, in their eyes, the supreme distinction.

This can be seen best in the work of Tönnies and some later German sociologists. Tönnies' distinction between *Gemeinschaft* and *Gesellschaft* is entirely a distinction between modern capitalist, rationalistic, contractual societies, and all pre-capitalist societies. The theme reappears in Simmel's *Philosophie des Geldes* (1902) which examines the specific cultural characteristics of a society oriented towards the maximum production and accumulation of wealth, and it underlies all Max Weber's work, in his fundamental concern with the increasing rationalization of social life. We may agree upon the significant features of industrial societies without accepting the kind of classification which puts all other societies in a single class.

Spencer and Durkheim, of course, were aware that societies might be classified in other ways. Spencer proposed to distinguish four types of society: (i) *simple societies*, (ii) *compound societies*, (iii) *doubly compound societies*, and (iv) *trebly compound societies*.[1] The types are distinguished primarily in terms of scale (or size), but also in terms of associated phenomena such as the more extensive division of labour, more elaborate political organization, developed ecclesiastical hierarchy, social stratification, etc. But the utility of the classification appears less when it is realized that the first three social types comprise only primitive societies, while all civilized societies are grouped together in the fourth class, which includes, according to Spencer, Ancient Mexico, the Assyrian Empire, the Roman Empire, Great Britain, France, Germany, Italy and Russia. Spencer recognized that this classification cut across the distinction between militant and industrial societies, and he outlined, in effect, a composite classification of eight types of society (although industrial societies are mainly to be found among the trebly compound societies). Moreover, Spencer warned that 'pure' types are difficult to find for many reasons, including survivals and a kind of societal miscegenation.

Durkheim also outlined, in similar terms to those of Spencer, while criticizing the latter's scheme, a classification of societies. He distinguished: (i) *simple societies* (the horde); (ii) *simple polysegmentary societies* (e.g. Iroquois tribes); (iii) *simply compounded polysegmentary societies* (e.g. the Iroquois confederation, the three

[1] H. Spencer, *The Principles of Sociology* (3rd rev. edn. 1885), Vol. I, Pt. II, Ch. X, 'Social types and constitutions'.

tribes which founded Rome); (iv) *doubly compounded polysegmentary societies* (e.g. the ancient tribes, the Germanic tribes).[1] Durkheim did not go beyond these examples, but A. Moret and G. Davy later attempted a more elaborate classification, in terms of scale and internal differentiation, in their book *From Tribe to Empire*.[2]

Most of these classifications implied an evolutionary scheme. Other evolutionists proposed classifications in terms of intellectual development. Thus Comte, having formulated his 'law of three stages', according to which human thought developed from the theological through the metaphysical to the positive stage, attempted to correlate material life, types of social unit, types of order, and prevailing sentiments with these intellectual phases. Hobhouse, in a similar way, distinguished five phases in intellectual development: (i) formation of the elements of articulate thought in primitive societies; (ii) proto-science in the ancient East (Babylonia, Egypt and ancient China); (iii) the stage of reflection in the later East (China, Palestine and India); (iv) the stage of critical and systematic thought in Greece; (v) the stage of 'experiential reconstruction', represented by modern science. In his *Morals in Evolution* (1906) Hobhouse attempted to correlate types of social institution (forms of political organization, family, property, and social stratification) with these intellectual stages. In the same work, however, he proposed two other classifications; a classification of primitive societies in terms of their economic level, and a general classification of societies in terms of the nature of the social bond. Using the latter criterion Hobhouse distinguished three types of society, based upon kinship, authority and citizenship respectively. In a later work, *Social Development* (1924), Hobhouse introduced other criteria, scale, efficiency, mutuality, and freedom, which should also enter into the classification of societies. Nowhere did Hobhouse attempt to bring the different criteria together in an ordered scheme of classification. Indeed, neither Comte nor Hobhouse can be regarded as having formulated a classification of actual societies. They were both primarily concerned with levels of civilization, and much of their work is an intellectual history of mankind. In this respect their schemes are less useful than those of Spencer and Durkheim, who attempted to define types of society as intelligible units of study.

A different approach to classification is that which distinguishes different forms of one or several major institutions of society. The

---

[1] E. Durkheim, *The Rules of Sociological Method*, Ch. IV, 'Rules for the constitution of social types'.
[2] English trans. London, 1926.

economic system has often been taken as the crucial institution, and the best known classification along these lines is that of Marx. In the Preface to his *Contribution to the Critique of Political Economy* (1859) Marx wrote that, 'In broad outline we can designate the Asiatic, the ancient, the feudal and the modern bourgeois methods of production as so may epochs in the progress of the economic formation of society'. Elsewhere both he and Engels referred to primitive communism, ancient society, feudal society, and capitalism, as the principal epochs in the history of mankind. If we combine these two schemes we have five principal types of society; primitive, Asiatic, ancient, feudal, and capitalist. This is a valuable and utilizable preliminary classification, which has in fact been widely used, tacitly or explicitly, by many sociologists. It needs however, a number of modifications and qualifications.

First, it is evident that the major types may include sub-types. Hobhouse, Wheeler and Ginsberg in their *Material Culture and Social Institutions of the Simpler Peoples* (1915) were able to classify more than four hundred primitive societies in terms of their economic level of development, and to show that the forms of other social institutions were correlated with the type of economy. In a similar way, we might distinguish subtypes within the other major types of society, although this seems to be more difficult, chiefly because the number of 'civilized' societies is so small compared with the number of primitive societies. However, it may be possible to distinguish sub-types of feudal society (European, Japan from the eleventh to the nineteenth century, etc.) and of capitalist society (early liberal, competitive capitalism and later oligopolistic capitalism characterized by the pre-eminence of large corporations). It may eventually prove fruitful to use the term 'industrial society' for the fifth type of society and to distinguish as sub-types various forms of capitalist and collectivist industrial society.

A second qualification involves distinguishing between this scheme of classification and the theory of social development with which it is associated in Marxist thought. The types of society which Marx defined may be arranged in a historical sequence, though the Asiatic type of society constitutes an exception and has been relatively little discussed by Marxist writers.[1] In this case, the important problem becomes that of explaining the transition from one type of society to another throughout the sequence. But the classification may also be used for other purposes; to establish general features of each type of society in relation to its economy, or even to discover

[1] *See* George Lichtheim, 'Marx and the "Asiatic Mode of Production"', *St. Anthony's Studies*, No. 14 (London, 1964).

universal characteristics of every type of social structure which might then be formulated in a general law.

The classification has also to be dissociated from a theory of economic determinism, but it may well be argued that Marx himself did not propound such a theory.[1] A classification of societies in terms of their economic systems can be justified if it is found that the societies in each class also broadly resemble each other in other respects (e.g. social stratification, political structure, family structure) and are therefore genuine classes of similar phenomena. To explain the correlation between the economic system and other social institutions is a matter for later sociological theory and investigation.

Finally, we should not expect to find 'pure' instances of the different types of society. It would be better to regard them as 'ideal types', in Max Weber's sense; i.e. as constructs which do not describe any actual society, but which are fruitful in the analysis and investigation of actual societies.[2] Weber himself provided an ideal type definition of capitalism, and the same kind of definition might be formulated for the other types of society, and their sub-types.[3]

In earlier chapters I have suggested that a comprehensive classification of societies would require the definition of types of society in terms of the system of institutions, the number and character of the social groups within society, and the nature of the predominant social relations. We can conveniently test some of the principles of classification which have been discussed by a brief comparison of India and other developing countries with some industrial countries.

The predominant types of social group and social relations were briefly considered in the previous chapter, and here the main emphasis will be upon the system of institutions. To which social type does India belong? Marx defined the Asiatic type of society as one which had an agricultural economy with small units of production, and at the same time a centralized state and bureaucracy, whose power rested upon its regulation of water supplies. He examined particularly the case of India: 'Climate and territorial conditions, especially the vast tracts of desert, extending from the Sahara through Arabia, Persia, India, and Tartary, to the most elevated Asiatic highlands, constituted artificial irrigation by canals and waterworks the basis of Oriental agriculture. . . . This prime necessity of an economical and common use of water, which, in the Occident, drove private enterprise to voluntary association, as

---

[1] *See* below, p. 301.

[2] On Weber's use of the ideal type, see Aron, *German Sociology*, pp. 72–5.

[3] Such a definition of feudalism was in fact provided by Marc Bloch in *La société féodale*, Vol. II, Book III, Ch. I, 'La féodalité comme type social'.

in Flanders and Italy, necessitated, in the Orient where civilization was too low and the territorial extent too vast to call into life voluntary association, the interference of the centralizing power of Government. Hence an economical function devolved upon all Asiatic Governemnts, the function of providing public works . . . These two circumstances in the Hindoo, on the one hand, leaving, like all Oriental peoples, to the central government the care of the great public works, the prime condition of his agriculture and commerce, dispersed, on the other hand, over the surface of the country, and agglomerated in small centres by the domestic union of agricultural and manufacturing pursuits—these two circumstances had brought about, since the remotest times, a social system of particular features—the so-called *village system*, which gave to each of these small unions their independent organization and distinct life'.[1] Later, in *Capital*, he observed that 'In Hindustan, one of the material foundations of the powers exercized by the State over the small and disconnected productive organisms of the country, has always been the regulation of the water supply'.[2]

Max Weber later used the same idea in his account of the differences between East and West in respect of the growth of towns and the emergence of a *bourgeoisie*. 'The distinction is based on the fact that in the cultural evolution of Egypt, western Asia, India and China, the question of irrigation was crucial. The water question conditioned the existence of bureaucracy, the compulsory service of the dependent classes upon the functioning of the bureaucracy of the King. That the King also expressed his power in the form of military monopoly is the basis of the distinction between the military organization of Asia and that of the West. In the first case the royal official and the army are from the beginning the central figures of the process, while in the West both were originally absent.'[3]

In recent years there have been several studies of what are variously called *irrigation civilizations* or *hydraulic societies*.[4] These studies

---

[1] Karl Marx, 'The British Rule in India' *New York Daily Tribune*, June 25, 1853.

[2] Karl Marx, *Capital* (Everyman edn.) ,Vol. I, p. 558. Marx did not analyse the Asiatic type of society in any detail, but he treated it more systematically in an early draft of *Capital* which has been published under the title *Grundrisse der Kritik der politischen Oekonomie* (*Rohentwurf*) (Moscow, 1939 and 1941); pp. 375–413.

[3] Max Weber, *General Economic History* (Eng. trans. 1950), pp. 321–22.

[4] See especially J. H. Steward (ed.), *Irrigation Civilisations: A Comparative Study* (Pan-American Union, 1955); and K. Wittfogel, *Oriental Despotism* (New Haven, 1957). See also the criticisms in E. R. Leach, 'Hydraulic Society in Ceylon', *Past and Present*, April 1959.

have been related to the general study of bureaucracy, but little has yet been done in the way of large scale comparative work on bureaucratically organized societies.[1] The concept of 'irrigation civilization' has been used by A. K. N. Karim in explaining the absence in India of Western type towns and of a *bourgeoisie* able to acquire social and political influence.[2] He writes, 'The primary function of the State was to look after the water supply. . . . Its power was built upon the control of water works. And to control, regulate and supervize public works, and collect land tax, the State stationed its agents at various local centres , which became the towns.'[3] These did not resemble the European medieval towns, with their commercial middle class, communal organization, and relative independence of the feudal state.[4] The greatest changes in Indian social structure came during the period of British rule. They were, briefly, the decline of public works and thus of the paternalistic state, the development of capitalist enterprise, and the growth of towns (not so much in relative size, as in social and political importance).[5] One sign of the emergence of a self-conscious urban middle class was the nationalist movement, which was created, organized and supported by the new professional groups and the commercial and industrial *bourgeoisie*.[6]

It is not enough, however, to characterize pre-British India as an 'irrigation civilization', with a centralized bureaucracy and a village system of production. The unity and stability of Indian society depended also upon two other factors, caste and religion. Here, the aspect of caste to be emphasized is not so much its rigid hierarchical character and the way in which it divided groups from each other, as its integrating function, closely connected with religion. M. N. Srinivas, in a discussion of Indian social structure, observes that 'caste guarantees autonomy to a community, and at the same time it brings that community into relation with numerous other communities all going to form a hierarchy. The importance of such an institution is obvious in a vast country like India which has been the meeting place of many different cultures in the past and which has always had considerable regional diversity. While the autonomy of a sub-caste was preserved it was also brought into relation with

---

[1] *See*, however, S. N. Eisenstadt, *The Political Systems of Empires* (New York, 1963)

[2] A. K. Nazmul Karim, *op. cit.*

[3] *Op cit.*, pp. 45–6.

[4] See H. Pirenne, *Medieval Cities* (*op. cit.*).

[5] The changes are considered in more detail in Chapters 17 and 18 below.

[6] See A. R. Desai, *Social Background of Indian Nationalism* (*op. cit.*), Ch. 11, especially pp. 171–80.

others, and the hierarchy was also a scale of generally agreed values. Every caste tended to imitate the customs and ritual of the topmost caste, and this was responsible for the spread of Sanskritization. . . . Caste enabled Hinduism to proselytize without the aid of a church'.[1]

Thus the separate village communities were integrated and maintained in a larger social and political system not only by the central bureaucracy which controlled water supplies, but also by a religious system of values expounded and interpreted by a priestly caste. How far there was anything similar in other 'irrigation civilizations' is a matter for more detailed comparative study. The work of K. Wittfogel suggests that many important similarities can be found, in Ancient Egypt, in Byzantium, and elsewhere, especially in the social functions of the priests and in the elements of caste revealed in detailed regulation of the division of labour.

The foregoing account indicates some features of traditional Indian society which enable us to classify it, however tentatively, as belonging to a particular social type. A similar account might be given of other societies which are now often grouped together as 'developing countries'. China, like India, has been studied as a hydraulic society, in which a highly developed bureaucracy ruled over village communities.[2] In quite a different category are many of the new African societies, which are emerging from a tribal form of society overlaid by colonial rule; or again, the countries of Latin America in which there are elements of a feudal structure, along with an exceptional degree of military intervention in political life. It is evident that any classification of types of society which took account of this diversity would be much more complex than the schemes proposed by the early sociologists, who derived their ideas largely from the experience of European history. There has been little effort, however, to work out any more complex classifications; on the contrary, sociologists seem to have reverted to one of the simplest distinctions made by early writers—that between industrial and non-industrial societies. Of course, there is a good deal of justification for the revival of this distinction. The developing countries, regardless of their past, are all attempting to bring about rapid economic growth, generally on the basis of industrialization; and they are profoundly affected, in a great variety of ways, by their relationships with the industrial societies.

[1] M. N. Srinivas, *Religion and Society Among the Coorgs of South India* (Oxford, 1952), Ch. 2, 'Social structure', p. 31.
[2] See Karl A. Wittfogel, *Oriental Despotism*; Max Weber, 'The Chinese Literati', in H. H. Gerth and C. Wright Mills (eds.), *From Max Weber*.

Nevertheless, this distinction is scarcely adequate by itself, however much it may correspond with important economic and political concerns of the present time. The course of development in the non-industrial countries will be strongly influenced by their traditional social structures as well as by the aims which they now set themselves, and we shall not understand the new developments properly unless we grasp the different conditions from which they begin. On the other side, in the case of the industrial societies, we have to recognize at least the existence of two different types: those societies with a collectivist economy and those with a capitalist economy (or the Soviet and Western types). Over the past decade much has been done to elaborate and refine the conception of an industrial society,[1] and more recently there have been some interesting discussions of the advent of a 'post-industrial society'.[2] But in spite of the fact that there are obviously some very general features of industrialism, it is not clearly established that the different types of industrial society are fundamentally alike in their social structures or that they are tending to become more alike.

One of the difficulties in comparing these types of industrial society arises from the fact that no comprehensive sociological studies of capitalism or of Soviet society are available. There is no work on modern society which equals, in scope and profundity, Marc Bloch's *Feudal Society*. Marx's *Capital*, although it was conceived as a sociological study, was never carried beyond the analysis of the economic system. Of later studies which attempt in some degree to deal with the social structure as a whole, rather than the purely economic aspects, the most useful are Max Weber, *General Economic History* (Chapters 22–30); W. Sombart, *Der moderne Kapitalismus*; J. Schumpeter, *Capitalism, Socialism and Democracy*; and John Strachey, *Contemporary Capitalism*. There is a still greater lack of sociological studies of Soviet society, in part because of the predominance of an extreme ideological concern to attack or defend this form of society; but much useful information is brought together in a recent work by Allen Kassof (ed.), *Prospects for Soviet Society* (New York, 1968). One other type of industrial society, that represented by the Fascist states, has still not been studied in detail, although there is an admirable study of Nazi Germany, of

---

[1] Notably in the works of Raymond Aron, Ralf Dahrendorf, and J. K. Galbraith. See also the discussion in Paul Halmos (ed.), *The Development of Industrial Societies* (Sociological Review Monograph No. 8, Keele, 1964).

[2] See especially Alain Touraine, *La société post-industrielle* (Paris, 1969). Some similar themes are discussed in Norman Birnbaum, *The Crisis of Industrial Society* (New York, 1969).

great sociological value, by Franz Neumann, *Behemoth* (New York, 1942).[1]

The lack of comprehensive studies of the types of industrial society is affected, in turn, by the relative dearth of large scale sociological studies of particular modern societies. In the case of Britain, for example, there is no systematic account of the social structure as a whole; the works available are largely descriptive and statistical, as in the case of A. M. Carr-Saunders, D. C. Jones, and C. A. Moser, *A Survey of Social Conditiions in England and Wales as illustrated by Statistics* (Oxford, 1958), and D. C. Marsh, *The Changing Social Structure of England and Wales, 1871–1961* (London, 1965), or journalistic, as in the case of Anthony Sampson, *Anatomy of Britain Today* (rev. edn., London, 1965).[2] For the USA, Robin Williams, *American Society* (2nd edn., New York, 1960) provides a more adequate sociological analysis; and some important aspects of the social structure are examined, from quite different points of view, in C. Wright Mills, *The Power Elite* (New York, 1956), and in S. M. Lipset, *The First New Nation* (New York, 1963). There have also been several recent works on Canadian society: Bernard R. Blishen, Frank E. Jones, Kaspar D. Naegele, and John Porter (eds) *Canadian Society: Sociological Perspectives* (rev. edn., Toronto, 1968); John Porter, *The Vertical Mosaic: An Analysis of Social Class and Power in Canada* (Toronto, 1965); Marcel Rioux and Yves Martin (eds), *French-Canadian Society* (Vol. I, Toronto, 1964)., As yet, however, there have been few such studies of the European societies; the most significant work to date is Ralf Dahrendorf, *Society and Democracy in Germany* (Garden City, N.Y., 1967).

This brief review of sociological studies of modern industrial societies brings to light an important contrast between the work and achievements of social anthropologists and sociologists. Anthropologists have provided excellent accounts of the social structure of many tribal societies (although one might wish that there were more studies of the same society by different anthropologists); but sociologists, dealing with large and complex modern societies, have found it much more difficult to portray and analyse the total social structure. Nevertheless, this is the kind of study which must increasingly be

---

[1] There is, however, one recent work which illuminates the differences between the three principal types of twentieth century industrial society—Fascist, Soviet, and Western capitalist—through a historical study of the alternative routes to modernization: Barrington Moore, Jr., *Social Origins of Dictatorship and Democracy.*

[2] Rather surprisingly, a study of English society published at the beginning of this century has a more sociological character: C. F. G. Masterman, *The Condition of England* (London, 1909).

attempted, if there is to be a basis for wider generalizations about industrial society and its sub-types.

Civilization and Culture

The terms 'civilization' and 'culture' are widely used, with a variety of meanings, in ordinary discourse and in sociological writing. The Oxford English Dictionary defines 'to civilize' as 'to bring out of a state of barbarism, to instruct in the arts of life; to enlighten and refine', and quotes in illustration Addison's line, 'To civilize the rude unpolish'd world'. 'Civilization' is then 'the civilized condition or state'. 'Culture' is defined as 'the training and refinement of mind, tastes and manners; the condition of being thus trained and refined: the intellectual side of civilization'. The terms have often been used in this way in general writing on the intellectual and artistic aspects of human society. Clive Bell in his *Civilization* (1928) employs them to refer to the condition of refinement or enlightenment of a small elite in society.[1]

Many of the early social scientists used the terms in a similar fashion to distinguish between 'savage' and 'civilized' societies, or between 'nature peoples' and 'culture peoples'; the point of division being the invention of writing. There are many examples of this usage in the works of the eighteenth century Scottish historians mentioned earlier, in L. H. Morgan's *Ancient Society* (1877) which distinguishes between 'savagery', 'barbarism' and 'civilization', and in the early anthropological literature. The usage persists in our customary differentiation between 'primitive' and 'civilized' societies, though the terminology here is only a matter of convenience.

Later, a different distinction was introduced; not between 'civilization' or 'culture' on one side, and 'savagery' on the other, but between 'civilization' and 'culture' as applicable to all human societies. The distinction was made most clearly and elaborately by Alfred Weber,[2] who differentiated between three processes in human history; social process, civilization, and culture. I shall discuss his general scheme later, in examining the problems of social change. By civilization he meant primarily scientific and technical knowledge and the command which they give over natural resources; by culture, the artistic, religious, philosophical and similar products of a society. A similar

[1] Raymond Williams, in his *Culture and Society* (London, 1958), not only gives an illuminating account of the varied and changing uses of the term 'culture', but also shows that it only came to be used at all in its wider sense with the advent of modern industrial society.

[2] *See* especially, A. Weber, *Kulturgeschichte als Kultursoziologie* (Leiden, 1935, 2nd rev. edn. 1950).

usage is the common distinction in anthropological and archaeological writing between 'material culture' and 'non-material culture'.

More recently, 'culture' has become a central concept in social anthropology, and has been given a very wide meaning. The major contribution here was that of Malinowski who defined culture as comprising 'inherited artefacts, goods, technical processes, ideas, habits and values'.[1] He also included social structure within the notion of culture, since 'it cannot be really understood except as part of culture'. In a later essay, Malinowski reiterated these views: culture 'obviously is the integral whole consisting of implements and consumers' goods, of constitutional charters for the various social groupings, of human ideas and crafts, beliefs and customs'. Further, 'the essential fact of culture as we live it and experience it, as we can observe it scientifically, is the organization of human beings into permanent groups'.[2] The most important feature in Malinowski's use of the term was his conception of culture as an integral whole, within which the functions of the various parts (institutions) could be studied.[3]

In other recent discussions the term 'culture' has been used in the same broad way,[4] but there has been a tendency to distinguish more strictly between culture and social structure, especially among British social anthropologists. Thus R. Firth says that these terms represent two ways of looking at the same phenomenon: 'social structure' refers to the relations between individuals and the form of those relations, while 'culture' refers to 'the component of accumulated resources, immaterial as well as material, which the people inherit, employ, transmute, add to, and transmit'; it is 'all learned behaviour which has been socially acquired'.[5] This seems a valid and useful distinction, which corresponds broadly with a

[1] B. Malinowski, 'Culture' in *Encyclopaedia of the Social Sciences* (New York, 1933). Actually, a similar definition had been proposed much earlier by Tylor, in his *Primitive Culture* (1871), where culture is regarded as 'that complex whole which includes knowledge, belief, art, law, morals, customs, and all other capabilities and habits acquired by man as a member of society'.

[2] B. Malinowski, *A Scientific Theory of Culture* (Chapel Hill, 1944), pp. 36, 43.

[3] For an appraisal of Malinowski's views, see Audrey I. Richards, 'The Concept of Culture in Malinowski's Work', in R. Firth (ed.), *Man and Culture* (*op. cit.*).

[4] See, for example, Clyde Kluckhohln, 'Universal categories of culture', in A. L. Kroeber (ed.), *Anthropology Today* (Chicago, 1953), pp. 507–23, and A. Irving Hallowell, 'Culture, Personality and Society', *ibid.*, pp. 597–620.

[5] R. Firth, *Elements of Social Organization* (*op. cit.*), p. 27. There is, however, still much variation in the use of the term 'culture', as may be seen from a survey of definitions and usages, A. L. Kroeber and C. Kluckhohn, *Culture* (Papers of the Peabody Museum of Harvard, XLVII (1), 1952).

distinction often made in sociology between the study of social structure (or the comparative study of social institutions) and the *sociologie de l'esprit*, i.e. what I should call the sociology of mind or culture, which includes as one important part the sociology of knowledge. In studying culture we are concerned with ideas and values such as are found in religious and moral codes, in literature, science, philosophy, art and music.

The term 'civilization' has not acquired the same central importance as 'culture' in either sociology or social anthropology, and it is used in a very general and imprecise way.[1] Alfred Weber's distinction between civilization and culture does not seem to have been widely adopted, although R. M. MacIver advanced it independently and has emphasized its significance.[2] Civilization has remained largely a historian's term, and is often used to describe what anthropologists would refer to as a culture; for example, in Burckhardt's *The Civilization of the Renaissance in Italy*. But in the work of Arnold Toynbee[3] the term 'civilization' is given a different meaning, which may contribute to a more precise sociological conception. Toynbee distinguishes twenty-one independent civilizations (which he then confusingly calls 'societies') as 'intelligible fields of historical study'. These 'civilizations' are distinguished from 'primitive societies', along lines which I mentioned earlier.[4] We need not be concerned here with Toynbee's view that only civilizations and not societies (which he refers to as nation-states, city states, and the like) are 'intelligible fields' of study.[5] From the sociologist's point of view the contrary is true: actual societies are the most intelligible fields of study.[6] But Toynbee's discussion is of great interest in drawing attention 'to the fact that distinct societies are related to each other by sharing a common culture and cultural tradition. The number of societies thus related may be a significant feature of social development. It should be noted that a similar conception of civilization was briefly formulated by Durkheim and Mauss, in their 'Note sur la notion de civilisation' (*Année Sociologique*, XII, 1913).

[1] There is a good discussion of the usages in *Civilisation, le mot et l'idée* (Centre international de Synthèse, Paris, 1930), with a contribution from a social anthropologist, Marcel Mauss.

[2] R. M. MacIver, *The Modern State* (1926), Ch. 10, ii, 'Civilization and culture'; 'Our culture is what we are, our civilization is what we use' (p. 325). *See also* R. M. MacIver and C. H. Page, *Society* (English edn. 1950), Ch. 21, 'Functional systems'.

[3] Arnold Toynbee, *A Study of History* (10 vols., London, 1934–56).

[4] For Toynbee's distinction see *op. cit.* I, pp. 147–9.

[5] *Op. cit.* I, pp. 44–5. Toynbee equates a 'society' with a 'political community' in a way that sociologists have learned to avoid.

[6] *See* above, p. 119.

They observed that although social phenomena could ordinarily be most usefully studied within well-defined units such as particular societies, there were some phenomena which transcended these limits and which they proposed to call 'phenomena of civilization'.

We can now suggest a consistent, though still broad and general, usage for the terms *culture* and *civilization*. By *culture* we mean the ideational aspects of social life, as distinct from the actual relations and forms of relationship between individuals; and by *a culture* the ideational aspects of a particular society. The distinction which A. Weber made between 'culture' and 'civilization' can be recognized by distinguishing between material and non-material culture. This terminology has certain advantages, since it differentiates two elements within culture as a whole, and does not lend itself to the rigorous and overemphatic distinction between two fundamentally different types of phenomena. A. Weber made the distinction because he wished to contrast the growth and diffusion of science and technology with the uniqueness and independence of cultural products in each epoch and place. But it is not demonstrated that there is no development in the cultural sphere, or that cultural products cannot be diffused; and at the same time it is evident that within a particular society the material and non-material elements of culture are closely interconnected.

Finally, by *a civilization* we mean a cultural complex formed by the identical major cultural features of a number of particular societies. We might, for example, describe Western capitalism as a civilization, in which specific forms of science, technology, religion, art and so on, are to be found in a number of distinct societies. I shall not attempt here to classify civilizations; but only remark that a sociological classification would probably differ in many respects from that of Toynbee, though the latter is a valuable guide.[1]

The concepts of 'culture' and 'civilization' are obviously important in the study of Indian society, for as I have already observed the unity of India was, during most of its history, a cultural rather than a social or political unity, in which the influence of religious and philosophical conceptions was very strong. As yet, there has been little sociological study of Indian culture. The vast literature on Hinduism is almost entirely theological and philosophical.[2] Most writers on the caste system have emphasized the part played by

[1] For example, it would hardly be possible to regard Western civilization throughout its history as a single type.

[2] It is noteworthy that a recent trend report on 'Sociology of Religions', *Current Sociology*, V (1), 1956, mentioned only three items under the general heading 'Hinduism'. This was due less to unfamiliarity with the literature than to the absence of sociological writing on the subject.

religion in creating and sustaining it. But there have been few other studies of the social implications of Hindu doctrines and beliefs. Max Weber, in his *Religionssoziologie* discussed the social role of the Brahmins and examined the economic ethic of Hinduism, which he contrasted with that of Protestantism.[1] Some recent works have examined the social doctrines of Hinduism, but they are still mainly concerned with the doctrines themselves (and with upholding their truth) rather than with the sociological effects of individuals being taught and holding specific beliefs and values. Thus P. N. Prabhu's *Hindu Social Organization* (2nd rev. edn., Bombay, 1954) examines Hindu teaching on certain aspects of social life, education, marriage, family life, and caste, but is very little concerned with actual social behaviour (either historical or contemporary) in relation to that teaching. A more distinctly sociological study, which sets out to analyse Hindu culture in the manner of the 'culture and personality' school,[2] is D. Narain's *Hindu Character* (Bombay, 1957). His examination of some major 'themes in Hindu culture' is supplemented by a study of films, childhood training, and folklore as expressed in proverbs. Narain depicts the passive and mild character of the Indian, which he connects with the emphasis upon duties in Hindu religion. He quotes the view of W. S. Taylor that the doctrines of *Karma* and rebirth tend 'to produce a feeling that all the experiences of life are too insignificant to be worried about, except those duties and rites which determine and so control the indefinite future', and to 'discourage effort in every sphere except that in which initiative is necessarily replaced by obedience to *Dharma*'.[3] He also quotes Nehru as expressing concern about 'this amazing capacity of the people to ask for help and their amazing incapacity to do something themselves'.[4] Narain's study is, however, too impressionistic to be quite convincing.

Such passivity and helplessness might be connected not only with the cultural tradition, but also with the characteristics of 'oriental despotism' and with the dominance of the joint family, which removes much of the burden of choice from the individual. This is an important field for new research, which should take into account variations between town and country, between different religious groups, castes and classes, and between generations. It is noteworthy,

[1] Max Weber, *The Religion of India* (Glencoe, 1959, English translation of the relevant parts of *Religionssoziologie*).

[2] See A. Irving Hallowell, 'Culture, Personality and Society' in A. L. Kroeber (ed.), *Anthropology Today* (*op. cit.*), pp. 597–620.

[3] W. S. Taylor, 'Basic personality in orthodox Hindu culture patterns', *The Journal of Abnormal and Social Psychology*, XL, 1948.

[4] Jawaharlal Nehru, reported in *Indian Express*, November 21, 1957.

for instance, that certain religious groups, Christians, Parsis, and Jews, are much more urbanized than the Hindus and seem to be more prominent in industrial and commercial activities.

One outstanding problem of present day culture in India and in other developing countries concerns the relationship between the traditional culture and the values and beliefs which have been introduced from the West. Here we can study empirically the question of the material and non-material elements in culture. The developing countries have imported from the West modern science, technology, and methods of business enterprise; but is it the case that the non-material culture has been unaffected and has remained unchanged? According to Alfred Weber's conception material culture is transmissible from one society to another, while non-material culture is unique, incommunicable, and bound to time and place. The developing countries may acquire science and technique from the West, but they will retain their own systems of religion and philosophy, their own forms of art, which, so far as they change at all, will change unpredictably through the influence of outstanding individuals working within the traditional culture. Weber's conception, as I have already said, exaggerates the independence of these two elements in culture. In India, for example, the existence of socialist and communist parties demonstrates the absorption of Western political philosophies and values. The Congress Party itself has a political doctrine which is largely inspired by Western sources. Further, the existence of parliamentary government in India shows the acquisition not merely of a system of government machinery, but also of political values and conceptions of how a political community should be organized. The same process has occurred in other countries of Asia and Africa. Elsewhere, in China and Cuba, the whole social structure is being refashioned under the influence of Marxist thought which, though it has been modified to take account of different structural and cultural conditions, is still manifestly a Western doctrine. It may be said that some of the new values can be related to particular elements in the traditional culture, but that is only because (contrary to Weber's view) there are many similarities in the doctrines of the major world religions, philosophies and ethical systems. The importance given to particular aspects of these doctrines may well vary with changes in material culture and in social structure.

This is not to deny that the cultures of India or China, of African or Latin American countries, still possess some unique features, but simply to propose that these should be considered in relation to other features which are by no means unique, and in relation to present social changes.[1] For the European, India, China, and other Asian countries, or the countries of Africa, are no longer 'mysterious'. They differ in important respects from the European countries (and from each other), but they are also similar in equally important respects. Their cultures are probably no more remote or strange for most Europeans than is the culture of medieval Europe.

These general observations provide a starting point for sociological inquiry. How are the diverse elements of culture, traditional and Western, perceived and grasped by individuals, and by individuals in different social groups? How do they appear in popular literature (science fiction against the *Ramayana*)? A book published in the late 1950s depicted, in a striking manner, the changes in the culture of the English working class.[2] There are, in the developing countries, fascinating opportunities for similar investigations, into films, radio and the Press, as well as literature.[3] In a more formal way, changes in education and in law bring about a modification of cultural values, and their influence will be discussed in later chapters. Sociological research in these various fields should be able to show how culture changes or persists, how new elements are incorporated or rejected, and how traditional elements are modified or abandoned.

But the formulation of this contrast and opposition between traditional culture and modern culture should not lead us into the error of treating each of these types of culture as it if were uniform, harmonious, and only capable of change in response to external forces. During the 1940s and 1950s many sociologists, under the influence of functionalist ideas, assumed too easily that the Western industrial countries were 'stable' societies, in which a 'modern' culture existed in a more or less settled form. Within the last decade this assumption has been upset by the emergence of vigorous and widespread movements directed against the established culture; for example, by the creation of a much more distinctive 'youth culture'.[4] Such problems of cultural conflict and transformation in both industrial and developing countries will be examined more fully in later chapters dealing with the forms of social control and with theories of social and cultural change.

[1] The mingling of indigenous and foreign cultural elements can be seen very well, for example, in the social doctrines of Gandhism, and in the ideas of 'African socialism'.

[2] Richard Hoggart, *The Uses of Literacy* (London, 1957).

[3] One study which illustrates to some extent this kind of inquiry is D. Lerner, *The Passing of Traditional Society: Modernizing the Middle East* (New York, 1964).

[4] For a discussion of this phenomenon in the USA see Jack Newfield, *A Prophetic Minority* (New York, 1966), and T. Roszak, *The Making of a Counter Culture* (New York, 1969).

Chapter 8

ECONOMIC INSTITUTIONS

Modern economic theories have not, on the whole, shown much interest in the study of economic structure, although many economic textbooks contain brief accounts of the organization of industry, the division of labour, the structure of enterprises, and so on. Economic sociology, on the other hand, is almost entirely concerned with problems of economic structure. The major fields of interest, which we shall examine in turn, have been the division of labour and occupational specialization, the property system, types of economy and structural changes (especially the process of industrialization), the structure of the industrial enterprise or factory, and industrial relations.

The division of labour

One of the best known of Durkheim's works is his study of the division of labour,[1] in which he analysed the social functions of the division of labour and sought to show how in modern societies, by contrast with primitive societies, it is the principal source of social cohesion or social solidarity. In the course of his enquiry, Durkheim distinguished two types of solidarity, mechanical and organic, which he associated with two types of law which he called repressive and restitutive. In a later part of the book Durkheim discussed abnormal forms of the division of labour in modern industrial societies; i.e. those forms which diminish rather than promote social cohesion. He distinguished two principal abnormal forms: the 'anomic' and the 'forced' division of labour. By the first he meant a condition of extreme specialization of labour in which the individual became isolated in his specialism; and particularly a condition in which there was a permanent division between capital and labour. Durkheim proposed as remedies the fostering of regular and prolonged contacts through professional associations and corporations, and through institutional arrangements for discussion and negotiation between capital and labour. By the second form Durkheim meant a condition in which individuals did not freely

---

[1] E. Durkheim, *The Division of Labour in Society* (*op. cit.*).

choose their occupations but were forced into them. He regarded this discrepancy between the abilities of individuals and the functions imposed upon them as a principal source of class conflict. Durkheim thought that modern societies could and would get rid of these abnormal forms of the division of labour, and it is interesting to observe the extent to which his expectations have been realized. In many industrial societies the relations between capital and labour have been institutionalized in elaborate procedures for consultation, negotiation and arbitration; and the choice of occupations has become wider for many people as a result of educational expansion and changes in the occupational structure. The effects have been to reduce, in some measure, the intensity of class conflict.[1]

Other sociologists have discussed the division of labour largely in its connection with social stratification. Marx outlined a theory of social stratification which made it the effect of the division of labour, and especially of what he called the 'first great distinction between manual and intellectual labour'.[2] G. Schmoller presented a more elaborate theory which defined classes as occupational groups created by the division of labour and maintained by heredity.[3] Such theories have an obvious relevance to the Indian caste system, in which differentiation is very largely in terms of traditional occupations. Indeed they have a greater relevance here than in the case of any other system of stratification, where what has to be explained is the aggregation of occupations in the broader groupings of estate, class or status groups.

From such concerns with the social consequences of the division of labour, much contemporary sociological work has derived. One derivation is the sociological study of occupations, which is particularly concerned with the connection between occupation and social status but also with the problems of the entry to occupations (and thus with one of the issues studied by Durkheim). This occupational sociology has concentrated especially upon the study of those influential and prestigeful occupations, the liberal professions.

A second derivation is the study of the minute division of labour in modern industry and its social and psychological consequences and implications. In a recent study, Georges Friedmann[4] has

[1] However, these changes have been interpreted in diverse ways. See below, pp. 194-7.
[2] See *The German Ideology* (English trans., 1938) and *Economic and Philosophical Manuscripts* [in T. B. Bottomore (ed.), *Karl Marx: Early Writings* (London, 1963)].
[3] G. Schmoller, 'Das Wesen der Arbeitsteilung und der sozialen Klassenbildung', *Schmollers Jahrbuch* XIV, 1890, pp. 45-105.
[4] G. Friedmann, *Anatomy of Work* (London, 1961).

135

examined the modern division of labour as it affects both work and leisure, and has given an excellent account of research in this field. He also examines critically Durkheim's theory of the social functions of the division of labour, and in a long statistical appendix presents data on the extent and character of specialization in a number of industrial societies.

The division of labour has not become so extensive in India as in the advanced industrial countries. Nevertheless, industrialization is bringing about similar difficulties and problems, and in the industrial areas research is called for. Moreover, a particular interest attaches to the effects of the growing division of labour upon the caste system. In the past, new castes were often formed where changes in technique occurred or where entirely new occupations came into existence. It is important to see how far this is taking place in the new industrial occupations, or on the contrary, whether caste divisions are giving way to trade union and class divisions.[1] At the same time it is of interest to study entry to the liberal professions in relation to caste distinctions, to see how far such distinctions are maintained in new forms.[2] A broader problem should also be mentioned. As organized in the caste system, the division of labour had the integrative functions which Durkheim emphasized. In the village economy caste, like the medieval guilds, ensured the performance of necessary functions (by passing on craft skills, etc.) and these functions were organized by the direct exchange of services between castes (the *jajmani* system). In an industrial and money economy, the division of labour becomes far more complex, and the exchange of services is accomplished through the market or central planning, or a combination of both. As a result, caste becomes so much the less important from the point of view of the division of labour; indeed like the medieval guilds caste groups may be a serious obstacle to economic development.[3] The caste system retains some integrating functions, on the cultural level, but these are likely to be less and less important as social cohesion comes to depend increasingly

[1] Hutton quotes a statement of Enthoven in 1932 concerning the formation of a new caste of chauffeurs (Hutton, *Caste in India*, p. 117): 'Modern India, having created a caste of chauffeurs from the menials who tend motor cars, is almost ripe for a Rolls Royce caste rejecting food or marriage with the Fords'.

[2] See the discussion, and references to other literature, in T. B. Bottomore, 'Cohesion and Division in Indian Elites', in Philip Mason (ed.), *India and Ceylon: Unity and Diversity* (London, 1967).

[3] On the general economic effects of caste, see V. Anstey, *The Economic Development of India*, pp. 52–9. There has been little detailed study of the influence of caste on the recruitment and training of workers in the recent period of industrialization.

upon the economic division of labour and the sentiment of nationality.

Property

Property, in Hobhouse's phrase, 'is to be conceived in terms of the control of man over things', a control which is recognized by society, more or less permanent, and exclusive.[1] Property may be private (individual or collective) or common. In his account of the development of property Hobhouse observed that there is some personal private property in all societies, but that in many primitive societies the principal economic resources are communally owned (e.g. hunting land, grazing land, pasture). In more developed agricultural societies private ownership comes to predominate. But Hobhouse pointed out that although tribal common ownership disappears, common ownership may be maintained for the joint-family. R. H. Lowie, in an excellent short account of property, which uses much comparative material from primitive and civilized societies, presents much the same view.[2] There is personal private property among all primitive peoples, including names, dances, songs, myths, ceremonial regalia, gifts, weapons, household implements. So far as the 'instruments of production' are concerned there are differences between hunters and food-gatherers, where the land is tribal property (not always well-defined), and agriculturalists and pastoralists. Among agriculturalists individual private property in land is frequently found, though the clan or tribe may still exercise some control over its use or alienation. In the case of pastoralists, land may be communally owned but not the livestock; 'the ownership of livestock strongly develops the sense of individual property'. (Lowie).

Common ownership by a joint-family occurs in many societies. In Europe, the Yugoslav *Zadruga* was a well-known example, but there were similar forms of property in other peasant societies. Most of these had given place to individual ownership by the early twentieth century. The nature of property rights in the Hindu joint-family in the Vedic period is not entirely clear. Macdonell and Keith argued that 'The (Vedic) passages all negative the idea that the property of the family was family property: it is clear that it was the property of the head of the house, usually the father, and that the other members of the family only had moral claims upon it

[1] L. T. Hobhouse, 'The Historical Evolution of Property, in Fact and in Idea', in *Property, its Duties and Rights* (ed. Bishop Gore, London, 1913).

[2] R. H. Lowie, *Social Organization* (London, 1950), Ch. 6, 'Property'.

which the father could ignore . . .'[1] But K. M. Kapadia has concluded that there is no clear indication in the Vedic literature that the patriarchal family was the only type of family organization.[2] Later, according to the same writer, there were tendencies towards the disintegration of the joint family, and the scope of individual property was broadened, but the old patriarchal tradition was utilized to strengthen the joint family. Thus, at no period was there common family property, but in later periods there were restraints upon the powers of the family head to alienate property.[3]

In general, with the development of agriculture, manufacture, and commerce, individual or collective ownership of productive resources was extended but some common ownership continued in most societies, e.g. in the manorial system of feudal Europe where the community retained a general control of cultivation and certain rights in the settlement of disputes. In Russia such community control lasted until the present century. The characteristic feature of all these property systems, as Hobhouse emphasized, was that they were concerned with property for use, and even where individual ownership was highly developed there remained some community control and responsibility for ensuring that no member became entirely destitute. Property for power, and unlimited individual acquisition of wealth was a product of capitalism; it reached its peak in nineteenth century Europe and North America, but was relatively quickly limited again by the community. The recent history of property is very largely a history of the imposition or re-imposition of community restraints upon the individual owners of economic resources, and in a later phase the deliberate redistribution or appropriation of such resources by the community.

A number of writers have attempted to distinguish the principal types of property system, or stages in the development of property. We have already mentioned Hobhouse's scheme, which has three phases; the first, in which there is little social differentiation, little inequality, and in which economic resources are owned in common or are strictly controlled by the community, the second in which wealth increases, great inequalities appear, and individual or collective ownership escapes from community control, and a third in which a conscious attempt is made to diminish inequality, and to restore community control. This scheme has some resemblances to the Marxist distinction into three stages; that of primitive classless

[1] A. A. Macdonell and A. B. Keith, *Vedic Index* (1912), I, p. 351.
[2] K. M. Kapadia, *Marriage and Family in India* (2nd ed. Bombay, 1958), p. 194.
[3] *Op. cit.*, pp. 200 *sqq.*

society, followed by class differentiation and the growth of inequality, and the final stage of a classless society at a higher level. Vinogradoff[1] distinguished four principal stages; the establishment of property rights in a tribal and communal context, the application of the notion of tenure to land, the development of individual appropriation, and finally the imposition of restrictions under the influence of modern collectivist ideas.

More recent writers have emphasized the complexity of property systems and have rejected the notion of a unilinear evolution. There have been a number of comparative studies of property in primitive societies, which illustrate the difficulty of determining the character and extent of property rights.[2] Nevertheless, the evolution of property in Western Europe is fairly clear; it has been well-documented by economic historians, and its recent phases are reflected in property ideologies from John Locke's natural right theory to the modern socialist doctrines.[3]

The history of property rights in India is less clear. The principal form of productive property was, until recently, land, and the tenure of land was regulated by Hindu customary law, later supplemented by Muslim law. Land tenure only became precisely determined during the period of British rule, after the Bengal Permanent Settlement Regulation of 1793. It is doubtful whether under Hindu law, as recorded in the Code of Manu, there were any proprietary rights in land. The King had a right to a share of the produce, and the cultivator had the right to be protected in the occupation of his land and to transmit this to his heirs. The version of Muslim law which was generally followed in India after the twelfth century seems to have created some proprietary rights.[4] But the Permanent Settlement of 1793 created in Bengal, and later in other parts of India, definite proprietary rights for the *zamindars*, who were originally revenue collectors employed by the Muslim conquerors and who thus became landed gentry.[5] Elsewhere, in Bombay and Madras, a different settlement (the *ryotwari* system) created a class of peasant proprietors. The general results of British legislation were, therefore, to establish clear proprietary rights in land, to make

1 P. Vinogradoff, *Historical Jurisprudence* (Oxford, 1920).

2 See especially, M. J. Herskovits, *Economic Anthropology*, Ch. 14–17, and R. H. Lowie, *op. cit.*

3 On the theories of property see Hobhouse, *op. cit.*, and R. Schlatter, *Private Property* (London, 1951).

4 For a short and clear account see Sir Benjamin Lindsay, 'Law' in L. S. S. O'Malley, *Modern India and the West*, Section on land law, pp. 115–27.

5 See the excellent study by S. Gopal, *The Permanent Settlement in Bengal and its Results* (London, 1949).

land an alienable saleable commodity and thus to bring it within the general property system of a capitalist economy.

Recent sociological studies of property in industrial societies have been largely concerned with two aspects; first, the distribution of property and its social effects, and second, the separation between the ownership and the control of industrial enterprises in modern capitalism. There have been numerous studies of the distribution of wealth and income. In Britain, R. H. Tawney's *Equality* (4th rev. edn., London, 1952) examines in detail the inequalities of wealth and income and their connection with the class system. H. Dalton, in an earlier study. *The Inequality of Incomes* (London, 1920), showed that the unequal distribution of wealth is a principal factor in producing inequalities of income. For the USA there is much information on the distribution of wealth and income in C. Wright Mills, *The Power Elite* (New York, 1956; Ch. 5, 'The very rich', and Ch. 7, 'The corporate rich') and more recently in F. Lundberg, *The Rich and the Super-Rich* (New York, 1968). These and other studies indicate that there has been some movement towards greater equality in many of the advanced industrial countries since the beginning of the twentieth century, though it has been more marked in respect of incomes than in respect of property. Thus, for example, in Britain, 1 per cent of the population owned 69 per cent of all private property in 1911–13, and still owned 42 per cent in 1960.[1] But the equalization of incomes has proceeded more rapidly, as a result of high progressive taxation and the expansion of social services.[2] In the present day communist countries the range of incomes seems to be similar to that in the capitalist democracies, although it is difficult to reach any certain conclusions in the absence of serious sociological research.

The separation of ownership and control in industrial enterprises is a phenomenon which has attracted much attention from sociologists concerned with the development of modern capitalism. It has resulted from the extension of the joint stock principle. The industrial capitalists of the early nineteenth century were both owners and

[1] See J. E. Meade, *Efficiency, Equality and the Ownership of Property* (London, 1964).

[2] However, the process of equalization seems to have been halted or reversed in most of the industrial countries during the 1950s, and at the same time it has been shown that the very poorest sections of the population have become relatively poorer. On the USA see Gabriel Kolko, *Wealth and Power in America* (rev. edn. New York, 1964), and Michael Harrington, *The Other America* (New York, 1962); on Britain see B. Abel-Smith and P. Townsend, *The Poor and the Poorest* (London, 1965). There is a good general discussion of the situation in Britain in R. M. Titmuss, *Income Distribution and Social Change* (London, 1962).

140

managers of their enterprises, but as the enterprises grew larger more and more capital had to be drawn from outside, and this was made possible by joint stock legislation. At present, the large companies which dominate the major branches of industry are managed and directed by individuals who do not own them. The owners of most of the capital are the thousands of small and medium shareholders who have little interest except in the profitability of the company and may not even know what it manufactures. In a well-known study, *The Modern Corporation and Private Property* (New York, 1933) A. A. Berle and G. C. Means examined in detail the large corporations of the USA. Their conclusions were the basis for later theorizing about the 'managerial revolution', and the transformation of capitalism.[1]

These changes have been exaggerated by some writers. Although the managers of modern industry do not own the enterprises outright, they usually have an important shareholding and they are wealthy men in their own right; there is no fundamental divorce between ownership of property and management of industry. P. Sargant Florence has shown, in his book *The Logic of British and American Industry* (London, 1953), that 'on average in large companies, twenty shareholders out of some ten to twenty thousand hold, in Britain and America, nearly a third of voting shares', and this is quite enough to give them control of the company. He argued that 'there is certainly evidence for believing that the managerial revolution has not proceeded as far as is sometimes thought (or stated without thought) and that leadership and the ultimate decision on top policy may remain in many companies or corporations with the largest capital shareholders'. C. Wright Mills, in *The Power Elite* (New York, 1956) shows how ownership and control are interwoven in American industry; he observes that 'the chief executives and the very rich are *not* two distinct and clearly segregated groups'.

Recent studies in Britain and the USA give a remarkable picture of the concentration of economic power. The large corporations dominate the economy; in the USA $0·2$ per cent of all the manufacturing and mining companies employ half of all the people working in those industries,[2] and in Britain 12,000 public joint stock companies are responsible for half the total economic activity, i.e. as much as the quarter million private companies, the nationalized

[1] See James Burnham, *The Managerial Revolution* (New York, 1941); A. A. Berle, *The Twentieth Century Capitalist Revolution* (London, 1955).

[2] See C. Wright Mills, *op. cit.*, J. K. Galbraith, *American Capitalism* (1952), and G. William Domhoff, *Who Rules America?* (Englewood Cliffs, N.J., 1967), Chapter 2.

141

industries, and other enterprises together.[1] The ownership of shares in the large corporations is *not* widespread; in Britain less than 5 per cent, and in the USA less than 7 per cent, of the adult population own any shares. Moreover, within the group of shareholders there is a distinction between the small group (less than 0·2 per cent of the total) which owns large numbers of shares and all the rest who own, individually, very small parts of the total stock. Finally, interlocking directorships concentrate still more, in the hands of large owners, the control of industry.

Types of economy

It was shown in an earlier chapter that the classification of societies has often been based upon a preliminary classification of economic systems. Such was the case with Marx's distinction of five major types of society: primitive society, ancient society, Asiatic society, feudal society, and capitalist society. In accordance with Marx's basic assumptions the distinction is made not only in terms of the level of technology and the mode of production, but also in terms of property and class relations. Rather similar classifications have been proposed by other writers, especially by the German historical economists and sociologists, such as Bücher and Sombart. This broad classification of types of economy seems to have been generally accepted, and there have also been a number of attempts to distinguish sub-groups within the principal types. Thus Hobhouse, Wheeler and Ginsberg[2] distinguished different types of economic organization among primitive societies, and went on to show that differences in other social institutions (stratification, government, etc.) were correlated with these. The distinction between food gatherers, hunters, pastoralists and agriculturalists, in the case of primitive societies, has become a commonplace. On the other hand, some doubt is thrown upon the correlations between the type of economy and the forms of other social institutions by more recent studies. For example, Daryll Forde, in a comprehensive survey of primitive societies,[3] shows that there is very considerable variation in institutions within the same economic type.

In the case of modern capitalism, H. Pirenne distinguished several stages in the 'social history of capitalism', in terms of the principal directions of economic activity and the social groups which took the leading role at each stage.[4] Sociologists, from Marx onwards, have

---

[1] For details see J. Strachey, *Contemporary Capitalism*, p. 23 *sqq.*

[2] *The Material Culture and Social Institutions of the Simpler Peoples.*

[3] Daryll Forde, *Habitat, Economy and Society* (London, 1941).

[4] H. Pirenne, 'The Stages in the Social History of Capitalism', *American Historical Review* XIX (3), 1914.

devoted much of their effort to the analysis of capitalism as an economic and social system. Aside from the debate on the origins of modern capitalism, most attention has been given to recent developments, and particularly to the growth of large scale enterprise. Marxist writers make a distinction between nineteenth century capitalism and the 'monopoly capitalism' of the twentieth century, which they connect with imperialism.[1] The phenomena to which they draw attention are generally recognized, but few sociologists accept in its entirety the Marxist scheme of explanation. The rapid growth of large enterprise, and the concentration of economic power, can be seen in all the industrial countries, whether their property system is one of largely private ownership, mixed public and private ownership, or complete collective ownership. Many sociologists would argue that the concept of 'ownership of the means of production' needs re-examination. In the USSR, as in Britain and the USA, a small number of individuals manage the giant enterprises upon which material well-being depends and decide the major economic issues as to the use of resources. In all cases they have great power, and it is increasingly difficult for the mass of the population to exercise control over their use of power. Contrary to the orthodox Marxist view, popular control may well be greater in some of the capitalist countries, where independent trade unions can bring pressure to bear upon managements, and where the competition among political groups prevents the emergence of a single, omnipotent elite.

In those capitalist countries in which some basic industries have been nationalized, difficult problems have arisen in the control of the public corporations which manage them. From the point of view of the employee and the ordinary citizen public bureaucracies may be no easier to deal with, and no more egalitarian or devoted to the common good, than private managements. In many Communist countries the cost of public bureaucracy has been painfully reckoned in recent years. We can see in these developments a confirmation of the importance of Max Weber's analysis of bureaucracy. In his essay on 'Politics as a vocation'[2] Weber suggested a parallel between the concentration of productive powers and the concentration of administrative powers. In discussing the development of the modern state he observed that the prince, in his conflict with the nobility, opened the way for the expropriation of the autonomous, private owners of executive power, those who possess in their own right the

---

[1] See, for example, P. Baran and P. Sweezy, *Monopoly Capital* (New York, 1966).

[2] In H. Gerth and C. W. Mills, *From Max Weber* (*op. cit.*).

143

means of administration, welfare, etc. 'The whole process is an exact parallel to the development of the capitalist enterprise through the gradual expropriation of the independent producers'. In the future development of industrial society Weber saw the danger that socialism might result, not in the liberation of man, but in his enslavement to an all powerful bureaucracy.

Sociological studies of a type of economic system have thus contributed notably to recent political controversies. John Strachey, in his *Contemporary Capitalism*, sees a conflict between political democracy and the oligarchic tendencies of modern capitalism. C. Wright Mills, in *The Power Elite*, notes the emergence of a 'mass society' in the USA, in which power becomes increasingly concentrated in the hands of the leaders of large scale organizations, in the economic field and elsewhere. In the totalitarian societies the process of concentration of power in a small elite reaches its zenith. These social changes have re-awakened interest in problems of the control of economic power through decentralization and 'industrial democracy' (which I shall discuss in the following section), and in the analysis of oligarchic tendencies in political organizations (which will be considered in the next chapter), as well as in the general characteristics of bureaucratic organization.

The study of types of economy shows well the value of a sociological approach, which attempts to view synoptically and to elucidate the complex interrelations between the property system, the organization of industry, social stratification and political organization. This is also apparent in the study of change from one type of economy to another. An early controversy in sociology, begun by Marx and continued notably by Max Weber, concerned the origins of capitalism.[1] It is impossible here even to summarize this debate; but we can formulate very roughly what seem to be

[1] There is now a considerable literature on this subject. The major contributions are: Max Weber, *The Protestant Ethic and the Spirit of Capitalism* (1904; English trans. London, 1930); W. Sombart, *Der moderne Kapitalismus* (3 vols., Munich, 1924–7; English trans. of some parts in F. L. Nussbaum, *A History of the Economic Institutions of Modern Europe*, New York, 1933); R. H. Tawney, *Religion and the Rise of Capitalism* (London, 1927); H. M. Robertson, *Aspects of the Rise of Economic Individualism: A Criticism of Max Weber and His School* (London, 1933); A. Fanfani, *Catholicism, Protestantism and Capitalism* (English trans. London, 1935; this book, while presenting a particular view, also gives a summary of the debate); K. Polanyi, *The Origins of Our Time* (London, 1944). The best Marxist accounts of capitalism will be found in M. Dobb, *Studies in the Development of Capitalism* (London, 1946), which deals at length with the origins and early development, and Paul Sweezy, *The Theory of Capitalist Development* (New York, 1942). There is a useful survey of the different conceptions of capitalism in W. Sombart, 'Capitalism', *Encyclopaedia of the Social Sciences*.

reasonable conclusions from it. The development of capitalism required a generalization of attitudes towards work and wealth which had previously been exceptional in human societies.[1] The social ethic of Protestantism aided the diffusion of such attitudes; thus it helped to accelerate the development of capitalism in Western Europe and North America, and may also have contributed certain specific characteristics (as Weber claimed). The importance of values and ideologies in the functioning of economic systems is brought out in later writing on the 'decline of capitalism'; as for example in J. A. Schumpeter's *Capitalism, Socialism and Democracy* where it is argued that the decay of capitalism will be largely the consequence of the rejection of 'bourgeois' values, not of economic breakdown. The argument recalls Max Weber's dictum: 'The Puritan wanted work to be his vocation; we are forced to want it', which expresses disillusion and suggests eventual hostility to the culture of capitalism.

Perhaps more significant is the recent development of a theory of industrial societies and industrialization which takes account of many social factors, including ideologies, and which represents at present one of the main points of convergence of economics and sociology. The writing in this field[2] emphasizes the distinction between two types of economy, industrial and non-industrial, and is concerned with industrialism rather than capitalism since it is evident that industrialization can occur in a variety of ways in different social and political contexts. W. Arthur Lewis[3] deals comprehensively with the economic and other factors involved in economic growth; the desire for goods, attitudes to work, the influence of property systems, social mobility, religion and family structure, the effects of population growth, and the role of government. A more specific problem of industrialization, the recruitment and training of labour for industrial employment in agricultural countries, has been exhaustively studied in W. E. Moore, *Industrialization and Labour* (New York, 1951). This is an outstanding problem in all non-industrial countries, for the agricultural worker who is brought into industrial work also moves from the village to the town, and

[1] On this see the concise discussion in R. L. Heilbroner, *The Great Economists*, (English edn. London, 1955) Ch. II, 'The economic revolution'.

[2] I have mentioned earlier as important contributions, R. Aron, *18 Lectures on Industrial Society* and W. Arthur Lewis, *The Theory of Economic Growth:* and a review of the now voluminous literature in Lyle W. Shannon, 'Social factors in economic growth', *Current Sociology*, VI (3), 1957. A contribution which provoked much discussion when it was first published is W. W. Rostow, *The Stages of Economic Growth* (Cambridge, 1960).

[3] *Op. cit.*

145

the process of adjustment to the new conditions may be long and difficult. In Europe, the problem of 'peasant workers' and their families has called forth much useful research in two countries of collectivist industrialization, Poland and Yugoslavia.

The study of economic growth has particular importance for India. The Indian economy is still primarily a village economy. At the present time more than four-fifths of the population live in villages, while 70 per cent are engaged in agricultural occupations. Industrialization began about 1850, and it progressed extremely slowly. Dr Anstey has referred to 'arrested economic development'[1] and it has been shown that the proportion of people living in towns hardly increased between 1881 and 1931, while the proportion of industrial workers in the total working population actually declined between 1911 and 1941.[2] Moreover, before 1947, industrial development was one-sided; the principal manufactures were in light industries, while iron and steel production was at a low level and heavy engineering practically non-existent. Since the achievement of independence industrialization has proceeded more rapidly.[3] At the same time, much effort has been devoted to raising the level of productivity (which was extremely low) in agriculture, as an indispensable basis for capital accumulation and industrial expansion.

We need not concern ourselves here with the purely economic aspects.[4] It is regrettable, however, that relatively little sociological research has yet been undertaken into these fundamental problems. A report of the United Nations has dealt generally with the underdeveloped countries, drawing attention to sociological and demographic factors in industrialization. It is apparent from the available studies that economic growth in India is impeded by numerous social factors; high fertility, the caste system, resistance to innovation founded upon religious beliefs, dependence of the individual on the joint family, and others. But is is not clear what importance should be attached to the different factors, and still less how their influence may be modified. There is no reason to suppose that the

---

[1] In the 1936 edition of her book *The Economic Development of India* (*op. cit.*).

[2] R. Mukerjee, *The Indian Working Class*, p. 2.

[3] See the account given in the *Third Five Year Plan: Draft Outline* (Delhi, 1960).

[4] The general economic problems have been discussed in W. Arthur Lewis, *op. cit.*; Colin Clark, *The Conditions of Economic Progress* (2nd edn. London, 1951); W. W. Rostow, *The Process of Economic Growth* (New York, 1952); Gunnar Myrdal, *Economic Theory and Under-developed Regions* (London, 1957). There is a good discussion of the problems in India in B. Datta, *The Economics of Industrialization* (Calcutta, 1952).

[5] UNITED NATIONS, Department of Economic and Social Affairs, *Processes and Problems of Industrialization in Under-developed Countries* (New York, 1955).

cultural values as a whole are opposed to economic and social development; for example, the growth of nationalism from the end of the nineteenth century was based in part upon a cultural renaissance. Hindu culture has, in fact, been able to absorb many elements from the Western industrial world, or to re-discover similar features in its own tradition. The ideal of asceticism, which would be a strong influence against economic development, is not the only ideal of Hinduism, nor at present the most prominent. There is every sign that economic progress is ardently desired, and that national planning, as well as government encouragement to private enterprise, is generally approved. But how these values affect the individual in his choice of occupation, and in his behaviour at work, is uncertain. What is known about the problem comes in the main from studies which were primarily concerned with other questions; from village studies and urban surveys. Yet industrialization and economic growth depend as much upon understanding these social factors as upon economic calculation, and sociological research can here make a major contribution.[1]

The industrial enterprise and industrial relations

Within the general field of study of industrial societies there has grown up in recent decades a more limited branch of study, now called industrial sociology, which has taken a prominent place in sociology as a whole by reason of the amount of research and the number of workers involved in it. Industrial sociology has been concerned with two aspects of industrial life; the internal organization of the enterprise and the social relationships existing there, and industrial relations in the wider sense of the relations between the different groups in industry, principally between owners and managers, supervisors and white collar workers, and manual workers.

Two recent books have surveyed a large part of the field of industrial sociology: W. E. Moore, *Industrial Relations and the Social Order* (New York, 1946), and Georges Friedmann, *Industrial Society* (Glencoe, 1955).[2] The authors give some indication of how sociological studies of industry developed. In the first place, there were practical problems of fatigue, boredom, absenteeism, and other

[1] The various forms of industrialization, and some recent studies in this field, will be considered more fully in a later chapter on social change.

[2] English trans. of *Problèmes humains du machinisme industriel* (2nd rev. edn. Paris, 1954). See also his later book, *Anatomy of Work*. There is a good survey of much recent research in S. R. Parker, R. K. Brown, J. Child and M. A. Smith, *The Sociology of Industry* (London, 1967).

factors which adversely affected output. The study of such problems became particularly urgent during the First World War with the growing demands upon industry, and it was at that time that, for instance, the first systematic enquiries (by psychologists) were undertaken in Britain. The next phase was the rise of the 'scientific organization of work' movement sponsored by the American engineer, Taylor, and enthusiastically received by manufacturers like Ford. A third phase was reached with the pioneer studies of Elton Mayo, the first which had a distinctively sociological character. All these studies were basically concerned with productivity, and with the psychological and social factors affecting it. From another direction, the trade unions and the labour movement, there was pressure to improve working conditions, to create a more humanly satisfying working environment, and to provide opportunities for individual advancement and promotion. These interests converged to favour sociological studies of social relations in the enterprise, particularly as the problems became more acute with the development of mass-production, conveyor belt production, and, very recently, automation.

The major themes of study, over the past ten years, have been the interpersonal relations in working groups and their influence upon productivity, the role of supervisors, problems of management and bureaucracy, the effects of specialized work and possible compensations in leisure time, and the problems created by technological change. Special attention has been given to particular groups of workers, such as young people, and women workers. The volume of research and writing is now vast, but the major results are well summarized in the books by Friedmann and Moore mentioned above.

Research in industry has covered publicly owned industries as well as private enterprise, and has been conducted in both capitalist and communist industrial countries, as well as in under-developed countries. It was mentioned earlier that the concentration of economic power had revived interest in the problems of 'industrial democracy'. This interest has been stimulated also by the discovery that the public ownership of industry did not resolve all the problems of the enterprise, or eliminate conflict (although authoritarian governments might suppress overt conflict); and by concern over the 'meaninglessness' of specialized industrial work, and its effects on the individual and on output. In fact, there have been numerous experiments, in recent years, in workers' participation in management or workers' management, and these experiments have been closely studied by sociologists. There is an account of some of this research in Friedmann, *Industrial Society*, in a symposium published by the International Sociological Association, and in a recent collection of papers on the Yugoslav system, all of which indicate the similarity of many of the problems in societies with different political régimes.[1]

The other aspect of industrial sociology, industrial relations in the broad sense, was for a time overshadowed by the studies within the enterprise. There was even some inclination, especially among American sociologists, to explain the wider industrial relations in terms of relationships within the factory, and to reduce the latter to problems of individual personality, familial relationships, etc., while entirely ignoring the broader institutional framework of property, the class system, and political institutions. But this phase has now passed. There have been numerous studies of the different groups involved in industrial conflict and negotiation, though these have tended to concentrate upon trade unions and to leave in some obscurity the structure and policies of the organizations of technicians, managers and owners. This is partly because the immediate postwar growth of trade unions, especially in Britain and the USA, and the more favourable social climate of the Welfare State, has given them greater power, while the extension of public ownership has created difficult problems of relationships between trade unions and the managements of nationalized industries. At all events there have been many investigations of trade union leadership and organization.[2]

The processes of negotiation, arbitration and conflict have also been studied, though not on the same scale. One outstanding analysis of industrial conflict is K. G. J. C. Knowles, *Strikes: A Study in Industrial Conflict* (London, 1952), which deals with the United Kingdom in the period 1911–1945 and attempts to correlate

[1] International Sociological Association, Symposium on 'Workers' Participation in Management', *Archives Internationales de Sociologie de la Cooperation*, I (2) 1957; M. J. Broekmeyer (ed.), *Yugoslav Workers' Self-Management* (Dordrecht, 1970). See also, on Britain, the publications of the Institute for Workers' Control, especially Ken Coates and Wyn Williams (eds.), *How and Why Industry Must be Democratised* (Nottingham, 1969).

[2] See, for a general study of the problem in Britain, V. L. Allen, *Power in Trade Unions* (London, 1954), and more recently the Report and research papers of the *Royal Commission on Trade Unions and Employers' Associations* (1966–67). In the USA there have been fewer studies of trade unions at the national level; one such study (of the international Typographical Union) is S. M. Lipset, M. Trow and J. Coleman, *Union Democracy* (Glencoe, 1955). One aspect of trade unionism which has become increasingly important is the growth of white collar unions; it is discussed very fully in Adolf Sturmthal (ed.), *White Collar Trade Unions* (Urbana, 1967).

strike activity with other social phenomena. There is no work of similar scope on other industrial countries, and there have been few attempts to make comparisons between countries or between historical periods, though two books make some contribution in this direction: A. Kornhauser, R. Dubin and A. M. Ross (eds.), *Industrial Conflict* (New York, 1954), and A. M. Ross and P. T. Hartman, *Changing Patterns of Industrial Conflict* (New York, 1960). I have referred in an earlier chapter to a number of sociological contributions to the study of negotiation and wage-determination which supplement the work of economists in this field.[1]

This brief review will illustrate the distinctiveness of a sociological approach, which consists in the attempt to study economic phenomena (and as will be seen later, those of other limited areas of social life) in the context of the social structure as a whole. The division of labour, property ownership, the type of economic system, and the character of industrial relations, as well as the political order and social stratification—viewed in the light of the historical changes which they undergo—may all be involved when we try to describe and understand a particular set of conditions or events in one society at a given moment of time.

[1] *See* above, p. 71.

Chapter 9

POLITICAL INSTITUTIONS

Political institutions are concerned with the distribution of power in society. Max Weber defined the state as 'a human community which successfully claims the monopoly of the legitimate use of physical force within a given territory'. Thus the state is one of the important agencies of social control, whose functions are carried out by means of law, backed ultimately by physical force. It is *one* association within society, and not society as a whole. And Weber made territoriality one of the characteristics of a political system. I discussed earlier the distinction established between 'civil society' and the state,[1] which was an important step in the formation of sociology as a science. The early sociologists, having established this distinction, proceeded to examine the relationship between civil society and the state, and to attempt a classification of political systems based upon the different forms of civil society. Their approach was evolutionary: they were interested in the *origins* and *development* of the state. Regarding the state as one association within society, and as characterized by definite territorial limits, and being acquainted through the growing literature of ethnography with primitive societies which seemed to have no political organization, they were naturally led to consider the question of origins; and some of them went on to speculate, under the influence of the philosophy of history, about the future of the state. This same philosophy of history (and the political revolutions of the age) determined their interest in the different historical forms of the state, especially in Western civilization. However little we may now be inclined to accept these schemes of unilinear evolution, the classification of political systems remains a primary task of political sociology, and much can be learned from the nineteenth century writers.

I shall consider first, therefore, the types of political system, and then discuss in greater detail political organization and political behaviour in present day societies, which can be directly observed

[1] *See* above, p. 17.

by the sociologist and social anthropologist and to which most of the literature is devoted.[1]

Types of political system

The evolutionary sociologists all made a distinction between those societies which had, and those which had not, a political system, but they made it in different ways and they diverged in their accounts of how the state originated. Spencer distinguished in his category of 'simple societies' some which had no headship, and others which had only occasional or unstable headship. It was only at the stage of 'doubly compound societies' that any elaborate political organization was to be found. Hobhouse distinguished between three types of society characterized by different fundamental social bonds: kinship, authority, and citizenship. In a later work,[2] he studied more closely the institutions of primitive societies, and demonstrated a correlation between the level of economic development, increasing social differentiation, and the emergence and consolidation of a regular political authority. This classification agrees, so far as it goes, with the Marxist scheme. Marx and Engels, having elaborated a classification of societies in which the state came into existence only at a stage of economic development where antagonistic social classes appeared, found confirmation of their views in the anthropological researches of L. H. Morgan. Engels' systematic formulation of the Marxist view in *The Origins of the Family, Private Property and the State* (1884) was based upon Morgan's work[3] and Marx's manuscript notes thereon.

The explanations of the emergence of the state were broadly of two kinds. Spencer and Comte regarded it as a consequence of the increasing size and complexity of societies, in which warfare was a major factor. According to Spencer, war consolidated the 'compound society' and still more the 'doubly compound society'. Comte attributed to warfare the 'first great mission' of bringing about the expansion of human societies and the establishment of settled political authority. These views agree in some respects with the theory of F. Oppenheimer who, criticizing Marxism, discovers the origin of the state *and* of social classes in the conquest of one tribe by another: 'the state is a juridical institution unilaterally imposed upon a conquered people by the conquerors, originally

[1] Law, as a type of social control dependent upon the existence of a state, will be discussed separately in Part IV below.

[2] *The Material Culture and Social Institutions of the Simpler Peoples (op. cit.).*

[3] L. H. Morgan, *Ancient Society.*

with the sole object of subjecting them to a tribute . . .'[1] In contrast, the Marxist theory accounts for the emergence of the state by differentiation into social classes within the community following the growth of productive forces and of wealth. The study of the simpler societies by Hobhouse, Wheeler and Ginsberg, while not proposing any explanation, shows a correlation between social differentiation and settled political authority.

Recent sociological and anthropological study has confirmed some of these distinctions and modified others. It is generally agreed that some primitive societies lack a political authority[2] and Lowie writes: 'The earliest communities must have been tiny, egalitarian groups corresponding to a Semang or Eskimo camp. Such a community was in the main a body of kindred . . .'[3] At the same time, the role of kinship in maintaining social unity should not be exaggerated, as it probably was by Hobhouse, Morgan and others. Maine, in his *Ancient Law*, argued that in early societies kinship was 'the sole possible ground of community in political functions'. Lowie remarks that this 'exaggerates the correct view that kinship has played an enormous part in the social life of aboriginal and archaic peoples', and he goes on to say: 'That the territorial tie is never wholly negligible is proved a fortiori by two extreme instances of kinship-dominated tribes, the Ifugao and the Yurok'.[4] One distinctive feature, in primitive and early societies, is that where a separate political authority exists it is closely bound up with kinship, religion and other institutions.

We need not be concerned here with the diverse accounts of political development given by the evolutionary sociologists, but two

[1] Franz Oppenheimer, *System der Soziologie*, Vol. II, Der Staat (1926).

[2] Recently I. Schapera has argued on the basis of a comparative study of four African tribal societies that political organization is more prevalent than many sociologists believe, and that this would be clearer if the insistence upon physical coercion as a criterion were abandoned. He observes that, '. . . organized force is only one of the mechanisms making for orderly life in any community, and to adopt it as the distinctive criterion of political organization would mean neglecting unduly the various others that help to unite people into self-governing groups'. I. Schapera, *Government and Politics in Tribal Societies* (London, 1956), p. 218. But the first part of this assertion has hardly ever been denied, and we have already noted here that the state is only one of the agencies of social control. Nevertheless, it is distinctive *because* it claims a monopoly of the legitimate use of violence; and it does not seem helpful to sociological analysis to abandon a distinction which enables us to differentiate not only between societies which have or do not have a state, but also between politically organized societies in terms of the degree in which the social order is maintained by force or by other means.

[3] R. H. Lowie, *Social Organization* (1950), Ch. 14, 'The State'. This is one of the best short accounts of political structure.

[4] Lowie, *op. cit.* This view is supported by Schapera's study; *op. cit.*, Ch. I.

points are worthy of attention. They discussed the problem of how small communities developed into larger societies, a problem which is of general sociological interest. Some like Spencer or Comte emphasized the part played by military conquest, and I shall discuss this later. Others stressed the integration brought about by economic or religious developments. Thus, Fustel de Coulanges, in his *Ancient City*, attributed the formation of the Greek and Roman cities to the elaboration of a more inclusive religion. Recent studies indicate that both conflict and co-operation have played an important part in different times and places.[1] This can be seen in the case of those primitive societies which have developed federations or leagues. And in the modern world it is evident that religion has been a significant factor in the political unity of many states; of India, the emerging Arab states in the Middle East, and Israel.

Secondly, the evolutionary sociologists agreed in recording the development, in Western civilization, from authoritarian states to less coercive types of political system, variously termed 'industrial society', 'citizenship', or the 'classless society'. Their optimistic views were later challenged, by Burckhardt, Spengler, Max Weber, and others. I shall not discuss here their historical prophecies. But in the course of making them they analysed the relations between political authority and other social phenomena (e.g. economic power, social stratification) in ways which are still valuable.

The types of political system which the nineteenth century sociologists distinguished were relatively few, and they were defined largely in terms of an evolutionary scheme which was relevant above all to Western civilization. Primitive and archaic societies, city states, feudal states, and modern democracies were the principal forms considered. Little was said about the Asiatic type of society and government which we discussed in an earlier chapter. At the present time it seems possible to outline a more comprehensive classification, which is presented schematically below:

Primitive societies
1. without a distinct and permanent political structure
2. with a distinct and permanent political structure, but strongly influenced by kinship and religion

City states
Empires based upon city states
Feudal states
Asiatic states with a centralized bureaucracy
Nation states

[1] For a general account see A. Moret and G. Davy, *From Tribe to Empire*.

154

1. modern democratic states
2. modern totalitarian states
Empires based upon nation states

This classification is largely descriptive, but it takes into account the scale of societies, the economic system, social stratification, religion, and other factors which have been seen to be important in determining political structure. It is probable that a more systematic classification, in terms of fundamental political relationships, could be established, using the material from modern political studies, but no such attempt has yet been made. This classification cannot here be discussed in detail, and in the following section I shall concentrate upon the political institutions of modern societies. But it may be useful to present some reflections upon the political structure of India in the past. Earlier, I discussed the application to India of the concept of 'Asiatic society'. This implied a political classification, since an essential feature of the Asiatic type of society is the existence of an authoritarian government ruling through a centralized bureaucracy. At the same time, however, we have to consider that this type of government is superimposed upon a large number of small, and to some extent self-governing, communities. Thus there are two levels of political organization and action. The centralized state may be little more than a tax collecting and public works agency; there is no fundamental political integration, but, on the contrary, a strong tendency for the separate units within the state to break away. In the actual development of political unity in India we can see at work the forces of conquest and co-operation discussed above. India was unified at various times by conquest, by the Maurya and Gupta Empires, the Muslim conquest, and most completely, by the British conquest. Yet in all these periods, and still more in the periods of breakdown of the central authority, the unity of the society was maintained by the caste system and religion. This has given a particular importance to the priesthood in the Indian state. Secular and religious authority were closely related, and the influence of the Brahmins seems to have gradually increased. 'From Vedic times the king had a priest attached to his person, the *purohita*; and this dignitary soon became his adviser in all matters of importance.'[1] Moreover, the law books were written and interpreted by Brahmins, and law in India retained until recently (and still retains in some respects) a strongly religious character.[2] The situation resembled that in other 'Asiatic societies' discussed by Wittfogel;

[1] K. Wittfogel, *op. cit.*, p. 98.
[2] *See* below, pp. 253–4.

155

Byzantium, the Inca Empire, ancient Egypt. The important political role of priests seems to have been connected in part with the rigid stratification system, which required religious justification. In later Indian history this political structure was complicated by the introduction of feudal type relations, after the Muslim conquest. These characteristics of the Indian polity are not only intrinsically worthy of study by the methods of historical sociology; political traditions also survive and influence the conduct of politics today. The village community and bureaucracy, religion, and the political role of the Brahmins have all helped to shape the political thought and political issues of modern India. Western political institutions, the legacy of British rule, are more obvious influences but they are not the only ones.

Contemporary political institutions and political behaviour
We can broadly distinguish, in the contemporary world, three types of political situation. First, there is the situation of tribal societies, which, under Western influence and often under Western control or guidance, are being industrialized and are seeking, or have recently acquired, more modern political institutions and forms of political expression. These are principally African societies. So far, there has been little sociological study of the changes which are taking place;[1] and although certain regularities can be detected, and similar problems identified, the data are insufficient for wide generalization.

Secondly, there is the situation of non-industrial countries of ancient civilization which are being industrialized after emancipation from colonial and feudal or autocratic rule. This category includes many of the countries of Asia and the Middle East, and, with some qualifications, the countries of Latin America. The political changes in these countries have been more closely studied, and I shall consider in some detail the case of India.

Thirdly, there are the industrial countries, in which sociology itself was born, and which have been the object of intensive sociological investigation. Here we have to distinguish between two principal types of political system: the democratic-capitalist or democratic socialist, and the communist-totalitarian (with some other variants of totalitarianism).[2] This distinction will be explored later. The

[1] Two valuable local studies should, however, be mentioned: D. E. Apter, *The Gold Coast in Transition* (Princeton, 1955), and A. L. Epstein, *Politics in an Urban African Community* (Manchester, 1957) (on Rhodesia).

[2] It is well known that the problems of terminology in describing contemporary political systems are considerable, since most of the available terms have an ideological and emotional significance. The terms I have employed above should be regarded, so far as possible, as being *purely descriptive.*

general political characteristics of modern industrial societies are: (1) the political community as a nation-state, (2) the existence of political movements, parties and pressure groups, (3) the election of the political executive by universal adult suffrage, and (4) the administration of public affairs by a large centralized bureaucracy.

The first of these characteristics has received relatively little attention from sociologists.[1] Indeed, it may be argued that the significance of the nation-state has been altogether under-estimated, especially in its bearing upon the development of capitalism. Similarly, nationalism as an ideology, and its connections with religion or class interests, have been much less closely investigated than have other political ideologies. Yet the force of nationalism in the modern world is very great, and creates problems in relation to international order. Some of the major problems of the present day arise from the contradictions between the need for an international political authority and the forces of new nationalisms and old and new imperialisms.

The study of political parties and elections has developed rapidly in the past few decades, along several different lines. The connection between political parties and social classes, which is the central conception of the Marxist theory of politics and the state, has been thoroughly investigated. The general relationship between class interest, party affiliation, and electoral choice is unmistakable.[2] Numerous enquiries have shown that the main political parties in most societies are perceived by the electors as representing class interests, and that most electors vote in accordance with what they take to be their own class interests. Nevertheless, the relationship is by no means as simple or precise as popular Marxist doctrine (and some varieties of intellectual Marxism) claim. Political parties are also seen as representing diverse elements in a national tradition, and as being concerned in some degree with general, rather than class or sectional, interests.[3] Moreover, not all individuals vote in accordance with their social class position as an external observer

[1] Among the few major contributions is F. Znaniecki, *Modern Nationalities: A Sociological Study* (Urbana, 1952). *See also* M. Ginsberg, *Nationalism: A Reappraisal* (Cambridge, 1961). The growth of national sentiment in India has been comprehensively studied from a sociological point of view by A. R. Desai in *Social Background of Indian Nationalism*.

[2] *See* especially the analysis of the situation in Britain by Richard Rose, 'Class and Party Divisions: Britain as a Test Case', *Sociology*, Vol. 2, No. 2, May, 1968.

[3] I have discussed the problem of a 'ruling class' in my *Elites and Society* (London, 1964), Chapter II. See also the more detailed analysis in Nicos Poulantzas, *Pouvoir politique et classes sociales* (Paris, 1968). I shall discuss some aspects of working class politics in Chapter 11 below.

might define it. In British General Elections since 1951, approximately one-third of those in the working class have voted for the Conservative Party, although this party is regarded by a large majority of electors as the party of the 'upper class'.[1] Over the same period some 20 per cent of those in the middle class have voted for the Labour Party. In the USA, although the class system differs in important ways from that in European countries, and class ideologies are less influential, a similar correlation between socioeconomic status and electoral choice has been demonstrated, but with the same or greater divergences. There are in particular important regional and religious influences upon party affiliation and electoral choice.[2] In France, which has experienced violent class conflicts and extreme political ideologies, similar divergences are manifest. The French working class, which is often conceived as politically homogeneous and firmly attached to the left wing parties, is nothing of the kind; in the elections of June 1951 only 63 per cent of the working class voted for the Socialist and Communist Parties.[3] Besides election studies, the studies of party membership also show the predominant but not exclusive influence of social class, or socio-economic status, upon political affiliation.

These detailed empirical investigations have raised doubts about a pure 'interest' theory of politics. They have suggested new problems of political motivation, and have drawn attention to the existence of more specific 'interest groups' than political parties (which in democratic societies have to make a wide appeal if they wish to obtain power); namely, what are now called 'pressure groups'. Such groups have important political functions in all modern societies, functions which may be either useful or harmful to the stability or progress of society. Where there is a stable political authority pressure groups may be a useful additional means for individuals to make known sectional desires or grievances, or to convey information which is valuable to the administration; where political authority is weak the more powerful pressure groups may usurp governmental

[1] On the question of class and party in Britain, see M. Benney, A. P. Gray, and R. H. Pear, *How People Vote* (London, 1956); and J. Bonham, *The Middle Class Vote* (London, 1954). See also two recent studies of conservative working class voters; R. T. McKenzie and A. Silver, *Angels in Marble* (London, 1968), and Eric A. Nordlinger, *Working Class Tories; Authority, Deference and Stable Democracy* (Berkeley, 1967).

[2] For a general discussion, see R. Heberle, *Social Movements: An Introduction to Political Sociology* (New York, 1951), especially Ch. 12. See also the detailed comparative studies, based upon much recent research, in S. M. Lipset, *Political Man* (London, 1960).

[3] M. Duverger, *Partis politiques et classes sociales en France* (Paris, 1955), p. 33.

functions or hold the rest of the community to ransom, as has happened in post-war France.[1]

Another interest in the study of political parties stems from the classical work of Robert Michels, *Political Parties*.[2] Michels, who was a colleague and friend of Max Weber, concluded from his study of modern mass parties that they were not, and could not be, democratically organized, in so far as they were engaged in a struggle for power. They were, on the contrary ruled by a small oligarchy in control of the bureaucratic apparatus. An elaborate study of British political parties has broadly confirmed Michels' view.[3] And several studies of the Communist Party in communist countries tend to support Michels' view that revolutionary parties more easily become bureaucratized and oligarchic than do others. A broad comparative study by M. Duverger[4] also brings out the oligarchic character of party leadership, especially in those societies which have a single-party system. Duverger also formulates a number of generalizations about the relation between the electoral system and the number of parties, with particular reference to the effects of proportional representation and the second ballot in France.

Michels' views were strongly influenced by Max Weber's more general conception of the growth of bureaucracy in modern societies. Since Weber wrote, bureaucracy has been increasingly studied, in public administration, in industry, in trade unions, as well as in political parties. There are many divergent lines of enquiry,[5] but one major emphasis has been on the separation between leaders and masses in modern large scale organizations of all kinds, and a second on the emergence of a bureaucratic or managerial ruling class.

The latter problem has been discussed especially in connection with the communist countries, and we may conveniently turn now to examine this second principal type of political system. Unfortunately, there has been little sociological thought or research in communist societies, except in Poland and Yugoslavia, until quite

---

[1] *See* for example, J. D. Stewart, *British Pressure Groups* (London, 1958); H. W. Ehrmann, *Organised Business in France* (Princeton, 1957).

[2] Leipzig, 1911, 2nd edn. 1925. English trans. Glencoe, 1949.

[3] R. T. McKenzie, *British Political Parties* (London, 1955).

[4] M. Duverger, *Political Parties* (English trans. London, 1955).

[5] See P. Blau, *Bureaucracy in Modern Society* (New York, 1956); S. N. Eisenstadt, 'Bureaucracy' *Current Sociology*, VII (2), 1958. There is a useful review of ideas and studies of bureaucracy in M. Albrow, *Bureaucracy* (London, 1970), while a more extensive analysis of theories of bureaucracy is to be found in Nicos P. Mouzelis, *Organisation and Bureaucracy* (London, 1967).

recently, and even now it is limited in scope. It is therefore, impossible to deal in the same precise and detailed way with their political institutions, or the political behaviour of their citizens. The most characteristic feature of these societies is the existence of a single party which monopolizes political power. This situation is justified in terms of Marxist theory as the expression of social unity resulting from the elimination of antagonistic social classes.[1] The dictatorship of the party is equated with the dictatorship of the proletariat in a transitional period during which the foundations of the ultimate classless society are being laid. According to the orthodox Marxist theory, after the achievement of the classless society the state, and presumably *all* political parties, will 'wither away'. Critics have assailed both the theory and practice of communism. It is pointed out that the coercive apparatus of the state has vastly increased in communist societies, to the detriment of individual liberty, and that the social distinctions between the leaders and officials on one side, and the mass of people on the other, are very great. In recent years, criticisms of the concentration of power have been made within the communist societies themselves, in the form of attacks upon 'Stalinism' and 'bureaucratic tendencies', and in one country, Yugoslavia, there have been attempts to decentralize political authority. The major sociological criticism of most orthodox Marxism is that it asserts, against the evidence, that political power is always based upon, and can only be based upon, economic power, and fails to analyse in a scientific and exact way, the notion of 'economic power'. The latter point was briefly discussed in the previous chapter, where I drew attention to the ambiguities in the notion of 'ownership of the means of production'. The assertion of a one to one causal relationship between economic power and political power goes back to the eighteenth century distinction between 'civil society' and the state, and to the impression made upon social theorists by the rapid emancipation of economic life from political regulation in the early stages of industrial capitalism. But in a broader historical perspective, while recognizing the important influence of economic structure upon other social institutions, we must also admit the relative autonomy of politics. This problem will be further discussed in a later chapter in connection with the Marxist theory of class. Here we may conclude by noting the sociological contribution to the study of political power represented by Max Weber's analysis of bureaucracy, and the more recent

[1] The single party system was justified in Nazi Germany and Fascist Italy as an expression of *national unity*. It is so justified at present in Spain and also in a number of developing countries.

studies of bureaucratic power,[1] and by Pareto's exposition of the theory of elites, in which the most interesting and useful parts are the historical analyses of political motivation and of struggles for power.[2] Contemporary sociologists have become acutely aware of the problem of power, and their enquiries, from the work of Weber, Michels and Pareto onwards, have contributed much to an understanding of the complexities of power and of the difficulties, in large scale organizations and mass societies, of controlling it. By comparison with this growing body of scientific knowledge, the propositions of popular Marxism appear naïve; they are the equivalent in social theory of Aristotelian physics.

Political sociology has dealt with a far greater range of subjects than can be discussed here. The detailed study of administrative behaviour and organization has resulted in much useful knowledge which can be, and is, applied to improve the efficiency of administration. The conflict of ideologies, within and between societies, has promoted studies of the social influences upon political beliefs. Karl Mannheim contributed greatly to this branch of the sociology of knowledge, notably in his classical essay on 'conservative thought'.[3] Socialist ideologies have been less studied, but C. Bouglé analysed the influence of social structure upon the emergence and spread of egalitarian ideas[4] and Raymond Aron has examined the social factors which affect the acceptance of Marxism.[5] These diverse studies have led to an increasing interest in the political role of intellectuals, especially in the particular situation of under-developed countries where intellectuals frequently represent modern Western culture and find themselves separated from, and in conflict with, the traditional cultural values of the mass of their fellow countrymen. This is one of the sources of tension in countries, such as India, which are undergoing industrialization and it may also be a source of political authoritarianism in so far as the cultural isolation of the intellectuals emphasizes the distinction between the elite and the masses.

One aspect of political behaviour, however, has been relatively neglected by sociologists; namely, the development of social move-

---

[1] For example, by K. Wittfogel and by M. Djilas, *The New Class* (London, 1957).

[2] V. Pareto, *The Mind and Society* (English trans. New York, 1935). The theory of elites is praised in James Burnham, *The Machiavellians* (London, 1943), and criticized in T. B. Bottomore, *Elites and Society*.

[3] English trans. in K. Mannheim, *Essays on Sociology and Social Psychology* (London, 1953).

[4] C. Bouglé, *Les idées égalitaires* (Paris, 1925).

[5] Raymond Aron, *The Opium of the Intellectuals* (Eng. trans. London, 1956).

ments. As I have indicated, parties and pressure groups have been quite thoroughly studied, but the more diffuse movements out of which they arise have received much less attention. One major reason for this neglect was the preoccupation during the 1950s with 'stable democracy'—that is, with the political systems of Western societies, regarded as having attained a more or less definitive form with their existing array of parties and interest groups—and on the other side with the 'totalitarian societies', similarly regarded as having a permanent character.[1] Only with the emergence, during the 1960s, of new radical movements in the industrial countries, and the continuing growth of revolutionary movements in the Third World, have sociologists begun to devote themselves seriously to the study of such phenomena.[2]

Politics in the Developing Countries

There are some political conditions which are common to most, if not all, developing countries; in particular, the problems of establishing a new political system, and of making government and administration effective in bringing about rapid economic growth, and a general improvement in levels of living, which is a major aspiration of the mass of the people. Many developing countries have one-party rule, arising out of the preeminence of a national liberation or revolutionary movement at the time when the new nation was formed. In many countries military officers have taken power, either because of the failure of other political forces, or because the military have already acquired a political role and see themselves as more 'modern' and efficient than other groups.[3]

But there are very diverse circumstances in which these problems are faced, and the distinction between different types of political situation which I sketched earlier (p. 156) can be refined to take account of more specific variations. If we disregard for the present

[1] The ideas about 'stable democracy' are critically examined in Brian M. Barry, *Sociologists, Economists and Democracy* (London, 1970), Chapters III and IV. The differences between the democracies and the totalitarian countries are formulated, in a more subtle and qualified way than by some other writers on the subject, in Raymond Aron, *Democracy and Totalitarianism* (London, 1968).

[2] There is a good account of the early stages of the radical movements, which took shape initially in the USA, in Paul Jacobs and Saul Landau (eds.), *The New Radicals: A Report With Documents* (New York, 1966). Right wing movements are examined in Daniel Bell (ed.), *The Radical Right* (2nd edn., New York, 1963). The general literature on social movements is limited. A useful earlier work is Rudolf Heberle, *Social Movements* (New York, 1951). I shall discuss revolutionary movements more fully in a later chapter.

[3] *See* Morris Janowitz, *The Military in the Political Development of New Nations* (Chicago, 1964).

purpose the factors of size and natural resources, and also the unique characteristics of each country, arising from its history, its geographical situation, or its particular relationships with other nations, we may distinguish, as I have argued elsewhere: '. . . four main categories of underdeveloped countries, within each of which there are important similarities of social structure and culture: (i) the African states; (ii) the Arab states of the Middle East and North Africa; (iii) the Asian states; and (iv) the Latin American states. The countries belonging to the first group have established themselves by means of anti-colonial struggles which have affected profoundly their political regimes. They have to face, in addition to the problems of economic development, those of consolidating a national community formed out of tribal groups whose existence within their frontiers is in some measure the result of the arbitrary division of Africa among the colonial powers. Among the countries of the second group, a number have been formed by independence struggles against direct colonial rule, but many others have enjoyed political independence for some time and have had chiefly to resist the indirect control of their economic resources by foreign powers. Their political problems are mainly those of breaking down feudal and autocratic systems of government, which are linked with highly inegalitarian and rigid class systems. The third group, that of the Asian countries, is characterized especially by the fact that these are, for the most part, countries of ancient civilization in which traditional social institutions are very strongly established. They are also countries which have liberated themselves very recently from colonial rule, and although they do not confront major problems of integrating tribal groups into a national community, as is the case with the African countries, they face some similar problems of national integration in so far as they are divided into castes or linguistic regions (as in India), or into ethnically and linguistically separate groups (e.g. Tamils and Sinhalese in Ceylon, Malays and Chinese in Malaya). The fourth group, that of the Latin American countries, differs in important respects from all the others. These countries are, for the most part, more advanced economically, and they are already urban rather than agrarian societies, although they have only recently begun to industrialize on a large scale; and they have been politically independent for a relatively long time. Thus, their political problems are not to the same extent those of national integration, although in some of them, such as Peru, the large Indian population has still to acquire full citizenship; nor has recent political activity been directly inspired by nationalism, although it has been directed increasingly against North American

163

economic influence in the region. The main problems are those created by industrialization, the rapid increase of population, and the rise of a labour movement within a political system in which the large landowners have long been dominant, and have often ruled through military dictatorships.'[1]

An examination of Indian politics will show in more detail some of the problems of the developing countries, even though India is exceptional in certain respects, particularly in having maintained a democratic system and avoided both authoritarian and military rule.[2] W. H. Morris-Jones, at the end of a comprehensive study of parliamentary government in India, observes that 'The "experiment" is working and parliamentary institutions are more firmly established in the way of life of the Indian people than they are in that of many a country in Europe'.[3] Political parties function more or less on the Western model, and illiteracy has not proved a serious obstacle to the exercise of electoral choice.

The predominance of all-India parties indicates the extent to which political unity is firmly established. Regional differences of culture and language have found political expression in debates on the number and delimitation of the states composing the Indian Union, but they have not until very recently given rise to important organized political movements. The influence of caste on political life has been variously assessed. Some writers suggest that it has been increasing in recent years, but the evidence is not clear. Morris-Jones refers to the conflict between Brahmins and non-Brahmins as a dominating factor in Madras politics.[4] The very small number of individuals from the scheduled castes elected to unreserved seats in the Indian Parliament suggests that few caste Hindus are willing to vote for untouchable candidates. On the other hand the Scheduled Castes Federation, which has contested the reserved seats, has not been very successful, and its lack of success suggests that the electorate is not well disposed towards parties which are organized

[1] T. B. Bottomore, *Elites and Society*, Chapter V.

[2] For studies of some other societies *see:* Franz Schurmann, *Ideology and Organization in Communist China* (Berkeley, 1967); Thomas Hodgkin, *African Political Parties* (Harmondsworth, 1961); P. C. Lloyd (ed.), *The New Elites of Tropical Africa* (London, 1966); S. M. Lipset and Aldo Solari (eds.), *Elites in Latin America* (New York, 1967). There are also a number of general and comparative studies: *see* especially, Peter Worsley, *The Third World* (2nd end., London, 1967), and Irving L. Horowitz, *Three Worlds of Development* (New York, 1966), Part III. S. P. Huntington, *Political Order in Changing Societies* (New Haven, 1968) presents a different view, emphasizing the need for political stability rather than processes of change.

[3] W. H. Morris-Jones, *Parliament in India* (London, 1957), p. 332.

[4] *Op. cit.*, p. 28.

explicitly on a caste basis. Indeed, voting in general elections shows a strong preference for the Western type parties.

A study of the 1951–52 election examined in some detail the influence of caste in different areas.[1] In Delhi, neither caste, class nor religious affiliation seem to have had an important influence on the electors, who voted heavily in favour of the Congress Party. The influence of caste and religion is of course stronger in the predominantly rural regions. The report on Rajasthan observes that 'caste, tradition, religious beliefs, even threats and bribes, influenced the voter even more than they did in other states'.[2] But a careful survey of a village in Gujarat, by A. H. Somjee,[3] shows that neither caste nor religion had a preponderant influence upon the voters' choice. Every caste in the village was divided in its political allegiance, and only one caste even attempted to influence its members to vote for a particular candidate. A major factor in the voters' choice was economic interest; the larger landowners voted mainly against the Congress Party, while Government employees and small landowners voted for it.

Studies of party composition, organization and ideology, which would give some indication of the different influences upon political affiliation have yet to be made.[4] At present, the members of all political parties seem to be drawn predominantly from the middle class, urban, younger categories of the population. A survey of the Praja Socialist Party in Bombay (1953) showed that of 469 'active' members, 136 were industrial workers and virtually all the others middle class.[5] The members of parliament seem, from the data available, to be drawn from an even narrower social circle; and among them members of the professions, especially law, are markedly predominant.[6] It is evident from various sources that intellectuals, in a broad sense, have dominated political life in India since independence, and that active participation in politics by the mass of the population such as occurred in the independence

[1] S. V. Kogekar and R. L. Park (eds.), *Reports on the Indian General Elections, 1951–52* (Bombay, 1956).

[2] *Op. cit.*, p. 234.

[3] A. H. Somjee, *Voting Behaviour in an Indian Village* (Baroda, 1959).

[4] There is a preliminary study, historical rather than sociological, in M. Weiner, *Party Politics in India: The Development of a Multi-Party System* (Princeton, 1957).

[5] Quoted in Weiner, *op. cit.*

[6] See the estimates by Morris-Jones, *op. cit.*, p. 120. In both the House of the People and the Council of States about fifty per cent of the members come from the professions. There do not seem to be any members in either House from the industrial working class or from the ordinary village workers. Another striking feature is the high proportion of members who are full-time party workers.

movement has only recently begun to revive, on a limited scale, with the emergence of peasant movements, especially in West Bengal. Students are the principal source of recruitment to active political work, and this fact accounts in part for the prevalence of factionalism in the major parties. Weiner suggests that the student cliques are continued into later political life, and that the clique and subsequently the faction assume for the individual 'many of the functions of the traditional joint family, caste system and village organization'.[1] Other studies however, find the prevalence of factionalism to be characteristic of the traditional village culture itself.[2]

Besides the influence of caste, which cannot be exactly determined on the basis of present knowledge, and the prevalence of factions, Indian political life has some other specific features which should be briefly mentioned. One is that the party system appears not to have assumed its final shape. Weiner has discussed the reasons for the existence in India of a multi-party system, when the electoral system is the 'simple majority single ballot' type which is generally favourable to a two party system.[3] The reservation of seats for the Scheduled Castes and Tribes has encouraged some minor parties, but the principal causes seem to be the dominant position of the Congress Party with its prestige resulting from the successful struggle for independence, and the consequent inability of any other party to conceive itself as a national opposition with a chance of attaining power; and the opposition between the traditional culture and Western civilization, which has given rise to the Hindu tradition-alist parties. Nevertheless, there has been a gradual movement toward a predominantly two party system, and this has been accelerated in the last few years with the split in the Congress Party between left-wing and right-wing groups. The left-wing, led by Mrs Gandhi, has formed alliances with other parties on the left, including the pro-Moscow Communist Party (with considerable success in the September 1970 elections in Kerala); while the right-wing has attempted to do the same with the Swatantra Party (which advocates a free enterprise, capitalist economy for India) and the Hindu traditionalist parties.

[1] *Op. cit.*

[2] See Oscar Lewis, *Group Dynamics in a North Indian Village; A Study of Factions* (Delhi, 1954,) and a Symposium introduced by R. Firth, 'Factions in Indian and Overseas Indian Societies', *British Journal of Sociology*, VIII (4), 1957. There is a very good account of the influence of factions, caste and other forces upon state politics in Paul R. Brass, *Factional Politics in an Indian State: The Congress Party in Uttar Pradesh* (Berkeley, 1965).

[3] *Op. cit.*, Chapter XI.

A second feature is the existence in India of a distinct pattern of political thought and behaviour, inspired by religious doctrine and Gandhian politics, which is directly opposed to the political arrangements represented by the Western style party system.[1] The influence of this pattern could be seen in the importance attributed to the village reform movement of Vinoba Bhave, and in the support which this movement attracted from prominent Western style political leaders, and notably Jayaprakash Narayan. At the same time, it is difficult to see this style of politics as a real alternative to the party system, and it seems to have declined in recent years. It reveals the clash of cultures in India, and perhaps its future will lie in emphasizing the ethical basis of ordinary politics rather than in proposing a solution of social problems 'beyond politics'.

We can see, from this examination of political institutions in India, similar problems to those in the economic field; the conflict between traditional social arrangements fixed in the caste system and religion, and the new relationships brought about by economic growth. It is also evident how the political bond may be reinforced by other social relations, or may come into conflict with them. In other developing countries, within other cultural and historical contexts, similar changes and problems are to be found which distinguish these countries as a whole from the industrial societies.

[1] This is referred to as 'saintly politics' by Morris-Jones, *The Government and Politics of India* (London, 1964), p. 52. For a good account of this tradition *see* D. M. Brown, *The White Umbrella: Indian Political Thought from Manu to Gandhi* (Berkeley, 1953).

Chapter 10

THE FAMILY AND KINSHIP

The nuclear family

The individual nuclear family is a universal social phenomenon. As Lowie writes: 'It does not matter whether marital relations are permanent or temporary; whether there is polygyny or polyandry or sexual licence; whether conditions are complicated by the addition of members not included in *our* family circle; the one fact stands out beyond all others that everywhere the husband, wife, and immature children constitute a unit apart from the remainder of the community.'[1]

The universality of the nuclear family can be accounted for by the indispensable functions it performs and the difficulty of ensuring the performance of these functions by any other social group. 'In the nuclear family or its constituent relationships we thus see assembled four functions fundamental to human social life—the sexual, the economic, the reproductive, and the educational.'[2] We may distinguish between the social and the psychological functions of the nuclear family. Kingsley Davis has distinguished four major social functions; reproduction, maintenance (of immature children), placement, and socialization.[3] Of these the first two, and the fourth, are most important, since placement in the sense of allocation to a position in the occupational system or the status hierarchy is not a universal function; it occurs in rigidly stratified societies (e.g. in a caste society) but not invariably, or even predominantly, in modern industrial societies. The psychological functions are primarily the satisfaction of the sexual needs of the marital partners, and of the need for affection and security, both for parents and for children. The family has often had other functions in addition to those we

---

[1] R. H. Lowie, *Primitive Society* (1920), pp. 66–7. There are a few possible exceptions to this generalization, the most frequently cited case being that of the Nayar of South India; see Kathleen Gough, 'Is the Family Universal?—the Nayar Case' in N. W. Bell and E. F. Vogel (eds.) *A Modern Introduction to the Family* (New York, 1960).

[2] G. P. Murdock, *Social Structure* (1949), p. 10.

[3] Kingsley Davis, *Human Society*, p. 395.

have mentioned. Murdock observes that: 'As a firm social constellation it frequently, but not universally, draws to itself various other functions. Thus, it is often the centre of religious worship, with the father as family priest. It may be the primary unit in landholding, vengeance or recreation. Social status may depend more upon family position than upon individual achievement. And so on.'[1]

Anthropologists have consistently emphasized the economic functions of the family in primitive societies. The bond between the father and mother is not only, or even predominantly, the sexual privileges accorded to married spouses, since many primitive societies allow unrestricted pre-marital sexual relations, and a number of societies allow extra-marital relations either unrestricted or more frequently with prescribed relatives. A major factor in maintaining the nuclear family is economic co-operation based upon division of labour between the sexes. Lévi-Strauss has given a graphic account of the miserable situation of unmarried individuals in the most primitive societies; he writes of the spectacle of a young man in a village of central Brazil, 'crouching for hours on end in the corner of a hut, gloomy, ill-cared for, terribly thin and, it seemed, in the most complete dejection . . . he seldom went out except to hunt alone, and at the family meals round the fire he would usually have fasted if a relative had not from time to time placed a small portion of food beside him which he ate in silence. When I asked what was the matter with him, believing that he had some serious illness, my suppositions were laughed at and I was told, "He is a bachelor".'[2] Economic co-operation also strengthens the ties between parents and children, and between siblings. The loss of these productive functions involving co-operative labour by the family members is a significant feature of the nuclear family in modern industrial societies, which I shall consider later.

The basic structure of the nuclear family, it has been held, depends upon incest taboos; from these it follows that the nuclear family is discontinuous over time and confined to two generations. A third generation can only result from the formation of new families by an exchange of males and females between existing nuclear families. 'In consequence . . . every normal adult in every human society belongs to at least two nuclear families—*a family of orientation* in which he was born and reared, and which includes his father, mother, brothers and sisters, and *a family of procreation* which he establishes by his marriage and which includes his husband or wife, his sons, and his

[1] G. P. Murdock, *op. cit.*, p. 11.
[2] C. Lévi-Strauss, *Les structures élémentaires de la parenté* (1949), p. 49.

daughters.'[1] The incest taboos, and their extensions outside the nuclear family, in rules of exogamy, together with rules of descent, are the source of all the complexities of kinship usages and terminology which I shall briefly consider later. Here we need simply note that the extended incest taboos establish interdependence between families, sibs, and clans, and thus play an important part in the integration of primitive societies.

Types of family structure

The universality of the nuclear family does not mean that family structure is everywhere the same. On the contrary, it is extremely variable. Kingsley Davis has listed some of the major items of variation in the marital relation (number of spouses, authority, strength of bond, choice of spouse, residence, etc.), in the parent-child relation, and in sibling relations.[2] We may, however, make a broad distinction between family systems in which the nuclear family is relatively independent, and systems in which the nuclear family is incorporated in, or subordinated to, a larger group, the polygamous or the extended family.[3]

The independent nuclear family is characteristic of modern industrial societies. Its predominance seems to be due to the growth of individualism, reflected in property, law, and general social ideals of individual happiness and self-fulfilment, and to geographical and social mobility. It has also been affected by the increasing State provision for individual misfortune; the individual is no longer so dependent upon his family in times of distress. The marked predominance of the relatively autonomous nuclear family is a recent phenomenon, and it has appeared most fully in the most advanced industrial societies, particularly the USA. The solidarity of this type of family

[1] Murdock, *op. cit.*, p. 13. I cannot discuss here the various explanations of the incest taboos; the problem has been examined by Lévi-Strauss, *op. cit.*, Ch. 2, and most comprehensively by Murdock, *op. cit.*, Ch. 10. But see the criticism in Edmund Leach, *Lévi-Strauss* (London, 1970), of Levi-Strauss' equation of exogamy with the converse of the incest taboo; and the discussion of the problem in Robin Fox, *Kinship and Marriage* (London, 1967).

[2] Kingsley Davis, *Human Society*, pp. 414–16.

[3] Murdock (*op. cit.*, p. 2) makes this distinction between the independent nuclear family and composite forms of the family. A *polygamous family* 'consists of two or more nuclear families affiliated by plural marriages, i.e. by having one parent in common'. An *extended family* 'consists of two or more nuclear families affiliated through an extension of the parent-child relationship . . . i.e. by joining the nuclear family of a married adult to that of his parents'. Murdock found, in the 192 societies of his sample for which information was adequate, that 47 had normally only nuclear families, 53 had polygamous but not extended families, and 92 had some form of the extended family.

depends largely upon sexual attraction and companionship between husband and wife, and companionship between parents and children.[1] This does not seem to be such a firm basis as the wider complex of rights and obligations (economic, sexual and so on) which exist in the extended family. The loss of economic functions is more important than most sociologists have recognized. Divorce is frequent in the USA, and has been increasing in most Western countries.[2] The solidarity of the independent nuclear family is greater where it includes young children, but as the children grow up the bonds tend to weaken again, first through the influence of peer groups, and later as a result of social and geographical mobility.

The composite forms of the family are to be found frequently in primitive societies, but also in many non-industrial societies. In Europe, the Yugoslav form of the extended family, the *zadruga*, survived until the beginning of the present century. Different types of extended family are still common in Asia, even in an industrialized country such as Japan.[3] In India, the joint family has existed since the earliest times. It was, in the past, a corporate body with property held in common, common worship of a tutelary deity, and authority exercised by the head of the family (usually the eldest male in the eldest male line). According to Hindu law the family property was not strictly impartible, but partition was infrequent and it was quite usual for families to comprise three or four generations living, working and eating together.[4] Besides property and work,

[1] One of the best known recent studies of the family, E. W. Burgess and H. J. Locke, *The Family: From Institution to Companionship*, emphasizes this point.

[2] See below, p. 177.

[3] See K. Ariga, 'The contemporary Japanese family in transition', *Transactions of the Third World Congress of Sociology* (London, 1956), Vol. IV. pp. 215–21, and K. Ariga, 'Problems of the Asian family system', *ibid.*, Vol. VIII, pp. 233–41. In the latter article Ariga discusses the role of the Japanese *dozoku* (familial aggregates) in economic life. In Japan '. . . the managing bodies which operated business were commonly familial. . . . A *dozoku* was composed of a main family and families which were dependent upon it and affiliated through consanguinity or some other kind of relationship with the main family. When the scale of an enterprise grew too large for such a *dozoku* to manage the entire business, the enterprise was organized into a joint stock company with *dozoku* members constituting the governing body of the whole organization. Thus the *Zaitbatsu* (financial cliques) of pre-World War II came into existence.' In the nineteenth century, until the land-tax reforms of 1873–6, family property (land, houses, etc.) was owned by the family as a unit, and there was little individual property. But since 1945 the influence of the composite family and the *dozoku* has declined.

[4] See H. S. Maine, *Ancient Law* (Everyman edn.), p. 154: 'As soon as a son is born, he acquires a vested interest in his father's substance, and on attaining years of discretion he is even, in certain contingencies, permitted by the letter of the

religion was an important force uniting the joint family, for its members included the dead and unborn as well as the living. As Prabhu writes, 'The living members of the family are, so to speak, trustees of the house which belongs to the *pitris*, the ancestors, in the interests of the *putras*, future members of the family. . . . The central idea here is the worship of the family (*Kula*) as a temple of sacred traditions (*parampara*)'.[1] One of the most important duties of the family members was to keep alive the sacred fire.[2]

These general characteristics may be illustrated from the very thorough study by M. N. Srinivas of the joint family among the Coorgs of south India, who consider themselves to be Kshatriyas, i.e. to belong to the second highest rank in the traditional caste hierarchy.[3]

'The *okka* or the patrilineal and patrilocal joint family is the basic group among Coorgs. It is impossible to imagine a Coorg apart from the *okka* of which he is a member. It affects his life at every point and colours all his relations with the outside world. People who do not belong to an *okka* have no social existence at all, and the elders always bring pressure on the parties concerned to see that children born out of wedlock obtain membership in their father's or mother's *okka*.

Membership of an *okka* is acquired by birth, and the outside world always identifies a man with his *okka*. His association with his *okka* does not cease even after death, because he then becomes one of a body of apotheosized ancestors (karanava) who are believed to look after the *okka* of which they were members when alive. The ancestors are worshipped, and offerings of food and drink (bharani) are occasionally made to them.

Formerly the boys in an *okka*, all sons of agnatically related males, grazed the *okka's* cattle together, hunted birds, and played

law to call for a partition of the family estate. As a fact, however, a division rarely takes place even at the death of the father, and the property constantly remains undivided for several generations, though every member of every generation has a legal right to an undivided share in it. The domain thus held in common is sometimes administered by an elected manager, but more generally, and in some provinces always, it is managed by the eldest agnate, by the eldest representative of the eldest line of the stock.'

[1] P. N. Prabhu, *Hindu Social Organization* (Revised edn., 1954), p. 219.

[2] There is an obvious parallel here between the Hindu family and the family in ancient Greece and Rome. See Fustel de Coulanges, *The Ancient City* (Doubleday, 1956), p. 42, 'The members of the ancient family were united by something more powerful than birth, affection, or physical strength, this was the religion of the sacred fire and of dead ancestors'.

[3] M. N. Srinivas, *Religion and Society Among the Coorgs of South India*. Ch. 5, 'The cult of the *okka*'.

games. When they grew up all of them jointly looked after the ancestral estate under the guidance of the head of the *okka*.

Membership of an okka determines to a very large extent the choice of a spouse. First of all, marital relations are forbidden between members of the same *okka*. Where agnation overflows the *okka*, the taboo extends to agnatic relatives who are not members of the *okka*. Again, children of sisters may not intermarry.

The ancestral, immovable property of an *okka* was formerly regarded as impartible. It usually descended from one generation of agnatically related males to another without being split up in the process. Partition did, however, occur when every adult member of the *okka* wanted it. But such cases were unusual—at least that is what one is told. Both the difficulty of partition and the preference for leviratic unions added to the strength of the *okka*. The members of an *okka* have to live together from birth till death. They are bound together by numerous strong ties, and they co-operate in performing common tasks. After death, they become ancestors who continue to show an interest in their *okka* and demand propitiation from their descendants. The *okka* is something very much more than the group of living members in it at any given moment. It is a continuum through time, and the body of living members at any particular moment form only points on it. Coorgs themselves clearly state that the *okka* has a longer life than its members. They are also aware that an individual lives, in a social sense, as long as his *okka*. There is a great desire for the continuance of the *okka*, and there is no greater calamity than its extinction. When an *okka* is threatened with extinction certain traditional devices are resorted to perpetuate it.'

In recent times the importance of the joint family has gradually declined. As Srinivas points out, the Coorg *okka* 'is a very much stronger institution than the joint family of the higher castes of south India. The theory of the impartibility of its traditional property and the preference for leviratic unions buttress it strongly against fission. Add to this the fact that a cross cousin is commonly chosen for marriage and it becomes almost impregnable'.[1] Even here, however, the joint family is said to be weakening.[2]

There are no such detailed studies of the joint family elsewhere in India (and especially in urban areas) for systematic comparisons to be made. However, the general causes of change in the joint-

[1] *Op. cit.*, p. 147.

[2] *Op. cit.*, p. 155. The solidarity of the nuclear family 'has been increasing at the expense of the solidarity of the *okka* of which it is a part. . . . The unity of the elementary (nuclear) families within the *okka* appears in certain non-ritual contexts. For instance, parents take sides with their own children against the children of another member of the *okka* in the frequent quarrels of children.'

family can be identified, and additional information is available from an urban survey and from other studies.[1] Economic changes have exerted an important influence, especially in the diversification of employment and the fostering of an individualistic, acquisitive spirit.[2] The latter is reflected in changes in the law of property. After the establishment of British rule in India there was increasing resort by Hindus to the power of testamentary disposition of property, and an Act of 1870 recognized will-making along the lines of English law. Later legislation further modified the legal position of the joint-family; the Gains of Learning Act (1930) recognized an individual right to property acquired through an education paid for out of family funds, while the Hindu Law of Inheritance (Amendment) Act of 1929 allowed matrilineal as well as patrilineal inheritance. The Hindu Succession Act, 1956, is a further step in the direction of establishing individual property rights.

The Report on the 1951 Census of India contains some information and comment on the condition of the joint-family. It is there argued, on the basis of a classification of households by number of members, that families 'do not continue to be joint according to the traditional custom of the country and the habit of breaking away from the joint family and setting up separate households is quite strong'.[3] I. P. Desai has criticized these conclusions on various

[1] See K. M. Kapadia, *Marriage and Family in India* (rev. edn. 1958), Ch. 12; the Symposium on 'Caste and Joint Family', *Sociological Bulletin* IV (2), September 1955, pp. 85–146, and *Census of India* (1951), Vol. I.

[2] O'Malley, 'The Hindu Social system' in O'Malley, *op. cit.* 'The joint-family is an institution which had its origin in an earlier order of society, when the country was thinly peopled, the population was mainly agrarian, and cultivation was capable of expansion to meet the needs of growing families. Each family depended on its own labour and the larger it was, the greater was the number of hands available for work. . . . The conditions favourable to it were those of a stable society, in which the members of a family lived in the same place and followed the same pursuits from generation to generation. The economic complex has been transformed during the last hundred years. A largely increased population has caused pressure on the soil. . . . There is no longer the same community of interests owing to the small size of holdings and the pressure of circumstances necessitating the adoption of different callings. . . . The extension of communications has facilitated migration, which may be periodic or permanent' (p. 384).

[3] *Census of India*, Vol. I Report, p. 50. The distribution of households is as follows:

Type of household	Percentage of household of each type in a Typical Village	Typical Town
Small (3 members or less)	33	38
Medium (4–6 members)	44	41
Large (7–9 members)	17	16
Very large (10 members and over)	6	5

grounds.[1] In the first place he shows, from the Census material for Bombay State, that if the distribution of individuals between types of household is examined, 40 per cent are found to live in medium households, 40 per cent in large and very large households, and only 20 per cent in small households. Secondly, he argues that many urban households enumerated as separate are in fact branches of joint families in the villages. Finally, he has a general argument to the effect that, with the changing external conditions, 'the former characteristics of the joint family such as co-residence, commensality, worship and even property are becoming less important as the criteria of jointness . . .'. 'The joint family sentiment does not vanish with the residential separation.' But this is not entirely convincing, for it seems reasonable to suppose that with the disappearance of the fundamental characteristics of the traditional joint family, the traditional sentiments would weaken, and no evidence is given to the contrary. In practice, what remains of the joint-family system may be only a much vaguer and less binding system of kinship relations. However, I. P. Desai has shown very clearly, in a study of the family in a small town in Saurashtra, that joint-family sentiment in fact remains very strong, and Kapadia also indicates, in his study of 513 graduate secondary school teachers in Bombay State,[2] that the majority (57 per cent) live in joint families, and that even more (61 per cent) are in favour of the joint family.

What is lacking as yet, apart from I. P. Desai's study, is detailed study of how the contemporary joint family functions, and of the kinds of relationships which exist in practice between its members, especially in urban areas. In the absence of such studies it is impossible to analyse precisely the processes of change, and the problem is often obscured by ideological battles between traditionalists (often idealizing the Hindu family, as their counterparts in Britain have idealized the Victorian family) and partisans of change. We can, however, see some of the factors which might account for the survival, even if in an attenuated form, of the joint family, and of sentiments favourable to it. Its importance as a productive unit has declined, but it still has important functions as a social service agency. Desai observes that an individual still looks to his joint family for help in case of illness or unemployment, and in old age; and frequently also for assistance in obtaining a good education. And Kapadia shows that the three principal grounds on which his respondents believed the joint family to be desirable were: (1) that the economic burden is shared; (2) that it is the only arrangement

[1] I. P. Desai, in the Symposium 'Caste and Joint Family', *op. cit.*, pp. 97–117.
[2] *Op. cit.*

175

for social security; and (3) that it fosters certain desirable qualities in the individual.

Marriage

The forms of marriage are as diverse as the types of family system. The basic structure of the nuclear family is little affected by the diversity of marriage customs; it is rather the differences between the independent nuclear family and the composite forms of the family which influence marriage. Where the extended family predominates plural marriage is likely to occur (since it is economically advantageous), the choice of a spouse will probably be made by the head of the family, economic transactions will accompany marriage, and divorce will probably be infrequent.[1] Where the nuclear family is relatively independent marriage will be monogamous, individuals will choose their own spouses, there will be few economic transactions connected with marriage, and divorce may be frequent.

There are, however, certain uniformities in marriage customs. Monogamy is the prevalent form of marriage in all societies, for the good reason that the sex ratio is approximately 1 : 1 in most times and places. As Samuel Johnson said, 'No man can have two wives, but by preventing somebody else from having one'. Polyandry (the marriage of one woman to two or more men) is so rare as to be, as Murdock says, 'an ethnographic curiosity'. It occurs sporadically in several societies but where it has any permanence it may be accompanied by female infanticide, as among the Toda of South India. Polygyny (the marriage of one man to two or more women) occurs more widely, and is made possible by a surplus of females due to higher mortality among males. Even where polygyny is allowed, however, monogamy is the prevalent form of marriage and usually only the wealthier and more powerful males have more than one wife. Divorce is controlled and limited in some fashion in all societies, since a very high rate of divorce would endanger the functions of the family in maintaining and socializing children. The regulation of divorce, and its prevalence, are affected by numerous factors. The influence of religion has been very strong in the sphere of marital relations, and some of the major religions, e.g. Hinduism and Roman Catholicism, have not allowed divorce. The actual

---

[1] Among primitive peoples divorce is relatively easy, but as Lowie observes: 'Considering the difficulty of getting a mate in many societies and the widespread notion of wedlock as a group covenant, there would be powerful deterrents to hasty rupture of relations caused by individual disillusionment or caprice. Intimately linked with these factors are the heavy economic obligations that attach to matrimonial arrangements' (op. cit., p. 112).

prevalence of divorce is influenced, as we noted earlier, by the extent to which wider family and kin groups are involved, and by the existence of economic obligations. It is also influenced by the presence of alternative means of sexual and emotional satisfaction, through plural marriage, or permitted extra-marital relationships. According to Hindu law marriage is a sacrament, not a contract, and it was formerly indissoluble (except in the case of some lower castes which had a custom of divorce, and in the case of conversion of one spouse to Christianity). But at the same time, polygyny was legal, and there existed legal forms of concubinage. These arrangements, of course, met the needs only of the male population. The law was first changed by the Bombay Prevention of Hindu Bigamous Marriages Act 1946, which enforced monogamy in Bombay State, and this had soon to be followed by legal provision for divorce (in the Bombay Hindu Divorce Act, 1947). Since then monogamy, and provision for divorce, have been extended to the whole of India by the Hindu Marriage Act, 1955.

In the Western industrial societies divorce has increased rapidly since the beginning of the twentieth century,[1] and much sociological research has been devoted to the problems of family 'instability'[2] and of predicting marital harmony.[3] The causes of the increase in divorce are not entirely clear, but a comparison with primitive societies and many non-industrial societies is suggestive. In these societies, marriage is entered into as an economic arrangement and in order to have children (for economic and religious reasons), and not simply for the satisfaction of sexual needs; moreover, it has the support of a wider kinship group, and the personal satisfactions of the two individuals who marry are not unduly

[1] In the USA the divorce rate per 1,000 population increased from 0·75 in 1900 to 2·58 in 1960; in England and Wales the rate per 1,000 population rose from 0·02 in 1900 to 0·15 in 1938, and 0·81 in 1962. The increase has been similar in other West European countries.

[2] The term 'unstable family' was first used by Le Play (in his study of European working class families) to refer to the type of family in which children left home on reaching maturity, and often lost contact with their family of origin, so that each family regularly broke up into smaller units and there was no such family solidarity as existed in the patriarchal family. The term seems now to be used more widely to include also the break-up of families through the separation of the marital couple. *See* the discussion by William J. Goode, 'Family Disorganization' in Robert K. Merton and Robert A. Nisbet (eds.), *Contemporary Social Problems* (2nd edn., New York, 1966).

[3] *See* the trend report by Reuben Hill, 'Sociology of Marriage and Family Behaviour 1945–56', *Current Sociology*, VII (1), 1958. In the USA, over twenty-eight per cent of all research was concerned with mate selection and marital adjustment (p. 7).

emphasized. In some Western societies, and especially the USA, a combination of monogamous marriage, a rigid Puritan ethic which strongly condemns pre-marital and extra-marital sexual relations, and an ideal of romantic love, has established a model of the marital relationship which is difficult, perhaps impossible, to realize. Marriage is no longer an economic partnership, and is no longer sustained by wider kinship groups. Finally, the desire for a numerous progeny is replaced by the deliberate aim of limiting family size. Thus, the marriage bond is reduced to a simple relation of mutual attraction, and this is less strong than the network of economic, ritual and kinship interests which unite the family in other societies. We may regard a relatively high divorce rate therefore, as a con- comitant of modern individualism, the pursuit of happiness, and strict control of sexual relations outside marriage. In practice, Western societies have greatly relaxed their control of sexual behaviour in the last few decades, and these changes may affect the divorce rate by diminishing the exclusive concern with sexual felicity in marriage.

Kinship

As I noted earlier, it is family exogamy, and the resulting fact that every normal individual is a member of two nuclear families (family of orientation and family of procreation), which gives rise to kinship systems. The ramifications of kinship are considerable. Each individual has primary relatives in the nuclear families to which he belongs; outside these families he can have 33 types of secondary relatives, 151 types of tertiary relatives, and so on in increasing numbers. No society, even among the Australian tribes where kinship had a very prominent role, has taken account of all the degrees of relationship in its kinship system. But societies may usefully be classified in accordance with the types or relationship which are emphasized, both in terminology and in behaviour. Lowie and Kirchhoff have distinguished four major types of kinship terminology, based on the treatment of the parental generation.[1] Murdock has a more elaborate classification of eleven 'types of social organization', in which six types are differentiated by kinship terminology, and the other five (characterized by kinship terms similar to the foregoing), are differentiated by descent.[2]

Social anthropologists have devoted much of their effort to analysing kinship systems of particular societies, and to the com-

[1] Lowie, *op. cit.*, p. 63.
[2] Murdock, *op. cit.*, p. 224. The whole of Ch. 8, 'Evolution of social organiza- tion', is devoted to analysis of these different types.

parative study of kinship. This interest reflects the fact that kinship is supremely important in primitive societies. It is a chief factor in maintaining social unity,[1] and it constitutes the framework within which the individual is assigned economic and political functions, acquires rights and obligations, receives community aid, etc. Usually, therefore, the most effective way to study the social structure of a primitive society is to begin with an analysis of kinship. The comparative study of kinship systems, which bulked large in the work of the early evolutionary anthropologists and sociologists, has received much less attention since that time, and as Lowie says, 'nearly everything remains to be done in this field'. Kinship systems have been classified in various ways (as by Lowie and Murdock), but it has proved extremely difficult to find any general framework of explanation which would account for the occurrence of particular types of kinship system. Murdock has emphasized the importance of the rule of residence, and has shown how this is itself influenced by economic, political and religious factors.[2] With such partial explanations we must for the present be satisfied. In recent years, however, there has been a renewal of theoretical discussion through the work of Lévi-Strauss and the structural anthropologists, who attempt to show the basic structure of kinship as a logical schema, in terms of the exchange of women between social groups.[3]

Modern sociologists have shown little interest in kinship, since it plays a smaller part in the life of the industrial societies which they have mainly studied. It may be that they have unduly neglected the phenomenon, due to their preoccupation (especially in the USA) with the urban middle class family, which exhibits most plainly the characteristics of the independent nuclear family. In the industrial working class, as a number of studies have shown, kinship is still important in controlling individual behaviour and as a system of mutual aid.[4] Moreover, kinship has played, and continues to play,

[1] Even where there is a political system and a conception of territoriality. See the discussion above, p. 153.

[2] Murdock, *op. cit.*, p. 202. 'It is in respect to residence that changes in economy, technology, property, government, or religion first alter the structural relationships of related persons to one another, giving an impetus to subsequent modifications in forms of the family in consanguineal and compromise kin groups, and in kinship terminology.'

[3] See C. Lévi-Strauss, *The Elementary Structures of Kinship* (London, 1969; English trans. of the revised edition of 1967, in which Lévi-Strauss replies to some critics), and the criticism in Edmund Leach, *Lévi-Strauss*, Chapter 6.

[4] In a study of working class districts of Paris, P. Chombart de Lauwe has shown in his book *Paris et l'agglomération Parisienne* (Paris, 1954), that kinsfolk usually live close together and that social relationships in leisure time are very largely between kinsfolk. A study in London, M. Young and P. Willmott, *Family*

179

a significant part in consolidating the unity of upper classes and of various types of elites. But when this has been said, it remains true that kinship and family structure do not have any fundamental influence upon the social structure of modern societies.

In earlier societies, and in the non-industrial societies of the present day, kinship is of greater significance. I have shown its importance in India, where despite the absence of a common residence and commensuality in many cases, the joint family survives as a group of kin whose members have specific rights and obligations in relation to each other, and is still highly regarded. Even here, however, caste and class are vastly more important than kinship in determining the individual's place in society. No doubt caste and the joint family are intimately connected, but caste still represents a structural principle very different from that of kinship.

The family and society

In the study of kinship and the family, as in other fields, the early sociologists and anthropologists were largely concerned with the construction of evolutionary schemes. Marriage and the family were supposed to have evolved from primitive promiscuity through various forms of plural marriage to monogamy. Kinship was regarded as having developed from matrilineal descent through patrilineal descent and patriarchy to a system of bilateral descent associated with the independent nuclear family. The hypothesis concerning the priority of matrilinear descent, and its connection with the lowest levels of primitive culture, was first put forward by Bachofen.[1] This was widely accepted, and broadly similar evolutionary schemes were proposed, by many scholars up to the beginning of this century.[2]

In more recent work the evolutionist approach has been abandoned. Anthropologists have concentrated upon the functional or historical study of particular kinship systems and forms of the family, while sociologists have for the most part limited their interest

and Kinship in East London (London, 1957) has also demonstrated the fact of residential propinquity, and has shown the important social role of the wife's mother.

[1] J. J. Bachofen, *Das Mutterrecht* (Stuttgart, 1861).

[2] The best known are J. F. McLennan, *Studies in Ancient History* (London, 1876), L. H. Morgan, *Ancient Society* (New York, 1877), H. Spencer, *Principles of Sociology*, Vol. I (3rd edn., London, 1885). Much later, Hobhouse, who was greatly influenced by Spencer, presented in his *Morals in Evolution* (1905) the same kind of evolutionary scheme. Morgan's work, as is well known, was the basis of Engels' *The Origin of the Family, Private Property and the State* (1st edn., Zurich, 1884) which provided the framework for all later Marxist writing on the family.

to the problems of the family in contemporary industrial societies. The belief in a single line of development has had to be given up in the face of anthropological evidence.[1] It has even proved difficult to find any general framework of explanation to account for the varieties of kinship usages and family structure, or for changes in kinship and the family. Nevertheless, as we have shown, it is possible to establish broad classifications of kinship systems and types of family. But kinship usages appear to vary in a more random and arbitrary way than do marriage and the family. In respect of the types of family, and changes therein, it seems possible to formulate a number of useful generalizations which relate them to other elements of social structure.

The first generalization concerns the nature of the relation between the family and society. The nuclear family, I said earlier, is a universal phenomenon because it performs indispensable social functions. It is a group of major importance in any society; but its importance is of a very specific kind. Human young remain immature for a period which is long in relation to the span of human life; during this time they must be maintained and socialized. This is the principal function of the nuclear family. Its performance is independent of the form of the family, of wider kinship arrangements, of marriage customs, of the type of control of sexual behaviour, or of the performance of additional functions by the family. All these vary with the variations in other social institutions. Moreover, the ways in which the nuclear family performs its major function are also determined by other elements in society. The family first socializes the child, but it does not originate the values which it imparts; these come from religion, nation, caste or class. Thus, the specific character of the nuclear family in any society is determined by other institutions; it does not determine them. Similarly, social change originates in other institutions, not in the family; the family changes in response. I shall consider this point more fully below, in connection with the effects of industrialization. Here it may be noted that the point I have made about the nuclear family has a wider application to *primary groups* as such. In an earlier chapter I examined the view of Cooley that such groups as the family, neighbourhood, etc. are primary above all in that they are 'fundamental in forming the social nature and ideals of the individual.[2] A study of the nuclear family shows that the proposition is false. The family transmits values which are determined elsewhere; it is an agent, not a principal. In primary groups we may

[1] See especially Murdock, *op. cit.*, Ch. 8.
[2] See above, p. 100.

181

perhaps more easily study the effects of major 'social forces', but we cannot, in this way, investigate the forces themselves or explain their action.

Another characteristic of the relation between the family and society has very often been neglected by modern sociologists. No other group in society is so much influenced by religious and moral codes. The fact is surprising. Cupidity and lust for power would seem to be as powerful individual impulses as sexual desire, and as potentially disruptive of the human community. At the present time human society appears to be more gravely threatened by nuclear warfare than by the increase in divorce or the spread of pre-marital sexual intercourse. Yet religious and moral codes have rarely given as much attention to economic and political arrangements as to sexual behaviour and the family.[1] This connection between the family and religion can be seen today in the pre-occupation in Western societies with sexual 'promiscuity' and divorce,[2] and in India in the concern about the future of the joint family. The connection has had two important consequences; first, that scientific research into sexual behaviour and family life has been difficult or impossible until recent years, and secondly, that it has been more difficult here than in other areas of social life to bring about rational changes.

While the influence of religions has usually been to preserve established forms of the family, changes in economic institutions have been a major factor in bringing about changes in the family. Durkheim once observed that the inadequacy of the 'economic materialist' conception of history was most evident in the study of the family.[3] But this is doubtful. While the early evolutionist schemes, including that of Engels, have to be rejected, it is un-deniable that more limited sequences of change can be discovered and that economic factors are prominent in these. The anthro-pologists (especially Lowie and Murdock) who have undertaken

[1] There are, of course, differences between the major religions. The emphasis upon the regulation of sexual behaviour is strongest in Judaism and Christianity. Hinduism and Buddhism pay relatively more attention to the problems of violence and self-assertion. Thus, for example, in the writings of S. Radhakrishnan on Hindu religion and philosophy there is much discussion of social problems, and particularly of violence and non-violence. See especially his *Religion and Society* (London, 1947).

[2] For an unbalanced indictment of the modern Western family, from the Christian point of view, see E. O. James, *Marriage & Society* (London, 1952), Ch. 10.

[3] In a review of E. Grosse, *Die Formen der Familie und die Formen der Wirtschaft*, in *L'Année Sociologique*, I, 1898.

comparative studies of kinship and the family have emphasized this point.[1] The influence of modern industrialism upon the family is universally recognized. The specific characteristics of the modern Western family are very generally attributed to the development of industrial society.[2] In India, the changes in the joint family are, as I have shown, closely connected with the emergence and growth of an industrial economy. K. M. Kapadia, in discussing recent trends affecting the Hindu family,[3] notes that British rule introduced a new economic order, ideology and administrative system, which began to transform Indian culture. Capitalism and liberalism alike emphasized individual effort and rationality, and the spread of these ideologies challenged the sentiments maintaining the joint family. Economic development was accompanied by the growth of cities and the breakdown of village isolation; these changes also stimulated individualism, and brought about a revolt against the inferior position of women in the joint family. Kapadia also shows how, in recent years, the development of social insurance has begun to diminish the importance of the joint family as an organization for social security.

The Indian joint family is not only changing in fact as a result of industrialization; it can be shown that it must change, because it is in many respects incompatible with the needs of economic development. First, it is inimical to individual independence and effort. Paradoxically, the joint family is both too broad and too narrow a community. It is too broad in so far as it restrains and restricts the individual, and especially the female members; too narrow in that it limits the range of the individual's social relations and loyalties and obstructs *national* unity and effort.[4] Again, the joint family

[1] Murdock, *op. cit.*, in discussing the determinants of kinship terminology specifies one of his assumptions as being '. . . that the forms of social structure are not determined by kinship patterns or terminology, or influenced in any major degree by them, but are created by forces external to social organization, especially by economic factors. It is assumed herewith, for example, that the available sources of food and the techniques of procuring it affect the sex division of labour and the relative statuses of the sexes, predisposing peoples to particular rules of residence, which can eventuate in the formation of extended families, clans, and sibs. It is further assumed that the prevailing types and distribution of property favour particular rules of inheritance, that wealth or its lack affects marriage (e.g. encouraging or inhibiting polygyny), and that these and other facts external to social structure can strongly influence rules of residence and marriage and through them the forms of social organization and kinship structure.' (p. 137.)

[2] See W. F. Ogburn and M. F. Nimkoff, *Technology and the Changing Family* (Boston, 1955).

[3] K. M. Kapadia, *Marriage and Family in India*, Ch. 12.

[4] Cf. K. M. Pannikkar, *Hindu Society at Cross Roads* (Bombay, 1955): 'There can be no denying that the organization of Hindu life on the basis of the sub-

tends to encourage a high birth-rate, since additional members appear, according to traditional views, to increase the power and the economic potential of the family; moreover, numerous births are a guarantee that there will be *some* descendants to perform the family religious rites. Thus, the religious and social ideas associated with the way of life of the joint family obstruct the imperative task of reducing the Indian birth rate.

In the long run, as industrialization progresses, there is no reason to suppose that the Indian family system will differ greatly from that which exists today in Western societies. This family structure implies a low birth rate (since mortality is also low), a short child-bearing period and consequent large scale employment of married women, the provision of education by the state, and the restriction of family functions which I discussed earlier. But in the short run industrialization itself depends in part upon how quickly the trans-formation of the joint family occurs. And this may depend largely upon the relation between the family and religion. K. M. Panikkar has argued[1] that neither caste nor the joint family has any basis in Hinduism. Others, however, regard the joint family as essentially a ritual group, and account in these terms for its continuing vigour. Sociological research has not yet shed much light upon the problem. It was noted earlier that recent surveys show the favourable attitudes towards the joint family to be founded (overtly, at least) upon utilitarian considerations. The part of religious sentiment in these attitudes has yet to be investigated.

caste or the joint family extinguishes the social sense, the feeling of obligation to a social whole, and thereby renders the conception of a unified Hindu society impossible' (p. 23).

[1] *Op. cit.*

Chapter 11

SOCIAL STRATIFICATION

The division of society into classes or strata, which form a hierarchy of prestige and power, is an almost universal feature of social structure which has, throughout history, attracted the attention of philosophers and social theorists. But it is only with the growth of the modern social sciences that it has been subjected to critical study and analysis. Sociologists have commonly distinguished four main types of social stratification; slavery,[1] estates, caste, and social class and status. I shall briefly examine the first two types, then consider at greater length the phenomena of caste and of social class, and finally discuss some general theories of social stratification.

Slavery
L. T. Hobhouse defined a slave as 'a man whom law and custom regard as the property of another. In extreme cases he is wholly without rights, a pure chattel; in other cases he may be protected in certain respects, but so may an ox or an ass'. He continued, '. . . if [the slave] has by his position certain countervailing rights, e.g. to inherited property, from which he cannot (except for some default) be dislodged, he becomes . . . no longer a slave but a serf'.[2] Slavery thus represents an extreme form of inequality, in which certain groups of individuals are entirely or almost entirely without rights.

[1] Many sociologists now prefer to treat slavery as an 'industrial system' rather than a system of stratification. There is some justification for this. Slavery divides a community into two distinct sections, and within the group of those who are not slaves there may be, and usually is, a system of ranks. Thus slavery does not, by itself, constitute a system of stratification. But this view is not entirely convincing, for several reasons, In feudal society, also, it may be argued, there is a fundamental distinction between serfs and free men, together with a system of ranks within the latter group. Secondly, every system of stratification may be regarded also as an industrial system; as it is, for example, in Marxist theory, where slaves, serfs and wage earners are all categorized as the 'direct producers' upon whose labour the whole social edifice rests. Finally, if we examine social stratification in terms of social inequalities we can legitimately compare and contrast slavery, serfdom, caste, and class.
[2] L. T. Hobhouse, *Morals in Evolution*, Ch. VII.

It has existed sporadically at many times and places,[1] but there are two major examples of a system of slavery; the societies of the ancient world based upon slavery (especially Greece and Rome), and the Southern States of the USA in the eighteenth and nineteenth centuries. H. J. Nieboer gave an excellent account of the social condition of the slave in such a system. 'First, every slave has his master to whom he is subjected. And this subjection is of a peculiar kind. Unlike the authority one freeman sometimes has over another, the master's power over his slave is unlimited, at least in principle; any restriction put upon the master's free exercise of his power is a mitigation of slavery, not belonging to its nature, just as in Roman law the proprietor may do with his property whatever he is not by special laws forbidden to do. The relation between master and slave is therefore properly expressed by the slave being called the master's "possession" or "property", expressions we frequently meet with. Secondly, slaves are in a lower condition as compared with freemen. The slave has no political rights; he does not choose his government, he does not attend the public councils. Socially he is despised. In the third place, we always connect with slavery the idea of compulsory labour. The slave is compelled to work; the free labourer may leave off working if he likes, be it at the cost of starving. All compulsory labour, however, is not slave labour; the latter requires that peculiar kind of compulsion, that is expressed by the word "possession" or "property" as has been said before.'[2]

The basis of slavery is always economic; it is as Nieboer argued, an industrial system. Along with the emergence of slavery there also appears an aristocracy of some kind, which lives upon slave labour. But it is, also, in the opinion of most writers, the inefficiency of slave labour which is responsible for the decline of slavery.

Along with this, however, there is another influence tending to the decline of slavery, which can best be traced in the ancient world. There is always a certain conflict between the conception of the slave as an *object* of property rights, and the conception of him as a human being *possessing* rights. We find, in both Greece and Rome, that with the development of debt-slavery a distinction is made between foreign slaves and slaves originating within the group. In Athens debt-slavery was prohibited by Solon, and ultimately it was abolished in Rome under the influence of the Stoics. Hobhouse pointed out that 'the formation of debtor-slaves has a certain softening influence upon the institution of slavery itself, for while the

[1] *See* the article 'Slavery' in the *Encyclopaedia of the Social Sciences*, which distinguishes between primitive, ancient, medieval and modern slavery.

[2] H. J. Nieboer, *Slavery as an Industrial System.*

captive slave remains an enemy in the sight of law and morals and is therefore rightless, the debtor or the criminal was originally a member of the community and in relation to him there is apt to arise some limitation of the power of the master'. In the ancient world, slavery was gradually modified by progressive limitation of the master's right of punishment, the securing of personal rights to the slave (marriage, acquisition and inheritance of property) and the provision for manumission. The latter was supported and encouraged by the Christian church in the Roman Empire and later in feudal Europe, at least so far as Christians were involved.

Estates

The feudal estates of medieval Europe had three important characteristics. In the first place, they were legally defined; each estate had a *status*, in the precise sense of a legal complex of rights and duties, of privileges and obligations. Thus, as has been said, 'to know a person's real position it was first of all necessary to know "the law by which he lived".' In the twelfth century, when serfdom was increasing and a legal theory of the feudal state was emerging, the English lawyer, Glanville, listed the disabilities of serfs as being: inability to appeal to the king for justice, absence of rights over their chattels and holdings, liability to pay the fines of *merchet* and *heriot*. The differences between estates can be seen also in the different penalties imposed for similar offences.

Secondly, the estates represented a broad division of labour, and were regarded in the contemporary literature as having definite functions. 'The nobility were ordained to defend all, the clergy to pray for all, and the commons to provide food for all.'

Thirdly, the feudal estates were *political groups*. Stubbs, in his *Constitutional History of England*, wrote: 'An assembly of estates is an organized collection . . . of the several orders, estates or conditions of man who are recognized as possessing political power.' In this sense the serfs did not constitute an estate. Classical feudalism knew only two estates, the nobility and the clergy. The decline of European feudalism after the twelfth century is associated with the rise of a third estate, not of the serfs or villeins, but of the burghers, who behaved for a long period as a distinctive group *within* the feudal system before they transformed or overthrew it.[1]

The system of feudal estates was more complex and varied, as well as less rigid, than this summary account can show. The distinctions within estates, and the political aspect of feudalism, are excellently portrayed in Marc Bloch, *La société féodale* (Vol. II,

[1] *See* H. Pirenne, *Medieval Cities*, especially pp. 112–19 and 122 *et seq.*

'Les classes et le gouvernemente des hommes'). The opportunities for individuals to change their position in society are considered in R. W. Southern, *The Making of the Middle Ages* (Ch. II) and in A. Lane Poole, *Obligations of Society in the Twelfth and Thirteenth Centuries.*

Some modern historians and sociologists have been much concerned with the similarities between the European feudal societies and other societies which might be considered as belonging to the same type. The social system of Japan from the twelfth century has often been described as feudal, for instance by Marc Bloch (*op. cit.*) and in R. Coulborn, *Feudalism in History.* The existence of feudalism in India is more controversial. It must be recognized, first, that even if feudal relationships existed during some periods of Indian history they certainly existed alongside, and were interwoven with, caste relationships, and this implies that the *social system* cannot be described, without important qualifications, as feudal. Secondly, the 'feudalism' of the Maurya, Gupta and Mogul empires, and of their periods of decline, obviously lacked some characteristics of European feudalism. All scholars agree that Indian 'feudalism' had as its basis independent village agriculture, not the manorial system: in the words of K. S. Shelvankar, 'Indian feudalism remained fiscal and military in character. It was not manorial'.[1] Many scholars hold also that the conception of royal power in India was so different from that in the West that it could not establish a feudal system. 'In India, the king did not, in theory, create subordinate owners of land, because he himself was not, in theory, the supreme owner of land. What he delegated to his intermediaries was only the specific and individual right of *zamin*, i.e. the revenue-collecting power.'[2] This view is not universally accepted,[3] but there is, at least, agreement on the fact that feudal relationships often developed more strongly when the empires were in decline, since in such periods revenue-collectors could more easily establish proprietary rights in land and usurp political and judicial functions.

The historical materials available at present are inadequate to determine the relative influence of the caste system, the central administration of irrigation, and the periodic emergence of feudal-type relationships. This is so even in the case of the Mogul period, and still more in respect of ancient India. For the early period, the necessary historical records will perhaps never be available, but

[1] K. S. Shelvankar, *Problem of India* (London, 1940), p. 79.

[2] A. K. Nazmul Karim, *Changing Society in India and Pakistan*, Ch. II.

[3] *See* D. D. Kosambi, *An Introduction to the Study of Indian History* (Bombay, 1956), Chapters 9 and 10, for some qualifications.

much could be done by social historians to elucidate the nature of social stratification in its connection with property and political authority from the establishment of Mogul rule up to the advent of the British.

Caste

The Indian caste system is unique among systems of social stratification. This is not to say either that it is wholly incomparable with other types of stratification, or that no elements of caste are to be found elsewhere. In the first place, caste possesses the common characteristic of being evidently connected with economic differentiation. This is apparent whether we consider the effective caste groups (*jatis*) or the four traditional *varnas* of Brahmins, Kshatriyas Vaisyas and Sudras. The *varnas*, as Senart observed in a classical study, originally resembled feudal estates in certain respects.[1] They were like estates both in the character, and to a great extent, in the hierarchical ordering of the groups (priests, warriors and nobles, traders, serfs), and also in the fact that they were not totally closed groups; individuals could move from one *varna* to another and intermarriage was possible.

The *jatis*, which developed later and which continued to grow in number through the extending division of labour, the incorporation of tribes, and to a lesser extent, the operation of factors such as religious innovation, are the basic units of the traditional caste system. In modern India there are some 2,500 *jatis* in each major region. The *jati* is the endogamous group, and the principal reference group of the individual, embodying a distinctive way of life and maintaining it by the exercise of customary and, in earlier times, juridical sanctions. The economic significance of the *jatis* is plain; they are for the most part occupational groups and in the traditional village economy the caste system largely provides the machinery for the exchange of goods and services.[2]

On the other hand, elements of caste can be observed in other societies where more or less strict segregation of particular groups occurs; for instance, segregation of those engaged in 'unclean' occupations, or of those belonging to a particular ethnic group. But such individual features do not constitute a caste system. The only cases in which a caste system has been established outside Hindu India are those of non-Hindu groups in India (e.g. Muslims) or of Hindu settlement outside India, notably in Ceylon.

[1] E. Senart, *Caste in India* (1894; English trans. London, 1930).
[2] The *Jajmani* system; *see* H. Wiser, *The Hindu Jajmani System: A Socio-Economic System* (Lucknow, 1936).

189

The sociological problem of caste is, therefore, to account for the existence and persistence of this unique type of social stratification. An explanation may be sought in two ways, either in terms of historical events or in terms of some factor or factors which are present in Indian society and not elsewhere. Any historical explanation is bound to be speculative in the present state of knowledge, and its value would consist chiefly in its incitement to fresh historical research.[1] One of the most plausible accounts so far offered seems to be that given by J. H. Hutton,[2] who suggests that the original Aryan invaders of India, with their distinct ranks, introduced the principle of social stratification into a society already divided into exclusive tribal groups by taboos connected with food, and that they took over and consolidated these taboos as a means of maintaining social distance between themselves and the subject population. In this manner the principle of stratified exclusive groups was reinforced, and provided with a powerful sanction in the shape of a religious and magical doctrine of pollution through food, and later, pollution through contact.

The second way of explaining caste, in terms of some other, specific feature of Indian society, involves a brief consideration of the relationship between *jati* and *varna*. Modern students of caste have emphasized the role of the magical and religious ideas of the *varna* system, as expounded in the ancient religious literature. M. N. Srinivas observes that the notions of *karma*, which 'teaches a Hindu that he is born in a particular sub-caste because he deserved to be born there', and *dharma*, the code of duties (or rules of the caste), 'have contributed very greatly to the strengthening of the idea of hierarchy which is inherent in the caste system'.[3] The concept of pollution, he says, is 'fundamental to the caste system' and every type of caste relation is governed by it.' K. M. Panikkar,[4] however, has argued from the distinction between *jati* and *varna* that the caste system has no basis in Hindu religion, and is rather the product of Hindu traditional law and of the weakness of the central political

[1] It should be observed also that a historical explanation would involve a reference to some generalizations or laws, whether psychological or sociological.

[2] J. H. Hutton, *Caste in India*, Ch. XI. The resemblance between *jati* and tribe has been emphazied by P. Rosas ('Caste and Class in India', *Science and Society*, VIII (2), 1943), who also cites historical examples of the easy transition from tribe to caste.

[3] M. N. Srinivas, *Religion and Society among the Coorgs of South India*, Ch. II. *See also* Louis Dumont, *Homo hierarchicus; essai sur le régime des castes* (Paris, 1966), in which the basis of caste is found in the religious distinction between 'pure' and 'impure'.

[4] K. M. Panikkar, *Hindu Society at Crossroads* (1955).

authority during much of India's history. But although this draws attention to other factors which may be important in sustaining caste, it is in the main a plea for a re-interpretation of Hinduism. In fact, the castes and sub-castes are directly related to the *varna*-system which, as Srinivas notes, provides an All-India frame of reference into which the myriad sub-castes of any region can be fitted, and at the same time embodies a generally accepted scale of values and prestige. The distinction which Panikkar makes between the influence of religion and that of law is hardly tenable, for Hindu traditional law is dominated by religious ideas. The notions of *karma*, *dharma*, and pollution have figured prominently in both religious and legal thought, and together they constitute a doctrine which is undoubtedly one of the principal sustaining forces of the caste system.

We may conclude, then, that an explanation of the caste system would involve reference to some general theory of social stratification, to the specific features of the Hindu religion, and possibly to other factors such as the fragmentation of Indian society and the maintenance of a traditional economy. Such an explanation might be tested, albeit with difficulty, by studies of the effects upon the caste system of the far-reaching economic and political changes in recent times. In fact, studies in this field have hardly begun. The empirical studies of the past decade or so have mainly contributed a more precise knowledge of the traditional caste system.[1] Almost all of them have been carried out in rural areas, where the impact of economic and political changes is weakest; even so, a number of studies reveal significant changes. Wealth and education have become accessible to members of lower as well as higher castes—although not perhaps on equal terms, S. C. Dube has shown how this affects a village community;[2] wealth, education, or personal qualities may bring an individual prestige and power despite membership of a low caste. But the changes have been brought about by external forces, and they do not yet seriously challenge the old order. Dube notes that '. . . the grip of the traditional system is still firm, and people from lower castes or others with humble origins must behave with considerable tact and discretion if they seek to enhance their influence and importance in the community'. Similarly, F. G. Bailey, in a study of a village in Orissa,[3] shows how the 'extending frontiers'

---

[1] This is made clear in the excellent survey of recent studies by M. N. Srinivas, Y. B. Damle, S. Shahani and A. Beteille: 'Caste', *Current Sociology*, VIII (3) 1959. *See also* the more recent work of Srinivas, *Caste in Modern India, and Other Essays* (Bombay, 1965).

[2] S. C. Dube, *Indian Village* (1955).

[3] F. G. Bailey, *Caste and the Economic Frontier* (Manchester, 1957).

of the economy and the polity bring about changes. With the development of trade, and of a money economy, land ceases to be the main source of wealth; the lower castes enrich themselves through trade and then use their wealth to buy land and so acquire prestige and power. The extension of government and administration also changes the balance of power; the lower castes in the village are no longer defenceless, for they can appeal, outside the village, to public officials and administrative bodies. But Bailey also concludes that caste in the village remains powerful, for it is still effective in hampering social mobility and in its ritual aspect it maintains the traditional hierarchy.

We should expect changes in caste to be greater in urban areas than in the villages, for economic change is greater there, the anonymity of town life facilitates social mobility, and the intellectual life of the town is more favourable to change. As yet, however, the paucity of studies of caste in an urban and industrial setting makes it impossible to determine how far new activities, associations and ideas—trade union, professional or political organizations and ideologies—have weakened the allegiance to caste. Some information about the prevalence of caste sentiment is provided by K. M. Kapadia in a study of graduate teachers in Bombay State.[1] He shows that while a high proportion of teachers express themselves in favour of intercaste marriages, even for their own children, there are in fact many agencies tending to maintain caste sentiment and caste endogamy. Thus caste foundations and charities are common, and many castes publish journals and organize social functions. One-third of the teachers subscribe to their caste journal and would like to participate in caste social activities. Kapadia concludes that 42 per cent of the group display fairly intense caste feeling.

The lack of urban studies accounts in part for the uncertainties and disagreements about whether caste is being strengthened or weakened in Indian society as a whole. Many sociologists have observed that caste associations have developed rapidly, especially in the towns. M. N. Srinivas writes: 'There is a good case for arguing that caste-consciousness and organization have increased in modern India. Witness for instance the proliferation of caste banks, hostels, co-operative societies, charities, marriage halls, conferences and journals in Indian towns'.[2] The influence of caste in politics is

[1] K. M. Kapadia, 'Changing patterns of Hindu marriage and family', *Sociological Bulletin* (Bombay), III (1), March 1954.

[2] M. N. Srinivas, 'The Indian Road to Equality', *Economic Weekly*, August 20, 1960

disputed, and it certainly varies from one region to another; there is no doubt that castes play an important part as electoral organizations and as vote collecting agencies, but empirical studies show that local castes are frequently divided on political issues, and that many other considerations influence political allegiance.[1] In the sphere of education and opportunities for occupational mobility it is clear that caste retains its importance; higher education is still mainly open to the higher castes.[2]

On the other side, there are general arguments about the effects of legislation, political democracy, and industrialization, all of which are held to be inimical to caste. Overt caste discrimination has certainly diminished, and the position of untouchables has improved, but it is doubtful whether the factors mentioned have weakened caste consciousness and allegiance. It may be claimed that they have not yet had time to do so; and industrialization, in particular, is not yet far enough advanced to have a decisive influence. But the effects of industrialization cannot be predicted with certainty, and comparisons with the Western countries may be misleading. In the European countries which became industrialized during the nineteenth century, the new industrial workers were not involved in any such close traditional bonds as those of caste and joint family, and they were not hampered in this respect in the formation of economic and political associations of a modern type. Moreover, neither workers nor industrialists were influenced by a traditional other-worldly religion. The actual connections between industrialization and changes in caste (and joint family) have therefore to be studied directly in India, and this calls for a new kind of research, which would be focussed upon urban areas rather than villages, and upon the crucial occupational groups of a modern industrial society rather than the traditional caste occupations. M. N. Srinivas, in the survey mentioned earlier,[3] specifies a number of topics which need to be investigated; the interrelation between caste and class, the relation of caste, class and rural-urban residence to utilization of educational facilities, the role of caste and class in bureaucracy, the part played by caste in trade unions and in political life at different levels, urbanization of selected castes in different parts of the country, the relation between caste and economic development, dominant castes in different parts of the country, hypergamous castes, and the role of purity-pollution ideas in the caste systems of North and South India. It is only

[1] See above, p. 164-5.

[2] *See* B. V. Shah, 'Inequality of Educational Opportunities', *Economic Weekly*, August 20, 1960.

[3] M. N. Srinivas, 'Caste', *Current Sociology*, VIII (3).

necessary to add that the religious ideas which support caste deserve to be systematically studied.

We have seen that the strength of caste, and the tendencies to change, have been variously estimated, while the evidence is neither abundant nor clear. But whatever may be said about the strength of castes themselves, and of the individual's attachment to his own caste, it may be claimed that the traditional *caste system* has been profoundly altered.[1] In that system each individual caste had its ascribed place and co-operated with other castes in a traditional economy and in ritual. No doubt, there was always some competition between castes and there were changes of position in the hierarchy of prestige; but there was no generalized competition. It is quite otherwise with the modern caste associations, which exist in order to compete for wealth, educational opportunities, and social prestige in a much more open society. These associations are, in fact, interest groups of a modern type; in Tönnies' sense, they are 'associations', while the traditional caste groups were 'communities'. It is easy to understand that they should have grown up on the basis of traditional castes, but equally that they contradict the caste system and may well give rise to, or be absorbed into, the secular groups of a modern society—trade unions, professional associations and social classes.

Social class and social status

A social class system differs radically from those systems which we have so far considered. Social classes are *de facto* (not legally or religiously defined and sanctioned) groups; they are relatively open, not closed. Their basis is indisputably economic, but they are more than economic groups. They are characteristic groups of the industrial societies which have developed since the seventeenth century. Considerable difficulties arise when the attempt is made to specify the number of social classes, or to define their membership precisely. However, most sociologists would probably agree in recognizing the existence of an upper class (comprising the owners of the major part of the economic resources of a society), a working class (chiefly the industrial wage-earners), and a middle class, or middle classes (a more amorphous group, often treated as a residual category, but including most white collar workers and most members of the liberal

[1] Cf. F. G. Bailey, *Tribe, Caste and Nation* (Manchester, 1960), pp. 190–1, and *Politics and Social Change: Orissa in 1959* (Berkeley, 1963), pp. 122–35, where the differences between castes and caste associations are very clearly described. *See also* André Beteille, *Caste, Class and Power: Changing Patterns of Stratification in a Tanjore Village* (Berkeley, 1965).

professions). In some societies the existence of a fourth class, the peasantry, would be recognized.

Disagreement among sociologists begins generally on the issues of the cohesiveness of the different classes, their role in society, and their future. These problems will be discussed later in considering some theories of social stratification. The different classes, and especially the middle class, have been extensively studied. On the working class, the classical work is G. Briefs, *The Proletariat*, which begins from a Marxist definition and expands it to differentiate more clearly between the working class and the white collar middle class. Subsequently, there was little research in this area until recent years when controversies about the effects of affluence upon the working class stimulated a number of studies, in France, Britain and the USA.[1] General studies of the middle class include C. Wright Mills, *White Collar*, and David Lockwood, *The Blackcoated Worker* (London, 1958); but there have also been many accounts of specific groups within the middle classes, and especially of the liberal professions. In the nature of things it has been less easy to study the upper class, and sociological writing here extends from theoretical and historical studies of elites to studies based upon statistical information about property ownership, income, educational privilege, etc.[2]

The picture of social stratification in industrial societies is complicated by the existence of *status groups* as well as social classes. Max Weber was the first to distinguish rigorously between the two, and to examine their interrelation. 'With some over-simplification one might thus say that "classes" are stratified according to their relation to the production and acquisition of goods; whereas "status groups" are stratified according to the principles of their *consumption* of goods as represented by special "styles of life".'[3] The notion of social status has been analysed by a number of recent writers, especially by T. H. Marshall. In one essay on this subject[4] Marshall examines the factors which produce differences in status, as well as different types of status—personal, positional, etc. More recently, he has discussed the changes in social stratification in

[1] *See* Alain Touraine, *La conscience ouvrière* (Paris, 1966); John H. Goldthorpe, David Lockwood, Frank Bechhofer, Jennifer Platt, *The Affluent Worker* (3 vols., Cambridge, 1968–70); John C. Leggett, *Class, Race and Labor* (New York, 1968). *See also* the excellent historical study by E. P. Thompson, *The Making of the English Working Class* (rev. edn., Harmondsworth, 1968).

[2] Of recent studies *see* especially C. Wright Mills, *The Power Elite*.

[3] Max Weber, 'Class, Status, Party', in *From Max Weber* (ed. H. Gerth and C. W. Mills).

[4] 'The Nature and Determinants of Social Status', *Year Book of Education*, (London, 1953).

capitalist societies, and has argued that there has been a shift from class organization to status organization, or as he terms it, from multibonded but unidimensional groups to multidimensional and unibonded groups.[1]

There have been many empirical studies of status groups, especially in terms of occupational differentiation; indeed recent investigations of social stratification and social mobility have been carried out largely in terms of occupational prestige scales.[2] The emphasis, in much recent sociology, upon studies of social status and mobility, reflects a variety of influences. The needs of research have favoured the use of occupational scales, since these facilitate the design and implementation of research projects. The predominance of American sociology has been an important influence; in the USA, which is unique among Western industrial societies in having no strong tradition of class organization or ideological conflict, sociologists have naturally been concerned with social stratification in those aspects which do characterize American society—status and mobility. But the singularity of American society has not always been recognized, so that some writers have simply confused status with class,[3] while others have attempted to analyse social stratification in all societies in terms of the American model.[4]

A third influence has been the actual changes in Western societies, resulting in a real abatement, though by no means a disappearance, of class differences and class conflicts. This process of change can only be clearly grasped, however, if the phenomena of class and status are first carefully distinguished and their interrelations then examined. I have discussed this problem briefly elsewhere, and have suggested that: 'Stratification by prestige affects the class system, as Marx conceived it, in two important ways: first, by interposing between the two major classes a range of status groups which bridge the gulf between the extreme positions in the class structure; and secondly, by suggesting an entirely different conception of the social

[1] 'General Survey of Changes in Social Stratification in the Twentieth Century', *Transactions of the Third World Congress of Sociology*, Vol. III, pp. 1–17.
[2] A pioneer study is D. V. Glass (ed.), *Social Mobility in Britain* (London, 1954). This investigation has given rise to similar studies in other societies: for example, *Modern Japanese Society: Its Class Structure*, by the Research Committee, Japan Sociological Society (Tokyo, 1958, in Japanese with an English summary); and more recently Peter M. Blau and Otis Dudley Duncan, *The American Occupational Structure* (New York, 1967), which also includes a very useful discussion of methodological problems.
[3] E.g. W. Lloyd Warner and P. S. Lunt, *The Social Life of a Modern Community* and *The Status System of a Modern Community* (New Haven, 1942).
[4] *See* below, p. 202.

hierarchy as a whole, according to which it appears as a continuum of more or less clearly defined status positions, determined by a variety of factors and not simply by property ownership, which is incompatible with the formation of massive social classes and with the existence of a fundamental conflict between classes. The relations between status groups at different levels are relations of competition and emulation, not of conflict. With the growth in numbers of the middle classes, which form an increasing proportion of the whole population, this view of the social hierarchy as a continuum of prestige ranks (or statuses), without any sharp breaks, and thus without any clear lines of conflict between major social groups, has acquired a much greater influence upon social thought and its diffusion has served to check the growth of class consciousness'.[1]

The analysis of social stratification in the contemporary Western capitalist societies is complex and difficult. Equal, and perhaps greater, difficulties appear in the study of the second type of modern industrial society, represented by the USSR and some of the People's Democracies. An initial obstacle is the absence of data concerning income distribution, educational opportunities, attitudes and group sentiments, in these societies, owing to the lack of any systematic sociological research.[2] Moreover, the social realities are here obscured by the fury of ideological warfare. Orthodox Marxists claim that in the Soviet type countries social classes, or at least a hierarchical system of classes, have been abolished with the abolition of private ownership of the means of production. Critics point to the existence of great economic inequalities, educational privileges, the monopolization of political power by a small elite, and other characteristics which together amount to a system of social stratification. Much of the theoretical controversy turns upon the relationship between class structure and political power, which was briefly mentioned in an earlier chapter,[3] and will be discussed again below. From this controversy it emerges clearly that the classical notion of social class, in Marxist and non-Marxist writing, is closely connected with the notion of political power and especially with the concept of a 'ruling class'. This connection, however, may give rise to two different lines of thought: one, the Marxist which makes political power dependent upon economic power, and the other which treats

[1] *Classes in Modern Society*, p. 26. *See also* my essay on 'The Class Structure in Western Europe', in M. S. Archer and S. Giner (eds.), *Contemporary Europe: Class, Status and Power*. (London, 1971).

[2] *See* however, Murray Yanowitch, 'The Soviet Income Revolution', *Slavic Review*, XXII (4), 1963; and Frank Parkin, 'Class Restratification in Socialist Societies', *British Journal of Sociology*, XX (4), 1969.

[3] *See* pp. 157–8.

the economy and the polity as interrelated systems each of which may at different times be either 'basis' or 'superstructure'.

These problems indicate the need for renewed study of social stratification. A useful starting point is to be found in the phenomena of political conflict. The social groups involved in such conflict may be either elites or classes. In Pareto's sociology, at least in its major concern with the 'governing elite', the terms 'class' and 'elite' were practically synonymous; and it was in the context of his own theory of the 'circulation of elites' that Pareto regarded the notion of class conflict as the most important of Marx's contributions to sociology. More recently, sociologists have used the term 'elite' to refer to smaller and more cohesive groups, which may be more or less closely connected with social classes as traditionally conceived.[1] Raymond Aron has provided one of the best studies of the relationship between elites and social classes.[2] He formulates the problem as one of the relation between social differentiation and political hierarchy in modern societies, and sets out to show that the 'abolition of classes' (in the classical sense of abolishing private ownership of the means of production) will not resolve the problems of social differentiation, formation of elites, and inequalities of political power. There are, indeed, some advantages in the conflicts of elites and classes in capitalist societies, since these restrict the power of the rulers at any particular time.

We may summarize this brief study by saying that the nineteenth century concern with problems of social class was closely associated with a concern about democracy and political power, but that the answers provided did not distinguish clearly enough between the two sets of problems. In the twentieth century sociologists, guided by Max Weber, but more strongly influenced by events themselves, have attempted to study political power directly, and to examine the ways in which elite groups recruit support, conduct political struggles and attain or fail to attain power, as well as the conditions in which a power elite is either controlled or uncontrolled. For such studies, social class is only one element in the situation, though an important

[1] Cf. G. D. H. Cole, *Studies in Class Structure* (London, 1955), p. 106: 'Not all elites rest on a class basis, or are to be regarded as class representatives; but some do and are, and a special importance attaches, in modern societies and especially in the older societies which have been developing from aristocracy towards some form of democracy, to the relations between classes and elites and to the differences that emerge with the increasing complexities of class structure'.

[2] Raymond Aron, 'Social structure and the ruling class', *British Journal of Sociology*, I (1 and 2) March, June 1950; pp. 1–15, 126–143. See also his 'Classe sociale, classe politique, classe dirigeante', *European Journal of Sociology*, I (2) 1960. See also my *Elites and Society*.

one.[1] At the same time, the study of social differentiation and social stratification has been broadened to take account of the phenomena of social status and social mobility which are for the most part only indirectly related to political power, but which are important in other ways.

Theories of social stratification

There have been two major attempts to formulate a general theory of social stratification, that of Marx and that of the functionalists. The main outlines of the Marxist theory are well known, although neither Marx himself nor any later Marxist thinker formulated it in a systematic way.[2] In this theory social classes are defined by their relation to the means of production (ownership or non-ownership) and this becomes the basis of the view that there are in every society two principal contending classes.[3] The nature of the classes depends upon the mode of production, and this in turn upon the level of technology, in different societies. Marx, as Schumpeter observed, was primarily interested in the *development* of classes, and we may add, in their role in bringing about social and political changes. His own empirical studies were concerned with the origins of the bourgeoisie and the establishment of capitalism, and still more with the formation and growth of the proletariat as a class within capitalist society. Marx first distinguishes the proletariat as a 'class in itself', an aggregate of individuals who are in the same economic situation, and then tries to show how it becomes a 'class for itself', i.e. how its members become aware of their common interests and political aims. In the *Poverty of Philosophy* and in *Capital*, Marx describes

[1] *See* the excellent discussion of this question in S. Ossowski, *Class Structure in the Social Consciousness* (London, 1963), Chapter XII.

[2] The theory has always retained a certain metaphysical vagueness. This is the case even in the chapter on social classes in N. Bukharin's *Historical Materialism* (English trans. London, 1926) which comes closest to a systematic exposition; and it is, of course, a very prominent feature in one of the major works of later Marxist thought, G. Lukács, *Geschichte und Klassenbewusstsein* (Berlin, 1923).

[3] In most of his scientific writings Marx analyses the class system in terms of two classes; but he also has a model of a three-class system, which he uses occasionally, and notably in the final unfinished chapter of *Capital*, Vol. III, where he began a formal analysis of class. In fact, there are two different models of a three-class system; one (for example in the chapter just mentioned) where Marx refers to capitalists, landowners and wage-earners as the three great classes of modern society (a conception taken directly from political economy, with its 'three factors of production') and another in which Marx distinguishes the capitalists who own means of production and employ wage labour, the middle class (or petty bourgeoisie) who own means of production but also contribute their own labour power, and the wage earners. There is an excellent study of these different conceptions in S. Ossowski, *op. cit.*, Chapter V.

the circumstances favourable to this growth of class consciousness; the concentration of industry, the development of communications, the increasing economic and social distance between the bourgeoisie and the working class, the increasing homogeneity of the latter as a result of the decline of skilled trades, etc.

Marx was well aware that social differentiation produced many other groups with conflicting interests in addition to the two principal classes,[1] but he did not seriously examine the difficulties which this presented for his theory. His neglect of the problem may be accounted for in various ways: that he regarded the relationship of the individual to property as a crucial determinant of social action, and was confirmed in this view by the actual character of contemporary social and political conflicts; that he was unduly influenced by a philosophical conception (derived from Hegel) of development through the contradictions and antagonisms of two opposed entities; or that his analysis of the existing class system was distorted by his political commitment to the ideal of a classless society. Probably all these factors had some effect, but the first seems most important. For Marx's theory of class had, and still has, great explanatory value in dealing with social and political conflicts. His conception of social classes should not be regarded as describing the given economic characteristics of particular aggregates of individuals. It is rather that the situation of individuals with regard to property provides a basis for statements about the probability of certain types of social, especially political, action. Max Weber was interpreting Marx in this sense and also indicating a line of criticism of the Marxist theory, when he argued that 'a class does not in itself constitute a community', but that class situations are brought about by communal action. The extent to which a class does in fact become a community will be affected by whatever integrates or divides its members, by the general character of the inclusive society, and by its relations with other social groups and classes. Marx made a number of specific predictions about the future development of capitalist society, and in terms of these he expected an increasing

[1] This is especially obvious in his political writings, e.g. *The Class Struggles in France* (1850), *The Eighteenth Brumaire of Louis Bonaparte* (1852), where he distinguishes as many as ten major groups involved in the political struggle. Elsewhere, he recognizes the growing importance of the middle classes (including the 'new' middle classes); for example, in the manuscript of *Theories of Surplus Value*, 'What (Ricardo) forgets to mention is the continual increase in numbers of the middle classes . . . situated midway between the workers on one side and the capitalists and landowners on the other. These middle classes rest with all their weight upon the working class and at the same time increase the social security and power of the upper class'.

community of the working class. Some of the predictions were wrong, and the working class in advanced industrial societies has failed to develop in the way that Marx expected. Marx and the Marxists assumed too readily that the transition from potential to actual community will in fact be made in the case of social classes, *and in that case alone.*

A more general criticism of the Marxian theory is that while it seems highly relevant and useful in analysing social and political conflicts in capitalist societies during a particular period, its utility and relevance elsewhere are much less clear. Yet the theory is supposed to be universally valid. It encounters many difficulties when applied to particular forms of social stratification such as the Indian caste system, and in many other cases its explanatory power is diminished by its insistence upon social class as the sole basis of political action.[1]

The functionalist theory of social stratification begins from the general presuppositions of functionalism which I discussed earlier. It has been succinctly and clearly stated in an article by Kingsley Davis and Wilbert E. Moore,[2] who present it as follows:

'Starting from the proposition that no society is "classless", or unstratified, an effort is made to explain, in functional terms, the universal necessity which calls forth stratification in any social system . . . the main functional necessity explaining the universal presence of stratification is . . . the requirement faced by any society of placing and motivating individuals in the social structure . . . Social inequality is thus an unconsciously evolved device by which societies ensure that the most important positions are conscientiously filled by the most qualified persons.'

We may disregard here the difficulties of functionalist explanation as such.[3] The theory is open to many specific criticisms. In the first place it assumes that stratification is universal, and this, so far as it implies the existence of a definite system of ranks in every society, is untrue. It also assumes that the 'most important positions' and 'most qualified persons' are unambiguously defined, independently of the influence of interested groups, in all societies. Next, it will be observed that the theory is conceived in terms of the rank-

[1] *See* above, pp. 157–8.
[2] Kingsley Davis and Wilbert E. Moore, 'Some principles of stratification', *American Sociological Review*, April 1945 (Reprinted in Wilson and Kolb, *Sociological Analysis*).
[3] *See* above, pp. 42–4.

ing of individuals, and that it does not explain the existence of well-defined social groups; status groups, elites, and classes. Moreover, the theory does not account for, but merely recognizes, the existence of different types of social stratification and processes of change from one type to another. Finally, it entirely neglects the role of force in establishing and maintaining systems of stratification, and thus has little to say about the relationship between social stratification and political conflict.[1]

Whereas the Marxist theory unmistakably reflects the character of social and political conflicts in nineteenth century Europe, the functionalist theory reflects equally clearly the social situation in the USA, where neither a working class political movement nor a working class ideology has ever become established, and where the social hierarchy has been conceived very largely as a system of loosely organized status groups, membership of which is related to individual abilities. The Marxist theory emphasizes conflict between large and stable groups, with strong community sentiments, while the functionalist theory emphasizes the integrating function of social stratification based upon individual merit and reward. The latter theory has many points of resemblance with Durkheim's theory of the division of labour, without the qualifications which Durkheim suggested in his discussion of the abnormal forms of the division of labour.

Neither of these two theories has the universality which it claims. An adequate theory would have to take more serious account of the variety of stratification systems, would regard social stratification as a derivative institution most closely linked with property and the division of labour, but also with war and religion, and would deal systematically with the connections between social stratification, political institutions and cultural phenomena.

[1] See also the criticisms made by M. M. Tumin, 'Some Principles of Stratification: A Critical Analysis', *American Sociological Review*, XVIII (4), 1953.

Notes on Reading for Part III

I. SOCIAL STRUCTURE

1. The concept of social structure

Lévi-Strauss, C. *Structural Anthropology* (New York, 1963).

Nadel, S. F. *The Theory of Social Structure* (London, Cohen & West, 1957).
The most thorough and systematic attempt to clarify the notion of social structure.

Radcliffe-Brown, A. R. 'On social structure', in *Structure and Function in Primitive Society* (London, Cohen & West, 1952), pp. 188–204.

Boudon, Raymond. *A quoi sert la notion de 'structure'?* (Paris, 1968).

2. Types of society

In the work of the earlier sociologists the classification of societies had an important place, and the student should be familiar with such classifications as those of Spencer, Marx, Durkheim, Tönnies, Maine, and Hobhouse, which are discussed in the text. In recent work there has been less interest in the problems of morphology, but some important contributions are referred to in the text. For a general review of attempts to classify societies the reader should consult:

Rumney, J. *Herbert Spencer's Sociology* (London, 1934), Ch. III, 'Types of society'.

Steinmetz, S. R. 'Classification des types sociaux et catalogue des peuples', *L'Année Sociologique III* (1898–1899), pp. 43–147.
A very thorough and comprehensive survey of the schemes of classification proposed up to that time, with a critical discussion of the uses and principles of classification.

As examples of studies of particular types of society from a broadly sociological point of view, the reader may consult:

Hobhouse, L. T., Wheeler, G. C., and Ginsberg, M. *The Material Culture and Social Institutions of the Simpler Peoples* (London, 1915).

Forde, C. D. *Habitat, Economy and Society* (London, 1934).

Fustel de Coulanges, N. D. *The Ancient City* (New English edn., New York, Doubleday, 1956).

Bloch, Marc. *Feudal Society* (London, 1961).

Wittfogel, K. A. *Oriental Despotism* (New Haven, 1957).

Sombart, W. 'Capitalism', in *Encyclopaedia of the Social Sciences*.

An interesting preliminary analysis of Indian social structure is to be found in A. K. Nazmul Karim, *Changing Society in India and Pakistan* (Dacca, Oxford University Press, 1956), Part I. Some particular features of the social structure are examined in K. A. Wittfogel, *Oriental Despotism*. There is a useful survey of modern Indian society in L. S. S. O'Malley, *Modern India and the West* (London, Oxford University Press, 1941), especially Ch. X 'The social system' and Ch. XVI 'General Survey'.

3. Culture and Civilization

For a discussion of the concept of culture see:

Kroeber, A. L., and Kluckhohn, C. *Culture* (Papers of the Peabody Museum of Harvard, XLVII (1), 1952).

Malinowski, B. 'Culture', in *Encyclopaedia of the Social Sciences.*

Malinowski, B. *A Scientific Theory of Culture* (Chapel Hill, 1944).

The use of the concept is exemplified in such works as:

Benedict, Ruth. *Patterns of Culture* (London, 1935).

On the notion of civilization, see:

Durkheim, E., and Mauss, M. 'Note sur la notion de civilization', *L'Année Sociologique*, XII, 1913.

Centre international de Synthèse, *Civilization: le mot et l'idée* (Paris, 1930).

Toynbee, Arnold J., *A Study of History*, Vol. I (London, Oxford University Press, 1934), Introduction, C. 'The comparative study of civilizations'.

II. ECONOMIC INSTITUTIONS

1. General works

Weber, Max. *Wirtschaft and Gesellschaft* (Tübingen, 1921–22) [English trans. of part, with an introduction by Talcott Parsons, *The Theory of Social and Economic Organization* (New York, 1947)].

Goodfellow, D. M. *Principles of Economic Sociology* (London, 1939).

Herskovits, M. J. *Economic Anthropology* (New York, 1952).

These two books provide good general accounts of economic institutions in primitive societies; they also discuss briefly the relation between economic and sociological/anthropological analysis.

For studies of capitalist economic systems from a sociological viewpoint, see:

Schumpeter, J. A. *Capitalism, Socialism and Democracy* (London, Allen & Unwin, 1943), Part II.

Veblen, Thorstein. *The Theory of Business Enterprise* (New York, 1904).

Strachey, John. *Contemporary Capitalism* (London, Gollancz, 1956).

Galbraith, J. K. *American Capitalism* (London, Hamish Hamilton, 1952).

On industrial societies, see the works by Aron, Dahrendorf and others cited in the text.

2. *The division of labour*

Durkheim, E. *The Division of Labour in Society* (English trans., Glencoe, The Free Press, 1947).

Friedmann, Georges. *Industrial Society* (English trans., Glencoe, The Free Press, 1955).

A general study of the problems of industrial work.

Friedmann, Georges. *The Anatomy of Work* (English trans., London, Heinemann, 1961).

A more detailed study of the division of labour in modern industrial societies. Chapter V examines Durkheim's theory in the light of recent trends. A long statistical appendix presents data on the division of labour in a number of advanced industrial societies.

Caplow, Theodore. *The Sociology of Work* (Minneapolis, University of Minneapolis Press, 1954).

A good introduction to the sociological study of division of labour, occupations and technology.

3. *Property*

A general view of property and theories of property can be obtained from:

Gore, Charles (Bishop of Oxford) (ed.). *Property: Its Duties and Rights* (London, Macmillan, 1913).

Lowie, R. H. *Social Organization* (London, Routledge and Kegan Paul, 1950), Chapter 6, 'Property'.

On the distribution of property in modern industrial societies, see, for example:

Tawney, R. H. *Equality* (4th rev. edn., London, Allen & Unwin, 1952).

Mills, C. Wright. *The Power Elite* (New York, Oxford University Press, 1956).

Kolko, Gabriel. *Wealth and Power in America* (New York, 1962).

Pollard, Sidney, and Crossley, David W. *The Wealth of Britain* (London, Batsford, 1968).

There has been much study of industrial property in capitalist societies. A classical Marxist study is Karl Renner, *The Institutions of Private Law and their Social Functions* (English trans., London, Routledge and Kegan Paul, 1949). The English translation has a valuable introduction and notes by O. Kahn-Freund, who discusses the changes in property and property law since Renner's work was first published (1904, revised 1928). The pioneer study of the modern business corporation is A. A. Berle and G. C. Means, *The Modern Corporation and Private Property* (New York, 1933). A more recent study of the ownership and control of industry will be found in P. Sargant Florence, *The Logic of British and American Industry* (London, 1953).

4. *The industrial enterprise and industrial relations*

An early, influential study is that of Elton Mayo, *The Human Problems of an Industrial Civilization* (New York, 1933).

Moore, Wilbert E. *Industrial Relations and the Social Order* (rev. edn., New York, Macmillan, 1951).

A good general study dealing with the social organization of industrial enterprises and with industrial relations in a broad sense.

Flanders, A., and Clegg, H. (ed.). *The System of Industrial Relations in Great Britain: Its History, Law and Institutions* (Oxford, Blackwell, 1954).

A collection of essays which provides a general view of industrial relations in Britain.

For accounts of alternative forms of industrial organization see: Paul Blumberg, *Industrial Democracy: The Sociology of Participation* (London, Constable, 1968); E. Mandel (ed.), *Contrôle ouvrier, conseils ouvriers, autogestion* (Paris, Maspero, 1970); and works mentioned in the text.

III. POLITICAL INSTITUTIONS

1. *Types of political system*

There are regrettably few sociological studies of political systems. On primitive societies the reader may consult I. Schapera, *Government and Politics in Tribal Societies* (London, Watts, 1956). *See also,* Georges Balandier, *Political Anthropology* (New York, 1970).

A good general account of European political systems will be found in H. Sidgwick, *The Development of European Polity* (London, Macmillan, 1913). R. M. MacIver, *The Modern State* (London, Oxford University Press, 1926) is also largely concerned with European states. The Greek city state is studied from a sociological point of view in G. Glotz, *The Greek City* (English trans., London, 1929). On the feudal state see Marc Bloch, *Feudal Society* (English trans., London, 1961), Part II. Many features of the political structure of Asian societies are discussed in K. A. Wittfogel, *Oriental Despotism.* There is a large literature on the modern democracies. The most useful works for the sociologist are probably, A. de Tocqueville, *Democracy in America* (English trans., London, 1835); James Bryce, *Modern Democracies* (2 vols., London, 1921); A. D. Lindsay, *The Modern Democratic State* (2 vols., London, 1943). Among more recent works see Raymond Aron, *Democracy and Totalitarianism* (London, 1968), and C. B. Macpherson, *The Real World of Democracy* (Toronto, 1965).

On Soviet society, see A. Kassof (ed.), *Prospects for Soviet Society* (London, 1968), and the collection of articles in Paul Hollander (ed.), *American and Soviet Society* (Englewood Cliffs, N.J., Prentice Hall, 1969).

For an excellent study of a totalitarian society see Franz Neumann, *Behemoth: The Structure and Practice of National Socialism* (New York, Oxford University Press, 1942).

2. *Theories of the state*

The Marxist theory of the development and role of the state is set out briefly in Marx and Engels, *The German Ideology* (English trans. of Parts I & III, London, 1938), and Engels, *The Origin of the Family, Private Property and the State* (English trans, London, 1940). A sociological theory of the state which owes much to Marxism is expounded in F. Oppenheimer, *The State* (English trans., New York, 1926). For more recent discussions, especially of the modern capitalist state, see Nicos Poulantzas, *Pouvoir politique et closses sociales* (Paris, Maspero, 1968); and Ralph Miliband, *The State in Capitalist Society* (London, Weidenfeld and Nicolson, 1969).

Different accounts of the development of the state are given by R. H. Lowie, *The Origin of the State* (New York, 1927), and L. T. Hobhouse, *Morals in Evolution* (London, 1905), Chapter III, 'Law and Justice'.

3. *Political parties and pressure groups*

The two classical studies of political parties are:

Michels, R. *Political Parties* (Glencoe, The Free Press, 1949) (English trans. of *Zur Soziologie des Parteiwesens in der modernen Demokratie*, 2nd edn., Leipzig, 1925).

Ostrogorski, M. *Democracy and the Organization of Political Parties* (English trans., 2 vols., London, Macmillan, 1908).

Among the recent general studies see especially:

Duverger, M. *Political Parties* (English trans., London, 1954).

Key, V. O. *Politics, Parties and Pressure Groups* (2nd edn., New York, 1950).

Heberle, R. *Social Movements: An Introduction to Political Sociology* (New York, Appleton Century Crofts, 1951).

This book deals with the ideologies, structure, and functions of political groups which aim at a fundamental change in the social order. It also discusses the major problems of electoral studies, and examines methods and techniques of research.

On Britain, see R. T. McKenzie, *British Political Parties* (2nd edn., London, 1963).

An introductory study of parties in India will be found in M. Weiner, *Party Politics in India: The Development of a Multi-party System* (Princeton, 1957). See also, W. H. Morris-Jones, *The Government and Politics of India* (London, 1964).

The study of pressure groups has attracted increasing attention. For a general survey see V. O. Key (*op. cit.*, above). Two recent studies in Britain are S. K. Finer, *Anonymous Empire* (London, 1958) and

J. D. Stewart, *British Pressure Groups* (London, Oxford University Press, 1958).

4. *Political behaviour*

There is now a considerable literature on electoral behaviour. For a general survey and bibliography up to 1954 see, G. Dupeux, 'Le comportement électoral', *Current Sociology* III (4), 1954–55. See also R. Heberle (*op. cit.*, above), D. E. Butler, *The Study of Political Behaviour* (London, 1958), and S. M. Lipset and S. Rokkan (eds.), *Party Systems and Voter Alignments* (New York, Free Press, 1967). For a general discussion based upon the study of a British election, see M. Benney, A. P. Gray and R. H. Pear, *How People Vote* (London, Routledge and Kegan Paul, 1956).

There have been numerous studies of particular elections in many countries (e.g. the Nuffield College series of studies of British General Elections), and of the electoral behaviour of particular social categories (e.g. women) and social strata (especially the middle classes). For details of these see Dupeux (*op. cit.*). There is a largely descriptive study of the Indian General Elections of 1951–52 in S. V. Kogekar and R. L. Park (eds.), *Reports on the Indian General Elections* 1951–52 (Bombay, Popular Book Depot, 1956).

The more general sociological and psychological study of political behaviour has languished somewhat with the proliferation of detailed electoral studies. A good introduction is still Graham Wallas, *Human Nature in Politics* (3rd edn., London Constable, 1931). *See also*, the works mentioned above by V. O. Key, R. Heberle, D. E. Butler; and references in the text to studies of social movements.

5. *Political ideologies*

The sociological conception of 'ideology' was first clearly formulated by Marx, and it has had a prominent place in later Marxist theory. For Marx's exposition see K. Marx and F. Engels, *The German Ideology*. The notion was later re-examined in a critical manner in Karl Mannheim, *Ideology and Utopia* (London, Kegan Paul, 1936), which provides the best general survey of the problem.

Two outstanding sociological studies of political ideologies are Mannheim's 'Conservative Thought' (Translated in Karl Mannheim, *Essays on Sociology and Social Psychology*. London, Routledge and Kegan Paul, 1953); and C. Bouglé, *Les idées égalitaires* (Paris, Alcan, 1899).

There are many expositions and critical studies of modern political doctrines, but few recent sociological writings on the subject. Political ideologies, and especially the relation between class membership and political beliefs, are discussed in the works by R. Heberle and M. Benney, *et al.* (see above). The role of intellectuals in politics is examined in Raymond Aron, *The Opium of the Intellectuals* (English trans., London, 1957), and from quite a different point of view in Noam Chomsky, *American Power and the New Mandarins* (New York, 1969).

Modern nationalism has received some attention; e.g. by F. Znaniecki, *Modern Nationalities: A Sociological Study* (Urbana, 1952). There is a sociological account of Indian nationalism in A. R. Desai, *Social Background of Indian Nationalism* (2nd ed., Bombay, 1954).

For a recent review of the literature, see N. Birnbaum, 'The Sociological Study of Ideology (1940–60)', *Current Sociology* IX (2), 1960.

6. *Bureaucracy*

The origin of modern studies of bureaucracy is Max Weber's work; see the essay on bureaucracy in H. H. Gerth and C. Wright Mills (eds.), *From Max Weber* (New York, Oxford University Press, 1946). Peter M. Blau, *Bureaucracy in Modern Society* (New York, Random House, 1956) is a clear and illuminating introduction to the subject. For a general survey of recent writing and a classified bibliography, see S. N. Eisenstadt, 'Bureaucracy and Bureaucratization', *Current Sociology* VII (2), 1958. *See also* the works by Albrow and by Mouzelis mentioned in the text.

IV. THE FAMILY AND KINSHIP

1. *Kinship*

Murdock, G. P. *Social Structure* (New York, Macmillan, 1949).
A comparative study, based upon the files of the Yale Cross-Cultural Survey, which discusses the major problems of kinship analysis. Also has chapters on the types of family and on the social regulation of sexual behaviour.

Fox, Robin. *Kinship and Marriage* (London, 1967).

Radcliffe-Brown, A. R. 'Introduction' to A. R. Radcliffe-Brown and Daryll Forde, *African Systems of Kinship and Marriage* (London, Oxford University Press, 1950), pp. 1–85.
An outstanding short survey of kinship and marriage. The rest of the volume contains valuable studies of the kinship systems and marriage customs of particular African tribes, by leading social anthropologists.

See also Chapter 4, 'Kinship' in R. H. Lowie, *Social Organization* for an excellent short analysis.

The most useful general work on kinship in India is K. M. Kapadia, *Hindu Kinship* (Bombay, 1947).

2. *Marriage and the Family*

On the history of marriage and the family, see:
Goodsell, W. *A History of Mariage and the Family* (London, 1934).
Westermarck, E. *Short History of Marriage* (London, 1926).

These two books give some account of the different types of family structure. On this subject, see also G. P. Murdock, *Social Structure*, Chapters I and II, and R. H. Lowie, *Social Organization*, Chapters 5 and 10. There is a large literature on particular types of family structure; the following books and articles may be consulted for a general view:

The ancient world. N. D. Fustel de Coulanges, *The Ancient City* (English trans., New York, Doubleday, 1956), Book II.

China. Olga Lang, *Chinese Family and Society* (New Haven, Yale University Press, 1946).

India. K. M. Kapadia, *Marriage and Family in India* (2nd edn., Bombay, Oxford University Press, 1958).

A. B. Keith, 'Marriage (Hindu)' in Hastings, *Encyclopaedia of Religion and Ethics.*

Modern European and American Family. E. W. Burgess and H. J. Locke, *The Family: From Institution to Companionship* (New York, American Book, 1953).

M. Sorre (ed.), *Sociologie comparée de la famille contemporaine* (Paris, 1955).

A collection of papers, mainly on the French family, but with some contributions on other European countries.

W. F. Ogburn and M. F. Nimkoff, *Technology and the Changing Family* (Boston, Houghton Hiffln, 1955).

Much recent sociological study of marriage and the family has been concerned with specific modern problems; marriage stability and divorce, child development, 'problem families', etc. There is a vast literature on these matters, some of which has been surveyed by Reuben Hill in 'Sociology of Marriage and Family Behaviour 1945–56', *Current Sociology* VII (1), 1958.

V. SOCIAL STRATIFICATION

1. *General*

Three short introductory studies offering different approaches are:

Bottomore, T. B. *Classes in Modern Society* (London, Allen & Unwin, 1965).

Includes a discussion of Marx's theory of class and a brief account of social stratification in Britain, the USA and USSR.

Mayer, Kurt B., and Buckley, Walter. *Class and Society* (3rd edn., New York, Random House, 1969).

Examines the principal types of social stratification and then studies in some detail the different aspects of social stratification in the USA.

Tumin, Melvin M. *Social Stratification: The Forms and Functions of Inequality* (Englewood Cliffs, N.J., Prentice-Hall, 1967).

Gives a particularly good account of evaluation and rewards in social ranking.

An interesting general study of types of social differentiation and stratification is O. C. Cox, *Caste, Class and Race* (New York, 1948). There is a useful collection of readings in R. Bendix and S. M. Lipset, *Class, Status and Power* (2nd edn., New York, Free Press, 1966). A wide-ranging survey of the literature up to 1952, concentrating however on modern societies, will be found in D. G. Macrae, 'Social Stratification', *Current Sociology* II (1), 1953–54. Recent research is well represented by the contributions to the Second and Third World Congresses of Sociology; see *Transactions of the Second World Congress of Sociology* (London, I.S.A. 1954, Vol. II. National and regional studies, occupations, social mobility, characteristics of different social strata, theoretical and methodological studies), and *Transactions of the Third World Congress of Sociology* (London, I.S.A. 1956, Vol. III, Changes in social stratification, social mobility and class structure, dynamics of social class). There is an excellent review of recent studies in the long Introduction to the new edition of Charles H. Page, *Class and American Sociology* (New York, Schocken Books, 1969); the original text is a good interpretation of the ideas of the early American sociologists.

The theoretical writing on social stratification is for the most part disappointing, except for some writing on social class and status (see below).

The Marxist theory has not been expounded anywhere in a coherent or satisfactory manner. It is best to read Marx and Engels, *The German Ideology* (English trans., London, 1938), and the *Communist Manifesto* (remembering that this is a manifesto, not a scientific essay). Among the more useful commentaries on Marx's theory are J. A. Schumpeter, *Capitalism, Socialism and Democracy*, Chapter II; R. Schlesinger, *Marx: His Time and Ours* (London, Routledge and Kegan Paul, 1950) Chapters X and XI; and S. Ossowski, *Class Structure in the Social Consciousness* (London, Routledge and Kegan Paul, 1963).

In recent years there have been attempts to construct a functionalist theory of social stratification, although functionalism as such is under critical attack (see Chapter 2 above). See especially, K. Davis and W. E. Moore, 'Some principles of stratification', *American Sociological Review* X (2), April 1945 [reprinted in L. Wilson and W. L. Kolb, *Sociological Analysis: An Introductory Case Book*, (New York, 1949)], and B. Barber, *Social Stratification* (New York, 1957).

2. *Slavery*

Article on 'Slavery' in *Encyclopaedia of the Social Sciences*.

Nieboer, H. J. *Slavery as an Industrial System* (The Hague, Nijhoff, 1900).

Recent contributions to knowledge about slavery in the ancient

211

world are conveniently brought together in the collection of essays edited by M. L. Finley, *Slavery in Classical Antiquity* (Cambridge, Heffer & Sons, 1960).

3. *Feudal estates*

See especially Marc Bloch, *La société féodale*, Vol. II, 'Les classes et le gouvernement des hommes'. (English trans., *Feudal Society*, 1961); and also his article 'Feudalism' in *Encyclopaedia of the Social Sciences*. A more specialized study dealing with the situation in England is A. Lane Poole, *Obligations of Society in the Twelfth and Thirteenth Centuries* (Oxford, 1946).

4. *Caste*

There are several general studies of the caste system and numerous studies of caste in particular regions or contexts. Of the general studies the following are most useful:

Hutton, J. H. *Caste in India* (2nd edn., Bombay, Oxford University Press, 1951).
The most systematic account of the caste system. In Part III there is a most useful discussion of theories of the origins of caste. Has a good bibliography.

Senart, E. M. *Caste in India* (English trans., London, Methuen, 1930).
An interesting study, first published in 1896, which emphasizes the resemblances between the original Aryan varnas and estates.

Srinivas, M. N., *et al.* 'Caste', *Current Sociology*, VIII (3), 1959.
An excellent review and evaluation of recent studies of caste, with an annotated bibliography. The introduction brings out very clearly the complexity of the caste system.

Srinivas, M. N. *Caste in Modern India, and Other Essays* (Bombay, 1965).
For a detailed study of changes in the caste system in an Orissa village see F. G. Bailey, *Caste and the Economic Frontier* (Manchester, Manchester University Press, 1957).

5. *Class and Status*

There is a vast literature on social class and social status.
Of the general studies, the following will be found useful:

Dahrendorf, Ralf. *Class and Class Conflict in an Industrial Society* (London, Routledge and Kegan Paul, 1959).

Marshall, T. H. *Citizenship and Social Class and Other Essays* (Cambridge, Cambridge University Press, 1950).

Marshall, T. H. (ed.) *Class Conflict and Social Stratification* (London, Le Play House, 1938).

Schumpeter, J. A. 'Social classes in an ethnically homogeneous environment', in *Imperialism and Social Classes* (Oxford, Basil Blackwell, 1951)

Veblen, Thorstein. *The Theory of the Leisure Class* (1899; new edn., New York, Mentor Books, 1953).

Weber, Max. 'Class, Status, Party' in H. H. Gerth and C. W. Mills (eds.). *From Max Weber; Essays in Sociology* (London, Kegan Paul, 1947).

Among the studies of stratification in particular societies see:

Cole, G. D. H. *Studies in Class Structure* (London, Routledge and Kegan Paul, 1955).

Mills, C. Wright. *The Power Elite* (New York, Oxford University Press, 1956).

Porter, John. *The Vertical Mosaic: An Analysis of Social Class and Power in Canada* (Toronto, University of Toronto Press, 1965).

There are also some useful short studies in the *Transactions of the Second and Third World Congresses of Sociology* mentioned above.

There have been many studies of particular classes and occupational groups in modern societies, especially of the middle classes and professional groups. A classical study of the working class is G. Briefs, *The Proletariat* (New York, McGraw Hill, 1938). On the middle classes see *Inventaires III. Classes Moyennes* (Paris, Alcan, 1939); G. D. H. Cole, *Studies in Class Structure*, Chapters III and IV; R. Lewis and A. Maude, *The English Middle Classes* (London, Penguin Books, 1953); C. Wright Mills, *White Collar: The American Middle Classes* (New York, Oxford University Press, 1951); and D. Lockwood, *The Blackcoated Worker* (London, Allen & Unwin, 1958).

The psychological aspects of social class are discussed in a perceptive way, using historical and contemporary data, in M. Halbwachs, *The Psychology of Social Classes* (London, Heinemann, 1958. Originally published in French in 1938).

On elites, see the relevant sections of V. Pareto, *The Mind and Society* (London, Jonathan Cape, 1935); G. Mosca, *The Ruling Class* (New York, McGraw-Hill, 1939); James H. Meisel, *The Myth of the Ruling Class: Gaetano Mosca and the Elite* (Ann Arbor, University of Michigan Press, 1958); C. Wright Mills, *The Power Elite* (New York, Oxford University Press, 1956); T. B. Bottomore, *Elites and Society* (London, C. A. Watts, 1964).

6. *Social Mobility*

The pioneer study by P. A. Sorokin, *Social Mobility* (New York, Harpers, 1927), provides a very comprehensive survey on the basis of data available at that time.

More recent data have been used for comparative purposes in S. M. Lipset and R. Bendix, *Social Mobility in Industrial Society* (Glencoe, The Free Press, 1959); and in S. M. Miller, 'Comparative Social Mobility', *Current Sociology*, IX (1), 1960.

A pioneer empirical study of a particular society is D. V. Glass (ed.) *Social Mobility in Britain* (London, Routledge & Kegan Paul,

1954). See also Alain Girard, *La réussite sociale en France* (Paris, P.U.F., 1961); and Peter M. Blau and Otis D. Duncan, *The American Occupational Structure* (New York, Wiley, 1967).

See also the studies reported in *Transactions of the Third World Congress of Sociology*, Vol. III, mentioned above.

Part IV

THE REGULATION OF
BEHAVIOUR

Chapter 12

FORCE IN SOCIAL LIFE

The regulation of behaviour in society, whether of individuals or of groups, is undertaken in two ways: by the use of force, and by the establishment of values and norms which may be more or less fully accepted by the members of a society as binding 'rules of conduct'. The term 'social control' is generally used by sociologists to refer to this second kind of regulation, in which the appeal to values and norms resolves or mitigates tensions and conflicts between individuals and between groups in order to maintain the solidarity of some more inclusive group. The term is also used to refer to the arrangements by means of which the values and norms are communicated and instilled.[1] We may distinguish, therefore, between the *types* of social control, and the *agencies* and *means* which are the vehicles of social control. The principal types of control are those which will be discussed in subsequent chapters: custom and opinion, law, religion, morals, and education (knowledge, science). The educational system also figures as an agency of social control, along with the political system, churches and other religious bodies, the family (in which the initial socialization of new generations takes place), and many other specialized organizations. Every social group, indeed, can be studied from the aspect of the social control which it exercises over its own members,[2] and the contribution which it makes to the regulation of behaviour in society at large.

Social control, in this sense, has to be contrasted with the regulation of behaviour by force. These two modes are not, of course, entirely separable in actual social life. The ultimate sanction of law is physical coercion, and physical force may enter more or less prominently into all the types of social control; public opinion may become mob violence, religious sentiment may turn to religious

[1] For a similar but more comprehensive definition see G. Gurvitch, 'Social Control', in G. Gurvitch and W. E. Moore (eds.), *Twentieth Century Sociology* (New York, 1945).

[2] Simmel's studies of social groups were very largely concerned with variations in the nature of social control in groups of different size. (See above, p. 100.)

persecution and the burning of heretics. On the other hand, physical coercion itself is usually most effective where it can be justified in terms of widely accepted values; and even in the most extreme case of rule by force (for example, in a military dictatorship) the ruling group itself must be bound together by other means. Nevertheless, the distinction is clear and important. In political philosophy it has long been represented in the opposition between those thinkers who conceive the state as based upon force and those who regard it as based upon consent. Social analysis is here connected with conceptions of what *ought* to be the basis of political obligation. Sociological researches have thrown new light upon the actual processes by which social order is maintained, and perhaps because these studies have concentrated upon primitive societies on one side, and upon modern democratic societies on the other, there has been a strong emphasis upon the normative aspects of the regulation of behaviour. In some modern sociological theories, such as that of Talcott Parsons, the element of physical coercion in social relationships is almost entirely neglected.[1] Yet it is contrary to our experience even of present-day societies to underestimate the role of force; in the modern world there are police states and colonial regimes (in a variety of forms) as well as democracies. And in the history of human societies the significance of violence, conquest and oppression is all too evident.

The sociological theories which emphasize the regulation of behaviour by values and norms also tend to be preoccupied with such regulation at the level of an inclusive society and to depict social control as a relatively harmonious, unified and stable system; while they treat conflicts between values as secondary phenomena under the heading of 'deviations'. Such a framework seems applicable only to very small and simple societies. I have already noted that every social group regulates the behaviour of its members, and in complex societies different social groups may be in conflict with each other, each seeking to extend its own values and norms over the whole society. Examples of such situations are to be found in the conflicts between social classes, between different religious groups, and between ethnic groups and nationalities.

In this chapter I shall be concerned with those conflicts between social groups which involve the use of force. I shall not discuss social conflict in a more general sense.[2] Nor shall I deal here with

[1] For a critical examination of this point *see* David Lockwood, 'Some Remarks on "The Social System" ', *British Journal of Sociology*, VII (2), 1956.

[2] I have discussed this briefly in an essay, 'Sociological Theory and the Study of Social Conflict', in John C. McKinney and Edward A. Tiryakian (eds.), *Theoretical Sociology* (New York, 1970).

individual violence, although the degree and trend of violence in a society may be an indicator of social problems.[1] Violent conflict between social groups has obviously had a very great influence upon the form of human societies by extending, destroying or modifying particular ways of life, and its causes and consequences deserve the most serious study. We may usefully begin by distinguishing two main types—violent conflict between whole societies (war), and violent conflict within a society (revolution and counterrevolution, civil war)—which I shall consider separately before looking at any more general features.

War

Modern sociologists have shown comparatively little interest in the study of war. As one writer has noted: '. . . until very recently . . . the study of war and peace attracted nothing like the degree of intellectual attention that has been devoted for three of four generations to economic analysis . . . and, whatever the reasons, there is no generally acknowledged corpus of theory . . .'.[2] The case was different with the early sociologists, and with a number of later thinkers up to the beginning of this century. Both Comte and Spencer assigned to war a very important role in the development of society. According to Comte: 'There was no other means, in the early stages, to bring about the indispensable expansion of human society, and to restrain within society a sterile warlike ardour incompatible with an adequate growth of productive work, except the gradual incorporation of civilized populations into one conquering nation.'[3] Similarly, Spencer argued that in the early stages of development those societies were most likely to survive which were most effectively organized for war: 'The social type produced by survival of the fittest will be one in which the fighting part includes all who can bear arms and be trusted with arms, while the remaining part serves simply as a permanent commissariat.'[4]

Both Comte and Spencer could take this realistic view of the historical importance of warfare partly because they believed the

[1] This aspect will be referred to in a later chapter. There is evidently much concern about the apparent growth of violence in the industrial countries, and in the USA it has been the subject of a large scale official inquiry: see the Report of the National Commission on the Causes and Prevention of Violence (Washington, DC, 1969). and the associated Task Force reports. See also the symposium on 'Collective Violence', *Annals of the American Academy of Political and Social Science* (September, 1970).

[2] Alastair Buchan, *War in Modern Society: An Introduction* (London, 1966).

[3] *Cours de philosophie positive*, Lecture 57.

[4] *Principles of Sociology*, Vol. II.

age of international war was now ending. They made a distinction between a military and an industrial type of society; in the former work was subordinate to war, while in the latter, represented by the modern Western nations, war is subordinate to work. As Comte rashly declared: 'At last the time has come when serious and lasting war must disappear completely among the human elite.'[1] Later writers such as Gumplowicz and Oppenheimer took a similar view of the importance of war in social development, without sharing the belief of Comte and Spencer that it was about to disappear from human affairs; and at the beginning of the twentieth century studies of war were stimulated again by the threat of renewed warfare among the advanced nations.[2]

Subsequently, as I have noted, the interest of sociologists in this field of study declined.[3] In part, this may have been due to a conviction that the subject was too vast and complex to be treated adequately in a more or less scientific manner; but this view is no longer plausible now that sociologists have embarked upon studies of equal scope and difficulty concerned with the nature of industrial societies or the process of modernization. Much more important, probably, was the abandonment of historical and comparative inquiries, and the adoption of a functionalist approach which diverted attention from problems of conflict to problems of the integration of particular societies. Whatever the reasons, the systematic study of war, and of conflict generally, languished for several decades; but it has revived strongly in recent years. This is due not only to changes in the whole theoretical orientation of sociology, but also to the recognition that war, in the nuclear age, is one of the most dangerous problems confronting mankind, and that a social science which ignores it can hardly claim to be comprehensive or fully relevant to the practical problems of human welfare.

Among the recent works the most wide-ranging and profound is Raymond Aron's *Peace and War: A Theory of International Relations* (New York, 1966). Aron discusses first the concepts and schemes

[1] *Op. cit.*, Lecture 57.

[2] *See*, for example, William James, 'The Moral Equivalent of War' (1910), and W. G. Sumner, 'War' (in *War and Other Essays*, 1911). This was also the period in which the theory of imperialist war was developed from the writings of J. A. Hobson, Lenin and others on imperialism. A number of the writings I have mentioned are usefully collected in Leon Bramson and George W. Goethals (eds.), *War* (New York, 1964).

[3] There were exceptions, of course. Morris Ginsberg published an essay on 'The Causes of War' in 1939 (in the *Sociological Review*; reprinted in *Reason and Unreason in Society*, 1947). P. A. Sorokin was almost alone, however, in dealing at length with war, as an integral aspect of his general social theory, in his *Social and Cultural Dynamics* (4 vols., New York, 1937).

of classification which are necessary in order to study war and peace systematically: power, force, the international system of states, different types of war and of peace. Then he considers some of the possible determinants of war, and the theories which have been offered about them, before turning, in the third part of the book, to a historical examination of the global system of states in the nuclear age. In the last section of the book he discusses some moral evaluations of war, and their political and strategic implications; and he raises the question of the possible alternatives to war as a means of regulating the relations between sovereign states, each of which is pursuing its own national interest. Two possibilities are peace through law, and peace through empire—either of which would involve, in different ways, a greater or lesser sacrifice of national sovereignty. A third possibility is peace through the balance of power as it now exists, but this may be difficult to maintain in conditions of rapid technological advance and of the spread of nuclear weapons. In a final note Aron criticizes the indiscriminate use of game-theory models in some recent studies and advocates paying more attention to 'reasonable policy' than to 'rational strategy'.[1]

Another interesting kind of inquiry is that which was undertaken by L. F. Richardson in an attempt to discover the correlates of war by means of a careful quantitative study;[2] and subsequently, to determine the influence of an arms race upon the probability of war.[3]

The recent studies of war and peace, which have brought together sociology and other social sciences under the general title of 'strategic studies', differ in important respects from the earlier sociological theories. They are no longer very much concerned with long-term evolutionary trends but devote their attention rather to modern war, and to the specific practical issue of avoiding a major war, through an analysis of the conditions and situations which may provoke it (for example, what Richardson called a 'runaway arms race'). Such studies draw upon historical and comparative investigations, but they do not aim at the construction of an ambitious general theory of war. What they have contributed so far is a clarification of ideas about the complex phenomenon of war and an indication of some of its proximate causes. Like sociology in general, sociological studies of war and peace do not provide the

[1] The limitations of game-theory are also pointed out in Anatol Rapoport, *Fights, Games and Debates* (Ann Arbor, 1960).
[2] *See* his *Statistics of Deadly Quarrels* (Pittsburgh, 1960).
[3] *Arms and Insecurity* (Pittsburgh, 1960).

grounds for a single correct course of action, but help to enlarge the area of rational choice and control.

It is understandable that most of the recent studies should have concentrated upon the dangers of a nuclear war between the super-powers, but this does not exhaust the subject matter of the use of force in international affairs. Indeed, from the point of view of the regulation of behaviour by force, the occurrence of limited wars fought with conventional weapons, and various kinds of military intervention by the super-powers (the USA in the Dominican Republic and in Vietnam, the USSR in Czechoslovakia), are more immediately significant. The problems which these examples indicate are not likely to be easily solved. They arise in part out of the general confrontation between power blocs, but they also reflect the permanent inequality in the international order between large and small nations; and we are still far from having a clear conception of how the rights of small nations can be guaranteed, let alone an effective practical policy.

Revolution and Counter-Revolution

The study of revolution was never neglected to the same extent as the study of war, largely because one important sociological theory—Marxism—treated revolution as a basic phenomenon of social life. Even in this case, however, modern revolutions and revolutionary movements were not very thoroughly or objectively studied, and the chief preoccupation of many Marxists seemed to be to uphold Marx's general idea of revolution against its critics.

In recent years the interest of sociologists in the study of revolutions has become much more widespread, and at the same time the implementation of such studies has encountered great difficulties. The interest is not difficult to explain: the twentieth century is, more than any other, a century of revolutions. The Russian and Chinese Revolutions have at least as great a historical and political significance as had the French Revolution, marking in a similar way the beginning of a new course of social development; while many revolutions in smaller countries (in Yugoslavia, Algeria, Cuba) have contributed new political ideas and models of new social institutions. The cumulative effect of these events, and the revival of radical and revolutionary ideas in the Western industrial countries themselves. have obliged sociologists to pay more attention to such phenomena.

The difficulties arise in two ways. In the first place, while sociologists, like most other men, condemn war and are apprehensive about the possibility of a conflict involving nuclear weapons—and thus agree broadly upon the aim of their studies as being the eventual

222

control or elimination of international warfare—there is no such agreement in respect of the use of force in revolutionary struggles. Sociologists may, and do, approach the study of revolutions with sympathy or aversion; they may become advisers to revolutionary leaders, or more frequently, it seems, to counter-insurgency agencies.[1] For various reasons, including the predominance of a conservative style of social thought during much of the postwar period, there has grown up an idea that a sympathy with movements of rebellion is somehow more ideological, and a greater threat to sociological objectivity, than is an attachment to the *status quo*. This is obviously not the case. Nor is it evidently true that violence and the use of force are more prevalent in revolutionary movements than in counter-revolutions or in the defence of an established order. It would be difficult, no doubt, to draw up a balance sheet of violence, but there are numerous historical examples of the savage repression of radical, or even reforming movements in modern societies, from the suppression of the Paris Commune to the armed attacks on the early trade unions (especially in the USA), and on quite a different scale, the Nazi movement, and the massacre of Indonesian communists in 1965–66; and it appears quite probable that the *status quo* is generally defended much more violently than it is attacked. Questions of moral attitude and political commitment thus become exceptionally intrusive in this field of inquiry, with the result that many sociologists have been deterred from entering it.

The second kind of difficulty is theoretical. The major theory of revolution—that of Marx—was concerned principally with the transition from feudalism to capitalism in Western Europe, and with the development of a revolutionary working class within capitalist society. But the twentieth century revolutions have taken place in peasant societies, while the revolutionary movement in the advanced capitalist countries seems (or seemed) to many sociologists to have subsided. As yet these events have not been incorporated into a revised Marxist theory, even though the peasant revolutions have often been led by parties which profess Marxism as their doctrine; nor has any alternative theory of social change dealt adequately with the new circumstances.

A revolution, in the words of Franz Schurmann and Orville Schell, '. . . is the sweeping away of an old order—an ancient political

---

[1] Some of the issues involved are well illustrated by the notorious 'Project Camelot'; they are discussed in Irving L. Horowitz (ed.), *The Rise and Fall of Project Camelot* (Cambridge, Mass., M.I.T. Press, 1967), and in Ralf Dahrendorf, *Essays in the Theory of Society* (Stanford, Stanford University Press, 1968), Chapter 10.

system, a traditional culture, an uncreative economy, a ruling class which only exploits, and a system of social organization which no longer satisfies men'.[1] It does not necessarily involve the use of force and armed conflict; but most modern revolutions have occurred through such conflict, either because the established rulers have used force to resist change or because the leaders of the revolutionary movement have encountered a situation in which their aims could be achieved very rapidly by force. The underlying causes of revolutionary movements and revolutions are conflicts of interest, principally between social classes as Marx's theory maintains; although many other elements may enter into the process—ethnic and religious differences, or nationalist sentiments. The success of a revolutionary movement depends upon diverse factors; Crane Brinton, elaborating upon ideas which were expressed at various times by Marx, particularly in his early writings, has suggested that the favourable conditions include economic progress in a society, bitter class antagonisms, desertion of the ruling class by the intellectuals, inefficient governmental machinery, and a politically inept ruling class.[2]

These notions enable us to understand, in some measure, the absence or failure of revolutionary movements in the Western industrial countries since the end of the nineteenth century. In particular, it is the fact that class antagonisms have not become more acute—but on the contrary have been limited by the growth of the middle classes, by the achievement of reforms through the activities of the labour movement, and in recent years by increasing prosperity—which explains these conditions. At the same time, the ruling classes in these societies have experienced few crises in which they have been wholly deserted by the intellectuals or have become demoralized to such an extent that they have lost control of events. Only on rare occasions—for example, following a military defeat in which the rulers were discredited, as in Germany in 1918—could a revolutionary movement develop. Or to take an example from a different sphere, the attempted revolution in Hungary in 1956 was only possible because the political leaders had been thrown into confusion by the revelations concerning the nature of Communist rule during the Stalinist period. The absence of any large scale revolutionary movements in most of the Western countries in this century does not mean that the opposition between classes—economic, cultural and ideological—has ceased to exist. At times, as

[1] Franz Schurmann and Orville Schell (eds.), *China Readings 2: Republican China* (New York, 1967), Introduction.
[2] Crane Brinton, *The Anatomy of Revolution* (New York, 1957).

in the 1950s, it has been muted, but it has always reappeared; and in recent years there has even been a revival of revolutionary ideas, not in the working class, but in the student movements. However, in spite of the example of the student inspired revolt of May 1968 in France, it seems unlikely that there will be any serious revolutionary movements in the Western industrial countries.[1] On the other hand, it is probable that there will be accelerated social and political change, broadly along the lines which the labour movement has followed, and this may be accompanied by sporadic violent conflicts in some societies.

In the predominantly peasant societies where revolutions have occurred the conditions which I mentioned earlier have generally prevailed: bitter class antagonisms resulting from the gross disparities of wealth, and from the autocratic rule of a small minority; the defection of Westernized intellectuals, often influenced by Marxism; the ineptitude of traditional ruling groups in dealing with economic problems and with the impact of more advanced societies. These revolutions, while inspired by Marxism and socialism, have also been intricately involved with anti-colonial, national liberation movements, and with the effort to modernize and industrialize which now characterizes all the countries of the Third World. Thus their achievement is not necessarily the creation of a socialist society as this was conceived in the West during the nineteenth century, but rather the successful implementation (at least in some cases) of a policy for rapid economic growth. At the same time they have had a great influence upon world politics, by reanimating revolutionary ideas elsewhere and to some extent giving them a new form, in which the violent conflicts which will bring about profound changes in the structure of society are seen not so much as conflicts between classes within capitalist society but as conflicts between the 'bourgeois' and the 'proletarian' nations. Clearly, these ideas involve a substantial revision of Marxist theory, such as has been attempted in diverse ways by H. Marcuse,[2] A. G. Frank,[3] and a number of other social scientists more or less closely associated with the radical movements of the 1960s. There is quite a different interpretation, which remains closer to the original Marxist scheme,

---

[1] There is a good discussion of this subject, with reference to the USA, in Barrington Moore, Jnr., 'Revolution in America?', *New York Review of Books*, XII (2), 1969.

[2] See particularly, *One-Dimensional Man* (Boston, 1964), and *An Essay on Liberation* (Boston, 1969).

[3] *Capitalism and Underdevelopment in Latin America* (2nd edn., New York, 1969).

insofar as it rests upon an analysis of the nature of internal class relations, in Barrington Moore's *Social Origins of Dictatorship and Democracy*, where 'three routes to the modern world' are distinguished and compared: the bourgeois revolution (England, France, USA); the revolution from above (Germany, Japan); and the communist revolution (Russia, China).

In recent years the growing preoccupation with the violent character of this century has led to a revival of interest in the notion of an aggressive instinct or propensity in human nature. This was, of course, discussed at a much earlier time. Simmel, in studying conflict, wrote that '. . . it seems impossible to deny an *a priori* fighting instinct',[1] and Freud, in an exchange of letters with Einstein on the prevention of war, asserted the existence of a destructive or aggressive instinct in human beings.[2] A study by Durbin and Bowlby concluded that '. . . the willingness to fight is so widely distributed in space and time that it must be regarded as a basic pattern of human behaviour'.[3] Recent biological and anthropological studies have generally supported the view that there is an aggressive instinct, resulting from natural selection, which is widely distributed among the vertebrates and is to be found among the primates, including man;[4] but most writers recognize that to posit such an instinct is far from providing a complete explanation of the occurrence of violent conflict. An aggressive instinct, like other instincts, can be regulated and controlled, as indeed must be the case, since men are not fighting all the time. As Durbin and Bowlby observe: 'Peaceful cooperation predominates—there is much more peace than war'. . . .

What has to be explained is the occurrence of violent conflict at particular times, and this can only be done by investigating the social conditions which lead to a situation in which groups of men determine (or have determined for them by their leaders) that they will fight to defend or promote their interests. In whatever way the causes of such conflicts are explained—and I have outlined above some of the theories of war and revolution—there can be no question about the significance which the use of force, in these different forms, has had in sustaining or destroying a particular social order, and in creating new types of society. Pareto took an extreme view when he argued that '. . . it is by force that social institutions are estab-

[1] G. Simmel, *Conflict* (1908; English trans., Glencoe, 1955).

[2] The letter was originally published in 1933; it is reprinted in Sigmund Freud, *Collected Papers*, Vol. 5, and in Bramson and Goethals (eds.), *War* (1964).

[3] E. F. M. Durbin, *et al.*, *War and Democracy* (London, 1938).

[4] See, for example, Konrad Lorenz, *On Aggression* (New York, 1966); and S. L. Washburn, 'Conflict in Primate Society', in Anthony de Rueck and Julie Knight (eds.), *Conflict in Society* (London, 1966).

lished, and it is by force that they are maintained',[1] but his argument, derived from Marx's theory, is still nearer to the truth than the conception which prevailed in sociology for some time, according to which men's behaviour is regulated only by values.

In the following chapters I shall be concerned with this second kind of regulation, but instead of taking the values and norms for granted, as is so often done in studies of social control, I shall also be concerned to examine the ways in which they emerge, change and are diffused or checked; or in other words, to look at the same phenomena from the standpoint of the sociology of mind.[2] In each particular study it is necessary to be aware of both aspects; to observe how the real situation and interests of a group influence its values (its doctrine or ideology), and how these values in turn influence its situation and the actual behaviour of its members. The case of social groups in conflict, and especially class conflict, brings out very clearly this double aspect of the phenomena. Social classes are the source of important ideologies, which then contribute to the cohesion of the classes in their struggles with each other. Further, each class seeks to make its own norms and values prevail in the society as a whole, and at certain periods in the history of a particular society we may be able to discern plainly the predominance of the values of specific classes. In other cases it may be the ideologies of particular religious or ethnic groups which become predominant.

The phenomena of social control are thus more complex and more difficult to analyse than many accounts of the matter would suggest. We have to take account, first, of the relation between force and social control in the regulation of behaviour and the maintenance of group cohesion. Secondly, we have to consider the relation between the different types of social control: custom, opinion, law, religion, morals, education, etc. Next, we must remember that socia lcontrol refers to systems of values and norms which undergo change, which are challenged and criticized by other systems, which are always in process of being built up or reconstructed, or which are declining and succumbing to criticism. This is true of social control both in total societies and in the social groups within a society. At the level of an inclusive society social control is a more or less precarious and temporary balance between

---

[1] V. Pareto, *Les systèmes socialistes* (Paris, 1902).

[2] I use the term 'sociology of mind' as the English equivalent of the French *sociologie de l'esprit* which includes besides the sociology of knowledge, the sociology of art, religion, morals, etc.

conflicting groups and ideologies; at the same time it is subject to external influences, receiving support from the civilization to which it belongs and being challenged by other civilizations. These broader aspects of the question should be borne in mind throughout the following discussion of particular types of social control.

Chapter 13

CUSTOM AND PUBLIC OPINION

Custom and public opinion may be considered together, since they have certain features in common and there are important connections between them. In the first place, they are to be counted among the less formal types of social control. They do not have the kind of systematic elaboration which we find in the case of law, morality or religion. There is a certain vagueness, and sometimes ambiguity, in regard to infractions of the code of behaviour which they prescribe, and in regard to punishments.

Custom has frequently been contrasted with law, and a distinction made between societies which possess law, in the sense of rules promulgated by a single recognized authority and sanctioned by definite punishments, and societies in which behaviour is regulated by traditional norms which are simply 'accepted' rather than sanctioned or enforced. I shall examine later the problems raised by this conception of law. Custom, as thus conceived, presents other difficulties. Conformity with custom is made to appear almost automatic, and indeed some early anthropologists, in their accounts of primitive societies, gave the impression that individual deviation from the customary rules was hardly conceivable.[1] This total and automatic submission to custom was explained largely by the force of habit, although some writers also referred to public opinion and supernatural beliefs as additional supports for conformity.[2]

This distinction between types of society in which behaviour is regulated by custom and law respectively is too simple and clear cut, and the explanations of the submission to custom are inadequate. It is one of the major contributions of Malinowski to have shown the complexity of social control in primitive societies, and to have

[1] E.g. R. R. Marett, *Anthropology* (p. 182) '. . . one reason why it is hard to find any law in primitive society is because, in a general way of speaking, no one dreams of breaking the social rules'. Such views underlay the emphasis upon the conservative, unchanging nature of custom, and the contrast between the 'cake of custom' which immobilizes primitive societies and critical, reflective thought which enables civilized societies to progress.

[2] E.g. L. T. Hobhouse, *Social Development* (1924).

provided a more satisfactory account of the influence of custom.[1] He argued, first, that 'besides the rules of law, there are several other types of norm and traditional commandment', such as morals, manners, rules of craftsmanship and ceremonial, and religious precepts. In discussing custom, he showed that neither the force of habit, nor respect for tradition, nor public opinion, nor the fear of supernatural beings, could entirely account for conformity. He emphasized the role of 'binding obligations' and 'reciprocity', as positive inducements to customary behaviour. As Schapera comments, '. . . life in a primitive community involves every individual in specific obligations to others, who in turn are similarly duty-bound to him. Those obligations he fulfils partly because of early training, and partly because of public opinion and self-interest: it pays him in various ways to do as he should, and if he does not he suffers loss of material benefit and of social esteem.'[2] Further, Malinowski combated the notion that in primitive societies submission to custom is automatic, by showing that contraventions of the social rules are frequent and motivated by considerations of personal advantage similar to those found in more complex societies.

Taken as a whole Malinowski's work made untenable the earlier conceptions of the 'tyranny of custom' and of the irresistible force of habit and early training. It implied also a greater degree of comparability between different types of society in respect of social control. While in primitive societies custom has a large influence, in civilized societies custom, habit, public opinion and reciprocity still play a part, but some of the major forms of behaviour are more strictly and precisely regulated by law, religion and morality. There are important differences, also, between civilized societies in which social change is taking place rapidly and those in which change is slow. The social life of the medieval European societies, feudal and absolutist, was regulated not only by an armed aristocracy, by the religious and moral doctrines of an organized church, and by law but also by custom and tradition. At the very end of the *ancien régime* the power of custom was recognized by conservative political philosophers, such as Burke, who argued that political wisdom consisted in following the traditions of one's society as embodied in its existing social institutions. The social structure of India, until the

---

[1] See especially his *Crime and Custom in Savage Society* (1926). Malinowski's own views on social control varied at different periods in his career; they are usefully discussed and evaluated in I. Schapera, 'Malinowski's Theories of Law', in R. Firth (ed.), *Man and Culture*.

[2] Schapera, *loc. cit.*

last two centuries, underwent few and gradual changes; and the importance of custom was correspondingly great. J. D. Mayne, in his classical work on Hindu law[1] argued that 'the great body of existing law consists of ancient usages, more or less modified by Aryan or Brahmanical influence', and observed that the greatest effect was given to custom by the Courts and by legislation under British rule.[2]

Even in modern industrial societies the importance of custom is far from negligible, for much religion and morality is customary rather than reflective, and ordinary social intercourse is largely regulated by custom and public opinion. But in most of these societies we should rather speak of 'customs' and 'opinions', for they are characterized by a diversity which springs from the existence of numerous competing and conflicting groups, and from the rapidity of social change. The present-day communist societies constitute an exception, in so far as they aim by a variety of means at the inculcation and enforcement of a single uniform pattern of behaviour. Some recent writers have seen in such societies an extreme form of the regulation of opinion and conduct towards which all industrial societies are tending, because of the concentration of power and the massive growth of effective media of mass persuasion. Thus, C. Wright Mills, in his book *The Power Elite*, observes that the USA has 'moved a considerable distance along the road to the mass society. At the end of that road there is totalitarianism, as in Nazi Germany or Communist Russia'. He distinguishes a mass society from a 'society of publics' by four characteristics: (i) far fewer people express opinions than receive them, (ii) the communications are so organized that it is difficult or impossible for the individual to answer back immediately or with any effect, (iii) the realization of opinion in action is controlled by authorities, (iv) the mass has no autonomy from the official institutions of society, but is permeated by agents of these institutions. In Britain, Richard Hoggart has recently studied the influence of 'mass culture' upon working class attitudes and opinions, and has emphasized the increase in 'passive acceptance'.[3]

But it remains true that in many modern societies there is a greater diversity of opinion, more rapid variation in opinion, and a larger number of voluntary groups engaged in formulating and influencing

[1] J. D. Mayne, *A Treatise on Hindu Law and Usage* (10th edn., 1938).
[2] The Judicial Committee of the Privy Council in the Ramnad case said: 'Under the Hindu system of law, clear proof of usage will outweigh the written text of the law'. Mayne, *op. cit.*, p. 47.
[3] R. Hoggart, *The Uses of Literacy* (1957).

opinion, than in other types of society. The phenomena of public opinion have been studied mainly by social psychologists, but before we consider their work reference should be made to some more general studies. A classical work of historical and sociological inquiry is A. V. Dicey's *Law and Opinion in England in the Nineteenth Century*,[1] which examines the influence of the highly articulate opinion represented in political and social doctrines upon legislation. A quite different analysis of the formation of attitudes and opinions is given by Pareto in his *Mind and Society*, where a fundamental distinction is made between 'logical' and 'non-logical' action. Pareto devotes most attention to the latter, and implicitly presents the view that almost all human behaviour is 'non-logical' in his sense, i.e. that it is the result of impulses or sentiments which he calls 'residues'. These residues are the driving forces of human action, but they are often camouflaged in doctrines and theoretical systems which Pareto terms 'derivations', and which Marxists would call 'ideologies'. Thus, for Pareto, opinions, which Dicey and others treated as more or less rational constructions (ranging from prejudices to philosophical doctrines) are merely rationalizations of the basic residues. Pareto does not, however, give a very convincing account of the nature and source of these residues upon which his whole analysis is based.[2]

The social psychological studies of opinion have concentrated upon more limited fields of inquiry.[3] Much research has been devoted to prejudice, especially race prejudice. These problems are briefly surveyed in Arnold M. Rose, *The Roots of Prejudice* (UNESCO 1952) and discussed more extensively in G. W. Allport, *The Nature of Prejudice* (Cambridge, Mass., 1954). Two particular studies should be mentioned. T. W. Adorno and others in *The Authoritarian Personality* (New York, 1950) examined the psychological characteristics determining extreme intolerance and prejudice, particularly in the form of anti-Semitism. G. Myrdal in *An American Dilemma*

[1] 2nd edn., 1926. A recently published work, edited by M. Ginsberg, under the title *Law and Opinion in the Twentieth Century* attempts to continue Dicey's study by tracing recent changes. As a collection of essays it lacks the unity and critical power of Dicey's book.

[2] For a criticism of Pareto's doctrine of 'residues' and 'derivations' see M. Ginsberg, 'The Sociology of Pareto' in *Reason and Unreason in Society*. Ginsberg has also provided, in his *Psychology of Society*, the best general analysis of the parts played respectively by reason and impulse in social behaviour.

[3] The subject is discussed in most textbooks of social psychology. In Kimball Young's *Handbook of Social Psychology* approximately half the work is devoted to public opinion, mass communication, and prejudice. (See also works listed in the Bibliography at the end of this Section.) Current research in this field can best be followed in the *Public Opinion Quarterly*.

(New York, 1944) studied comprehensively the situation of Negroes in the USA, and in discussing prejudice brought out the conflict between a widely held 'egalitarian ideology' and the concurrently held opinions concerning the 'inferiority' of Negroes.

Another important field of inquiry has been that of political opinions, which was briefly considered in an earlier chapter.[1] Here the contributions of social psychology have been chiefly in revealing the distribution and fluctuation of opinions; not in providing explanations. It seems evident that in the formation of political opinions the social situation of individuals and the nature and control of the means of communication are especially important. On the other hand, social psychology should be able to elucidate some of the factors in the rise of new currents of opinion and mass movements; such movements for example, as National Socialism, or more recently the revival of radical movements, and in particular the growth of a distinctive student movement. In fact, little has been done to investigate such phenomena from the psychological[2] aspect.

These observations on the study of political opinions have a wider bearing. It is necessary to study public opinion in modern societies from different aspects and at different levels. First, there is the need to determine the actual distribution of opinions on different types of issue, and to follow the changes in this distribution. A considerable contribution has been made to this kind of study by the organizations which undertake, as a regular activity, surveys of public opinion; e.g. the 'Gallup Poll' and others in the USA, the British Institute of Public Opinion, the Institut Français d'Opinion Publique. These surveys, however, can deal only with relatively simple opinions on very clearly defined issues; they can discover little about the ways in which opinions are supported, or connected with other opinions and beliefs, and they cannot distinguish between identical opinions in terms of the degree of rational conviction with which they are held. Moreover, they can do little to explain, as against describing, the fluctuations in opinion, or to trace the connections between opinion and behaviour. To deal with these problems we have, secondly, to examine the actual ways in which public opinion is formed; and this requires a study of opinion-forming agencies and of the procedures by which opinion is influenced.

[1] *See* above, p. 161.
[2] There is, however, a very one-sided account of the student movement in Lewis Feuer, *The Conflict of Generations* (New York, 1969). A more balanced study drawing upon much sociological and psychological research is Charles Hampden-Turner, *Radical Man* (Cambridge, Mass., 1970).

233

Among the more important agencies are the mass-media (film, radio and television, the press) and the major voluntary associations which aim at the establishment of particular norms, either directly through the pressure of public opinion or indirectly through legislation brought about by public opinion. In recent years, the mass-media have been increasingly studied, but it cannot be claimed that the extent and nature of their influence is yet clear. There is some evidence that the press and radio have little effect in changing political opinions, but the diversity of opinions certainly depends upon their finding expression through the mass-media.[1]

The influence of associations in forming and changing opinions has been examined very largely by the students of pressure groups.[2] A classical study of this kind is P. H. Odegard, *Pressure Politics: The Story of the Anti-Saloon League* (1928) which describes and analyses the means by which the Anti-Saloon League succeeded in bringing about prohibition in the USA. Concerning the individual's acceptance or rejection of opinions and beliefs, much has been learned from commercial advertising techniques, and more recently from general studies of communication. The rapid growth of advertising in modern societies has led social psychologists to pay increasing attention to it, and quite apart from scientific study many psychologists are now employed as advisers on advertising techniques.[3] Political propaganda itself shows increasingly the influence of the advertising and public relations expert; a great distance separates the socialist pamphlets of the nineteenth century from the glossy election brochures of the British Labour Party in the 1950s and the professional television presentations of the 1960s.

Finally, it is necessary to consider how the content of public opinion is affected by values and norms derived from law, religion, morality, or custom, and on the other hand by social interests. Public opinion constrains and directs the behaviour of the individual, but in what way is public opinion itself formed? It is obviously relevant to this question to examine the agencies and techniques

[1] In recent years there has been a growing concern with the influence of television, especially commercial television. One of the questions raised is that of the effect of television violence on violent behaviour in society. More generally, however, commercial television may be seen as generating or reinforcing passive and conformist attitudes (as Marcuse has argued), which stifle criticism and dissent. See, for example, Robert MacNeil, *The People Machine* (London, 1970).

[2] *See* above, pp. 158–9.

[3] See A. M. and E. B. Lee, *The Fine Art of Propaganda* (New York, 1939), and Vance Packard, *The Hidden Persuaders* (London, 1957).

which influence opinion, which I have just discussed, but there remains a problem as to the source of the values which public opinion upholds. No doubt, the source is frequently custom and tradition; and public opinion, though it may influence law, often lags behind it. An example may be seen in some of the current problems of caste in India. The notions of 'untouchability' and 'unclean castes' are essential elements in the traditional doctrine of the caste system. Religious and moral reformers, influenced very often by values coming from outside Hinduism, have attempted to eliminate such ideas from Hindu religious teaching and from popular thought. The Indian Constitution of 1950 abolished 'untouchability' as a legal status, but in actual social relations the condition still exists. The behaviour of the individual, in this particular context, is guided by customary values and public opinion, rather than by law. In the long run, no doubt, law, religious and moral teaching, and education will modify customary attitudes and opinions. It would be of great sociological interest to study the ways in which opinions on this issue are affected by changes in the values expressed by the more formal types of social control, and how, on the other hand, change is resisted by particular social groups which appeal to traditional values.

There are problems of a similar kind on other societies. Public opinion is mutable, there are divergent and sometimes contradictory customs and traditions which are invoked, and there are diverse and competing interest groups which seek to spread their ideologies. It is difficult, without field research of the intensive kind which social anthropologists practise, to discover the nature and force of the different pressures upon the individual. Opinion surveys can do little more than provide a broad framework for further inquiry. There is a need to examine on one side the formal symbolic systems of law, religion, and scientific knowledge, and on the other to study, by close and continuous observation, the behaviour and opinions manifested in the life of social groups which can conveniently be directly observed. The relevance of many small group studies is evident here,[1] but much could also be learned from studies of neighbourhoods, economic enterprises, and local occupational groups, if they were undertaken from this point of view.

All studies of social control lead eventually to the issue of the relation between the individual and society, and to the problem of freedom and coercion. This concern, which is unmistakably the central reference point in the work of all the classical sociologists

[1] *See* above, p. 102.

is particularly apparent in the work of Durkheim,[1] and in the later writings of Karl Mannheim.[2] I shall return to it in a later chapter on sociology and social policy after discussing the other principal types of social control.

[1] *See* especially, *Professional Ethics and Civic Morals* (English trans., 1957).

[2] *Man and Society in an Age of Reconstruction* (1940), Part V, and *Freedom, Power and Democratic Planning* (1952).

Chapter 14

RELIGION AND MORALITY

The early sociological studies of religion had three distinctive methodological characteristics; they were evolutionist, positivist and psychologistic. These features may be illustrated from the work of Comte, Tylor and Spencer. In Comte's sociology one of the fundamental conceptions is the so-called 'law of three stages' according to which human thought has passed, historically and necessarily, from the theological stage (primitive and early society), through the metaphysical stage (medieval society), to the positive stage (modern society, beginning in the nineteenth century). Comte treats theological thinking as intellectual error which is dispersed by the rise of modern science; he traces, within the theological stage, a development from animism to monotheism; and he explains religious belief in psychological terms by reference to the perceptions and thought processes of early man. It is true that Comte later propounded his own 'religion of humanity' and thus recognized, in some sense, a universal need for religion, but he did not succeed in bringing these later ideas into harmony with his fundamental conceptions.

The work of Tylor and Spencer was much more rigorous, and it shows more clearly the features I have mentioned.[1] Both thinkers were concerned to explain, in the first place, the origin of religion. They believed that the idea of the soul was the principal feature in religious belief and set out to give an account, in rationalist terms, of how such an idea might have originated in the mind of primitive man. According to this, men obtained their idea of the soul from a misinterpretation of dreams and death; Spencer refers to 'that original theory of things in which, from the supposed reality of dreams, there resulted the supposed reality of ghosts; whence developed all kinds of supposed supernatural beings'.[2] From this point, Spencer goes on to describe the development of religious institutions in the different stages of society. As with Comte, the explanation of religious phenomena is in terms of psychological dispositions, intellectual error, and the evolution of social life.

[1] E. B. Tylor, *Primitive Culture* (London, 1871; 3rd revised edn., 1891); H. Spencer, *Principles of Sociology*, Vol. III (London, 1896).
[2] Spencer, *op. cit.*

Other social theorists of the nineteenth century approached the study of religion in a similar way. Marx held that religion originated in the fear and anxiety provoked by natural phenomena, and that it was an illusion which would ultimately disappear. But he also made a new departure in considering the role of religious doctrines as ideologies in different types of society; that is, the part played by religion in social control. Frazer also approached the problem from the point of view of evolutionary theory and positivist or rationalist philosophy. He made a distinction between magic and religion; the former involving an assertion of man's power over natural processes ('a spurious system of natural law as well as a fallacious guide of conduct'), and the latter 'a belief in powers higher than man and an attempt to propitiate or please them'.[1] He conceived the intellectual progress of mankind as a passage from the age of magic to the age of religion, and then to the age of science; but he recognized that magic and religion were frequently intermingled even in civilized societies, and that in modern societies a substratum of magical beliefs persisted.

An alternative approach to the study of religion was first formulated by Durkheim in his book *Les formes élémentaires de la vie religieuse* (1912),[2] although it had been propounded earlier in a less coherent form by Fustel de Coulanges (who was at one time Durkheim's teacher).[3] Durkheim argued that in all societies a distinction is made between 'sacred' and 'profane' things. Religion is 'a unified system of beliefs and practices relative to sacred things, that is things set apart and forbidden—beliefs and practices which unite into one single moral community called a Church all those who adhere to them'. In Durkheim's theory the collective aspects of religion are emphasized; the function of religious rituals is to affirm the moral superiority of the society over its individual members and thus to maintain the solidarity of the society. 'The god of the clan can be nothing but the clan itself.' Durkheim, in the first part of his book, criticized the work of the earlier anthropologists and sociologists on the grounds that their explanations of religion were psychological (in terms of individual sentiments), not sociological, and that they made religion an illusion whereas in his view nothing so universal and important in human society could be illusory. Nevertheless, his

---

[1] Sir J. G. Frazer, *The Golden Bough* (abridged edn., London, 1945).

[2] E. Durkheim, *The Elementary Forms of Religious Life* (English trans., 1947).

[3] Fustel de Coulanges, *The Ancient City*, shows the influence of religion in creating larger social groupings and maintaining them in existence. A similar approach is to be found in the work of W. Robertson Smith, especially in his *Lectures on the Religion of the Semites* (London, 1894).

own theory makes religion equally an illusion, for as Lowie asks: in what sense are natural phenomena less real than society?[1]

If, however, we eliminate from Durkheim's theory its philosophical pretension to explain the 'essence' of religion, and its rejection of any psychological contribution to the understanding of religious phenomena, we are in possession of a functionalist account of religion which has a definite, though limited, usefulness. Later anthropologists, among them Malinowski and Radcliffe-Brown, have shown in field studies how religion works in primitive societies to maintain social cohesion and to control individual conduct.[2] Durkheim's emphasis upon ritual as against belief was salutary in turning the attention of anthropologists away from exegesis of exotic religious ideas to the observation and description of religious behaviour.[3]

In the study of civilized societies Durkheim's theory has proved less helpful, for here religion is as frequently a divisive as a unifying force. That is to say, while it unites particular groups it may provoke conflict between these groups within the larger society. There are, of course, many instances of inclusive societies which are unified by religion—the states of medieval Christendom, some Islamic states and Hindu India (which I shall consider more closely below); but in modern industrial societies particularly there is considerable religious diversity and some religious conflict. Secondly, in civilized societies, and especially in modern societies, beliefs and doctrines have more importance than ritual, for men tend to unite or divide upon propositions rather than upon sentiments.

These features have meant that the sociological study of religion has diverged from that of social anthropology. It has been characterized especially by a concern with the ethical doctrines of the world religions. This approach is illustrated, in different ways, by the work of L. T. Hobhouse and Max Weber. Hobhouse's sociology as a whole is concerned with the influence of intellectual development upon social institutions. Within this general intellectual development Hobhouse gives particular attention to the development of moral ideas; thus, in discussing religion in his major work *Morals in Evolution* he is entirely concerned with the moral codes of the major religions and especially of Christianity. These moral codes are examined as doctrines and are analysed in a largely

[1] R. H. Lowie, *Primitive Religion* (1924).
[2] A. R. Radcliffe-Brown, *The Andaman Islanders* (1922); B. Malinowski, *Magic, Science and Religion and Other Essays* (1948).
[3] For a discussion of this point see A. R. Radcliffe-Brown, 'Religion and Society' in *Structure and Function in Primitive Society*.

philosophical way; their relation to social behaviour is then considered in very general terms. Max Weber's treatment of religious beliefs differs in important respects.[1] In the first place, it is not based upon any evolutionary scheme. Secondly, it is largely concerned with a single major aspect of religious ethics, namely their connections with the economic order. Weber examines these connections from two points of view; the influence of particular religious doctrines upon economic behaviour, and the relation between the position of groups in the economic system and types of religious belief. Thirdly, he is less concerned with ethical doctrines as expounded by theologians than with these doctrines in their popular form as they guide everyday behaviour. Weber's best known work, *The Protestant Ethic and the Spirit of Capitalism*, which was the starting point for his studies of religion, aims to show the part played in the origin and development of modern capitalism by Calvinist ethics. The thesis has been well summarized by Raymond Aron:[2] '. . . The Calvinist, never certain that he is one of the elect, looks for signs of his election in his earthly life, and he finds them in the prosperity of his enterprise. But he is not permitted to enjoy leisure as a result of his success, or to use his money in the pursuit of luxury or pleasure. Thus he is obliged to re-employ his money in his business, and the formation of capital takes place as a result of this ascetic obligation to save. Moreover, only regular and rationalized work, exact accounting which makes possible a knowledge of the state of the business at every moment, and pacific commerce are consistent with the spirit of his morality. For the Calvinist is master of himself, distrusts instinct and passions, is independent and has confidence only in himself, and studies and reflects upon his actions as the capitalist must do. . . . (But) Weber did not believe that 'ideas rule the world'; he presented the case of Protestantism as a favourable example which enabled one to understand the way in which ideas act in history. The theological and ethical conceptions of the Protestants were influenced in their formation by various social and political circumstances, and further, they had no direct influence upon economic affairs. But ideas have their own logic, and they give rise to consequences which may have a practical influence; thus the dogmas of Calvinism, established in the consciousness of individuals belonging to particular groups, brought about a particular attitude to life and a specific form of behaviour'.

[1] Max Weber, *Gesammelte Aufsaetze zur Religionssoziologie* (3 vols., 1922–3). Many of these essays have now been translated into English (see the bibliography at the end of this Part).

[2] Raymond Aron, *German Sociology*, pp. 94–5.

In his later studies of religion (Judaism, China, India) Weber followed the same line of enquiry, examining the religious doctrines of particular social groups, and the social (especially economic) consequences of particular attitudes to life derived from religious systems. It is of especial interest here to consider his observations on religion in India.[1] In the first place, he examines the relation between modern, rational business activity and religious beliefs, showing the appeal to traders and businessmen of such religious cults as Jainism, Parsiism, and Vallabhacharya. Orthodox Hinduism, on the other hand, which makes contemplation the supreme religious value accessible to man, restrains rather than stimulates business activity. Secondly, Weber emphasizes the importance of caste as the institutional framework of Hinduism. 'Caste, that is the ritual rights and duties it gives and imposes and the position of the Brahmans, is the fundamental institution of Hinduism.' The interconnections of caste and Hinduism are now generally recognized. M. N. Srinivas in his book on the Coorgs, writes that: 'The structural basis of Hinduism is the caste system which occasionally even survives conversion to Christianity or Islam'.[2] He also observes that the spread of Hinduism in India has proceeded by 'Sanskritization' of the ritual and belief of tribes or other non-Hindu groups and at the same time by the incorporation of these groups as castes within the caste system. 'The complete absorption of any group of people into the Hindu fold is indicated by their becoming a caste.'

Thus, caste may be regarded in one aspect as the church organization of Hinduism, without which the latter could not have maintained itself or spread.[3] At the same time, this feature also explains the inability of Hinduism to expand outside India. As Sir Charles Eliot observed, '. . . its small power of expansion beyond the seas (is) explained by the fact that it is a mode of life as much as a faith . . . a convert cannot enter the fold by any simple ceremony like baptism. The community to which he belongs must adopt Hindu usages and then it will be recognized as a caste, at first of very low standing but in a few generations it may rise in the general esteem. A Hindu is bound to his religion by almost the same ties that bind him to his family. Hence the strength of Hinduism in India. But such ties are hard to knit and Hinduism has no chance of spreading abroad unless there is a large colony of Hindus surrounded by an

[1] Max Weber, *The Religion of India*.
[2] *Op. cit.*, p. 212.
[3] Cf. Srinivas, *op. cit.*, p. 31, 'Caste enabled Hinduism to proselytize without the aid of a church'.

241

appreciative and imitative population'.[1] The ability of Hinduism to expand in India was also increased by its tolerance in the matter of religious belief. As S. Radhakrishnan writes, '. . . Hinduism developed an attitude of comprehensive charity instead of a fanatic faith in an inflexible creed. It accepted the multiplicity of aboriginal gods and others which originated, most of them, outside the Aryan tradition, and justified them all. . . . Hinduism is wholly free from the strange obsession of the Semitic faiths, the obsession that the acceptance of a particular religious metaphysic is necessary for salvation . . .'.[2] Hinduism spread by the gradual Sanskritization of tribal beliefs and rituals, but it was also willing to leave much in the original beliefs and rituals untouched, allowing them, so to speak, to wither away as the newly incorporated group sought to improve its status in the caste hierarchy by purifying its customs and ideas. This tolerance, however, was an additional reason for the failure of Hinduism to spread elsewhere; though tenaciously defended as a way of life Hinduism lacks missionary fervour as a system of beliefs. It could not be expected, either, that it would give rise to a sect so convinced and ruthless as the Puritans in Western Europe. On the contrary, with the exception of Buddhism, which spread outside India, all the sects and reforming movements in Hinduism have been assimilated again into the main tradition, often as new caste groups.

Since the work of Durkheim and Max Weber, few theoretical contributions have been made to the sociological study of religion. Social anthropologists, as I mentioned earlier, have based their studies largely upon Durkheim's theory. In sociology, Weber's influence has been predominant, and has stimulated two principal, and related, lines of enquiry; one concerned with the characteristics, doctrines and social significance of religious sects, and the other with the connection between religious doctrines and social classes. An important early contribution came from his friend, Ernst Troeltsch, whose book on *The Social Teachings of the Christian Churches*[3] complemented Weber's writings by giving a more detailed account of the social ethics of different Christian churches and sects. In the same field of concern with sectarian movements is R. Niebuhr's *The Social Sources of Denominationalism*. More recently there have been detailed empirical studies of particular sects, in terms of their relations with and responses to the social milieu in which they exist,[4]

[1] Sir Charles Eliot, *Hinduism and Buddhism* (London, 1921), Vol. I. Introduction, pp. xxxvii.

[2] *The Hindu View of Life.*

[3] In German 1912; English translation 1931.

[4] *See*, for example, B. R. Wilson, *Sects and Society* (London, 1961).

and also, especially in the work of H. Desroche in France, as precursors of socialist political groups.[1]

The second line of enquiry has also dealt with issues which Weber formulated. First, there has been a continuing debate on the significance of the Protestant ethic in the origin and growth of modern capitalism.[2] Secondly, there has been more intensive and exact study of the differences between social classes in religious belief and observance. Thus, there has gradually emerged a very useful *sociography of religion;* it is particularly advanced in France, where G. Le Bras has inspired many descriptive and quantitative studies.[3] This kind of study has been pursued in a wider context, that of the process of secularization which, it is generally agreed, has been taking place in Western societies over the past century. In this process it is apparent that secularization has affected the working class more than other classes. Thus, in Britain the 1851 Census (the only one in which a question about religious affiliation has been included) showed that the official church, the Church of England, had already lost many adherents to the Nonconfomist churches and sects, and many of these were working class or lower middle class people.

Throughout the latter half of the nineteenth century and during the twentieth century church attendance, and to a lesser extent religious belief, has steadily declined, and it has declined most in the working class. One survey has shown that whereas one-fifth of middle class informants say they never attend church, almost one-third of working class informants say this; and at the other end of the scale the proportion of those in the middle class who say they attend church frequently is two and a half times as great as that in the working class.[4] The same phenomenon has been observed, in a

---

[1] *See* especially, H. Desroche, *Les Shakers américains* (1955).

[2] Among the major contributions to this controversy are: R. H. Tawney, *Religion and the Rise of Capitalism* (London, 1926), A. Fanfani, *Catholicism, Protestantism, Capitalism* (English trans., London, 1935), H. M. Robertson, *Aspects of the Rise of Economic Individualism* (London, 1933).

[3] *See* F. Boulard, *Premiers itinéraires en sociologie religieuse* (Paris, 1954). Professor Le Bras' own work has ranged very widely, from historical studies of Catholicism in France to studies of religious belief and observance in contemporary France and then to studies of other world religions. His major writings are collected in *Etudes de sociologie religieuse* (2 vols., Paris, 1955, 1958). The exact description and measurement of religious practice has made some progress in other countries more recently. There is now published an *International Yearbook for the Sociology of Religion* (Köln-Opladen, 1965 on), and a *Sociological Yearbook of Religion in Britain* (London, third volume, 1970), which bring together surveys of religious affiliation and practice, and more general studies.

[4] T. Cauter and J. S. Downham, *The Communication of Ideas* (London, 1954).

more extreme form, in France, where the Catholicism of the upper and middle classes contrasts with Marxism as the dominant creed of the working class. In both Britain and France the recognition of this decay of religion in the working class led to the organization of working class missions, in Britain especially at the end of the nineteenth century (e.g. the Salvation Army), and in France at various times, most recently in the form of the *prêtres ouvriers*. These features of the process of secularization, although generally recognized, have only just begun to be systematically studied. A recent work by Bryan Wilson, *Religion in Secular Society* (London, 1966) reviews the theological and sociological discussions of secularization, presents information on the decline of religious belief and practice, and briefly compares the situation in Britain and the USA.

It is interesting to observe here that the USA constitutes an exception to the account we have given of secularization. In American society religious belief and observance have tended to increase rather than decline, and church attendance is high; at the same time class differences in the extent of religious practice are slight. Here also, sociological explanation is for the most part lacking, although one important study, W. Herberg, *Catholic, Protestant, Jew* (New York, 1955) proposes an explanation along Durkheimian lines in terms of the needs of immigrants' descendants for a community to which they can refer for moral rules and purposes.

Another theme in Max Weber's sociology of religion, and more prominently in the work of Troeltsch, was the social significance of religious sects. As we have noted, there has been a number of recent studies of particular sects, but one other general feature deserves some mention; namely, the proliferation of sects in some modern societies. In Britain and the USA during the past century innumerable new sects have been founded, and many of them have flourished.[1] This may reflect an 'individualization' of religious belief, which should perhaps be considered along with secularization as an outstanding feature of the religious situation in industrial societies.

About religious belief and observances in contemporary India there is little precise information. India is predominantly Hindu; some 85 per cent of the population are Hindus, 10 per cent Muslims, and the remainder Christians, Sikhs, Parsis, etc. There has been intermittent religious conflict, between Hindus and Muslims, and

[1] For example, in England and Wales between 1851 and 1952 the number of places of worship of 'other denominations' (i.e. denominations considered too small for listing separately by the Registrar-General) increased nine-fold; a much greater proportionate increase than occurred in any of the larger denominations.

between Sikhs and Hindus (though in this case the conflict was mainly political, with the aim of creating a separate Punjabi speaking state); and as I have noted earlier Hinduism has given rise to Hindu traditionalist parties and movements. Nevertheless, India is securely established as a secular or multi-religious state.[1]

In the past, religious sects and reforming movements were largely re-absorbed into the main tradition of Hinduism. But with the social and economic changes now occurring it seems unlikely that such assimilation will be possible. Insofar as Hinduism is closely linked with caste and the joint family it must be affected by changes in those institutions; and they are now being modified by economic development, by political decisions, including changes in the law of property which facilitate individual ownership, and by the spread of new social doctrines. The impact of nationalist and socialist ideas must already be considerable, and an enquiry carried out in this field would be of great interest. More generally, it would be valuable to study, even in particular areas, the nature and intensity of religious belief and observance, giving attention to variations between specific social categories and groups, such as men and women, age groups, educational categories and social strata.[2]

The sociological study of morals had, at the outset, some features in common with the study of religion. In particular, it was guided by evolutionist and positivist ideas. Two classical works of an evolutionist character are L. T. Hobhouse, *Morals in Evolution* (1905) and E. Westermarck, *The Origin and Development of Moral Ideas* (1906). Although differing in their conceptions of the source and basis of moral ideas, these two thinkers largely agreed in their accounts of the development of morals and especially in the conclusion that the history of mankind was marked by moral progress. Hobhouse claimed to show that moral ideas had developed towards the ideal of a rational ethic, and to establish a broad correspondence between this evolution of morals and general social development. Westermarck, although giving more emphasis to the similarity in the moral rules of different societies (primitive and civilized), also considered that in the course of social evolution moral ideas have become more enlightened and that the influence of reason upon morality is likely to increase in the future. This approach to the study of moral rules was first criticized, and then

[1] On this subject, *see* G. S. Sharma (ed.), *Secularism; Its Implications for Law and Life in India* (Bombay, 1966); and Donald E. Smith, *India as a Secular State* (Princeton, 1963).

[2] The relation between religion and changes in law is studied in detail in J. Duncan M. Derrett, *Religion, Law and the State in India* (London, 1968).

largely abandoned, by later sociologists. Various influences contributed to this change; a general rejection of the evolutionist approach, scepticism about social progress, new philosophical views on the character of moral judgments, and doubts about the value of associating sociology and social philosophy as closely as Hobhouse, in particular, had done.

The last of these issues was also important in French sociology, where the influence of Comte led to attempts to construct a normative 'science of morals'. This was an important aspect of Durkheim's sociology, the whole of which was quite evidently dominated by a concern with the moral and social problems of France at the end of the nineteenth century. The most influential expression of this positivist endeavour was probably the book by Lucien Lévy-Bruhl, *La morale et la science des moeurs* (1903). Both Durkheim and Lévy-Bruhl argued that moral rules could be derived from a science of morals; Lévy-Bruhl in the work just cited, and Durkheim principally in the preface to *The Division of Labour in Society*, and in his essay on 'La détermination du fait moral'.[1]

Recent sociologists have given up the attempt to formulate a sociological moral theory. For the most part, they have also ceased to concern themselves with the general direction of moral development or progress. A notable exception is Morris Ginsberg, who in a recent essay,[2] first criticizes social scientists who have assumed a necessary connection between the diversity of moral codes and ethical relativity, and philosophers who have regarded moral judgments as emotive and consequently neither true nor false; and then goes on to propose an examination of moral variations in terms of 'differences of level'. He argues persuasively that different levels can be distinguished in terms of such characteristics as the universality of rules, the range of experience embodied in the rules, the rationality of underlying principles, and the extent of self-criticism, and that development from lower to higher levels can be traced; although, as he concedes, it is 'the higher that decide that they are the higher'. Ginsberg recognizes that the comparison of moral codes can only be made in terms of very general and abstract moral ideas, and that the actual 'moral life' or 'way of life' of a particular society may be extremely complex and comprise divergent elements. In fact, when we examine moral codes in this way as the effective complexes of values which regulate behaviour it becomes extremely difficult to make any classification in terms of levels of development. Moreover,

---

[1] English trans. in E. Durkheim, *Sociology and Philosophy*

[2] 'On the Diversity of Morals', in *Essays in Sociology and Social Philosophy*, Vol. I.

the existence of divergent elements in the moral systems of complex societies renders more doubtful the identification of the dominant moral ideas. It might be argued, indeed, that one characteristic of the development of morality, at least in some modern societies, is the increasing diversity of moral beliefs within each society.

Most recent sociologists and anthropologists who have made any study of moral codes have confined their attention to particular societies. Anthropologists seem to have been relatively successful in describing comprehensively, and with some impartiality, the system of social control, including morality, in the societies which they study, though it should be noted that few anthropological studies are tested by other independent observations. Sociologists, because of the diversity and conflict of moral codes in more complex societies, have had a more difficult task, and their interpretations are notoriously controversial. What is presented as the 'central value system' of a society often turns out to be little more than the individual sociologist's own prejudiced view of the society in which he lives. It should be added that many sociological and psychological accounts of moral values fail to distinguish between the values which are asserted in a formal way and the values which actually guide behaviour in everyday situations of moral choice. However, a number of sociological studies, avowedly 'interpretative' in their approach, do illuminate some aspects of morality in advanced industrial societies. A prominent theme in these studies is the decline of the Protestant ethic. In the USA, David Riesmann, in *The Lonely Crowd*, and W. H. Whyte, in *The Organization Man*, have described and analysed the change from social behaviour directed by individual self-reliance and self-assertiveness, to behaviour ruled by the wish to conform and to be fully accepted by the social group. According to Whyte, whereas the Protestant ethic in America emphasized the 'pursuit of individual salvation through hard work, thrift, and competitive struggle', the new Social Ethic 'makes morally legitimate the pressures of society against the individual'. It involves 'a belief in the group as the source of creativity; a belief in "belongingness" as the ultimate need of the individual; and a belief in the application of science to achieve the belongingness'.[1]

These studies are concerned with American society, but they indicate some more general features of morality in modern societies. The separation between morality and religion is one prominent feature in the cultural changes of the past century, both in the sense that a clear distinction has been made between ritual and moral

[1] *See also* T. Roszak, *The Making of a Counter-Culture*, for a discussion of another 'new morality' which has made its appearance in the last decade.

247

rules, and in the sense that, with the decline of religious belief, it has been necessary to find a new basis and content for the moral rules. To some extent this separation has shown itself in the fact that religion has become more an individual and private matter (as indicated by the multiplication of sects and the spread of personal religion not involving church membership), while morality has become more social, in that it is increasingly concerned with social justice rather than individual virtue. This change of emphasis is apparent even in the moral doctrines of religious organizations, which are much more concerned with social relations and social problems than ever in the past. W. H. Whyte, in discussing the religion of the 'organization man', observes that there is a disposition to tone down the doctrinal and ritual aspects of religion, and to emphasize above all the utility of religion in solving social problems and creating fellowship.

This increasing concern with social morality has had two consequences which are more evident in European societies than in America. The first is a greater tolerance of diversity in such individual behaviour as is not connected with major social controversies. The social sciences have also played a part in this, by disclosing some of the external factors influencing conduct, and thus diminishing the scope of moral praise and blame. The second consequence is that moral codes have become closely associated with political doctrines. Moral disagreements are now very frequently political disagreements, and moral beliefs are largely incorporated in political ideologies. In all these respects there is great scope for sociological studies of morality which have hardly yet been attempted. Such studies would have to take account of the influence upon moral codes of the development of modern science (including social science) and its popularization,[1] and to relate the diversity of moral codes to the conflict of political doctrines, tracing in particular the influence of nationalism, socialism, and other modern ideologies.

In India, as in some other developing countries, the changes in morality which we have just discussed are as yet hardly apparent. Morality is still closely associated with religious belief, and moral and ritual rules are interfused. Caste and the joint family have so far resisted the growth of individualism, and a traditional social ethic prevails. Nevertheless, some significant precursors of change can be seen, in the rise of modern political doctrines such as nationalism and socialism which expound new conceptions of morality, and in re-interpretations of traditional Hindu ethics. One such

[1] On one aspect of this question see Jack D. Douglas (ed.), *The Impact of Sociology* (New York, 1970).

re-interpretation is to be found in the writings of S. Radhakrishnan, especially in his *Hindu View of Life*, which expounds the moral teaching of Hinduism in relation to issues which have become particularly significant in the modern world, violence and war, social equality, and the position of women. Equally, in the writings of Gandhi, Hindu religion and ethics are presented in the context of contemporary social and political problems; and the distinctive traditional valuation of asceticism is attenuated into a rejection of the excessive luxury and pleasure seeking of the highly industrialized countries. There is in present-day India a deep-rooted conflict between traditional moral conceptions and the aspirations expressed in the political movements for economic growth and social reform, and it is an open question how far reformulations of the traditional morality will be adequate to incorporate these new purposes. In this conflict, intellectuals occupy an important place, since they, in particular, are caught between the traditional culture and Western social and political doctrines. The secularization of learning, and its social consequences, which Karl Mannheim discussed in a fascinating essay on the European intelligentsia,[1] are now apparent in India. This conflict of ideas will determine Indian culture in the future and it deserves more attention from sociologists than it has yet received.

[1] K. Mannheim, *Essays on the Sociology of Culture*, Part II, 'The Problem of the Intelligentsia'.

Chapter 15

LAW

The sociology of law

The study of law has always involved some consideration of the general character of social institutions and societies. Traditionally, however, legal theory in Europe was based upon a philosophical conception of natural law, and was thus closely associated with moral philosophy and theology. The beginnings of a sociology of law can be traced to Montesquieu's *De l'esprit des lois* (1748). Montesquieu still discussed law partly in terms of 'natural law', but he also described and compared the laws of different societies, and related the differences to the diversity of conditions, both geographical and social, of these societies.

From the middle of the nineteenth century, with the emergence of sociology as a distinct discipline, the sociological study of law progressed rapidly, although it assumed diverse forms. Marx and the later Marxists undertook their critique of law as an ideology which conceals class divisions at the same time as it promotes the interests of the dominant class. A major work of Marxist scholarship, Karl Renner's *The Institutions of Private Law and their Social Functions*,[1] examines how the functions of the legal norms which regulate property, contract, succession and inheritance change with changes in the economic structure of capitalist society, yet without necessarily altering the formulation of the legal norms themselves, which thus come to obscure the significant social relationships of developed capitalism.

Other sociologists, and jurists influenced by sociological ideas, began to study legal rules in the context of the theories of social evolution which dominated European social thought in the latter part of the nineteenth century.[2] H. S. Maine, in his *Ancient Law*,

[1] Originally published in *Marx-Studien* I (1904). A revised version was published as a book in 1928, and an English translation appeared in 1949, with a long Introduction by O. Kahn-Freund, who discusses the changes in law and society which have occurred since Renner's work was first published.

[2] Many of them were particularly influenced by the German historical school of jurisprudence founded by Savigny; this is notably the case with Comte, Spencer and Maine.

made a distinction between 'static' and 'progressive' societies, and argued that 'the movement of progressive societies has hitherto been a movement from status to contract'. He meant by this, as he explained elsewhere, that 'the individual is steadily substituted for the family, as the unit of which civil laws take account'. Maine considered that these changes were brought about by non-legal factors, since 'social necessities and social opinion are always more or less in advance of Law'. and he examined under three headings, Legal Fictions, Equity, and Legislation, the agencies by which, in progressive societies, law is brought into harmony with society. Emile Durkheim's conception of the development of law is similar in important respects to that of Maine, for his distinction between 'repressive' and 'restitutive' law resembles that between 'status' and 'contract'. Repressive law is characteristic of societies in which the individual is scarcely distinguished from the group to which he belongs; while restitutive law is typical of modern societies in which the individual has become a distinct legal person able to enter freely into contractual relationships with other individuals. L. T. Hobhouse, in conformity with his general evolutionist approach, dealt systematically with the development of law and justice,[1] from private redress and the blood feud, through the stage of composition for offences, to the stage of civilized justice. In discussing the latter Hobhouse records not only the establishment of the notion of individual responsibility (following Maine), but also the influence of increasing class differentiation until recent times. He also discusses changes in the character of punishment, and examines the relations between law, religion and morals. Another study, by an outstanding jurist, which is similar in its approach, is P. Vinogradoff, *Historical Jurisprudence*.[2] Max Weber's studies of law showed, in the view of Roscoe Pound,[3] a much clearer understanding of the nature of law than those of earlier sociologists, and they have had a greater influence in the growth of a sociological jurisprudence, since Weber's conception of law as being concerned with the adjustment of conflicting values is close to the jurist's conception of law in terms of the adjustment of conflicting interests. Weber, although not an evolutionist, was also interested in the classification of types of law and in the development of law in Western societies. He conceived this development as an increasing rationalization of law, accompanying the general rationalization of life in industrial societies as a

[1] L. T. Hobhouse, *Morals in Evolution*, Ch. 3.
[2] Oxford, 1920.
[3] Roscoe Pound, 'The Sociology of Law' in G. Gurvitch and W. E. Moore, *Twentieth Century Sociology*.

result of the growth of capitalist economic enterprise and of bureau-cracy.[1]

A particular problem which emerged from the evolutionist studies concerned the existence of law in primitive societies. Some of the earlier sociologists and anthropologists made a sharp distinction between primitive societies governed entirely by custom, and civil-ized societies ruled primarily by law.[2] It was a major contribution of B. Malinowski to emphasize the study of social control as a whole, and to distinguish the different types of rules which regulate behaviour in primitive (as in civilized) societies. Malinowski's definitions of law and his account of primitive law are no longer generally accepted,[3] but they greatly influenced the study of law as a type of social control in primitive societies and did much to clarify the whole sociological discussion of social control. At the present time a widely accepted definition of law is that proposed by Roscoe Pound: 'social control through the systematic application of the force of politically organized society'.[4] In this sense law exists in many primitive societies. R. H. Lowie gives examples of developed systems of administration of justice, particularly among African Negroes.[5] Recently, Max Gluckman has studied in detail the judicial process among one African people, the Lozi of Barotseland,[6] and has shown how closely it corresponds with the judicial process in Western societies, in the modes of reasoning and in the underlying concepts. However, in the case of more primitive peoples, law may be entirely lacking; for example, the Eskimo, as Lowie observes, 'closely approach anarchy'.

The anthropological studies have brought out clearly an aspect of the sociology of law which is emphasized by Roscoe Pound in his survey of the subject.[7] The earlier writers largely identified law with 'laws' or legislation, and their distinction between primitive and civilized societies was based upon the absence of legislation in the former. But jurisprudence and the sociology of law, as Pound says,

[1] Max Rheinstein (ed.), *Max Weber on Law in Economy and Society*, esp. Ch. 8.

[2] See above, pp. 229–31.

[3] *See* I. Schapera, 'Malinowski's Theories of Law' in R. Firth (ed.), *Man and Culture*.

[4] Roscoe Pound, *loc. cit.* Cf. E. A. Hoebel, *The Law of Primitive Man* (Cambridge, Mass., 1954): 'A social norm is legal if its neglect or infraction is regularly met, in threat or fact, by the application of physical force by an individual or group possessing the socially recognized privilege of so acting.' (p. 28.)

[5] R. H. Lowie, *op. cit.*, Ch. 7.

[6] Max Gluckman, *The Judicial Process among the Barotse of Northern Rhodesia* (Manchester, 1955).

[7] Roscoe Pound, *loc. cit.*

have to be concerned with three things: (i) the legal order, i.e. a regime of adjusting relations and ordering conduct by the systematic application of the force of a politically organized society: (ii) the authoritative principles and guides to the determination of disputes in a society, a code of precepts based upon accepted ideals; and (iii) the judicial process[1] and the administrative process. The scope of the sociology of law is thus very wide and it overlaps with other fields of sociological study. It is not concerned only with types of legal system and their development but with the character of legislation (and thus with some problems of political sociology and social philosophy), with the judicial process and the social influences upon it, and with the administration of justice involving problems of punishment which are also the concern of criminology and moral philosophy. I shall consider some aspects of these problems later in this chapter.

Law in India

Indian law has a number of features which are of interest to the general sociology of law. A pre-eminent characteristic is the historically close connection between law and religion. Maine observed that '. . . India has not passed beyond . . . the stage at which a rule of law is not yet discriminated from a rule of religion'.[2] Max Weber discussed the same feature, but gave a somewhat different emphasis by referring to a dominant 'priesthood' which 'was able to regulate the whole range of life ritualistically, and thus to a considerable extent to control the entire legal system', and by maintaining that 'according to prevailing *Hindu* theory, all law is contained in the Dharma-Sutras'.[3] Maine considered that all early law was characterized by lack of differentiation between legal and religious rules and he made explicit comparisons in this respect between Hindu and early Roman law. In *Ancient Law* he argued that the absolute predominance of religion in Hindu law only gradually emerged.[4] In later works he illustrated this development in the case of the property rights of married women, which were slowly restricted under religious influence,[5] and attributed the general development to the important

[1] The importance of studying the judical process was first clearly stated in B. Cardozo, *The Nature of the Judicial Process* (Yale, 1941).

[2] *Ancient Law*, p. 14.

[3] Max Rheinstein (ed.), *loc. cit.*, p. 234.

[4] 'Among the Hindus the religious element in law has acquired a complete predominance. Family sacrifices have become the keystone of all the Law of Persons and much of the Law of Things.' (*Ancient Law*, p. 113). See also J. Duncan M. Derrett, *Religion, Law and the State in India* (London, 1968).

[5] *Early History of Institutions* (pp. 321–6).

place of ancestor worship in the Hindu religion, which invested almost all legal rules and relationships with a religious significance as family rituals.[1] J. D. Mayne, in his *Hindu Law and Usage*,[2] takes a similar view, arguing that 'Hindu law is based upon immemorial customs, which existed prior to, and independent of, Brahminism', but that as Hinduism spread and the influence of the Brahmin caste grew, law was increasingly dominated by religious conceptions.He adds that while the great codes, such as that of Manu, and the outstanding commentaries such as the Mitakshara, were addressed primarily to Brahmins and acquired increasing authority for all Hindus with the spread of Brahminism,[3] nevertheless many local usages remained distinct and retained their authority.[4] In addition, there grew up particular systems of law for certain occupational groups, especially in trade and commerce and also, as Weber observes, the castes came to establish their own laws and to acquire autonomy in the administration of justice through their possession of a highly effective means of compulsion, namely expulsion.[5]

The influence of British rule upon Indian law was complex. In the administration of justice it established a centralized system, by the creation of British courts and by the removal of judicial functions from the caste *panchayats*. But the law administered was still customary and largely Hindu law. Until 1864 the British judges were obliged to consult the pundits attached to their courts on all disputed points of law. Subsequently, with the growth of knowledge of the Hindu codes and texts, the British judges themselves decided points of law, and it has been argued that in their determination to administer Hindu law without introducing any changes they imparted to it a rigid character which it had not previously had, by their exclusive reliance upon ancient authorities.[6] At the same time, some legal changes were deliberately brought about where Hindu customs directly conflicted with the moral ideas of the rulers, as in the cases of child marriage and the immolation of widows. Beyond this, British rule necessarily introduced into India new cultural values and ways

[1] This is examined at length in *Early Law and Custom* (1883).
[2] Tenth edition.
[3] Which we have referred to earlier as 'Sanskritization'.
[4] Mayne, *loc. cit.*, pp. 5–9.
[5] Max Rheinstein (ed.), *op. cit.*, p. 327.
[6] J. D. Mayne, *loc. cit.*, p. 44. 'The consequence was a state of arrested progress, in which no voices were heard unless they came from the tomb'. K. M. Kapadia illustrates this with reference to the Hindu joint family, observing that the British Courts were accepting, for nineteenth-century conditions, the law as it had been expounded in the eleventh and twelfth centuries (*Marriage and Family in India*, pp. 247–51).

of life, and especially, new forms of economic activity. The development of industry, trade, urban centres and Western education brought about changes in opinion which ultimately affected law through the growing body of legislation. One general tendency of legislation has been to extend the legal rights of the individual; for example, the right to retain personal earnings by the Gains of Learning Act, 1930, and the right of women to a share in the property of the joint-family, by the Hindu Law of Inheritance (Amendment) Act. 1929 and the Hindu Woman's Right to Property Act, 1937. Since independence the process has continued and fundamental changes in the law of inheritance have been brought about by the Hindu Succession Act, 1956. In this respect, Indian law shows a development from 'status' to 'contract', similar to that which Maine traced in Western societies. This has been accompanied by an increasing rationalization of law, both in the administration of justice and in the body of legal rules themselves. The rationalization of the legal rules was promoted first by the endeavours of British judges to reconcile conflicting texts, and later by the growth of systematic legislation, especially since the attainment of independence, to deal with the social problems of a developing industrial society. This recent development exemplifies the process which Max Weber termed 'substantive rationalization'; that is, the elaboration of a type of law appropriate to the expediential and ethical goals of the political authority concerned. And since this political authority is no longer predominantly influenced by a priestly caste, the rationalization is taking place, as it did in Western Europe, by the separation of religious commands from legal precepts for the settlement of those human conflicts which have no religious relevance.[1]

Law and social change

Many writers, among them Maine, Hobhouse, Vinogradoff and Max Weber, whose writings we have briefly considered, have distinguished between types of legal order, and have discussed aspects of the development of law over longer or shorter periods. Their work constitutes the basis for modern sociological studies of particular systems of law, and of specific changes in legal systems. A particular interest attaches to the changes which have occurred in the modern world, with the transformation of Western capitalist societies, the emergence of Soviet-type societies, and the establishment of new independent nations.

The first of these changes has been brilliantly analysed by W. G.

---

[1] Max Rheinstein (ed.), *op. cit.*; J. Duncan M. Derrett, *op. cit.*

Friedmann.[1] He begins from the observations made by Dicey in a classical study of law and opinion in nineteenth century Britain,[2] that Benthamite reforming legislation which had been intended merely to do away with inequalities which interfered with free competition, could be extended, and was being extended, to deal with the new inequalities arising out of that competition. The increase in social legislation and the rise of the labour movement tended to halt or reverse the process which Maine had referred to as the movement from status to contract. Friedmann has summarized the outcome of these changes in the mid-twentieth century (with reference to Britain, but with a wider bearing) in the observation that: 'Freedom of contract, in so far as it survives today, no longer pertains to the individual'. He shows how the role of property in bargaining has been modified, first, by changes in the relations between employer and worker through the abolition of the crime of conspiracy, the recognition of collective bargaining, social security legislation and changing legal interpretations by the courts of the employment contract, and secondly, by direct limitations on the use of private property (stricter interpretation of abuse of rights, limitation of patent rights, statutory obligations imposed upon owners of industrial property, and public ownership). The functions of contract itself have changed with the development of the 'standard contract', resulting from economic concentration, the substitution of collective for individual bargaining, and the expansion of the welfare, social service, and industrial management functions of the state.

These changes in law are evidently connected with the more general change, in Western societies, from *laissez faire* and individualism towards some form of collectivism. In an essay published in 1930 and significantly entitled 'The new feudal system', Roscoe Pound observed that: 'Today the typical man (i.e. the wage earner or salaried employee) finds his greatness not in himself and in what he does but in the corporation he serves'. More recently, this aspect of modern Western societies has been discussed and analysed at length, especially by American sociologists and social commentators, who have introduced into the social sciences such expressions as 'the other-directed man', 'the organization man', to refer to the typical individual of mass society.[3] The contrast is great with those nineteenth century figures, the independent capitalist entre-

[1] W. G. Friedmann, *Law and Social Change in Contemporary Britain* (London, 1951); see also his later work, *Law in a Changing Society* (London, 1959).

[2] *See* above, p. 232.

[3] *See above* p. 247.

preneur, or the anomic individual, who attracted the attention of sociologists like Weber and Durkheim.

The Soviet-type societies present many similar features. Here too the legal situation of the individual is largely determined by his status in a particular group; and in these societies the groups themselves are organized in a more inflexible official hierarchy. Such societies have, in addition, experienced difficulties in maintaining a rule of law, because of the extreme concentration of political power. It is interesting that the reaction against Stalinism in the USSR has given rise to doctrines of legal positivism, which are critical of any sociological interpretation of judicial decisions.[1] Such doctrines are no doubt intended to establish and support a rule of law, but in the absence of any sociological studies of the administration of justice they also conceal important social pressures upon the judiciary which, in the USSR, as elsewhere, frequently arise from conceptions of 'public policy' formulated by political organizations.

In the under-developed societies which have experienced nationalist revolutions, in some cases against colonial rule, other features are apparent. There is a continuous rationalization of law, by codification or the introduction of foreign codes (e.g. at an earlier stage, the adoption of the Swiss Code in Turkey), and by the growing proportion of systematic legislation in relation to customary and traditional law. In some societies, as for example India, there is an increasing separation of law from religion and morality. Associated with this is the emergence and growth of a legal profession (whose members have in many cases been educated in the West) distinct from the priestly caste which formerly had a monopoly in interpreting the law. Finally, in those societies where kinship groups were an exceptionally important element in the social structure (and this is so in such countries as India and China, as well as in tribal societies) there is apparent the kind of development, which Maine traced historically, from 'status' to 'contract', in which the individual rather than the family or other kin group comes to be treated as the basic legal entity. This development, however, takes a different form from that in the nineteenth century European societies, since in most

---

[1] *See* S. F. Kechekyan, 'Social Progress and Law' in *Transactions of the Third World Congress of Sociology*, Vol. VI. 'Soviet juridical science refutes such propositions (i.e. of the 'sociological' school of jurists) aimed at justifying the arbitrary actions of the judge and administrative discretion. . . . . Socialist law proceeds from the precept that it is the duty of the judge and administrative bodies to follow exactly and implicitly the directives comprised in law and in the normative acts issued on the basis of the laws.'

cases the growth of contractual relationships is limited by the extent of economic planning and the provision of social welfare services.[1]

In Western societies the changes in law which we have considered came about partly as a result of economic concentration, partly as a result of changes in class relations and in the character of the state. During the nineteenth century law could be studied, as by Marx, as an ideology which reflected the interests of a ruling class; class influences upon law could easily be discerned in the character of legislation and of judicial decisions and in the nature of the penalties inflicted for offences against private property. But the Welfare State in Britain and the similar régimes in other West European countries are far removed from this state of affairs. The rise of the labour movement, the extension of the franchise, the spread of social reform and egalitarian doctrines, all brought about radical changes in legislation, in the social atmosphere which influences judicial decisions, and in the general class structure of these societies.[2] In consequence, law now functions more impartially in the regulation of conflicts between individuals or groups, so far as class interests are concerned; but a new and serious problem has emerged in the relationship, in legal conflicts, between the individual and large organizations, whether public or private.

One of the most significant changes over the past century in almost all societies has been the growing mildness of punishment. Hobhouse, in *Morals in Evolution*, referred to the barbarity of the criminal law in Europe down to the nineteenth century, but observed that from the end of the eighteenth century many individual reformers and reform movements (among the latter especially 'the Society of Friends, French Rationalists, English Utilitarians and the Evangelicals') began to have an effect in disseminating more humane views. The changes have been most rapid in the present century, both in the reform of the criminal law and in penal reform. They have been brought about by the combined action of diverse influences. In the first place, as Hobhouse noted: 'As society becomes more confident in its power to maintain order, the cruelty and callousness that are born of fear are seen in a new light. More humane influences make themselves felt, and from that moment excessive severity begins to militate against the proper execution of the law. . . .' Secondly, the generally greater stability of modern societies, resulting from the extension of rights, the reduction of class differences, and rising material standards, has been a favourable

---

[1] *See*, for a discussion of some of these issues, J. N. D. Anderson, *Family Law in Asia and Africa* (London, 1968).

[2] *See* above, pp. 196–7.

condition for the spread of humanitarian ideals, which received powerful support from the labour movement. There have been many setbacks even in the recent progress of humanitarian ideals—the Fascist regimes, the Stalinist period of Soviet-type societies, some colonial regimes, some political regimes established by nationalist revolutions, and above all the mounting horror of modern warfare— yet on balance the ideals are more firmly and widely held and are more clearly expressed in legal systems. Finally, the social sciences themselves, and especially sociology and psychology, have played an important part in bringing about reforms, by their direct influence upon policy makers and their influence upon public opinion. A new discipline, criminology, which is to a large extent a specialized and applied branch of sociology,[1] has grown rapidly during the present century, and has begun to affect legal thought and the general public discussion of punishment and penal institutions.

Law in the system of social control

At various points in this chapter I have referred briefly to the relations between law and other means of social control, and between law and social structure. These relations have been the subject of much controversy and deserve a fuller examination.

It is well established that early law, and primitive law, are not clearly distinguished from religious and moral precepts and doctrines. Maine refers to an early state of society in which a rule of law is not yet discriminated from a rule of religion. Firth, in discussing the regulation of conduct in primitive societies, observes: 'If a system of European law is intelligible only by reference to the changing practices of the people, their system of ethics, their institutional structure, their judges' ideas of what is 'reasonable', and non-legal factors which lead them to keep it or break it, how much more must this be so in the case of a primitive people without such a clear-cut scheme?'[2] Even in some more advanced societies law, religion and morals are still largely fused; for example, classical Hindu society represents an extreme form of the permeation of law by religion. It is very largely, indeed, among the European societies that we can trace the growth in thought and social practice of a clear distinction between religion, morals and law which is now taken for granted. This distinction does not, however, imply a complete autonomy of the three forms of control. In most societies moral rules are still strongly influenced by religious conceptions, and in all societies law is based upon moral notions. This is evident in the

---

[1] It is discussed more fully from this aspect in Ch. 20 below.
[2] R. Firth, *Human Types*, p. 137.

sphere of legislation, which always derives from social doctrines and ideals; but equally, in the administration of justice and in judicial decisions there has almost always been reference to the fundamental moral ideals of the society, in terms of 'reason', 'natural law', 'equity', or in recent times 'public policy', as well as to the written or traditional law.

The dependence of law upon morals, sometimes religiously interpreted,[1] does not make the distinction between them any less important. The domains of law and morals are not co-extensive. There are many legal rules which concern matters of expediency rather than morality; on the other hand, there are many things which might generally be regarded as morally desirable but either cannot be brought about by law or would lose their moral character if they were so brought about. But where the two domains overlap law seems to be determined rather than determining; it serves to consolidate a social order and way of life which has been brought into existence by moral and political doctrines or by unwilled changes in social structure. Thus, the changes in law in European societies since the nineteenth century can be attributed, as we have seen, to changes in economic structure and class relations, to the rise of the labour movement, and to the spread of democratic, socialist and humanitarian doctrines. In modern India, again, changes in law are resulting from economic development, and from the spread of modern social and political doctrines. In a more general way, the maintenance of a legal order depends upon the moral climate of a society. The effectiveness of legal regulation never rests solely upon the threat of physical sanctions, but upon a general attitude of respect for law, and for a particular legal order; and this attitude itself is determined by moral approval of law as embodying social justice.

The specific character of the legal regulation of conduct may, however, be considered from another aspect. In general, legal rules are more precise than moral rules and legal sanctions are more definite and frequently more effective than those of morality.[2] As Bertrand Russell has remarked, the good behaviour of even the most

[1] As, for example, in some European countries in which Roman Catholicism is the predominant religion, and the law relating to marriage and divorce is influenced or determined by religious rules.

[2] Durkheim, and later Radcliffe-Brown, distinguished between 'diffuse' and 'organized' sanctions, the latter being those of law. Cf. K. N. Llewellyn and E. A. Hoebel, *The Cheyenne Way* (1941), where the distinction between legal and moral sanctions in a primitive society is carefully examined. In this and other writings Llewellyn argues that law is more imperative than normative— 'Law has teeth'.

exemplary citizen owes much to the existence of a police force. It is hardly possible, and certainly not useful, to conceive a society of any degree of complexity in which social behaviour would be regulated entirely by the moral sanctions of praise and blame. Contemporary international relations provide an illustration of the importance of law in social control. It may well be true that the moral unity of mankind is now greater than ever in the past, at least in the sense that a moral duty towards all men, irrespective of their nationality, race, religion, etc., is more or less clearly recognized by many people in all countries. But these moral sentiments are largely ineffective in regulating the relations between societies when clashes of interest or doctrine occur, because they have not been precisely stated in legal rules, and above all because they are not supported by any legal sanctions. During the twentieth century, there have been attempts through international political organizations to lay the foundations of an international legal order, but they have made little progress in face of national sovereignty. Sanctions are easily imposed when the interests of powerful nations coincide, but then justice is not always done; and when justice needs to be done there is lacking any international authority with power to constrain.

This discussion indicates the importance of law, which, though it rests upon moral sentiments and is influenced by the institutional arrangements of a socie.y, brings about by the precision of its rules and sanctions, a degree of certainty in human behaviour, which cannot be attained through other types of social control. Moreover, law may have an independent influence upon social behaviour, at least in the sense that it establishes generally in a society attitudes and conduct which were initially those of a small minority of reformers. Thus in the USSR law has established models of behaviour which were, at first the aspirations of a small group of revolutionaries. In Western Europe, the varieties of democratic Welfare State have been created by systematic legislation, guided by the doctrines of social reformers. Such changes would have been less effective if they had depended entirely upon moral opinion and moral sanctions.

Chapter 16

EDUCATION

Durkheim defined education as 'the action exercised by the older generations upon those who are not yet ready for social life. Its object is to awaken and develop in the child those physical, intellectual and moral states which are required of him both by his society as a whole and by the milieu for which he is specially destined'.[1] This action, the socialization of new generations, necessarily takes place in all societies, but it assumes many different forms in respect of the social groups and institutions involved, and in respect of its own diversity and complexity.

We may consider, first, the extent to which education is a specialized social activity. In the simplest societies, where there is in any case little specialization of function, education is not organized as a separate activity; it is provided by the family, the kin group and the society as a whole through participation in their everyday routines of living. But in many primitive societies above the simplest level formal instruction is given at puberty, before initiation as an adult member of the society. Lowie gives as an example the educational scheme of the Yaghan (Tierra del Fuego): 'Each Yaghan novice gets two sponsors, who supervise his conduct throughout the several months' seclusion. Physically, each boy or girl has to learn rigorous self-control . . . For moral instruction the neophytes jointly listen to some venerable tribesman's lectures. In addition to mass instruction, each boy or girl is tutored by some close relative who has noted defects in the pupil's character and now takes pains to correct them . . . Finally, there is true vocational preparation. The girls' training, to be sure, amounts to little more than rounding out previously acquired skills . . . The boys, however, are relatively backward at corresponding tasks of adult life, and hence require schooling'.[2]

In more developed societies, formal education acquires greater importance, the period of systematic instruction increases, and a specialized occupational group of teachers is formed. Thus, in ancient India, formal instruction was provided by the Brahmins.

[1] E. Durkheim, *Education et sociologie* (Paris, 1922).
[2] R. H. Lowie, *Social Organization*, pp. 195–6.

'The pupil's first introduction was at the age of 5. He commenced by learning the alphabets for the first time, and this was open to the children of all ages. Then followed the ceremony of tonsure, which was followed by the student initiation ceremony at the normal age of 8 for a Brahmin, 11 for a Kshatriya, and 12 for a Vaisya . . . The entire educational system was based upon this ancient system of studentship which laid more emphasis on life than on learning or instruction. It was based upon constant personal contact between teacher and pupil, bound together by a spiritual tie, living in a common home . . . The student, after his initiation, entered into a new life whereby he was re-created by his teacher and had to undergo a twofold course of discipline—physical and spiritual'.[1] This educational system, however, extended to only a small minority of the population; and it was conducted by a hereditary priesthood chiefly concerned with the transmission of religious doctrines and largely excluding secular instruction. 'Throughout the centuries the Brahmins, who were the repositories of learning and the directors of Hindu life, continued to brood upon and to elaborate the sacred texts and to transmit their study in religious institutions—*tols* and *vidyalayas* and *chatuspathis*—to succeeding generations'.[2] Technical skills were imparted chiefly through the family and the occupational group, in informal and practical ways. This was very largely the case in all societies before the rise of modern science and industry, but the predominance of religious education was greater in India than in Western or Islamic societies, or in China.

The disorder accompanying the decline of the Mogul Empire brought about a deterioration and contraction of the educational system, and the subsequent establishment of British rule in India. though it made possible educational progress, also created new problems. At first the British rulers supported traditional Hindu schools and promoted the establishment of new schools and colleges; but in 1835 the decision was taken that the Government should aim at the promotion of European literature and science in India, that the medium of instruction should be English, and that the Education Fund should be employed on English education alone.[3] This policy

[1] Sobharani Basu, 'Forest Universities of Ancient India', *Year Book of Education* (London, 1957), pp. 316–32.

[2] J. R. Cunningham, in L. S. S. O'Malley, *Modern India and the West*, p. 138.

[3] This decision was the work of Lord William Bentinck, first Governor-General of India, and of Lord Macaulay, Chairman of the Education Committee. As early as 1829 Lord William Bentinck had written in a letter to the Committee of Public Instruction that he had 'no hesitation in stating to your Committee and in authorizing you to announce to all concerned in the superintendence of your native seminaries that it is the wish and admitted policy of

263

received the support of many Indian reformers, among them Raja Ram Mohan Roy, and generally of the new commercial middle class; but as D. P. Mukerji observes, it tended to reinforce the separation of the upper classes from the rest of society.[1] True, those responsible for education reiterated in the education dispatch of 1854 that, 'our object is to extend European knowledge throughout all classes of the people'; but they also proposed to continue with the same methods: 'This object must be reflected by means of the English language in the higher branches of instruction and by that of the vernacular languages of India to the great mass of the people'. Furthermore, in practice effort was concentrated upon the education of the upper and middle classes, and relatively little progress was made in establishing an adequate system of primary education.[2] Thus in 1881–2 it is estimated that 1 in 10 boys and 1 in 250 girls between the ages of 5 and 12 years attended school, and most attended for such short periods as not to become permanently literate. In 1939, 90 per cent of the population were still illiterate. Undoubtedly, therefore, the educational system tended to maintain and even increase the gulf between the upper classes and the mass of the population, and to make this separation more complete by transforming it into one of language and general culture.

However, such divisions exist in many societies. Wherever there is a system of social stratification, there is a corresponding differentiation within the educational system. This is the case even in some primitive societies; the Maori, for example, had commoners' schools during the winter, but also 'sacred colleges' which were open only to the nobility, especially the elder sons of chiefs. In most literate societies, literacy has been limited to the upper social strata. Modern industrial societies, which established mass literacy for the first time, did not by this means remove the educational distinctions between different social strata. These were maintained by the existence of different types of schools for the various social groups, such as the English 'public schools', reserved for children of the upper class,

the British Government to render its own language gradually and eventually the language of public business throughout the country . . .'. Lord Macaulay, in his famous Minute, argued that, 'We must at present do our best to form a class who may be interpreters between us and the millions whom we govern, a class of persons Indian in blood and colour but English in tastes, in opinions, morals and intellect'.

[1] D. P. Mukerji, *Modern Indian Culture*, Ch. 4, 'Education and Social Mobility'.

[2] It should be remembered, however, that British educational policy in India was not dissimilar from that in Britain itself, where in 1850 less than half the children of school age went to school. In Britain there was no national system of primary education until 1870, or of secondary education until 1944.

or by the unequal distribution of opportunities for higher education.

Higher education in most Western countries traditionally involved the languages and culture of classical Greece and Rome, and this reinforced the distinction between the educated gentleman and the rest of society. Such cultural differences have persisted, in an attenuated form, into the twentieth century; they underly the conflict between the 'two cultures', literary and scientific, and in some societies have constituted an obstacle to the development of technical education. As Lowie says: 'Historical accident had lent distinction to verbal felicity, while manual dexterity and whatever savoured of the utilitarian had long ranked low in the social scale'.[1] Besides this broad division between elites and masses, between education for intellectual and for manual occupations, there has existed a more refined graduation of educational facilities. Thus, in England before 1944, the educational system can be broadly characterized as having provided elementary education for working class children, secondary (grammar school) education for middle class children, and public school (fee-paying) education for children of the upper and upper middle classes. The Education Act of 1944 modified without destroying this differentiation; it is still largely the case that upper and upper middle class children go mainly to public schools, middle class children to secondary grammar schools and working class children to secondary modern schools, and this is only gradually being changed by the development of comprehensive schools.[2]

It should be observed that this kind of educational differentiation exists in all modern societies, however much they may be committed to egalitarian and welfare policies. The communist countries have made large claims for their success in establishing social equality, but to take one instance, while the progress of education in the USSR since 1917 has been extremely rapid, it has not resulted in the elimination of educational privilege. During 1958 a number of

[1] R. H. Lowie, *Social Organization*, p. 208.

[2] *See* J. Floud, A. H. Halsey and F. M. Martin, *Social Class and Educational Opportunity*, on school entrants. The authors also discuss the reasons for the continuing inequalities, and the problems of differences in educational performance between middle class and working class children. On the Universities, see R. K. Kelsall, *Report on an Inquiry into Applications for Admission to Universities* (London, 1957). For a general discussion of these aspects of education in Britain *see* D. V. Glass, 'Education', in *Law and Opinion in the Twentieth Century*. A useful survey of educational inequalities in the USA is to be found in Everett C. Hughes, 'Educational Selection in the United States of America' (1958). A number of studies of educational selection in different societies are brought together in A. H. Halsey, J. Floud, and C. A. Anderson (eds.), *Education, Economy and Society* (London, 1961).

speeches and memoranda in connection with the reform of the Soviet educational system provided data which had hitherto not been available, and which showed that only 55 per cent of children actually completed the ten year educational course by reaching the eighth grade in schools, and that in the institutions of higher education in Moscow only one third of the students were of working class or peasant origin, the other two thirds coming from families in a relatively small social stratum, the intelligentsia. In India, since the achievement of independence, there has been considerable progress in the expansion of educational facilities, and with the development of village schools and of educational opportunities for children of lower castes, there is substantially more equality of access to education. Yet there are still notable inequalities; basic education which incorporates Gandhi's ideas on the combination of intellectual and manual work is provided for most children (and most do not go beyond the primary stage of education), but the upper classes of Indian society still send their children to English type grammar and public schools.

These data, taken from different modern societies, show that educational differences are closely related to social stratification. Other types of social differentiation, between the sexes, ethnic groups, or religious groups, have also frequently been associated with differences in kind or quality of education. In most societies until recently women had much less chance than men of obtaining higher education, and this is still the case in India. Africans, in the Union of South Africa, and in many colonial territories, have very limited opportunities even for secondary education; and in the USA the Negroes, although their situation has improved, are still educationally handicapped. In many societies, at different times, religious minorities have been discriminated against in education as in other respects.

Thus the function of education in preparing the child for a particular milieu in society (as Durkheim defined it) has traditionally meant preparing him for membership of a particular group in the social hierarchy. The experience of modern egalitarian policies indicates that it is very difficult to eliminate this feature, not least because the intellectual and social criteria frequently overlap; the children of high status families are in general better qualified for higher education, because of a variety of advantages which they enjoy. It may be that in the more egalitarian societies of the future, when social equality has come to be taken for granted, these difficulties will cease; but it seems more likely that so long as there is educational selection privileged groups will always be emerging within society and that only deliberate policy and contrivance will succeed in maintaining a rough equality.

So far I have been largely concerned with educational differentiation, that is, with the transmission to younger generations of different codes of behaviour, largely influenced by social class. But as Durkheim observed, education also prepares the child for life in society as a whole, by transmitting common social traditions through the language, religion, morals and customs of the society. The inculcation of national values has been especially apparent in modern societies, and was for long reflected in the social prestige of teachers. The French *instituteur* who was given his title in the Revolution of 1789 ('celui qui institue la Nation'), acquired under the Third Republic a remarkable prestige and importance.[1] In the USA the schoolma'am played a similar role from the end of the nineteenth century in transforming the children of immigrants into 100 per cent Americans. The way of life which is taught may derive from different sources. In France, under the Third Republic, an attempt (to which Durkheim contributed by his writings) was made to teach a secular morality, but its principal result was to establish a deep division, and conflict, between the state schools and the Catholic schools and eventually between the adult generations which they produced. In Britain the 1944 Education Act imposed as a statutory obligation that in every school the day shall begin with collective worship and religious instruction shall be given; and official circulars and pamphlets have emphasized the Christian tradition as a foundation of the British way of life. The schools in communist societies instil into their pupils the social and political doctrines of Marxism. In India, the whole conception of basic education is founded upon the social philosophy of Gandhi, itself inspired by Hinduism, and almost all public discussions of education link the present with the traditional Hindu system of education.

The emergence of new nation-states and the growth of nationalism in nineteenth century Europe were concurrent with the spread of literacy and in most societies they resulted in an increasing emphasis upon indoctrination in the educational process. The same phenomenon has reappeared in the twentieth century, in those societies which have attained independence from colonial rule or have constituted themselves as modern nation-states, but it has been countered by other influences. The diffusion and acceptance of the ideal of the underlying unity of mankind, despite international conflict, has brought greater tolerance of cultural diversity and genuine efforts

[1] There is an excellent study in R. Thabault, *Mon Village* (Paris, 1944), especially. p. 220 *seq.*, 'Portrait de l'instituteur'.

to conceive and present each specific cultural tradition as a single element in a larger and richer whole. At the same time, while educational differentiation within societies has remained, increasing social mobility through the educational system has tended to break up the dominant national culture, and to create diversity. In India, the British system of education had, besides its disadvantages, one extremely good effect in establishing for the first time, opportunities of higher education for members of the lower castes. The growth of science and the rapidity of social change have also affected the codes of behaviour taught in educational institutions, imparting to them, in some modern societies, a tolerant or tentative character which may have as one result adolescent and adult aimlessness. A balance between firm traditions and standards of behaviour, tolerance, adaptability to change, and the spirit of free enquiry, is difficult to attain; and some of the failures of modern education (exacerbated by other social influences) in its prime function of socialization can be seen in the youth problems which are prevalent in all industrial societies. A country such as India, which is just embarking upon a period of rapid change, may well experience such difficulties in an acute form and there is indeed much evidence of inter-generational conflict over social values, expressed in opposition to arranged marriages, in student indiscipline, and in general juvenile lawlessness.[1]

These problems raise a larger question about the effectiveness of formal education as a means of social control. In earlier societies, where literacy was highly valued as a basis of prestige and power, teachers were also highly regarded; moreover, the teachers themselves usually came from high status families. Formal education imparted to a minority destined to rule and administer society a definite code of morals and behaviour. In China, the examinations 'tested whether or not the candidate's mind was thoroughly steeped in literature and whether or not he possessed the *ways of thought* suitable to a cultured man . . .' and in the eyes of the Chinese masses 'a successfully examined candidate and official was by no means a mere applicant for office qualified by knowledge . . . He was a proved holder of magical qualities . . .'[2] In this respect, although not a priest, he resembled the Hindu *guru* who was a spiritual counsellor as well as teacher and official. With the achievement of

[1] It is a general feature of the societies undergoing rapid industrialization that children tend to become the teachers of their parents (thus reversing the normal process of education). For a short account of the problems in various societies, see Margaret Mead (ed.), *Cultural Patterns and Technical Change*, pp. 268–78, 'Fundamental Education'.

[2] Max Weber, 'The Chinese Literati', in Gerth and Mills ,*From Max Weber.*

mass literacy in modern industrial societies the social prestige of the teacher tended to decline, for he was no longer set apart as the literate man; moreover, teachers for the primary levels of education were themselves recruited from the lower social strata. In addition the growth of business established the pre-eminence of wealth in conferring prestige and power. As an Indian educationalist writes of present-day India, 'In sharp contrast to the past when teachers were honoured however poor or powerless they may have been, contemporary India places a disproportionate emphasis on monetary standards'.[1] The values professed by the teacher are no longer authoritative; they have to compete with the values presented to the child by his family, peer group, and the media of mass communication. Neither sociologists nor social psychologists have yet given much attention to the conflicts between different codes of behaviour and different agencies of social control in contemporary societies.[2] Yet there are manifest conflicts between family and school, arising from social mobility (e.g. in many Western societies the conflict between the working class standards of the family and the middle class standards of grammar school and university), from the secular character of state education as contrasted with the religious values of the family (or vice-versa), or from inter-generational differences in outlook; and there are equally serious conflicts between school and peer group, and between school and mass media. British education in India was frequently criticized for its secular character: 'It is criticized as being alien to the Indian temperament, which is essentially religious, and as offending against the cherished conviction that religious and moral instruction is a necessary part of education. To it are ascribed a decline or disappearance of respect of youth for age, a denial of the natural authority of parents over their children and of teachers over their pupils, a widespread disregard of religious and social sanctions, and a growth of moral laxity'.[3] But the experience since the achievement of independence shows that there are more general influences at work. While there may not be any general conflict between Hinduism and modern science,[4] there is certainly conflict between the way of life of an industrial society based upon science and the traditional way of life which is

[1] Humayun Kabir, *Education in New India* (London, 1956).
[2] An earlier American study, W. Waller, *The Sociology of Teaching* (New York, 1932), has many illuminating observations on the conflict between family and school, but it has not been followed up.
[3] O'Malley, *Modern India and the West*, p. 665.
[4] Much less than between science and other world religions which impose upon their adherents, as philosophical Hinduism does not, definite beliefs of a cosmological and historical kind.

intimately bound up with Hinduism. Recent educational planning in India has in fact largely followed the British precedent by placing the major emphasis upon the secular aspect of education, the communication of modern knowledge, and by leaving aside the problems of moral and religious instruction.

Education as a type of social control

Helvétius, referring to education in eighteenth century France, observed that men 'are born ignorant, not stupid; they are made stupid by education'. This is not the modern view. There may still be societies in which men's minds are stupefied by dogmatic instruction which inclines them to accept uncritically the views of political or religious authorities; but the general character of formal education has been profoundly changed by modern science and technology. The greatest difference between primitive and early societies, and modern industrial societies, is perhaps that in the former education is largely concerned with transmitting a way of life,[1] while in the latter, because of the mass of available knowledge, the application of science to production, and the elaborate division of labour, formal education not only preponderates in the process of education as a whole, but is largely devoted to the communication of empirical knowledge. One aspect of this change is indicated by the observation that in modern societies the content of education is less literary and more scientific. A second major difference is that whereas in earlier societies a relatively unchanging way of life and sum of knowledge were transmitted, the scientific knowledge communicated by modern education is expected to change; moreover, education is increasingly required to prepare individuals for a changing rather than a static world.[2]

It is from this aspect that we can regard formal education in modern societies as communicating independently ideas and values which play a part in regulating behaviour. Malinowski rightly men-

[1] The accounts given above of formal education in primitive societies, in China, and in ancient India, all show that more emphasis was laid upon moral training for social life than upon learning and instruction.

[2] However, a considerable volume of criticism of education in the industrial countries has developed in the past decade. On schools, *see* Paul Goodman, *Growing Up Absurd* (New York, 1960); and Annette T. Rubinstein (ed.), *Schools Against Children* (New York, 1970). There is now a vast literature on the role and organization of universities; *see*, for diverse views, Alexander Cockburn and Robin Blackburn (eds.), *Student Power* (Harmondsworth, 1969); Julian Nagel (ed.), *Student Power* (London, 1969); S. M. Lipset and Philip G. Altbach, *Students in Revolt* (Boston, 1969); Eric Ashby and Mary Anderson, *The Rise of the Student Estate in Britain* (London, 1970); Christopher Jencks and David Riesman, *The Academic Revolution* (New York, 1968).

tioned this feature in its rudimentary form in primitive societies when he included the 'rules of craftsmanship' as an element in social control. Modern science and technology are not only the basis of infinitely more complex rules of craftsmanship but also of a general rational approach to nature and social life, which has an increasingly important role in establishing and maintaining social co-operation. More than this, scientific thought has, over the past three centuries, implicitly or explicitly criticized the ideas propounded in religious and moral doctrines and has largely been responsible for the changes which the latter have undergone. The whole rationalization of the modern world with which Max Weber was pre-occupied, is connected with the development of science. And since the chief vehicle of this development, at least during the past century, has been the educational system, we can legitimately speak of formal education as a type of social control.

There is, however, still another way in which education has contributed independently to the regulation of conduct, and that is in the early socialization of the child. The work of educational reformers such as Montessori and Froebel, has brought about great changes in the education of young children. Certainly these reforms in part reflect moral notions external to the educational system, but in part they have been influential in changing moral ideas in society at large. So far as they were connected with scientific studies of the development of children, such as those of Piaget, they arose from the development of the social sciences. Moreover, being based upon this observation and analysis of the actual development of children's activities, needs and problems, they can be regarded as having arisen very largely within the educational sphere itself, as independent discoveries. We should observe, also, that the changes in the formal education system have themselves brought about changes in family socialization, aided by the spread of social science knowledge. In this sense the formal education of children has genuinely originated new forms of regulation of behaviour.

Education in a broad sense, from infancy to adulthood, is thus a vital means of social control, and its significance has been greatly enhanced in the last two decades by the rapid expansion of education at all levels in the developing countries, and by the equally rapid growth of secondary and higher education in the industrial countries. Through education new generations learn the social norms and the penalties for infringing them; they are instructed also in their 'station and its duties' within the system of social differentiation and stratification. In modern societies, where formal education becomes predominant, and where an important occupational group of teachers

271

comes into existence, education is also a major type of social control (as the source of scientific knowledge) which is in competition and sometimes in conflict with other types of control. This conflict may become particularly acute with the extension of higher education to a much larger proportion of the population, as the experience of the last few years has shown in Europe and North America; and the educational system may increasingly provide one of the main sources of change and innovation in the social norms.

Notes on Reading for Part IV

War

See especially the following general studies which have been referred to in the text:

Aron, Raymond. *Peace and War: A Theory of International Relations* (New York, Doubleday, 1966).

Bramson, Leon, and Goethals, George W. (eds.) *War: Studies from Psychology, Sociology, Anthropology* (New York, Basic Books, 1964).

Buchan, Alastair. *War in Modern Society: An Introduction* (London, Watts, 1966).

Richardson, L. F. *Statistics of Deadly Quarrels* (Pittsburgh, Boxwood Press, 1960).

Wright, Quincy. *A Study of War* (2nd edn., Chicago, University of Chicago Press, 1965).

There is a useful collection of papers dealing with war in primitive as well as modern society, with aggression, and with alternatives to war, in Morton Fried, Marvin Harris, and Robert Murphy (eds.), *War: The Anthropology of Armed Conflict* (New York, Doubleday, 1968).

In addition to the studies of war there has been some interesting and relevant work on the role of the military in society: see, for example, S. Andreski, *Military Organization and Society* (revised edn., London, Routledge and Kegan Paul, 1968); S. E. Finer, *The Man on Horseback: The Role of the Military in Politics* (London, Pall Mall Press, 1962).

Revolution and Counter-Revolution

The following general studies deal with the subject from various aspects:

Arendt, Hannah. *On Revolution* (New York, Viking Press, 1965).

Eckstein, Harry (ed.). *Internal War* (New York, Free Press, 1964).

Friedrich, Carl J. (ed.). *Revolution* (New York, Atherton Press, 1966).

Brinton, Crane. *The Anatomy of Revolution* (rev. edn., New York, 1957).

Meisel, James H. *Counter-Revolution: How Revolutions Die* (New York, Atherton Press, 1966).

Meusel, Alfred. 'Revolution and Counter-Revolution', *Encyclopaedia of the Social Sciences* (New York, McGraw-Hill, 1934), Vol. XIII.

Wolf, Eric R. *Peasant Wars of the Twentieth Century* (New York, Harper and Row, 1970).

There is a large literature on particular revolts, revolutions and counter-revolutions; the following works illuminate diverse aspects of these phenomena:

Carr, E. H. *The Bolshevik Revolution, 1917–1923* (London, Macmillan, 1950), Vol. I.

Luxemburg, Rosa. *The Russian Revolution* (Ann Arbor, University of Michigan Press, 1940).

Reed, John. *Ten Days That Shook the World* (new edn., Harmondsworth, Penguin Books, 1966).

Trotsky, Leon. *The History of the Russian Revolution* (Ann Arbor, University of Michigan Press, 1957).

Lefebvre, Georges. *The Coming of the French Revolution* (Princeton, Princeton University Press, 1947).

Rudé, George. *The Crowd in the French Revolution* (Oxford, Oxford University Press, 1959).

Fitzgerald, C. P. *The Birth of Communist China* (Harmondsworth, Penguin Books, 1968).

Hobsbawm, E. J. *Primitive Rebels* (Manchester, Manchester University Press, 1959).

Guevara, Che. *Guerrilla Warfare* (New York, Monthly Review Press 1961).

Social control

A pioneer study, which established the general use of the term, is E. A. Ross, *Social Control* (New York, 1901). Among other earlier studies the most useful and interesting are W. G. Sumner, *Folkways: A study of the Sociological Importance of Usage, Manners, Customs and Morals* (Boston, 1906) and C. H. Cooley's discussion in parts of *Social Organization* (1909) and *Social Process* (1918).

G. Gurvitch, 'Social Control' in G. Gurvitch and W. E. Moore (eds.), *Twentieth Century Sociology*, provides a short review of studies in this field and an analysis of the major problems. Another valuable recent discussion is Roscoe Pound, *Social Control through Law* (1942). A good introduction to the subject, with particular reference to primitive societies, is R. Firth, *Human Types*, Ch. V. 'The regulation of conduct'.

Some of the outstanding contributions to the study of social control are to be found in the writings of B. Malinowski; *see* especially his *Crime and Custom in Savage Society* (London, 1926), and his Introduction, (pp. xvii–lxxii) to H. I. Hogbin, *Law and Order in Polynesia* (London, 1934).

Custom, public opinion

On custom *see* the works of B. Malinowski and W. G. Sumner quoted above.

Public opinion is discussed in most textbooks of social psychology; for example, Kimball Young, *Handbook of Social Psychology* (rev. edn., London, 1957), Ch. 14. For a short introduction to the subject *see* A. Sauvy, *L'opinion publique* (Paris, 1956). There is a more elaborate treatment in D. Katz, *Public Opinion and Propaganda* (1954) and W. Albig,

Modern Public Opinion (1956). For valuable earlier discussions see W. Lippmann, *Public Opinion* (New York, 1922) and M. Ginsberg, *Psychology of Society* (London, 1921).

The reader should also consult some of the particular studies mentioned in the text.

Religion

Wach, Joachim. *Sociology of Religion* (Chicago, 1944).
A general survey.
Birnbaum, Norman, and Lenzer, Gertrud (eds.). *Sociology and Religion* (Englewood Cliffs, Prentice-Hall, 1969).
A valuable collection of readings with commentary and bibliography.
Radcliffe-Brown, A. R. 'Religion and Society' in *Structure and Function in Primitive Society.*
An excellent short statement of a modified functionalist view.

Among the classical studies of religion *see*:

Frazer, Sir J. G. *The Golden Bough* (London, 1890), especially Chapters I–V. An abridged version of these chapters has been published under the title *Magic and Religion* (London, 1945) and provides a useful short account of Frazer's views.
Tylor, E. B. *Primitive Culture* (London, 1871). Tylor's evolutionary account of religion was criticized by Andrew Lang; see *Magic and Religion* (London, 1901), and *The Making of Religion* (3rd edition, 1909).
Spencer, H. *Principles of Sociology*, Vol. III (London, 1896), Ch. I–XVI.
Weber, Max. *Gesammelte Aufsätze zur Religionssoziologie* (3 vols., Tübingen, 1923). Most of these are now available in English as follows: *The Protestant Ethic and the Spirit of Capitalism* (London, Allen & Unwin, 1930).
The Religion of China: Confucianism and Taoism (London, Allen & Unwin, 1952).
Ancient Judaism (London, Allen & Unwin, 1953).
The Religion of India: The Sociology of Hinduism and Buddhism (London, Allen & Unwin, 1958).
Troeltsch, E. *The Social Teaching of the Christian Churches* (English trans., London, Allen & Unwin, 1931).
Tawney, R. H. *Religion and the Rise of Capitalism* (2nd ed., London, 1937).
Complements and criticizes Max Weber's account of the relations between Protestantism and capitalism. For additional references to the literature on this subject see above, p. 144.
Durkheim, E. *Elementary Forms of the Religious Life* (English trans., 4th impression, London, Allen & Unwin, 1960).
There have been several critical studies of Durkheim's theory; *see* especially M. Ginsberg, 'Durkheim's Theory of Religion' in *Essays in Sociology and Social Philosophy*, Vol. I.

Radcliffe-Brown, A. R. *The Andaman Islanders* (Cambridge, 1922).
An outstanding functionalist study of a primitive religion.
Malinowski, B. *Science, Magic and Religion and Other Essays* (selected
and with an introduction by R. Redfield, Glencoe, 1948).
Lowie, R. H. *Primitive Religion* (London, 1936).
Contains a comparative analysis of four types of primitive religion, a
good critique of earlier theories of religion, and a general discussion of
the social influence of religion.
James, W. *The Varieties of Religious Experience.*
A classical study of the psychological aspects of religion.
The American Journal of Sociology, May 1955. Sixtieth Anniversary
Issue, Part II.
Contains six papers on religion from early issues of the Journal, including
papers by Simmel, Sumner, and Albion Small; and a foreword on the
sociological study of religion by Everett C. Hughes.

There have been few major studies of religion in the recent period. An
outstanding anthropological study is E. Evans-Pritchard, *Nuer Religion*
(Oxford, 1956). In sociology there have been numerous small-scale
sociographic studies of church membership and religious participation;
there is a useful survey of such studies and presentation of the statistical
data in M. Argyle, *Religious Behaviour* (London, 1958). *See also Current
Sociology,* V (1) (1956), 'Sociology of Religions', and the reports on
sociological studies of religion in various countries in *Archives de Sociologie
des Religions* (Paris), Vol. I (1957). For sociological interpretations of
modern Western religions *see* especially G. Le Bras, *Etudes de Sociologie
religieuse* (2 vols., Paris, 1955 and 1958), and W. Herberg, *Protestant,
Catholic, Jew* (New York, 1955).

The psychological study of religion seems to have lapsed since Freud's
contribution and the earlier psychoanalytic discussions (*see* S. Freud,
Totem and Taboo (London, 1950), *Moses and Monotheism* (London,
1939) and *The Future of an Illusion* (London, 1934). There are few
references to religion in most textbooks of social psychology, and only
minor studies of the psychology of religious belief or conversion. There
is an interesting discussion of psychological aspects of religion in two
books by R. Bastide; *Sociologie et Psychanalyse* (Paris, 1950) especially
pp. 46–56, and *Eléments de Sociologie religieuse* (2nd ed., Paris, 1949).

On religion in India, *see:*

Weber, Max. *The Religion of India* (cited above).
Eliot, Sir Charles. *Hinduism and Buddhism* (3 vols., London, 1931).
A classical work which is largely concerned with doctrines and history,
but which also contains much illuminating sociological discussion.
Radhakrishnan, S. *Religion and Society* (London, Allen & Unwin, 1935).
Srinivas, M. N. *Religion and Society among the Coorgs of South India*
(Oxford, O.U.P., 1952).
An excellent anthropological study of religious belief and ritual among

one group of Hindus, with a chapter which discusses the more general sociological characteristics of Hinduism.

Morality

There are a number of comparative studies of moral codes. For the evolutionist approach, *see* L. T. Hobhouse, *Morals in Evolution* (7th edn. London, 1951; with a new introduction by M. Ginsberg), and E. Westermarck, *The Origin and Development of Moral Ideas* (London, 1906). The writings of Max Weber on religion (cited above) are very largely concerned with the moral codes of the world religions. Among recent comparative studies *see* especially M. Ginsberg, 'On the Diversity of Morals' in *Essays in Sociology and Social Philosophy*, Vol. I, and A. Macbeath, *Experiments in Living* (London, 1952).

There is a good discussion of the relation between the science of morals and moral philosophy, and a review of some attempts to construct a 'scientific morality' in G. Gurvitch, *Morale théorique et science des moeurs* (2nd edn., Paris, 1948).

In the field of social psychology there are numerous studies and discussions of attitudes and opinions, but few worthwhile studies of moral beliefs. There is much of sociological and psychological interest on morality and religion in H. Bergson, *Les deux sources de la morale et la religion* (Paris, 1933). The psychology of morals was discussed at length by V. Pareto, *The Mind and Society* (English trans., 4 vols., London, 1935).

Flugel, J. C. *Man, Morals and Society* (London, 1945) is an interesting study from a psychoanalytic point of view. *See also* M. Ginsberg, *Psychology of Society* (London, 1921).

The moral codes of Indian society are examined in the works on Hinduism and Buddhism cited above, but also particularly in S. Radhakrishnan, *The Hindu View of Life* (London, 1927).

Law

The most useful general works on the sociology of law are:
Ehrlich, E. *Fundamental Principles of the Sociology of Law* (New York, 1942).
Rheinstein, M. *Max Weber on Law in Economy and Society*.

An excellent short survey of the major contributions, and analysis of problems, is Roscoe Pound, 'Sociology of Law' in G. Gurvitch and W. E. Moore (eds.), *Twentieth Century Sociology*.

Friedmann, W. G. *Legal Theory* (London, 1957) is a stimulating discussion of a wider field, which has several chapters on the sociological contributions to the study of law. *See also*, W. G. Friedmann, 'Sociology of Law', *Current Sociology*, X/XI (1), 1961–62; and Vilhelm Aubert (ed.), *Sociology of Law* (Harmondsworth, Penguin Books, 1969).

277

A valuable work of reference, containing both readings and cases, is S. P. Simpson and J. Stone, *Law and Society* (3 vols., St Paul, Minnesota, 1948–50).

On primitive law *see* Malinowski (works cited above), E. A. Hoebel, *The Law of Primitive Man* (Cambridge, Mass., 1954), and particular studies mentioned in the text.

On law and social change, *see* for general studies of the development of law, H. S. Maine, *Ancient Law* (London, 1861) and P. Vinogradoff, *Historical Jurisprudence* (Oxford, 1930). The best studies of change in a modern legal system, in relation to social structure and social doctrines, are A. V. Dicey, *Law and Opinion in England in the Nineteenth Century* (2nd edn., London, 1926), and W. G. Friedmann, *Law and Social Change in Contemporary Britain* (London, 1950).

There has been little sociological writing on Hindu Law, except in the earlier comparative studies by Maine and Max Weber (referred to in the text). A standard work on Hindu law is J. D. Mayne, *A Treatise on Hindu Law and Usage* (11th edn. edited by N. C. Aiyar, Madras, 1950). S. V. Gupte, *Hindu Law in British India* (1947) gives a good account of the effects of British rule. *See also* the recent work by J. Duncan M. Derrett, *Religion, Law and the State in India* (London, Faber and Faber, 1968).

Education

The major work on the sociology of education is still Durkheim's *Education et sociologie* (Paris, 1922; English trans., 1956). N. Hans, *Comparative Education* (rev. edn. London, Routledge and Kegan Paul, 1958) is a useful study of different types of educational system. Many aspects of the relation between education and society are examined, on a comparative basis, in A. H. Halsey, J. Floud and C. A. Anderson (eds.), *Education, Economy and Society* (London, 1961). For a general survey of writing up to the late 1950s *see* Jean Floud and A. H. Halsey, 'Sociology of Education', *Current Sociology*, VIII (3), 1958.

Much sociological study of the educational system has been devoted to its connection with social stratification and social mobility. The most comprehensive work dealing with Britain is Jean Floud, A. H. Halsey and F. M. Martin, *Social Class and Educational Opportunity* (London, Heinemann, 1956). *See also*, on particular aspects of the problem, Brian Jackson and Dennis Marsden, *Education and the Working Class* (London, Routledge and Kegan Paul, 1963), and the study by J. W. B. Douglas reported in *The Home and the School* (London, MacGibbon and Kee 1964) and *All Our Future* (London, MacGibbon and Kee, 1969). Some data for the U S A are given in Everett C. Hughes, 'Educational Selection in the United States of America' (mimeographed 1958), and in Harold Howe, *Equality of Educational Opportunity* (Washington, D.C., 1966). Some aspects of educational selection in France are examined in P.

Naville (ed.), *Ecole et société* (Paris, 1959) and more recently in P. Bourdieu and J. C. Passeron, *Les héritiers* (Paris, Editions de Minuit, 1964).

There have been relatively few sociological studies, since Durkheim's work, which have dealt with the types of education, the functions of education in social control, the structure of educational institutions, or the social role of teachers. On the last subject, however, *see* Thorstein Veblen, *The Higher Learning in America* (New York, 1918), and the stimulating book by F. Znaniecki, *The Social Role of the Man of Knowledge* (New York, 1940). As I noted in the text there has been a revival of interest in the structure of universities in particular, and some of the recent literature is mentioned on page 270, note 2. The social effects of scientific knowledge have been discussed by several writers; from a Marxist point of view by J. D. Bernal, *The Social Function of Science* (London, 1939); more briefly, but in lively fashion, by Bertrand Russell, *The Impact of Science on Society* (London, Allen & Unwin, 1952). *See also* V. Gordon Childe, *Society and Knowledge* (London, Allen & Unwin, 1956). There has also developed a more general interest in the role of intellectuals in society; *see*, for example, Lewis A. Coser, *Men of Ideas* (New York, 1965).

Part V

SOCIAL CHANGE

Chapter 17

CHANGE, DEVELOPMENT, PROGRESS

From its beginnings sociology was closely connected with the philosophy of history and the interpretations of the rapid and violent changes in European societies in the eighteenth and nineteenth centuries. The Scottish historians and philosophers (in particular, Ferguson, Millar, and Robertson), the French *philosophes* (Voltaire, Turgot, Condorcet), the German historians and philosophers (Herder, Hegel), were all concerned to explain or interpret the social and political revolutions of their age, within the framework of a general theory of history. Their influence was profound and can be seen plainly in later writers such as Saint-Simon and Buckle, and in the work of the first sociologists, Comte, Marx and Spencer. Even later in the nineteenth century a historical or evolutionary approach was dominant in sociology and anthropology. Max Weber presented no theory of universal history, but it is evident that all his sociological work was inspired by a historical concern with the origins and significance of modern Western capitalism and more widely by his preoccupation with the increasing rationalization of social life and its implications for human freedom. Durkheim rejected Comte's evolutionary sociology, but his own outline of a classification of societies is conceived in terms of an evolutionary scheme, and his *Division of Labour in Society* is concerned with a process of development from primitive to modern societies. Hobhouse was more immediately indebted to Comte and Spencer, and the whole of his sociological work is clearly directed by a philosophical conception of social progress.

In these earlier sociological theories, the notions of 'change', 'evolution', 'development' and 'progress' are sometimes confused, or combined in a single concept; in other cases, a distinction is made between them but they are treated as logically related terms. Subsequent criticism has been largely concerned with the fittingness of the terms in their application to social phenomena, and with the character of the relations between them. The notion of social evolution was taken directly from the theories of biological evolution which, in the nineteenth century, powerfully reinforced the influence

283

of the philosophy of history upon sociology. Spencer in his *Social Statics* (1850) and at greater length in his *Principles of Sociology* propounded an analogy between society and an organism and between social and organic growth, but in his account of social evolution he paid little attention to the more specific features of the biological theory; i.e. its definition of evolution as 'descent with modifications' and its explanation, in the Darwinian theory, of the mechanism by which evolution takes place. Similarly, Tylor in his *Primitive Culture* (1871) used the term 'evolution' in a very imprecise way: 'On the one hand the uniformity which so largely pervades civilization may be ascribed, in great measure, to the uniform action of uniform causes; while on the other its various grades may be regarded as stages of development or evolution, each the outcome of previous history and about to do its proper part in shaping the history of the future'.

Modern writers have indicated the differences between the biological theory and the various theories of social evolution. W. F. Ogburn, while not entirely rejecting the concept of social evolution, observes: 'The attempts to find laws of heredity, variation and selection in the evolution of social institutions have produced few results either vital or significant'.[1] Similarly, V. Gordon Childe writes that '. . . it is essential not to lose sight of the significant distinctions between historical progress and organic evolution, between human culture and the animal's bodily equipment, between the social heritage and the biological inheritance. Figurative language, based on the admitted analogy, is liable to mislead the unwary. . . . Man's equipment and defences are external to his body; he can lay them aside and don them at will. Their use is not inherited, but learned, rather slowly, from the social group to which each individual belongs. Man's social heritage is not transmitted in the germ-cells from which he springs, but in a tradition which he begins to acquire only after he has emerged from his mother's womb. Changes in culture and tradition can be initiated, controlled, or delayed by the conscious and deliberate choice of their human authors and executors. An invention is not an accidental mutation of the germ-plasma, but a new synthesis of the accumulated experience to which the inventor is heir by tradition only. It is well to be as clear as possible as to the sort of differences subsisting between the processes here compared'.[2]

The weaknesses of the analogy between biological and social

---

[1] W. F. Ogburn, *Social Change* (New York, 1922), p. 57.
[2] V. Gordon Childe, *Man Makes Himself* (3rd edn., London, 1956), pp. 16–17.

evolution, had, of course, been realized earlier, and some sociologists preferred to use the term 'social development' to refer to the process of historical change. Even so, the distinction was not rigorously maintained. L. T. Hobhouse, for example, seems to have used the terms as synonyms in most of his writings, although he criticized certain aspects of Spencer's evolutionary theory.[1] Moreover, in his *Social Development* (London, 1924) he proposed four criteria of development, namely, increases in scale, efficiency, mutuality and freedom, which he then explicitly related to criteria of biological evolution.[2] Many other sociologists have used the criterion of scale in their accounts of social development; as we saw earlier both Spencer and Durkheim did so in their classification of societies, within an evolutionary framework.[3] Recently, V. Gordon Childe has suggested that 'the continuity between natural history and human history may allow numerical concepts to be introduced into the latter. Historical changes can be judged by the extent to which they have helped our species to survive and multiply'.[4] This is close to the idea of changes in the scale of a society, although as Durkheim pointed out, the latter involves more than growth of population. Another frequently used criterion of development is that of the extent of social differentiation, which is discussed by Spencer and Durkheim, as well as by Hobhouse in his account of efficiency and mutuality, and is treated as the principal criterion by MacIver and Page.[5]

The term 'development' is, however, no more precise than the term 'evolution', in its application to social phenomena. In ordinary usage development means 'a gradual unfolding; a fuller working out, of the details of anything; the growth of what is in the germ' (Oxford English Dictionary). It is in this sense that we can speak of the development of a child, or of a disease. But it is difficult to speak in the same way of social development, for we cannot always, with any certainty, refer a particular phenomenon to its germ, or clearly distinguish in a particular process between development and decay. There are only two (related) social processes to which it seems possible to apply the term 'development' with any accuracy; namely the growth of knowledge and the growth of human control over the natural environment as shown by technological and economic

[1] Introduction to *Development and Purpose* (London, 1913).
[2] The last two of these criteria are also related to his conception of progress; *See below*, p. 288.
[3] *See above*, pp. 118–9.
[4] *Man Makes Himself*, p. 12.
[5] R. M. MacIver and C. H. Page, *Society* (London, 1952), Ch. 27.

efficiency. It is, indeed, these two processes which have figured most prominently in developmental or evolutionary accounts of human society.[1]

In most recent sociological writing the term 'development' has been used in quite a different way; first, to differentiate two broad types of society—on one side the prosperous industrial societies and on the other side all those societies (very diverse in other respects) which are predominantly rural, agricultural and poor—and secondly, to describe the process of industrialization or modernization. This current notion of development has several distinctive features. It is not dependent upon a general theory of social evolution or development covering the whole span of human history, but deals with a specific kind of change, occurring at the present time or in the recent past, which can be represented in a simple historical model as a movement through three stages: traditional society, transitional society, modern society. Furthermore, studies of development in this sense have concentrated particularly upon economic growth, and in so doing they have brought out what was implicit in many of the earlier theories; namely, that the growth of knowledge and of control over nature—or in other words, the development of human powers of production—is the most significant element in the transformation of society. In some forms, however, this idea has given rise to a technological determinism which ignores many important aspects of social structure.

The fact that recent studies do not appeal to a general theory of development does not mean that they neglect entirely comparative and historical inquiry. In a symposium entitled *The Challenge of Development*[2] several contributors make explicit comparisons between the present industrialization of developing countries and the earlier industrialization of Western societies. This approach may

[1] There are other difficulties which are indicated in the brief discussion of the term 'development' by Ernest Nagel, 'Determinism and Development' in D. B. Harris (ed.), *The Concept of Development* (1957). Nagel points out that the term has not only a backward reference in the suggestion that something latent or hidden is progressively made manifest, but also a prospective one; 'it possesses a strong teleological flavour'. This is apparent in the examples we have given; e.g. the development of a child is related to some known characteristics of the adult human being. In the case of social phenomena we can relate the development of knowledge to a condition of more extensive and exact knowledge, and the development of control over nature to such things as survival and population size. But the development of society as such can hardly be related to any prospective condition of society except in terms of a moral ideal, and development then becomes synonymous with progress.

[2] Published by the Eliezer Kaplan School of Economics and Social Sciences, The Hebrew University, Jerusalem, 1958.

sometimes lead to the error of supposing that the developing countries will follow exactly the same path as did the present industrial countries, but a number of writers have pointed out that there are substantial differences.[1] A more general problem arises from the idea of a transition from traditional to modern society, for this suggests that 'modern industrial society' is in some way the terminal point of development. This has two important consequences: first, that the changes going on in industrial societies tend to be neglected, as has certainly been the case over the past few decades; and secondly, in a more specific way, that the contrast between capitalism and socialism as stages of development, or alternative forms, *within* modern industrial society, is either obscured or deliberately excluded.

The conception of development as a single great transformation, bound up with the advance of science and technology,[2] owes much to the methodology of Max Weber; it concentrates upon particular processes of change and the emergence of a particular type of society, and leads to the formulation of explanations and interpretations in terms of specific historical circumstances and general concepts about human action rather than in terms of comprehensive 'laws of development'. But it may be questioned whether industrial society or modern society can be treated in exactly the same way as Weber treated capitalism; namely, as a single, highly specific form of society. Indeed, one of the most illuminating studies of modernization—Barrington Moore's *Social Origins of Dictatorship and Democracy*—argues convincingly that there are three main routes to the modern world: by a bourgeois revolution, by a Fascist revolution from above, and by a peasant revolution. Moore also considers a possible fourth route, represented by the development of

[1] In the symposium I have mentioned, for example, an essay by Talcott Parsons, 'Some Reflections on the Institutional Framework of Economic Development' begins from Weber's analysis of capitalism in order to emphasize the *different* circumstances of present day industrialization. Parsons summarizes his argument in the following way: 'There is, perhaps, an understandable common-sense presumption to the effect that the conditions under which an important phenomenon of social structure has once developed are the same as those which will be most favourable to its repetition at a later time. My main argument has been that for the case of an industrial economy this is probably not true . . . in the first place industrialism *had to develop* . . . (as in the West) in essential independence from the main political organization of the society . . . (But in the present industrialization) governments, within the framework of the ideological symbols of nationalism and 'socialism', are likely to be by far the most important agencies.' (pp. 134–5). This question is also very thoroughly discussed in Guy Hunter, *Modernizing Peasant Societies* (London, 1969).

[2] *See* the writings of Raymond Aron on this subject, and also Ernest Gellner, *Thought and Change* (London, 1964).

India since independence. The importance of these distinctions is that they show not merely the different origins (influenced by the relations between classes in a given society), but also the different structures and possibilities of further development, of the various types of industrial society.

The earlier conceptions of social evolution and social development which I have discussed were also intimately connected with the idea of progress.[1] In the case of Comte and Spencer this is so obvious as to need no illustration. L. T. Hobhouse proposed a distinction between social evolution and social progress,[2] but his work was clearly dominated by a concern with progress. 'To form by a philosophic analysis a just conception of human progress, to trace this progress to its manifold complexity in the course of history, to test its reality by careful classification and searching comparisons, to ascertain its conditions, and if possible to forecast the future—this is the comprehensive problem towards which all sociological science converges and on the solution of which reasoned sociological effort must finally depend'.[3] It is not clear whether a precise distinction can be made between the notions of development and progress in their application to social changes. In Hobhouse's account the two processes coincide, and no example is given of general social development which is not progressive, although of course Hobhouse does show that growth in a *particular* sphere of social life may have undesirable consequences elsewhere.

Since the end of the nineteenth century the idea of progress has fallen into disfavour or neglect, not only in sociology but more generally in the *Weltanschauung* of intellectuals in Western societies. This is a phenomenon which itself deserves sociological study. Both intellectual and social influences have been important. Intellectually, there has been the persistent effort to make sociology a 'value-free' science, and during the same period the growth in philosophical thought of 'ethical relativism'; together they have produced a widespread belief that the sociologist can and should avoid value judgments, and that this self-restraint is made all the easier by the fact that values are in any case not matters of judgment. But the social influences may have had a greater effect. Here we should take into

[1] For the history of the idea of progress, *see* J. B. Bury, *The Idea of Progress* (London, 1920).

[2] 'By evolution I mean any sort of growth; by social progress, the growth of social life in respect of those qualities to which human beings attach, or can rationally attach, value.' *Social Evolution and Political Theory* (London, 1911) p. 8. In this book, which is infrequently mentioned, Hobhouse gives an admirably clear account of his sociological approach and principal conclusions.

[3] Introduction, *The Sociological Review*, I (1), p. 11.

account not only the frequently alleged pessimism, arising from the nature and extent of modern war and from the experience of recent totalitarian regimes, but also a quite different phenomenon, the uncertainty about what ends are worthwhile in societies which already enjoy high standards of living. So many of the aims of the nineteenth century disciples of progress have been achieved, yet without giving all the satisfaction which was anticipated; and the doubt arises whether any state of society likely to result from human effort would be ultimately satisfying. At the least, there is a recognition that once the major social evils of ignorance, poverty, and oppression have been largely overcome, the ends and means of progress become more complex and less easy to determine.

In this respect, there is an immense difference between the Western industrial countries and the low income countries in most of the rest of the world. In the latter the evils of poverty, ill-health, ignorance, and sometimes oppression are still almost untouched, and as C. P. Snow has recently observed it is absurd for Western intellectuals to expound their own scepticism concerning progress to the people or political leaders of such countries. There, at least, the line of progress is unmistakable, and sociologists in particular would be well occupied in studying the various pre-conditions for overcoming the present great (and increasing) disparity in levels of living between rich and poor countries. It is relevant here that one sociological system—Marxism—which has remained firmly attached to a general theory of progress, exerts its strongest appeal in the under-developed countries of Asia and Africa.[1]

There is one sense in which sociology is necessarily connected with the idea of progress; namely that as a discipline it must be justified in part by the contribution which it can make to human progress. Beyond this, it may be one of the important contributions of sociology to human knowledge to have elucidated the character and potentialities of modern industrial society. In the earlier universalistic theories of progress, such as those of Comte and Spencer, there is a particular concern with modern societies; and in later sociological writings this is still more evident. Hobhouse argued that, 'through science . . . (modern civilization) is beginning to control the physical conditions of life, and . . . on the side of ethics and religion it is forming those ideas of the unity of the race, and of the subordination of law, morals and social constitutions generally to the needs of human development which are the conditions of the control that is required. It seemed of secondary importance that

[1] In Europe, also, Marxism has been most influential in the relatively poorer countries; not in the most industrialized.

there should have been little or no progress in other respects, provided that this essential condition of future advance had been realized'.[1] Similarly, Marx treated modern capitalism as a critical period in human history, from which the rational control of human life could begin; and he devoted himself to the comprehensive study of this specific historical phenomenon rather than to the speculative elaboration of a historico-philosophical theory of social development. Nevertheless, the theory of progress as such belongs to the philosophy of history rather than to sociology. It is pre-eminently an interpretation of human experience, an attempt to discover, in a quasi-religious sense, the meaning of history. The achievement of progress, however it may be conceived, does not depend upon any such interpretation, but upon knowledge of the conditions and ways of social change, and of the circumstances of particular societies. Yet a philosophy of history in which speculation is informed and controlled by sociological knowledge may still have an important role in setting the objectives for sociological thought and enquiry.

The difficulties encountered in the theories of evolution, development or progress, as well as changes in the climate of opinion, led to a general adoption of the term 'social change' to refer to all the historical variations in human societies. The diffusion of this more neutral term was aided by the publication, in 1922, of W. F. Ogburn's *Social Change*. In this work, after discussing conceptions of social evolution, and examining in detail the role of biological and cultural factors in social change, Ogburn made a distinction between material and non-material culture and advanced the hypothesis of 'cultural lag' according to which changes in the adaptive culture (i.e. a part of the non-material culture) do not synchronize exactly with the changes in material culture and thus become a source of stresses and conflicts. Ogburn's analysis has some affinity with earlier studies; in particular, with A. Weber's distinction between culture and civilization,[2] and with the distinction made by Marx between 'basis' and 'superstructure'. Ogburn's treatment of the problems is different, especially in the attention which he pays to the process of invention, but he has in common with the writers mentioned that he concentrates upon the changes which have originated in the sphere of material production since the advent of modern industrialism. It is indeed within such a context that most recent studies of social change have been made. Thus we have numerous studies of the demographic trends in industrial societies, of changes in the family, in the class

---

[1] *Development and Purpose*. Introduction.
[2] *See above*, p. 127.

structure, in law and religion.[1] But there has been lacking, for the most part, any systematic consideration of the interrelations between the various changes, or any comparative study of changes occurring in different times and places, or finally any general view of the main directions of change such as was formulated in earlier theories by Hobhouse, Marx, or in a more tentative way, Max Weber. Only in the recent discussions of 'development', and the still more recent revival of interest in the prospects for radical change in the industrial societies, is it possible to discern a new attempt to formulate a more general theory of social change.

It is not to be expected that the ideas we have been considering here should have had their counterparts in the social thought of India or of other developing countries. In India, there were neither intellectual nor social conditions favourable to the appearance of theories of change, evolution or progress. Indian society itself, constituted by the predominant groups of caste, joint family and village community, was relatively static before the period of British rule introduced Western technology and Western conceptions of progress. At the same time Hinduism propounded an ideal which withdrew men's attention from material improvement at the same time as it sanctioned and justified the established social order. Indian culture, as has often been observed, has been essentially religious and other-worldly in its orientation. Moreover, even disregarding these specific characteristics of Hinduism, we may agree with Bury that the doctrine of progress could not arise so long as the religious doctrine of Providence was in the ascendant,[2] and even go further in suggesting that theories of progress and development could only become influential in societies where religious doctrines in general were challenged and where the secularization of social life was already advanced. Such conditions have only begun to emerge in India in very recent times, and the clash between secular and religious doctrines is in an early phase, which has also acquired a particlar character from the circumstance that secular thought was for long represented by the foreign rulers of the society.

Theories of social change

The theories of social change which have so far been propounded have been closely associated with philosophical interpretations of history. They can be classified in various ways, but it is convenient to make a preliminary distinction between linear and cyclical theories.

[1] These have been discussed in earlier chapters.
[2] *Op. cit.*, pp. 21–2.

Among the linear theories the most significant are those of Comte, Spencer, Hobhouse and Marx. Comte's theory, which derives from Saint-Simon, and more remotely from Condorcet, explains social change as the outcome of man's intellectual development, which is formulated in the 'law of three stages' as a progress from theological modes of thought, through the metaphysical mode to the positive mode of thought represented by modern science. This intellectual progress is accompanied by moral development, especially the growing predominance of altruism over egoism, and by changes in social institutions. 'Human activity, as I have long since shown, passes successively through the stages of Offensive warfare, Defensive warfare, and Industry. The connection of these stages with the preponderance of the theological, the metaphysical or the positive spirit respectively, leads at once to a complete explanation of history'. Recent criticisms of Comte have been largely concerned with the deterministic character of his theory,[1] or with its 'totalitarian implications'.[2] It is open to objection on other counts; its claim to have discovered the laws of social evolution, its assumption concerning the influence of intellectual development upon moral ideas, and its assertions, unsupported by any detailed evidence, of a close correspondence between the state of knowledge and the type of social structure. But Comte's analysis of the influence of modern scientific knowledge retains some value, as does his discussion of the characteristics of industrial society and their bearing upon the prevalence of war.[3]

Spencer's theory of social change was in some respects more comprehensive, and was based upon more adequate empirical data, than that of Comte. Spencer recognized more fully the variety of factors involved in social change, and also the difficulties of demonstrating evolution in each particular society. On the latter question he observed that '. . . though taking the entire assemblage of societies, evolution is inevitable, it cannot be held inevitable in each particular society or indeed probable'.[4] In discussing the actual course of social evolution he regarded as important features the increasing differentiation of function within societies, and the increasing size of societies (the latter brought about largely by warfare). But his analysis of social change ultimately depended upon a theory (long since rejected) of cosmic evolution, according to which there is a

---

[1] Isaiah Berlin, *Historical Inevitability.*

[2] F. A. Hayek, *The Counter-Revolution of Science.*

[3] *See,* on this aspect of Comte's theory, Raymond Aron, *War and Industrial Society* (London, 1958).

[4] *Principles of Sociology,* Vol. I, p. 107.

universal movement from 'an indefinite unstable homogeneity' to a 'definite stable heterogeneity'. Spencer did not in fact show how the societies he studied might be systematically arranged in an evolutionary sequence.[1]

L. T. Hobhouse was strongly influenced by both Comte and Spencer, but his theory of social change was worked out in a much more rigorous way and his use of historical and anthropological data was more scholarly and critical. From Comte he took the idea that the development of the human mind was the crucial factor in social development, but he did not accept Comte's dogmatic positivism, and he was able to support his account of mental development with a much sounder psychological theory (to which he made independent contributions). Thus he distinguishes five stages in the intellectual history of mankind,[2] and sets out to demonstrate the growth of rationality in all spheres of thought rather than accepting Comte's too simple contrast between theology, metaphysics and science. He was also indebted to Comte for a method which involves studying the development of particular spheres of social activity through the whole history of mankind, and not the development of particular societies or type of society. Except in the case of primitive societies Hobhouse does not attempt a systematic classification of societies, nor does he examine in detail any specific process of social change. The principal criticism of his sociological approach is that which Durkheim brought against Comte; namely, that he deals with an abstraction, humanity, and not with actual societies as intelligible objects of study. From Spencer, Hobhouse adopted the notion of social evolution or development as a process of increase in scale, complexity, and internal differentiation. Thus, his conception of social change is that the development of mind brings about social development (estimated by the criteria mentioned); and further that since this mental development includes a development of moral ideas towards the ideal of a rational ethic, which transforms the major social institutions, it can be regarded as progressive.

1 For a general account of Spencer's theory *see* J. Rumney, *Herbert Spencer's Sociology* (London, 1934). Spencer's major influence was in America rather than England, and there is a good critical account of the theory of social evolution in R. Hofstadter, *Social Darwinism in American Thought*. Spencer's ideas have recently been revived by Talcott Parsons in *Societies: Evolutionary and Comparative Perspectives* (1966).

2 These were: (i) the beginnings of articulate thought in pre-literate societies (ii) proto-science in the ancient East (Babylon, Egypt and ancient China), (iii) the stage of reflection in the later East (from the eighth to the fifth centuries BC in China, Palestine and India) (iv) the stage of critical and systematic thought in Greece, and (v) the development of modern scientific thought from about the sixteenth century.

In Marx's theory of social change two elements in social life have a pre-eminent place; the development of technology (productive forces) and the relations between social classes. Briefly, the theory states that there corresponds to a particular stage in the development of productive forces a definite mode of production and system of class relations, which is stabilized and maintained by the dominant class. But the continuing development of productive forces changes the relations between classes, and the conditions of their conflict, and in due course the hitherto dominated class is able to overthrow the existing mode of production and system of social relationships and to establish a new social order.[1] Marx himself only sketched his theory of historical change; he used it as a 'guiding thread' (or as we should now say, a hypothesis) for research, and devoted his powers to the analysis of one complex historical phenomenon, the emergence and growth of modern capitalism. Few later Marxists have added a great deal to Marx's ideas; on the contrary, by their vulgarization of the ideas to constitute a simple dogmatic faith they have largely obscured the importance of Marx's contributions to sociology. Among these contributions are the conception of sociology as a *critical discipline* which would reveal the contradictions and potentialities within every existing form of society; and the exemplification of a historical-sociological method through an analysis of early capitalism unsurpassed by any other social thinker. As a hypothesis, or conceptual framework, Marx's historical theory is open to criticism; in particular, that it is most relevant and fruitful where Marx himself applied it, in the study of capitalism (though even here it requires qualification), and that it is less helpful in the study of other historical periods and transformations. It is worthy of remark here that while later Marxist historians have discussed *ad nauseam* the transition from feudalism to capitalism, there has been little serious Marxist analysis of the emergence of feudalism, or of certain other types of society.

The linear theories which I have discussed had the great merit that they delineated, in one form or another, a number of significant cumulative changes in human social history; the growth of knowledge, the increasing scale and complexity of societies, and in modern times the growing movement towards social and political

[1] 'At a certain stage of their development, the material forces of production in society come in conflict with the existing relations of production, or—what is but a legal expression for the same thing—with the property relations within which they had been at work before. From forms of development of the forces of production these relations turn into their fetters. Then occurs a period of social revolution.' Karl Marx, *A Contribution to the Critique of Political Economy* (1859), Preface.

equality. They all recognized the particular significance of the changes which occurred in Europe from the seventeenth century, and which subsequently influenced the social life of mankind throughout the world, the development of modern science and industry. The cyclical theories of social change depict other aspects of human history, but they ignore these fundamental facts. Pareto, in *The Mind and Society*,[1] presented in his theory of the circulation of elites an interpretation of history according to which social change is brought about by the struggle between groups for political power, and there are alternating periods of harsh rule by a vigorous and newly triumphant elite, and of mild, humanitarian rule by a declining elite. The theory rests upon the assertion of biological differences between groups within society (derived from the racist theories of Ammon and others), and is supported by little historical evidence. Pareto only seriously investigates one instance of the circulation of elites, namely in ancient Rome, and his conception of political change wholly ignores the growth of democratic government in modern times (which he particularly detested).[2] More recently, P. Sorokin and Arnold Toynbee have presented theories which have some cyclical features. Sorokin, in his *Social and Cultural Dynamics* (4 vols. New York, 1937) while recognizing the occurrence of linear processes, draws attention to other cyclical processes which occur within human societies. He also makes a distinction between three broad types of culture, Ideational, Idealist and Sensate, which he conceives as succeeding each other in cycles in the history of societies. Toynbee's theory is expounded in *A Study of History* (10 vols. London, 1934–54). Its cyclical character is expressed in the conception of the growth, arrest and decay of civilizations; but the theory is, perhaps, in a more fundamental sense, linear, for according to Toynbee the different civilizations 'though they are certainly separate individuals, are also representatives of a single species and are also engaged upon an identical enterprise. . . . The differentiating Yang-movement of growth is leading towards a goal which is a Yin-state of integration'.[3] The process of growth and decay of civilizations is a vehicle of progressive religious revelation, and its consummation a 'communion with God'. In the work of both Sorokin and Toynbee the mass of historical analogies, and the oracular style, obscure the analysis of historical change, despite the

---

[1] English translation, 4 vols., New York, 1935.

[2] Pareto's theory is outlined, more or less sympathetically, in James Burnham, *The Machiavellians* (London, 1943) and is cogently criticized in F. Borkenau, *Pareto* (London, 1936).

[3] *Op. cit.*, Vol. III, p. 390.

many illuminating comments upon particular social transformations. They represent a return to philosophy of history in the grand manner.

In the theories I have considered, whether linear or cyclical, relatively little attention was given to the analysis of particular processes of social change or to the discrimination of the factors involved in social change. The major exceptions are Marx and Sorokin: the former studied in great detail one historical transformation, and the latter has discussed at length the different factors which produce change. In the next chapter I shall turn to this more detailed analysis.

Chapter 18

FACTORS IN SOCIAL CHANGE

General considerations

A sociological analysis of social change requires in the first place a model more precise and less ambitious than the general theories we discussed in the last chapter, which would make possible the formulation of problems and the systematic presentation of results. In their book, *Character and Social Structure*, Gerth and Mills have outlined such a model, in terms of six major questions which can be asked about social changes: (i) what is it that changes? (ii) how does it change? (iii) what is the direction of change? (iv) what is the rate of change? (v) why did change occur or why was it possible? (vi) what are the principal factors in social change?

In dealing with the first of these questions it is useful, I think, to define social change as a change in social structure (including here changes in the size of a society), or in particular social institutions, or in the relationships between institutions. Following the distinction proposed earlier between social structure and culture, we might then employ the term 'cultural change' to refer to variations in cultural phenomena such as knowledge and ideas, art, religious and moral doctrines, etc. Obviously, social and cultural changes are closely linked in many cases; for example, the growth of modern science has been closely associated with changes in economic structure. In other cases, however, the relations may be less close, as in changes of fashion, or changes in the forms of artistic creation.

The question concerning the manner, direction and rate of change require for their answer historical description and interpretation, such as have been provided, for example, in the various accounts of population changes, of the increasing division of labour in industrial societies, of the changes in the character of the modern Western family and so on. Discussion of the direction of change need not involve any value judgments; the diminishing size of the family, and the increasing size of economic units, are matters of historical fact. But in other cases, the direction of change may be less obvious and may become the subject of divergent interpretations. Moreover, the change itself may be one which is difficult to observe in a detached way, e.g. the increase in the divorce rate, or the extension of 'bureaucracy'; and discussions of the direction of change are then likely to become closely involved with moral evaluations. Finally, when it is a matter of analysing changes in the total structure of a society, whether it be a historical or present day society, the line of demarcation between the critical analysis and the expression of a social philosophy becomes obscure and uncertain, and can perhaps never be rigorously established. This is apparent if we consider the widely divergent accounts of the changes taking place in the British Welfare State, or in the USSR since the death of Stalin, or in India since the attainment of independence; or, on a larger scale, the contradictory accounts proffered by Marx and Max Weber of the dominant trends of change in capitalist societies.

The rate of change has always interested sociologists, and it is a commonplace to refer to the acceleration of social and cultural change in modern times. W. F. Ogburn was one of the first to examine the phenomenon systematically and to undertake quantitative studies of the rate of change, especially in the sphere of technological inventions.[1] He also focused attention upon the discrepancies between the rates of change in different sectors of social life; the hypothesis of 'cultural lag' is concerned with a major disharmony between the rapid growth of technology, and the slower transformation of familial, political and other institutions and of traditional beliefs and attitudes (religious, moral etc.). In recent years these problems have acquired greater importance, with the emergence of industrialization of underdeveloped countries as a major issue in world politics.[2] Research has followed two principal lines; sociological studies of the changes in social structure and culture induced by industrialization and the structural disharmonies of the transition period, and psychological studies of the adaptation of individuals to rapid social changes.[3] The problems have also been studied in the industrial societies, both in the context of changes in

[1] *Social Change (op. cit.)*, Part II. *See also* W. F. Ogburn and M. F. Nimkoff, *A Handbook of Sociology*, Ch. 26, and S. C. Gilfillan, *Sociology of Inventions* (Chicago, 1935).

[2] There is a good review and discussion of research on these problems in Africa in *Social Implications of Industrialization and Urbanization in Africa South of Sahara* (UNESCO, 1956. Prepared by the International African Institute, London). For Asian countries, see the five studies collected in *The Social Implications of Industrialization and Urbanization* (UNESCO, Research Centre on the Social Implications of Industrialization in Southern Asia, Calcutta, 1956). For a more general study see B. Hoselitz, *Sociological Aspects of Development* (Chicago, 1960).

[3] On the latter, *see* Margaret Mead (ed.), *Cultural Patterns and Technical Change* (UNESCO, 1953), especially Part V, pp. 279–303.

the family, in social stratification, in religious and moral ideas, in law, etc., and from the aspect of *attitudes*, the reactions of the individual to social change, and the implications and consequences in education, crime and delinquency, and mental health. On the other hand, there has been relatively little study of the differences between societies in which change has been rapid but continuous, and societies in which revolutionary and abrupt changes have occurred.

The problem of why change occurred, or why it was possible, is closely linked with the general problem of the factors in social change and raises very complex issues concerning social causation. Gerth and Mills briefly discuss some of these issues, as for example, the role of individuals in bringing about social change, and the relative influence of material factors and of ideas. In a recent essay, Morris Ginsberg has undertaken a systematic analysis of the factors which have been invoked by different writers to explain social change:[1] (i) the conscious desires and decisions of individuals (exemplified by the development of the small family system in Western countries); (ii) individual acts influenced by changing conditions (e.g. the decline of villeinage in England between 1300 and 1500); (iii) structural changes and structural strains (including as one instance the contradictions between forces of production and relations of production emphasized by Marxists); (iv) external influences (culture contact, or conquest); (v) outstanding individuals or groups of individuals; (vi) a confluence or collocation of elements from different sources converging at a given point (e.g. in revolutions); (vii) fortuitous occurrences (e.g. the Norman Conquest of England, the Black Death in the fourteenth century, the British conquest of India); and (viii) the emergence of a common purpose The final section of the essay contains an illuminating discussion of the concept of cause in social science, and its connection with teleology.

Much recent sociology, under the influence of functionalism, has disregarded problems of change or has presented them in such a way as to suggest that social change is something exceptional. The emphasis has been upon the stability of social systems and of systems of values and beliefs, and upon consensus rather than diversity and conflict within each society. It is clear, however, that all societies are characterized by both continuity and change, and that a major task of sociological analysis is to discover how the two processes are related to each other. Continuity is maintained by force and by the social controls which I discussed earlier, and especially by educa-

[1] M. Ginsberg, 'Social Change', *British Journal of Sociology*, IX (3), September, 1958.

tion, formal and informal, which imparts the accumulated social heritage to new generations. On the other hand, there are also certain general conditions which make for social change; the most important being the growth of knowledge and the occurrence of social conflict. The growth of knowledge has not been continuous, nor has it occurred at the same rate in all societies; but since the seventeenth century there has been a more or less steady growth which has now affected all societies. This has become a major condition of recent social change. Conflict, as a condition of social change, may be regarded from different aspects. In the first place, conflict between societies has played an important part historically in bringing about larger social units (as Comte and Spencer recognized), in establishing or re-inforcing social stratification (as Oppenheimer argued), and in diffusing social and cultural innovations. In modern times inter-national conflict has profoundly influenced the economic and poli-tical structure of societies, social policies, and norms of behaviour but these phenomena have hardly received the attention they deserve.[1] Secondly, conflicts between groups within society have been, and are, a major source of innovation and change. Among these conflicts, that between social classes, although it has not had the universal and decisive influence attributed to it by Marxists, has been an important agent of change, particularly in modern times. The establishment of political democracy in Western Europe has been very largely the outcome of class struggles. Finally, we should consider the conflict between generations, which has received much less than its due attention from sociologists.[2] Continuity in society, I have noted, is maintained by imparting the social tradition to new generations by the process of socialization; but socialization is never complete in the sense that new generations exactly re-enact the social life of their predecessors. Always there is criticism, rejec-tion of some aspects of tradition, and innovation. In modern times these features become more prominent because of the general changes which are taking place in the environment, and because of the diversity of norms and values, which allows the new generation

[1] *See above*, Chapter 12.

[2] Karl Mannheim was one of the few sociologists to see the importance of the subject, which he discussed in an illuminating essay, 'The Problem of Generations' (1927); published in English in Karl Mannheim, *Essays on the Sociology of Knowledge* (London, 1952). Since I first wrote this comment (in 1962) the conflict between generations has become a major theme of discussion; the problem which it presents is that of understanding how the more or less universal phenomenon of youthful revolt can acquire, in certain periods, a very great and even preponderant influence in promoting social and cultural change.

to choose, in some degree, between different 'ways of life' or to re-combine diverse elements in the culture in new patterns. It is a significant feature of the industrial societies that a distinctive youth culture and organized youth movements appear, which oppose in various ways the cultural values of the older generations; but the phenomena of inter-generational conflict are also apparent in societies such as India which are undergoing extremely rapid change from one type of society to another.

The early theories of social change, which I examined in the previous chapter, tended to emphasize a single factor in the causation of change. For the most part, however, they were not mono-causal theories (as they are sometimes classified), nor were they deterministic in any strict sense, as has been alleged by some recent critics.[1] Comte and Spencer both conceived of some ultimate law of social evolution (the development of mind for Comte, and a cosmic process of differentiation for Spencer), but in examining actual social change they took into account many factors, not least the conscious and deliberate acts of individuals. Spencer, for example, did not confine his studies to differentiation within societies, but considered the effects of knowledge, warfare, and other factors in bringing about social change. Marx's theory has often been condemned as mono-causal and deterministic, but his account of social causation is in fact extremely complex, involving several related but distinct phenomena—the forces of production, relations of production, class relations and ideologies. Moreover, his doctrine of political action is the very opposite of a deterministic theory. In later theories, such as those of Hobhouse, Toynbee and Sorokin, the complexity of social causation is fully recognized; and Sorokin, in particular, examines very carefully the various factors involved in social change.

Nevertheless, these theories raise a number of broad problems which need to be considered. The first is that concerning the part played respectively by individuals and by 'social forces' in inducing change. It should be remarked that the term 'social forces' does not refer to any forces which are entirely distinct from the acts of individuals, but to values and tendencies which are resultants of the interaction of individuals yet which confront any single individual as something external to him and relatively impervious to his individual criticism or influence. Thus the voluntary acts of individuals enter as constituents into 'social forces'; in this sense any individual may contribute to social change, although the effects may only be perceptible when a number of individuals begin to act in

[1] For example, Isaiah Berlin, *Historical Inevitability.*

a new way (for example, in limiting the size of their families). A different problem is that of the influence of outstanding individuals. At one extreme, it may be held that all important social and cultural changes are brought about by men of genius; at the other, that men of genius owe all their influence to the fact that they incarnate or represent the dominant social forces or tendencies of their time.[1] Neither of these extreme views is acceptable. For one thing, the influence of outstanding individuals may be greater in some spheres of social life than others; for example, greater in the field of artistic creation than in that of technology.[2] It would be arbitrary, however, to deny the personal influence of great men in the sphere of morals, religion, politics or economics. In the modern world, Lenin in Russia, and Mahatma Gandhi in India (as well as more recent political leaders such as Mao Tse-tung) have had a profound influence and it would be difficult to demonstrate that our world would have been the same had they not lived and acted as they did. Of course, they too were influenced by their environment, and their authority arose in part from their ability to formulate and interpret the latent aspirations of large numbers of people; but they were also charismatic leaders in Max Weber's sense, owing their positions of leadership to personal qualities, and imposing upon events the imprint of their own values.

A second major controversy has concerned the role of material factors and ideas in social change. Marxists, it is claimed, attribute a primary influence to material, economic factors, while others (e.g Comte, Hobhouse) give pre-eminence to the development of thought. One of the principal disputes in sociology is that between Marx and Weber concerning the origins of modern capitalism, in which Weber argued, not that 'ideas rule the world', but that in some historical situations ideas or doctrines may independently affect the direction of social change. It would be a mistake in any case, to establish a simple opposition between material factors and ideas, for material factors as such do not enter into social behaviour. In Marx's own theory of change the 'forces of production' are a determining element, but they are no more than the applications of science and technology; and the development of the productive forces can only mean the growth of scientific and technical knowledge and ideas. The fundamental problem is to determine the ways in which the growth or

[1] The latter view, in its Marxist version, is well expounded by G. V. Plekhanov, *The Role of the Individual in History*.

[2] Though there are evidently social influences upon art; *see* Max Weber's essay on the development of Western music, in *Wirtschaft und Gesellschaft*, and A. Hauser, *The Social History of Art*.

arrest of knowledge and thought affect society, whether through the influence of science upon economic relationships and class structure, or through the emergence of new religious, moral or philosophical doctrines, and how these diverse strands are connected in particular sequences of change.

Recent sociological studies of social change have dealt with more limited problems and have not aimed to provide any general explanation of change. But they have perhaps gone too far in dispensing with any conceptual scheme which would make possible comparative studies and partial explanations. Later in this chapter I shall consider whether a typology of social change might be constructed which would fill this gap.

Social change in the developing countries

The study of social change in the developing countries can be approached in various ways. Ideally, we should be able to apply to this particular case a general theory encompassing the processes of change in all societies; but as I have indicated there is no such theory which is widely accepted, and the most common approach in recent work has been to treat the developing countries as a present day instance of a particular kind of change from traditional society to modern industrial society. However, even if we accept this framework for understanding the changes which are going on in these societies there are still many distinctions to be made and alternative interpretations to consider. The traditional structure and culture of a society will obviously influence the nature of the changes which take place, and here we can distinguish broadly between developing countries in four main regions: Asia, Africa, the Midde East and Latin America.[1] Again, the origins of the process of development—whether it has begun from a social revolution or in a more gradual way—will profoundly affect its course. So too will the nature of the relations—economic, political and cultural—between a developing country and one or more of the industrial countries. The recognition or neglect of these factors colours the diverse interpretations of development, and it is not too difficult to criticize some economic and sociological theories of the last decade which ignored the colonial past, the economic dominance and political influence of the advanced industrial countries at the present time, and the differences between revolutionary and non-revolutionary change, in their accounts of the development process.[2] In addition to

[1] *See above*, Chapter 7.

[2] Some pertinent criticisms will be found in the essay, previously cited, by A. Gunder Frank,' Sociology of Development and Underdevelopment of Sociology'.

these factors of a traditional civilization, historical experiences affecting whole regions of the Third World, and present day international relations, it is essential finally to take account of particular elements in each individual country, so that any account framed in general sociological terms needs to be complemented by historical and anthropological studies and by detailed sociological surveys.

The case of India will illustrate some of these points. Two elements have played a decisive part in bringing about social change in India; first, Western science and technology, and secondly, social planning. The influence of technology has been apparent in diverse areas of social life. By the improvement of living conditions and medical care it has affected the mortality rate, and is thus largely responsible for the rapid growth of India's population. The introduction of capitalist industry brought about changes in the property system[1] and in the division of labour, and gave rise to new social strata and classes which played an important part in the political development of India.[2] In earlier chapters I have traced some of the effects of industrialization upon the joint-family, property, law, and the caste system. But technology did not only bring about change indirectly through the gradual transformation of economic relationships; technology and the scientific thought which was its basis constituted a new view of the world which came into conflict with the traditional culture. Moreover, British rule introduced into India social as well as technological inventions (a new system of government and administration, judicial procedures, forms of education), and new cultural values such as rationalism, and later on, egalitarianism and socialism.

The concept of 'cultural lag' has great relevance to India. The development of a modern capitalist economy brought into existence some social movements which rejected traditional Indian culture and others which set out to reform and modernize it; but it is by no means the case that the social institutions and cultural values of present day India are adapted to the way of life of an industrial society, whether capitalist or socialist. The large joint-family is not a useful or necessary institution in a modern society where individual mobility is considerable and the provision of welfare services a public responsibility. A caste system is incompatible with the

---

[1] Notably the establishment of individual private property in land. The effects have been studied very thoroughly in the case of Bengal; see S. Gopal, *The Permanent Settlement in Bengal and Its Results* (London, 1949) and Ramkrishna Mukherjee, *The Dynamics of a Rural Society* (Berlin, 1957), Ch. 1. Similar changes occurred elsewhere with the growth of commercial agriculture and the erosion of tribal ownership of land; see P. C. Lloyd, *Africa in Social Change*, Chapter 3.

[2] *See* especially, A. R. Desai, *Social Background of Indian Nationalism.*

rationality, mobility, and egalitarianism of a democratic society; in India, the principle of caste is unmistakably in conflict with the assumptions of the political regime, with the educational system, and with the needs of industry. Yet caste and the joint-family are fundamental elements in Hinduism, and thus in the traditional culture; as they become weaker so also do the cultural values of the past. Popular Hinduism itself is being directly influenced by the rationalization and secularization which accompany the growth of industrial society. The strains involved in this transition are, and have been for some time, apparent in the situation of Indian intellectuals who have to reconcile the divergent claims of two cultures, and in the conflict between generations. Many of the younger educated Indians dislike the caste restrictions upon marriage, are opposed to arranged marriages, and resent the patriarchal authority of family elders; yet they usually accept, in practice, the traditional forms of behaviour, moved by family loyalty and affection, and perhaps also by uncertainty as to the outcome if they choose a different path. There are other conflicts similar to those which occur in industrial societies, notably conflicts between social strata and classes. Caste, like every system of social stratification, involves economic differentiation and economic interest groups, although in the past these features have been partly obscured by the ritual significance of the institution. In conditions of economic change the privileged groups are led to resist innovations which would diminish their own prestige and economic advantage. These various conflicts are, in one sense, sources of change, but they may also retard change over a longer or shorter period, or even produce stagnation or regress. It is *not* a sociological law that every society can be successfully industrialized, although sociological research may well contribute to ensuring success, and to reducing its costs in tension, dis-orientation and suffering.

Social planning, in India as elsewhere, overrides to some extent the conflicts I have mentioned. It represents the factor in social change which has been described as the emergence of a common purpose. There is now, in almost all societies, central economic and social planning intended to promote social well-being. The extent and forms of planning vary widely from one society to another but the objectives and implications are similar. For the first time in human history, the mass of the people are drawn into a process of rational and deliberate transformation of their social life; social change has been brought, to some extent, under human control. The Indian Constitution of 1950 defined the purposes of the new political system as being to establish social, economic and political

305

justice, liberty of thought, expression, belief and worship, equality of status and opportunity, and fraternity. The Government Planning Commission, established in the same year, was conceived as a major agency for achieving these purposes, although its work has been somewhat narrowly restricted to economic problems. An excellent recent study by S. C. Dube[1] surveys the changes brought about by one of the principal activities of the Planning Commission, the Community Development Programme (annd also less the intensive National Extension Service), and examines some of the obstacles to change which these activities have revealed. In a detailed study of one Project in Uttar Pradesh, covering 153 villages, Dube shows that the more strictly technological innovations, such as improved seeds, fertilisers, improved breeds of animals, and so on, were accepted fairly readily, especially where the effects became apparent in a short time, as for example in higher cash prices for crops; but that the innovations which had, or were likely to have, repercussions on the social structure, or the cultural values, met with resistance. Thus, new agricultural techniques, co-operative methods of farming, measures to improve sanitation, and educational ventures, aroused much less interest and in some cases were opposed. In a general evaluation of the Project, Dube observes: 'Modest as they may appear, these projects have introduced certain ideas that will be long lasting. The people are slow and extremely cautious in accepting innovations, but on a limited scale they too make some experiments and watch their results carefully. Some of the project-sponsored innovations in the field of agriculture and rural health, though they appear to have been rejected or very reluctantly accepted today, may finally establish themselves in about a decade from now. Signs of a psychological change, too, are evident, although they cannot be attributed in every instance or even primarily to the project. There is an unmistakable change in the people's level of expectation, and with the gradual removal of barriers between them and the government substantial progress can be expected.

However, the Project studied here appears to have done little to further even the traditional modes of co-operation in these communities'.[2]

Dube establishes clearly the importance of communication between the government representatives who are seeking to induce change, and the villagers to whom the new ideas are addressed. The problems of communication involve several factors: the perceived character of those who originate the communications, the

[1] S. C. Dube, *India's Changing Villages* (London, 1958).
[2] *Op. cit.*, p. 151.

form and content of the communications themselves, and the response of the recipients. In the first of these problems the role of the Village Level Worker is crucial, and constitutes an important subject for sociological research.[1] The form and content of communications pose a general problem of balance between continuity and change; communication is more effective where it can be related to existing aspirations (e.g. for economic betterment), or to traditional cultural norms (e.g. the improvement of breeds of cattle presented in terms of the traditional religious valuation of cattle). Finally, the response of the villagers is determined largely by the local elites and opinion leaders, and the successful induction of change depends very much upon identifying such leaders (formal and informal) and convincing *them*, in the first place, that the changes are desirable.

In recent years the assessments of the Indian way of development have become much more critical than they were during the 1950s in the heyday of Nehru's leadership. Thus Barrington Moore, while he singles out India as the example of a fourth alternative route to the modern world—contrasted with the bourgeois and Fascist revolutions of the past, and with the communist revolutions of recent times—deals not only with the factors which made this kind of industrialization possible, but also with what he calls 'the price of peaceful change'—the very slow rate of economic development which makes the success of the venture doubtful. In similar fashion Gunnar Myrdal, in his massive study of South Asian countries, *Asian Drama* (New York, 1968), arrives at the conclusion that 'much of the momentum in Indian planning has been lost', while fundamental problems of land reform, modernizing village structure, raising levels of agricultural output, and controlling population growth remain unsolved.

On the other side, however, we should take account of some of the benefits of peaceful change. India, unlike many other developing countries, has not succumbed to authoritarian rule, whether it is that of a military elite or of a revolutionary party. In India the hundred flowers, which soon withered in China, can still bloom. It is not for a sociologist to pronounce a verdict upon these different courses of development. They are matters of political choice, and to some extent of necessity, if a situation occurs in which economic growth is halted and the aspirations of the mass of the people are frustrated by the incompetence and corruption of ruling groups. But the sociologist has still a responsibility to see the process of development as comprehensively as possible, recognizing the

[1] Dube, *op. cit.* Appendix I gives an illuminating account of the work and problems of the Village Level Worker.

diversity and complexity of its goals, and not reducing them to a simple matter of technological and economic growth.

Types of social change

The construction of a typology of social change would have great value at the present time. In the first place, it would set in perspective the problems of development in the Third World and enable us to avoid at least one prevalent error, which consists in assuming that the industrial countries have attained a definitive form, while the developing countries are simply trying to catch up with them. It would be much more accurate to regard the late 20th century world as being involved in a general process of exceptionally rapid change, in which the transformations in one part of the globe influence profoundly the course of events elsewhere. This idea is indicated very clearly in Irving L. Horowitz, *Three Worlds of Development* (New York, 1966), where an attempt is made to see the connections between social changes in the first world of the capitalist democracies (especially the USA), in the second world of the Soviet societies (especially the USSR), and in the third world of the non-industrial societies.

Secondly, however, the working out of a typology would lead us on to still more general questions concerning social changes in past as well as present societies; for example, the development of Western capitalism, the rise and decline of earlier civilizations and empires. This would provide a wider basis for comparison and generalization, and would restore to sociology the kind of historical awareness which has been so conspicuously lacking in the past few decades. And lastly, at a time when large numbers of people are becoming more aware of the potentialites for change in present day societies, and when young radicals of diverse persuasions urge the most sweeping transformations of culture and social structure, it would undoubtedly be useful to have even a very tentative scheme of classification which would reveal some of the causes, limits and consequences of social change. The formulation of such a scheme seems possible in terms of four major problems:

1. Where does social change originate? A distinction can first be made between *endogenous* and *exogenous* change, i.e. change originating within or outside a particular society. In practice, the origin of change cannot always be assigned wholly to one or the other category; but to take a modern example, it is evident that the changes now occurring in under-developed societies have originated very largely outside these societies, and are the product of Western

308

technology which was introduced in most cases by conquest. The problem which has then to be posed is whether there are significant differences between processes of change which are either internally or externally induced. It seems probable that there are such differences, especially in the relationships which are established between the agents of change and the rest of the population.[1] A second aspect of this question concerns the problem of where the changes begin within a particular society (regardless of their more remote origin); i.e. which institutions first undergo change. Two other problems are involved here; that of the factors in social change, and that of the social groups which initiate change. Historical evidence may permit us to classify processes of change according to the spheres or groups in which they begin; economic, political, religious, etc., and to study more closely how change is diffused from one sphere to another. It is in this context, for example, that Marx's theory of social change through class conflict needs to be reconsidered.

2. What are the initial conditions from which large-scale changes begin? The initial conditions may profoundly influence the course of social change; it cannot be assumed, for example, that the formation of ancient empires, of feudal states, or of modern capitalist societies, occurred in the same ways or can be accounted for in terms of a single generalization. In the contemporary world, industrialization is a very different process in tribal societies (as in Africa), and in societies of ancient civilization such as India or China. It is different again according to the size and complexity of the society. The sociological analysis of industrialization as a particular process of change would be greatly helped by a typology of under-developed societies themselves.

3. What is the rate of change? Social change may occur rapidly in some periods, or in some spheres, and more slowly, perhaps imperceptibly, in others. The rate of change may also be accelerating or decelerating. Ogburn and Gilfillan, whose work was referred to earlier, have shown that in industrial societies the rate of technological change, as measured, for example, by the numbers of patents issued, has been increasing. An important distinction is that between processes of gradual change and processes of revolutionary change (as a particular form of rapid change). In the economic and technological spheres it is not too difficult to identify revolutionary changes, and to trace their causes and effects. Gordon Childe has admirably

[1] *See* footnote 1 on p. 287 above, referring to the economic framework of changes in underdeveloped societies. This question also raises the issue of the role of elites in social change, which I have discussed in *Elites and Society*.

309

described what he terms the 'neolithic revolution', the introduction of a food producing economy;[1] and economic and social historians have documented and analysed the phases of the modern industrial revolution.[2] Political and social revolutions, however, have been considered for the most part in historical, descriptive terms, while comparative and analytical studies have been lacking. There is, of course, a Marxist theory of social revolution but it has not been very effective in stimulating sociological research. The twentieth century social and national revolutions have been closely linked with war, although the connections have not been systematically explored. At the same time, they have revealed the important role of intellectuals, as well as social classes, in revolutionary movements.[3]

4. To what extent is social change fortuitous, causally determined, or purposive? The principal distinction here is one which I have already discussed in considering social planning. In one sense, of course, almost all social changes are purposive, since they result from the purposive acts of individual men. But such acts may have unintended consequences, because the individual actions are not coordinated and may actually impede or distort each other as, for example, in situations of conflict. In such conditions, which have been those of most societies until recent times, change may be causally determined, or there may also be quite fortuitous elements in it, but it is not purposive in the sense that it achieves the purposes of all, or most, of the individuals who are involved. Change may more properly be termed purposive in the case of modern societies where, as Ginsberg suggests, a common purpose emerges and may be realized by degrees through a process of planned social change. Even here, of course, fortuitous events may have an influence, and there may be (since planners, like other men, lack omniscience) many unintended consequences. It is plain, however, that human beings now have a greater control than in the past over the natural and the social conditions of their life; the social sciences are themselves a product of the aspirations for control over the direction of social change and have contributed greatly to its establishment.

[1] V. Gordon Childe, *Man Makes Himself*, Chapter V.
[2] The changes in the economic system and in social attitudes are vividly presented in R. L. Heilbroner, *The Great Economists* (London, 1955), Ch. 1. A more sociological examination of the different phases in the industrial revolution is given by Georges Friedmann, *La crise du progrès* (Paris, 1936), especially Ch. 1.
[3] *See* the discussion in Chapter 12 above.

Notes on Reading for Part V

The idea of progress

Becker, Carl. 'Progress', *Encyclopaedia of the Social Sciences.*
Bury, J. B. *The Idea of Progress* (London, 1920).
Ginsberg, Morris. *The Idea of Progress: A Revaluation* (London, 1953).

Social evolution and development

The notions of evolution and development as applied to human societies have not received the systematic examination they deserve. Much of the discussion is still at the level of the functionalist criticisms (presented in an extreme form by Malinowski) of 'conjectural history'. There is a critical survey of evolutionary theories by P. A. Sorokin, 'Sociocultural Dynamics and Evolutionism' in Gurvitch and Moore (eds.) *Twentieth Century Sociology.* 'Social Darwinism' has been discussed, or historically surveyed, by a number of writers; *see* especially:

Ritchie, D. G. *Darwinism and Politics* (London, 1885).
Hofstadter, R. *Social Darwinism in American Thought* (Philadelphia, 1945).
Ginsberg, M. 'The concept of evolution in sociology', *Essays in Sociology and Social Philosophy*, Vol. I.
> Examines some of the crucial problems. *See also* the stimulating discussion in V. Gordon Childe, *Man Makes Himself*, Chapters I and II.
MacIver, R. M. *Social Causation* (Boston, 1942).
> Presents a good analysis of the notion of cause as applied to social change.
Popper, K. R. *The Poverty of Historicism* (London, 1957).
> A major criticism of evolutionary theories on grounds of logic and method.

The concept of development as used in recent discussions of 'developing countries' is expounded from different points of view by:

Aron, Raymond. *The Industrial Society* (London, Weidenfeld and Nicolson, 1967), Chapters I and II.
Gellner, Ernest. *Thought and Change* (London, Weidenfeld and Nicolson, 1964).
> Includes a good critical examination of general evolutionary theories.
Horowitz, Irving L. *Three Worlds of Development* (New York, Oxford University Press, 1966).

The literature on economic growth is now very large, but the following books provide an introduction to the main issues:

Lewis, W. Arthur. *The Theory of Economic Growth* (London, Allen & Unwin, 1955).

Myrdal, Gunnar. *Economic Theory and Under-developed Regions* (London, Duckworth, 1957).
Bhagwati, Jagdish. *The Economics of Underdeveloped Countries* (London, Weidenfeld and Nicolson, 1966).
Agarwala, A. N., and Singh, S. P. (eds.). *The Economics of Underdevelopment* (New York, Oxford University Press, 1963).

Social Change

Ogburn, W. F. *Social Change* (New York, 1922).
  See the discussion in the text.

Reference should be made to the works of Pareto, Toynbee and Sorokin cited in the text. In addition, there is a useful short exposition of Sorokin's concept of social and cultural change in F. R. Cowell, *History, Civilization and Culture* (London, 1952).

On the Marxist theory see Marx and Engels, *The German Ideology*, N. Bukharin, *Historical Materialism*, and Edmund Wilson, *To the Finland Station* (London, 1940).

There are a number of anthropological studies of social change in primitive societies; *see* especially the following which also consider some of the general problems of analysing social change:

Malinowski, B. *Dynamics of Culture Change* (Yale, 1945).
Wilson, G. and M. *The Analysis of Social Change* (Cambridge, 1945).
Mead, M. *The Changing Culture of an American Tribe* (New York, 1932).
Kroeber, A. L. *Anthropology* (New York, 1948), Chapters 10–12.
Firth, Raymond. *Social Change in Tikopia* (London, Allen & Unwin, 1959).

On social change in particular regions and countries of the Third World *see* the following works:

Karim, A. K. Nazmul. *Changing Society in India and Pakistan* (Dacca, 1956).
Lloyd, P. C. *Africa in Social Change* (Harmondsworth, Penguin Books, 1967).
Myrdal, Gunnar. *Asian Drama* (New York, Pantheon Books, 1968).
Schurmann, Franz. *Ideology and Organization in Communist China* (rev. edn., Berkeley, University of California Press, 1970).
Frank, A. Gunder. *Capitalism and Underdevelopment in Latin America* (New York, Monthly Review Press, 1967).
Veliz, Claudio. *Obstacles to Change in Latin America* (London, Oxford University Press, 1965).

Part VI

APPLIED SOCIOLOGY

Chapter 19

SOCIOLOGY, SOCIAL POLICY AND SOCIAL PLANNING

The formation of social policy

Sociology was conceived by many nineteenth century thinkers as providing the theoretical foundation for a comprehensive applied science. Such views were especially prevalent in France, where the idea of a natural science of society was transmitted from the *encyclopédistes* through Saint-Simon and others to Comte, who believed that sociology, as the summation of positive science, could establish universal laws of social behaviour by reference to which all disputes about social policy might be settled. The 'anarchy of opinions' would then come to an end in social matters as it had done in the case of natural phenomena. Durkheim, although he rejected much of Comte's sociology, was nonetheless a positivist in the Comtean tradition, who wished to establish an applied moral and political science on the basis of a theoretical science of society.

Marxism, as it has actually developed in the practice of Communist parties, has much in common with Comte's positivism. There is the same appeal to historical laws, and the same claim that an elite instructed in the science of society can resolve definitively all practical social problems and guide mankind infallibly along the path of social progress.

At the present time few sociologists (and even fewer social anthropologists) would regard their discipline as a developed theoretical science capable of being applied to social affairs in the way that theoretical physics or chemistry is applied to the control and transformation of the material world. They are deterred, in the first place, by the fact that after more than a century of sociological and anthropological thought and research few, if any, important sociological laws have been discovered. In this situation the question of applying general laws can hardly arise. They may also doubt the value of the analogy between natural science and sociology in respect of their practical application; for it is inconsistent with our ordinary notions of ourselves as individuals, and with our respect for other human

315

beings, to think of sociological principles being directly applied by 'experts' to the shaping of social life, as physical principles are applied to the construction of roads and bridges. For this reason, and for others to be discussed later, there can be no 'social engineering'. This is not to deny, however, that sociology can be systematically applied in a number of different ways, and at different levels. In this chapter I shall first consider in general terms the contribution of sociology to social policy, and then examine its role in social planning; in the following chapter I shall discuss some of the sociological research which has aimed to provide solutions to specific social problems.

The first important contribution to be noted is that of *descriptive sociology*, which has provided much exact and reliable information upon those matters of social policy with which politicians, administrators and social reformers have to deal. Among the earliest sociological researches, especially in Britain, were the surveys (including official surveys) of poverty and other problems of urban life, carried out from the mid-nineteenth century onwards.[1] Such surveys, and particularly those of Booth[2] and Rowntree[3] at the end of the nineteenth century, showed in detailed and rigorous fashion the extent and nature of poverty in an industrial society. Moreover, Booth and Rowntree were able to indicate some of the causes of extreme poverty; the lack of regular employment, and the accidents or illnesses suffered by wage-earners. These and similar researches undoubtedly influenced social policy, and a later study by Rowntree and Lavers (in 1951)[4] showed how the policies of the Welfare State (in particular, the maintenance of full employment and more adequate national provision for the emergencies of illness or accident) had almost entirely eradicated primary poverty.[5] Studies of this kind do not, of course, have quite the same importance in underdeveloped countries, where poverty is a very general condition, the alleviation

[1] There were earlier surveys (*see* p. 18 above), but their number grew rapidly during the latter part of the nineteenth century.

[2] Charles Booth, *Life and Labour of the People in London* (17 vols., London, 1902).

[3] B. Seebohm Rowntree, *Poverty: A Study of Town Life* (London, 1901).

[4] B. Seebohm Rowntree and G. R. Lavers, *Poverty and the Welfare State* (London, 1951).

[5] In the 1960s there has been a rediscovery of poverty in the affluent Western societies. These studies—for example, Michael Harrington, *The Other America* (New York, 1963), and B. Abel-Smith and P. Townsend, *The Poor and the Poorest* (London, 1965)—do not deal so much with 'primary poverty' as with the condition of social groups which have fallen behind the general level of well-being. The questions they pose concern the extent of economic inequality in the industrial societies.

of which depends, in the first place, upon increasing the total national product by industrialization and the improvement of agriculture. Nevertheless, in these countries too, there exist conditions of exceptional poverty which need to be investigated; in India, for example, the situation of particularly depressed castes and tribes,[1] of refugees,[2] and of beggars.[3]

In a number of other spheres sociologists have provided essential data for the formulation of rational policies. Population studies have not only furnished exact information on population size, fertility and mortality, but have also indicated some of the social factors responsible for demographic changes. Studies of social mobility, which reveal the extent and forms of mobility in different societies and show the connections between mobility and such factors as family size, educational opportunity, and occupational structure, provide essential knowledge for educational reforms, besides contributing to the discussion of more remote ends of social policy.

But although the growth of sociological research since 1945 has added greatly to the body of precise information on social matters, our knowledge is still deficient. As D. V. Glass pointed out some years ago,[4] important social policies are still formulated and implemented without any research into the ends or means proposed (as in the case of the New Towns policy, which established in an arbitrary fashion the size and density of the towns); and major social services are administered without much attempt to discover whether they meet the needs for which they were designed, or meet them in the most effective way, or indeed whether the needs themselves have not changed in a rapidly changing society. Similarly, R. M. Titmuss has drawn attention to the lack of social research which would 'identify and measure the more subtle and complex needs of today and their distribution among the different sections of the population'.[5]

In few countries has social (as distinct from economic) research yet become firmly established as a normal part of government and administration; although it has gained a more prominent place in the last decade. In India comprehensive planning has favoured

[1] On these there is much information in the Reports of the Commission for Scheduled Castes and Tribes.

[2] *See* R. N. Saksena, *Refugees* (Bombay, 1961).

[3] *See* M. S. Gore *et al.*, *The Beggar Problem in Metropolitan Delhi* (Delhi, 1959).

[4] D. V. Glass, 'The Application of Social Research', *British Journal of Sociology* I (1), 1950.

[5] R. M. Titmuss, 'Social Administration in a Changing Society', in *Essays on the 'Welfare State'* (London, 1958).

social research. The Research Programmes Committee of the Planning Commission has played an important part in encouraging and sponsoring research in a number of fields which directly concern government planning;[1] and the Programme Evaluation Organization has made a promising beginning with studies of the effectiveness of Plan projects in several areas. The Central Institute of Study and Research in Community Development, which was established in 1958, has so far been largely concerned with the training (in a broad sense) of key personnel in the community development programme, through 'orientation courses' of four weeks' duration, and systematic research has only recently been planned. The work of the Institute is potentially of great importance, for not only does it deal with a vast and crucial area of Indian social life (village development and agricultural production), but it brings together legislators, administrators, research workers and those engaged in the programme activities for wide-ranging discussions of problems, policies and achievements.

Some similar developments may be noted in Western Europe. In Britain, for example, the Government Social Survey has made numerous surveys on behalf of Government departments; the Department of Scientific and Industrial Research has sponsored much social research into industrial problems, and the Home Office has established a research section to conduct studies in the field of crime and delinquency. The Danish Parliament established, in 1958, a National Institute of Applied Social Research to undertake a continuing programme of research on problems of social welfare. But much remains to be done if the social sciences are to make their full contribution to administration in modern societies. It would be useful, in the first place, to review the range of social data at present collected by governments, and to examine the use which is made of such information and the influence which it has upon social policy. This would provide a starting point for an extension and rationalization of government social research, which should ultimately lead to the establishment of national research centres. The Danish National Institute of Applied Social Research is the first instance of such a centre, but the Research Programmes Committee in India, the Government Social Survey in Britain, and similar agencies in other countries might well develop in this direc-

[1] *See Research for Planning 1955–59.* The research projects approved cover the following fields: Land reform, agricultural economics, savings, investment and employment, small-scale and cottage industries, urban surveys, social welfare, public administration, macro-economic aspects of development, decentralization and regional development, resources for development, benefits of irrigation projects.

318

tion. The functions of such a national research centre would be to conduct specific enquiries needed for policy making, but also to collect on a regular basis information on the major aspects of social life, and to publish it in the form of surveys of social conditions. Most governments now collect basic economic information which they publish regularly along with general surveys of the economic situation. But it is essential, in a modern society, to extend this service to a much wider range of social questions, which should include crime and delinquency, dependency, housing, health, education, levels of living and family budgets.[1]

The role of the sociologist in policy-making also needs to be reconsidered. This is no doubt only one aspect of a more general problem concerning the relation between 'scientists' and 'administrators' in the multifarious activities of modern governments; but the position of sociologists (and of other social scientists, with the possible exception of economists) has been exceptionally disadvantageous. Those engaged in social research for government seem to have had, as a rule, little say in defining the scope of particular enquiries, or in relating the results to policy decisions. Their discoveries are simply used by those who have the main responsibility for policy-making and administration, and the latter may be as much influenced by the 'conventional wisdom' as by the results of systematic enquiry, if they know nothing about the background and further implications of the research.

The contribution of descriptive sociology should not be limited to providing information which is useful at the stage of formulating and introducing new social policies; it is equally important in evaluating the operation and achievements of these policies. But there are still few evaluation studies of this practical kind.[2] The Programme Evaluation Organization in India has made a modest beginning with such studies, but so far as I know it has no counter-

[1] The value of such data-collection and survey is shown by the United Nations *Report on the World Social Situation* (1961), but such international surveys would be easier to make and more comprehensive if there were more adequate publication of national data.

[2] The recent report by a Danish Government Committee on the Establishment of an Institute for Applied Social Research observes; 'It is the view of the Committee that the legislature, the administration and the general public has not at hand sufficient material for analysis of the functioning of the social services, their effects on the individual and other effects, *inter alia* on the national economy. The material at hand does not give sufficient basis for judgment whether the means used, in money or in organization, are put to the best possible use and are invested in the most important points . . .'. Quoted in Henning Friis, 'The Application of Sociology to Social Welfare Planning and Administration', *Transactions of the Fourth World Congress of Sociology*, II, pp. 65–6.

part elsewhere. A few research institutes in other countries have, in recent years, undertaken enquiries in this field (for example, of the reactions of individuals and families to re-housing in new areas, and of 'consumer' attitudes towards the health services and education), but these are isolated instances, and there are few signs of any systematic programme of research. It is surprising that even in those countries which have embarked upon radical planned changes in economic and social life, little advantage has been taken of the opportunities for social experiments which would allow a more exact evaluation of different policies. The use of experiment in social affairs is, of course, limited both by its cost and by the obligation to respect the interests and rights of those individuals who would be affected by it; nevertheless, there are many spheres in which small scale experiments could be made without great expense and without harming individuals. The community development programme in India, for example, would undoubtedly be helped by evaluation studies based upon experiments with different types of administration, different sequences and forms of innovation, and different means of communicating ideas, in development projects. Similarly, there is scope for experiment in town planning, in the provision of education, in policies concerned with juvenile delinquency, in the treatment of offenders, and many other spheres. Indeed, some policies in these various fields are often referred to as 'experimental', but in fact thay almost always lack the essential feature of an experiment, namely the systematic comparative examination of the results produced by different courses of action.

I have already noted, especially in connection with the surveys of poverty, that the sociologist has not always been restricted to the precise description of a social phenomenon, but has on occasion been able to indicate its probable cause or causes. In much of the applied research of recent years the intention has clearly been to go beyond description, useful though that may be, to discover causes and to propose specific solutions. This aim is less ambitious than that of the early sociologists, who thought in terms of a body of theory which could be applied everywhere and infallibly in the solution of practical problems; for all that is now claimed is that some particular and limited causal relationship may be discovered by sociological analysis. Nevertheless, the results even of these more modest endeavours are open to question; it has proved difficult in the extreme to establish causal connections between social phenomena in the complex situations with which social policy has to deal. The difficulties can best be seen in relation to particular problems and I shall, therefore, defer an examination of them to the next chapter.

320

It is not only those who may be called professional sociologists who make use of sociological knowledge. The social sciences generally have begun to influence social policy in another way, through their part in the education and training of those who are concerned with the formation and execution of policy. Sociology now has an important place in the training of social workers, and it is becoming recognized as a useful element in the training of industrial managers, personnel officers, teachers, and public officials responsible for the administration of social welfare services or of publicly owned enterprises. The value of sociology for these occupations is not, in most cases, that it provides the individual with sociological principles which he can apply directly to the solution of practical problems. It is rather that the individual who has acquired a broad general knowledge of different types of social structure and culture, has studied in greater detail the structure and history of his own society, and has learned something of the methods by which data on social matters may be collected and evaluated, is thereby enabled to form more reasonable judgments and to make wiser decisions in dealing with the social problems which he confronts.

The increasing use of sociological research, and the desire of sociologists themselves to make a practical contribution, raises questions not only about how sociology *can* be applied but also about how it *ought* to be applied. In the preceding discussion I have taken for granted that the social policies are themselves good or desirable. But this assumption conceals a host of problems, which should be briefly noticed, though they cannot be fully examined here. For my part I consider that sociologists in the practical application of their discipline are necessarily committed to the improvement of social life, or, in the language of earlier writers, to social progress; and that this commitment prescribes for them certain fields of enquiry while proscribing others. An analogy may be drawn between applied sociology and medicine, as has been done by A. W. Gouldner in an informative essay.[1] Gouldner distinguishes between an 'engineering' approach and a 'clinical' approach in applied sociology. The former is characterized by the fact that the client's formulation of the problem is accepted by the sociologist, who is concerned only to discover efficient ways of solving the problem; the latter by the fact that the sociologist (like a doctor) is not restricted, and is generally recognized as not being restricted, to the client's own definition of the problem, which he may indeed regard as one of the symptoms of the underlying difficulties. In recommending the clinical approach Gouldner

[1] A. W. Gouldner, 'Explorations in Applied Social Science', *Social Problems*, III (3), 1956.

is concerned partly with the effectiveness of the method, and partly with the values which should guide applied sociological research. He does not, however, consider an important difference between medicine and applied sociology. The practice of medicine is founded upon the doctor's commitment, which is in the great majority of cases precise and unambiguous, to maintain health and combat disease. Applied sociology is not based upon any such precise commitment, for 'social welfare' or 'improvement' may be matters, not of direct and unanimous appraisal but of conflicting judgments. The terms 'social health' and 'social disease' (or 'social pathology') which are sometimes employed are ambiguous and largely inappropriate; for it is not so much the health of a society (defined perhaps as its ability to survive) as the quality of its life which is a matter of concern, and on the other side, what are taken to be diseases may subsequently be seen as unavoidable disorders accompanying healthy growth,[1] or more commonly, they may be differently evaluated by different observers.[2]

I do not wish to conclude either that there is no intelligible standard by which applied sociology may be guided, or, in the opposite sense, that it is the business of sociologists themselves to declare authoritatively what constitutes welfare or progress. It should be recognized, in the first place, that very often the difficulties I have mentioned do not arise; there is near unanimity on the definition of many social evils. But where there is no agreement sociologists can make a practical contribution by clarifying the points of controversy, by assessing in the light of facts the received interpretations of a social problem, and especially, by viewing alternative social policies in relation to the structure of society as a whole. In the latter case, sociologists necessarily produce ideas and data which become materials for social criticism, because they are obliged to take account of the influence upon social policy of established inequalities in the wealth and power of different social groups, and to describe how, in turn, different kinds of policy work to the advantage or disadvantage of particular groups. The exclusive insistence, in much

[1] Cf. E. Raab and G. J. Selznick, *Major Social Problems* (New York, 1959); 'It is apparent that the absence of social problems is not necessarily the mark of an ideal society. . . . Nor does the intensification of social problems necessarily signify that a society is moving in a backward direction. The contrary may indeed be true. A society which permits no change and no progress tends almost by definition to have fewer social problems. In a changing society . . . some social problems may be symptoms of a change for the better' (p. 5).

[2] For example, the greater sexual freedom which has come to exist in many Western societies in recent times is regarded by some as a symptom of social decline, by others as a manifestation of a more rational and tolerant social order.

recent sociology, upon a rigorous 'scientific method', has tended to create an unduly conservative outlook; the existing framework of society is accepted as given, because it is too complex for scientific study, and all the resources of a truly 'scientific' sociology are then marshalled for the investigation of small-scale problems carefully isolated from the wider social structure. It is desirable, therefore, to emphasize once more as the distinctive feature of sociological thought that it attempts to grasp every specific problem in its whole social context, and to conceive of alternative social policies which affect the entire life of society.[1]

The critical function of sociology can best be seen in its least tangible, but perhaps most important, influence upon social life; that which is exerted through the instruction of the general public, or at least, of that part of the public which has a sustained interest in social and political affairs. Here sociology provides a framework of concepts, and a basis of exact knowledge, for the intelligent discussion of political issues.[2] The usefulness of sociological enquiry from this point of view is admirably illustrated in R. M. Titmuss, *Essays on 'The Welfare State'*. In an essay on 'The social division of welfare', Titmuss explains some of the assumptions which have guided recent thinking about social policy in Britain, and particularly the assumption about the extent to which social welfare plans have been implemented and about the effects which the social services have had in redistributing income from rich to poor. His analysis

[1] This view of the practical uses of sociology which was, perhaps, rather eccentric in the late 1950s has now become almost fashionable. Many, especially of the younger sociologists, now assert the need for 'criticism', and deplore the extent to which sociological research is tied to established institutions, either of business or of government. This welcome change of outlook does not, however, resolve all the problems. A sociologist should not accept existing society as unalterable, but neither should he set himself up as an inspired prophet. Some of the issues raised in this chapter are carefully examined in the context of recent developments, in Piet Thoenes, *The Elite in the Welfare State* (London, 1966), and in Irving L. Horowitz (ed.), *The Rise and Fall of Project Camelot* (Cambridge, Mass., 1967).

[2] Cf. Gunnar Myrdal, 'The Relation between Social Theory and Social Policy', *British Journal of Sociology*, IV (3), September 1953: 'My thesis is that, while there was little participation on the part of social scientists in the actual technical preparation of legislation and still less in administering induced social changes, their influence was nevertheless very considerable, and that this influence was due in the main to their exposition and propagation of certain general thoughts and theories' (p. 215). Myrdal mentions among those who influenced social policy in this way, Malthus, Ricardo, Marx, Darwin, Spencer and Keynes. Later, as he says, social scientists (and particularly economists) were drawn increasingly into administration; but he would not deny that the propagation of 'general thoughts and theories' is still one of the important ways in which they influence policy making.

reveals the many difficulties which confront the modern search for equality, and the ever-renewed sources of social inequality and dependency. He is sceptical about the egalitarian effects of the social services, since the latter are too narrowly defined, and other types of collective provision which tend to increase inequality, are left out of account. The three distinct systems of social service (social, fiscal and occupational) taken together are, he says, 'enlarging and consolidating the areas of social inequality'. In other essays in this volume Titmuss examines the age structure of the population in relation to some popular views on the burden of dependency involved by the ageing population, and some of the problems created by the conflicting standards of behaviour expected of the working class father in the family and in industry. These essays contribute directly to informed public discussion of major issues of social policy, and they are firmly grounded in modern sociological thought and research.

Another example may be taken from the field of educational policy. Recent discussions of education, in Britain and in other industrial societies, have had to take account of sociological investigations which show the connections between social class origin, educational opportunity, and achievement. In so far as public policy, or the policies of particular social groups, aim to establish equality of opportunity in education, and to extend and improve the national system of education, they must use the results of sociological research which show the sources and mechanisms of inequality, and the factors in poor scholastic performance, and which suggest ways of eradicating them.

In this critical function, and as a source of deliberate social change, sociology has differed greatly from social anthropology which, as an applied discipline, has been closely connected with colonial administration. Evans-Pritchard has observed that '. . . if it is the policy of a colonial government to administer a people through their chiefs it is useful to know who are the chiefs and what are their functions and authority and privileges and obligations. Also, if it is intended to administer a people according to their own laws and customs one has first to discover what these are'.[1] Firth has emphasized the help which anthropological studies can give to the administrator who has to deal with the problems of social change resulting both from internal development and from contact with the colonial power.[2] Both writers acknowledge that anthropology could only be applied within the limits of the colonial government's settled policy.

[1] E. E. Evans-Pritchard, *Social Anthropology* (London, 1951), pp. 109–10.
[2] Raymond Firth, *Human Types* (rev. edn., London, 1956), Chapter VII.

It is also worthy of note that social anthropologists and sociologists have stood in quite different relations to their subject matter. The members of primitive societies do not, on the whole, read the anthropological monographs which are written about them; whereas some members of industrial societies do read the works of sociologists. Thus, a sociologist often arouses, and expects to arouse, some response in some of the people he is studying and this influences his study. It is the ending of the colonial system, much more than the fact that so many tribal societies have now been exhaustively studied, which accounts for the present transformation of social anthropological studies, and for the *rapprochement* between social anthroplogy and sociology in respect of theoretical work and applied research.

The practical influence of sociology may be wider than has yet been indicated. Beyond the public which has a sustained interest in social affairs, a larger section of the population may be led, through the media of mass communication and the educational system, to consider some social problems in a more dispassionate and objective way, and to recognize and reject irrational opinions and policies. It seems likely, for instance, that sociology has contributed in this way to the diminution of race prejudice and discrimination,[1] and to the more humane consideration and treatment of criminals.

In these various ways—by the exact description of social problems, the search for causes and remedies, the training of social workers and administrators, the education of public opinion, the revelation of inequalities and privileges and of the political controversies to which they give rise—sociology has in fact contributed to the realization of the ideal which was formulated, in a manner too dogmatic and naïve, by its founders: the participation of all men in the control of their social conditions of life, a self-directing humanity. In the following section I shall briefly consider one of the most distinctive modern manifestations of such self-direction, namely, the process of planned social change.

Social planning

There is some degree of social planning in all modern societies. Up to the present it has been conceived almost exclusively in terms of the control and direction of economic activity, and sociologists have had a small part in the process. This is the case even where, as in the underdeveloped countries, the sociological aspects of economic

[1] At the very least it has provided a basis for educational publications directed against race prejudice; *see*, for example, the UNESCO series of booklets on race.

325

growth are particularly apparent. But the relevance and importance of sociological knowledge is becoming more widely recognized; there is now a considerable literature on the social aspects of economic growth, and those economists who have been most concerned with problems of economic development have drawn extensively upon sociological theory and research.[1]

In India, the research programmes of the Planning Commission have recognized that sociologists can make an important contribution to economic planning. But sociologists have not yet availed themselves fully of the opportunities, either in carrying out detailed studies, or in examining on a broader scale the aims and difficulties of Indian planning. One notable exception is C. S. Dube's admirable study of village development,[2] the conclusions of which deserve to be quoted at some length:

'While planners and administrators must share the primary responsibility for the formulation and implementation of the rural development projects, the social scientist can give them incalculable help in the areas of social organization, human relations, culture and values touched by the plans. . . . The sociological studies recommended above should present integrated analyses of culture and social organization in representative village communities in the different linguistic and cultural regions of India. Besides portraying the social organization, attitudes, and values of the people, they should lay special emphasis on trends and motivations in change. An attempt should be made to discover the groups that function as agents and carriers of change in the village communities. The problem of selectivity in the acceptance of ideas and innovations offered by the outside world also deserves a fuller investigation. Another area of research, having great theoretical and practical possibilities, is that of leadership and decision-making in the village communities. In this connection problems of group dynamics and factionalism will also have to be critically analysed. Traditional forms of co-operative activities in village India also merit a serious study.

'The crucial significance of communication in a programme of rural community development has been brought out earlier in this study. This field holds out challenging possibilities of social science research. It is necessary to discover the existing channels of communication in rural India, and to assess the role and function of different categories of agents of communication. It is equally essential to find out what types of themes and appeals work effectively in these communities. The response of the different segments of village

[1] See especially the writings of Gunnar Myrdal and W. Arthur Lewis.
[2] S. C. Dube, *India's Changing Villages*.

population to different modes of communication needs to be evaluated carefully. The role of school education in the communication and diffusion of modern ideas also deserves to be assessed. Empirical research in this field is very necessary for developing an adequate and effective communication programme.

'Another field in which the social scientist could make a useful contribution to the rural community development movement in India is that of preparing empirical case-studies of specific projects and field situations. The importance of such studies as an instructional aid in the training programmes of village welfare workers has been emphasized time and again by this study. A good case-study, which analyses the complex attitudes, beliefs and values, and assesses clearly the role of each in a specific field situation, is one of the most satisfactory methods of introducing the prospective extension agent to the problems and complexities of his task. The hypotheses emerging from these studies could be an invaluable aid to those engaged in evaluating the programme. They could be further tested in the wider and more general evaluation studies for making meaningful formulations and generalizations . . .

'The participation of the social scientist in training programmes for development workers could also be encouraged. He can make a distinct contribution to the success of these programmes by offering his concrete, practical insights into the village situation and thus correct the somewhat unbalanced view of the village scene held generally by the administrator.

'Finally, another important area for the fruitful collaboration between planners and social scientists is that of planning, analysis, and evaluation of 'Pilot Projects' to be undertaken on an experimental basis. A carefully designed pre-project survey by the social scientist should precede the formulation and initiation of the Pilot Projects.'

In a number of other fields connected with social planning in India, the value of sociology has been increasingly recognized, both in research and in the training of personnel. Sociology occupies an important place in the training of social workers,[1] and it is becoming more important in the training of Village Level Workers and other officials responsible for the rural development programme.

The wider aspects of the application of sociology in planned social change have not been much discussed.[2] It is evident that the sociologist has so far been primarily an external critic, pointing to

[1] *See* M. S. Gore, *Sociology and Social Work* (Bombay, 1962).
[2] But *see* the Symposium on Sociological Aspects of Social Planning, by Gunnar Myrdal, S. Ossowski and Charles Bettelheim, in *Transactions of the Fourth World Congress of Sociology*, Vol. II (London, 1959).

some of the reasons for failures and difficulties in the achievement of economic plans. This is well brought out in S. Ossowski's discussion of inadequacies and mistakes in post-war planning in Poland.[1] In India, the economic problem is fundamental at the present time, and sociologists can make their most useful practical contribution by enquiring into the influence of traditional culture, caste and family upon agricultural and industrial production, and by studying the most effective means of attaining the desired ends in specific planning projects. They have a duty also, to investigate the economic and social effects of rapid population growth, and the means of controlling such growth. It goes without saying that in these researches sociologists will need to collaborate with other social scientists—economists, demographers, anthropologists and psychologists—and that they will have to devote attention to the ways in which this collaboration can best be made effective, for the idea has often remained a pious wish or has been made real only as a juxtaposition of quite independent studies.

It should not be supposed that the sociologist will always be confined to the role of critic, important though this is, or that he will restrict his studies to the social factors in planned economic growth. Industrialization and economic growth give rise to new social problems, of crime, mental illness, boredom and dissatisfaction in industrial work, the uses of leisure, which he is called upon to study. Social planning itself creates problems of bureaucracy and centralization, of the relationship between the individual and the community, between public authorities and voluntary associations, which have become major subjects of sociological enquiry.[2]

There is, finally, a more general connection between sociology and social planning. The growth of sociology has been in part responsible for extending the notion of planning from the idea of a planned economy to that of a planned society. At the same time, sociology has responded to developments in political thought and practice. As Nehru wrote, in connection with the discussions in the National Planning Committee in 1938: 'The original idea behind the Planning Committee had been to further industrialization . . . But no planning could possibly ignore agriculture, which was the

[1] *See* previous note.
[2] The difficulties of planning have become more apparent during the past decade. *See*, for example, the discussion by Gunnar Myrdal in *Asian Drama*, Vol. II, Part IV, with reference to South Asian countries; and also some recent studies of the economic failures in Cuba, by Leo Huberman and Paul Sweezy, *Socialism in Cuba* (New York, 1969), and by René Dumont, *Cuba est-il socialiste?* (Paris, 1970). Much useful discussion of the problems of planning has taken place in Yugoslavia, in Poland, and in Czechoslovakia during 1967–68.

mainstay of the people; equally important were the social services. So one thing led to another and it was impossible to isolate anything or to progress in one direction without corresponding progress in another. The more we thought of this planning business the vaster it grew in its sweep and range till it seemed to embrace almost every activity. That did not mean we intended regulating and regimenting everything, but we had to keep almost everything in view even in deciding about one particular sector of the plan.'[1] It is part of the business of the sociologist to aid in 'keeping everything in view', by defining clearly, and describing precisely, the interconnections among social phenomena of different kinds, thus making planning more effective and helping to avoid unintended and undesired consequences. While not necessarily a critic, he also provides the means of criticism. In both respects, he serves an end to which both sociology and planning have been historically committed: the growth of human freedom and rationality.

[1] Jawaharlal Nehru, *The Discovery of India*, p. 402.

Chapter 20

SOCIAL PROBLEMS

Although there is a variety of ways in which sociology may be applied, as I have endeavoured to show in the previous chapter, it is plain that many sociologists, and most of those who are engaged in practical social work, think of applied sociology pre-eminently in terms of its capacity to provide (or at least to suggest) remedies for particular social evils. The attempt has rarely been made, however, to show exactly how sociological principles, concepts or data have been used, or might be used, in a direct way to solve practical problems.[1] The actual state of affairs may be illustrated from the experience of the International Sociological Association in undertaking a systematic review of the application of sociological knowledge in a number of different fields.[2] The authors of the principal papers found so few instances of the direct and successful application of sociology to the different problems with which they dealt that they had to confine themselves for the most part to reviewing current research or reflection upon methodological questions.

But even if it is impossible to point, as yet, to any problems solved with conspicuous success by means of sociological reasoning or research, it is still useful to consider what has been accomplished on a modest scale, and what may be expected and hoped for if socio-

[1] It is worthy of note that despite much talk of an applied science there are very few books or journals which deal at all thoroughly with applied sociology. A journal actually entitled *Applied Sociology* enjoyed a brief existence in the USA from 1921–27. At the present time the most useful and interesting journals in this field are *Social Problems* (published by the Society for the Study of Social Problems), and *Trans-action* (published since 1964) which has responded to the new mood of the 1960s by taking up in a serious critical fashion the study of a wide range of social and political issues. Among the few books which even attempt to discuss social problems in a systematic relation with sociological theory and research, two are particularly valuable: E. Raab and G. J. Selznick, *Major Social Problems* (2nd edn., New York, 1964); and Robert K. Merton and Robert A. Nisbet (eds.), *Contemporary Social Problems* (2nd edn., New York, 1966).

[2] *See Transactions of the Fourth World Congress of Sociology* (London, 1959), Vol. II.

logical studies are intelligently developed. Let us begin by examining what constitutes a social problem. Raab and Selznick say that this is 'a problem in human relationships which seriously threatens society itself or impedes the *important* aspirations of many people.'[1] They go on to say, about the first aspect: 'A social problem exists when organized society's ability to order relationships among people seems to be failing; when its institutions are faltering, its laws are being flouted, the transmission of its values from one generation to the next is breaking down, the framework of expectations is being shaken. The widespread contemporary concern with juvenile delinquency, for example, is only partly that delinquency is the doorway to crime or is a threat to personal safety and property. It is also a fear that society is failing to transmit positive social values to its youth . . . It is seen, in other words, as a breakdown in society itself.'[2] On the other hand, Barbara Wootton, in her *Social Science and Social Pathology*,[3] defines more narrowly what she terms 'social pathology': it includes 'all those actions in the prevention of which public money is spent, or the doers of which are punished or otherwise dealt with at the public expense'. Her intention is to define the field of study as sharply as possible, and to avoid the difficulties which arrive from divergent subjective ideas of what are to be regarded as 'social problems'. But this definition restricts the field unduly, in that it refers only to actions, and not to situations, and includes only such actions as attract the attention of the state at a particular time. Thus it excludes from consideration many important situations and kinds of behaviour which are very widely regarded as constituting social problems; e.g. poverty, some types or degrees of industrial conflict, and in modern times, war. I shall, therefore, adopt here the broader definition proposed by Raab and Selznick.

Among the great array of problems thus defined there are two—crime and delinquency, and industrial relations—which have been investigated with exceptional thoroughness; and the research carried out in these fields reveals very clearly both the difficulties and the potentialities of sociology as an applied science. Crime and delinquency have perhaps attracted more public attention than any other problem in the industrial countries in recent years, partly because of the continued increase in their incidence, partly because other problems (such as poverty) seemed to have declined in importance. An examination of the achievements of sociological research in this sphere is greatly helped by the work of Barbara Wootton, already

[1] *Op. cit.*, p. 4.   [2] *Op. cit.*, p. 6.   [3] London, 1959.

331

SOCIOLOGY

mentioned, which provides a very comprehensive review and analysis of recent work. Wootton selects twenty-one major investigations for consideration,[1] and finds that they refer to twelve different factors as being possibly associated with criminality or delinquency: (i) the size of the delinquent's family, (ii) the presence of other criminals in the family, (iii) club membership, (iv) church attendance, (v) employment record, (vi) social status, (vii) poverty, (viii) mother's employment outside the home, (ix) school truancy, (x) broken home, (xi) health, (xii) educational attainment.[2] She shows that none of these factors can be regarded as causes, in any strict sense, and arrives at the general conclusion that 'this collection of studies although chosen for its comparative methodological merit, produces only the most meagre, and dubiously supported, generalizations'.[3] Similar views have been expressed by other investigators; thus John Mack observes that 'the total of possible factors which may be specially connected with delinquency is limited only by the patience of the investigator and by the number of methods extant and professionally favoured at the time of the investigation. It is now generally accepted that all that these comparisons can establish is the fact of correlation, the fact that delinquency is frequently accompanied by defective home discipline and by temperamental instability, and by intellectual disabilities such as backwardness and dullness, and so on'.[4]

It is now widely held that the main positive contribution of research in this field has been to show that many popular explanations of crime and delinquency are untenable. As Barbara Wootton observes:

'Up till now the chief effect of precise investigations into questions of social pathology has been to undermine the credibility of virtually all the current myths. Solid evidence that irreligion, or lack of interest in boy's clubs, or life in the squalor of a problem family or a mother's absence at work have the corrupting effects that they are said to have, or that the younger one embarks on a career of crime, the longer one is likely to stick to it, or that the delinquencies of the young are "all the fault of the parents", or that problem families repeat themselves generation after generation—solid evidence

[1] On grounds of methodological soundness.
[2] *Op. cit.*, Chapter III, pp. 81–135.
[3] *Op. cit.*, p. 134.
[4] John Mack, 'Juvenile Delinquency Research: A Criticism', *Sociological Review* 3 (47), July 1955, quoted by Gordon Rose, 'Trends in the Development of Criminology in Britain', *British Journal of Sociology*, IX (1), March 1958.

for any of this is conspicuously lacking; and any evidence that can be found has a way of falling to pieces after closer inspection.'[1]

Similarly, Hermann Mannheim writes, in the course of a short survey of American criminology: 'It was not only laborious, it was also courageous and unpopular to prove that it was in fact not the immigrant but the American-born white who was largely responsible for the high crime rate; that American society rather than the Negro had to bear the blame for much of Negro crime . . . And, lastly, it may have required more than just ordinary courage to show, as the late Edwin H. Sutherland did that some of the most powerful American business enterprises were in fact "habitual criminals" . . .'[2]

Such findings are useful, both in restraining public authorities from inappropriate remedial action, and over a longer period in influencing public opinion, but they can hardly be said to provide a firm basis for practical measures to deal directly with the problems. Among workers in the field who are trying to enhance the practical value of their studies, two principal lines of thought may be distinguished at the present time. There are those who argue that students of crime and delinquency have so far only mapped out in a very general way the main areas of social life which produce delinquency, and that the next stage will be to distinguish different types of delinquency and to seek the specific causes of each type.[3] This view implicitly re-states Durkheim's rule that every social fact has a single cause, and that where a phenomenon appears to have several causes this is an indication that we are dealing, not with a single phenomenon, but with several distinct phenomena, each one of which has its own specific cause.[4] But the rule is only re-stated, without considering its difficulties and without showing how it might actually be applied in the study of crime and delinquency. The difficulties have long been recognized in connection with Durkheim's

[1] *Op. cit.*, p. 326.

[2] Hermann Mannheim, 'American Criminology: Impressions of a European Criminologist', *British Journal of Sociology*, V (4), December 1954.

[3] See Gordon Rose, 'Trends in the Development of Criminology in Britain', *British Journal of Sociology* IX (1), March 1958, p. 62.

[4] See *The Rules of Sociological Method*, Ch. VI. Durkheim in fact gives as examples of phenomena which appear to have several causes, suicide and crime; and he argues 'if suicide depends upon more than one cause, this is because there are in reality several types of suicide. And it is the same with crime'. The application of the rule 'one effect—one cause' is shown in great detail in Durkheim's study of suicide.

own study of suicide; first, that there is something arbitrary in his distinction between different types of suicide,[1] and secondly, that the causal connections which he establishes are by no means as solid or convincing as might be wished. Most sociologists today would be more inclined to accept J. S. Mill's contention that social phenomena depend upon a 'complication of causes' than Durkheim's criticism of it; and the investigator of a social problem may feel that he would be helped more by some kind of vector theory than by a theory which involves a one-to-one relationship between a phenomenon and its cause. Unfortunately, although much social analysis is couched in terms of 'factors', 'forces' and 'pressures', which are alleged to produce a particular happening or condition,[2] there has been little progress in measuring the various acting forces with precision, in order to make prediction possible. Moreover, the forces or factors involved may be so numerous and heterogeneous that their interconnections can never be properly disentangled.

The second line of thought, recognizing these difficulties of causal explanation, proposes a different approach. It is well formulated by Barbara Wootton, in a passage which deserves to be quoted at length:

'Much of the research reviewed in these pages is inspired by the hope that the connections between various manifestations of social pathology and other specific phenomena may prove to be a cause-and-effect relationship; and that the elimination of causes will result in a cure. It cannot, however, be said that this type of enquiry has been very successful. The generalizations that have been reached are shaky; few of them are supported by the work of any considerable numbers of investigators; and even in those that do recur, the quantitative variations are apt to be very large. Many of these generalizations, moreover, are quite untenable as causes . . . By contrast, the record of experiments in prediction is much more encouraging, and is also rapidly improving. Yet, as has already been observed, the predictive factors used by some of the most successful enquiries are obviously far removed from 'causes' as we have defined them. The demonstrably reliable findings of the Mannheim and Wilkins enquiry,[3] which shows that previous

[1] That is to say, the distinction seems to be determined not by observable differences in the phenomena under examination, but by some pre-conception of the possible causes.

[2] For example, the notion of 'cross-pressures' influencing the individual's political allegiance.

[3] H. Mannheim and L. T. Wilkins, *Prediction Methods in Relation to Borstal Training* (London, 1955).

334

experience of an approved school or of probation, together with frequent changes of job, augur badly for an offender's post-Borstal record can hardly be interpreted to imply that the abolition of approved schools and of the probation system, or the enactment of a law forbidding employees to discharge themselves would improve the outlook. And, although it is true that the factors used by the Gluecks[1] in their predictive tables (such as inconsistent discipline in the home) could more credibly be regarded as causes of delinquency, the validation of these is still awaited.

'The moral seems to be that it is in their role as the handmaidens of practical decision that the social sciences can shine most brightly. Prediction may be a less ambitious goal than causation but it is certainly more often within the reach of our present capacities and techniques. Though still unable to say much about the why or wherefore of any given social events, we may yet be in a position to indicate which of a limited range of decisions is most likely to produce required results; and the reason for this is just the fact that the range of possible alternatives is so closely limited. The factors for instance, which throw light upon the relative success of alternative methods of dealing with particular types of offenders are much more manageable than are the multifarious observations necessary to establish why people commit the crimes that they do.[2]

Other social scientists have come to similar conclusions. Sargant Florence makes a distinction between 'applied science' and 'operational research'. He writes, 'When a science . . . is called applied it seems to assume that a body of general theory, principles or doctrine has been built up by 'pure' science . . . which is fairly certain. It is then only a question of applying the general theory by deduction to a particular case . . . Operational research, on the other hand, does not necessarily assume any theory or principle to be certain or reliable and deduce from it. The official definition of operational research as 'the use of the scientific method to provide executives with an analytical and objective basis for decisions' (First Report of the Committee on Industrial Productivity, 1949, p. 17, Cmd. 7665) clearly stresses method rather than doctrine.'[3] And L. T. Wilkins, who co-operated with H. Mannheim in the prediction

[1] S. Glueck and E. Glueck, 500 *Criminal Careers* (New York, 1930).

[2] *Op. cit.*, pp. 323–35.

[3] P. Sargant Florence, 'Patterns in Recent Social Research', *British Journal of Sociology*, I (3), September 1950.

study on Borstal training, has advocated an extension of prediction methods in operational research.[1]

It is unnecessary to choose between these two approaches in the sence of excluding one of them entirely; for research can well be pursued along both lines. But in considering their relative importance in the whole strategy of research, two further points need to be made. In the first place, operational research is *not* applied sociology. It is a procedure which appears to depend upon commonsense or practical wisdom, rather than upon any specialized sociological knowledge or sociological mode of thought. Its connection with sociology consists chiefly in the use of techniques of enquiry derived from sociology, and of statistical methods which have been largely employed in sociological research.[2] By all appearances it could well proceed in the absence of any sociological (or psychological) theories or descriptions. For in this case it is not, as Barbara Wootton claims, the *social sciences* which 'shine most brightly' as handmaidens of practical decision; it is only certain *techniques of investigation* which do so, while the social sciences (as bodies of theory and description) play little part. Even in the matter of practical guidance the contribution of operational research, at least in the form of prediction studies, is not quite so promising as has been claimed. For the ability to predict success or failure in a course of action does not always imply the ability to solve the social problem to which the action relates. The study of Borstal training, which Wootton particularly cites, is a case in point; for the social problem is constituted by the 'failures', and the successful prediction of failure provides no clue to its causes or, consequently, to the remedies.

Secondly, in the attempts to formulate causal explanations of crime and delinquency, extremely heterogeneous factors have been juxtaposed or associated. Thus, explanations may be offered which refer to a range of individual psychological characteristics (temperamental instability, mental backwardness, etc.), and to a variety of social circumstances (divorce, parental discipline, criminal environment, etc.). In this particular field of study the general problem of the relation between psychological and sociological explanation is very acutely posed; but there are few works in which the problem is even clearly formulated, and none, to my knowledge, in which a plausible theoretical model encompassing both sets of data has been constructed.

[1] 'Some Developments in Prediction Methodology in Applied Social Research', *British Journal of Sociology*, VI (4), December 1955.

[2] It will be shown later that 'applied sociology' is often conceived in terms of a method of investigation.

The second field of applied research which I propose to consider is that concerned with industrial relations. The principal aim of research has been to discover the causes of industrial conflict, in the individual enterprise and on a national scale, and of other impediments to high productivity such as high rates of absenteeism, illness, labour turnover, etc. The same difficulties of causal explanation as in the study of crime and delinquency have been encountered, but there are additional difficulties which arise from the ramifications of industrial problems.

Before considering these questions I should like to take up the point made earlier, that the principal contribution of sociology is generally seen as consisting in skilled investigation. This is very apparent in industrial sociology. The authors of a recent survey of sociological reseach in industry[1] observe that 'it is often the case no doubt, that to the firm which calls upon his services, the sociologist appears less as the possessor of a particular kind of knowledge which is capable of application, than as a person trained in the use of certain tools (interview etc.), or indeed as one who has the advantage of appearing neutral to everyone concerned'.[2] This is very close to the view advanced by Barbara Wootton according to which the contribution of the social sciences to practical life is found in a scientific attitude and in the use of certain techniques of enquiry. This conception is very prevalent. In the sphere of medical research, for example, it has been claimed that 'Many physicians approach sociologists, if they approach them at all, as I did, thinking of them as people with technical skill in interviewing and questionnaire construction'.[3] But a contribution of this kind can only be regarded as a very minor part of applied sociology, more especially since these techniques of investigation are common to all the social sciences. Clémens and Evrard recognize this, and while admitting that there are few instances of the successful application of sociological principles to solve specific problems, they make a case for applied industrial sociology in respect of its contributions to improved organization. The contributions are of two kinds: first, studies of the social structure of business enterprises which make possible improvements in the authority system, the system of communication, the constitution of working groups, etc.; and secondly, training

---

1 René Clémens et Pol Evrard, 'La connaissance sociologique et son application à la vie industrielle', *Transactions of the Fourth World Congress of Sociology*, II, pp. 1–12.

2 *Op. cit.*, p. 3.

3 Mary E. W. Goss and George G. Reader, 'Collaboration Between Sociologist and Physician', *Social Problems*, 4 (1), July 1956.

courses for managers and supervisors. Clémens and Evrard regard the latter as the more successful development: 'It is in the sphere of training for those who hold positions of authority in industrial life, that the most serious attempts to apply sociology in a systematic way are to be found. The ever more numerous training courses for managers, technicians and supervisors, or for trade union officials, constitute an important factor of social change in modern industry . . .'[1] But this favourable assessment would not receive universal assent. As William F. Whyte observes: 'To be sure, important changes in human relations have taken place in industry, but there is little reason to believe that they have come to any considerable degree through research and through training that has been based upon such research. There have been hundreds of thousands of human relations training programmes in industry. To my knowledge, only two of them have been subjected to the sort of solid research evaluation which would measure their effectiveness. In one case, an International Harvester programme, workers' reactions to the foreman who had been trained were slightly more negative after the programme than they had been before. In the other case, Detroit Edison, there was a loss registered in one division which was more than counterbalanced by a gain in another'.[2]

The inadequacy of applied research in industry is due, Whyte suggests, to the failure to take account of the wider social context of industrial problems. Similar criticisms have been expressed more fully by Georges Friedmann, who has made an outstanding contribution to the study of problems of industrial work in relation to different types of economic and political system.[3] Some of the principal difficulties of applied research in this field arise, then, from the fact that in investigating the causes which have produced a practical problem, we encounter a network of interrelated factors which extends far beyond the limited situation in which the problem itself occurs. The study of obstacles to greater productivity, of resistances to technological change, of ways to increase the efficiency of management, or of the prevention, limitation or peaceful settlement of industrial conflicts, leads inescapably to the consideration of much broader questions concerning the property system, social stratification and occupational mobility, family structure, ideologies and cul-

---

[1] *Op. cit.*, p. 3.

[2] William F. Whyte, 'Problems of Industrial Sociology', *Social Problems*, 4 (2), October 1956, pp. 148–60. The article as a whole sets out admirably the problems of applied research and makes some excellent suggestions for more effective studies.

[3] See especially his *Industrial Society* (Glencoe, 1956).

tural traditions.[1] Furthermore, when this intricate web of circumstances is explored it may disclose not only the 'complication of causes' in the production of a specific social problem but also interconnections among social problems such that the solution of one problem may require the prior solution of others, or that the solution of one may impede the solution of another or even create a new problem.

In seeking to apply his knowledge, therefore, the sociologist has to contend with two kinds of difficulty: first, that of establishing precise causal connections, and secondly that of delimiting a problem without doing violence to its relations with important general features of the social structure and culture. The consideration of these difficulties leads, I believe, to a recognition that there are different types of social problem, varying both in their importance and in the extent to which they can be resolved. Some social evils are, in the strict sense, ineradicable. Durkheim argued that crime is a 'normal phenomenon' in human societies which could only be eliminated by social controls and sanctions so repressive as to destroy many other cherished values; and further, that each type of society has its own 'normal rate' of crime. The high rates of crime and delinquency in modern industrial societies may therefore be the counterpart of the relative laxity of social control in these societies. Similarly, high divorce rates may be explained, in part, as the outcome of the pursuit by individuals of other ends—personal freedom, an ideal romantic love—which are in themselves good. In the under-developed countries, many social problems have to be seen at the present time as concomitants of the disturbing processes of industrialization and urbanization. It should not be concluded that in these cases social research is futile. Sociological studies may encourage a more realistic approach to such problems, and in particular restrain those immoderate moral denunciations which often exacerbate the difficulties. They may also, at the least, suggest means of diminishing the evils without harm to other social values, and more effective ways of dealing with their consequences. Thus, modern criminology is concerned to discover ways of reducing crime and delinquency, and more successful treatment methods for offenders. Studies of marriage and divorce aim to provide knowledge of the factors predisposing to marital conflict and divorce, which can be used, in

[1] Although such ramifications are particularly evident in the case of industrial problems, they can also be traced in other areas. The rates of crime and delinquency in a society may be influenced by a dominant way of life which emphasizes very strongly economic competition and individual achievement judged in terms of wealth, or by inadequate provision for public education.

marriage counselling and in other ways, to reduce the incidence of such problems or to find solutions to them without breaking up the family.

There are other social problems which can be solved or which constitute such a grave danger to human society that a radical solution has to be sought. In the first category comes the problem of poverty in economically developed societies. Here, the solution requires from the sociologist primarily an investigatiom of the facts, in the course of which one or a small number of factors may be revealed as the cause of the problem. In other cases, the causation may be much more difficult to discover, but sociological research may at least eliminate some popular but erroneous beliefs about the causes, and provide a sufficient description of the problem situation to be a useful guide in dealing with it. Experiments with different remedial measures and careful evaluation of the results, as well as operational research, may make it possible to resolve or control the problem even though we remain largely ignorant of its causes. In the second category, of supremely dangerous problems, the pre-eminent example, in this age of nuclear weapons, is war. No one is likely to suppose that sociologists alone, or sociologists and psychologists together, will provide a universally acclaimed solution. Equally however, no-one will contest that a war fought with nuclear weapons would be an immense and probably final disaster for mankind, that sociological and psychological research can at least contribute significantly to understanding how crucial situations of tension and conflict develop and so help responsible leaders to avoid them, and that sociologists ought consequently to make an exceptional effort to investigate the problems of war and peace, and to disseminate their findings as widely as possible. It is sad that so few have undertaken the task,[1] even though it is so formidable, so exposed to the incursion of political strife, and so little assimilable to the neat research designs of much current enquiry.

This last example brings out very clearly a feature which I have tried to bring into relief at various places in this and the preceding chapter. The sociologist can rarely solve a problem directly or propose a policy which is exactly appropriate, even when he is sure what is wrong; for every solution of a problem and act of policy is a political decision. It expresses the resolve of a social group to maintain or to change a particular way of life, and to act in accordance with certain social ideals. The sociologist may supply information, elucidate the context of problems, point to causes or conditions, indicate the advantages and costs of alternative courses of action; in

[1] But *see* the discussion in Chapter 12 above.

the longer term, his studies may, and I believe do, influence social ideals themselves. But in the last resort political decisions rest upon judgment, or political wisdom, and upon interests. To suppose otherwise, and to assign sociologists the role of philosopher kings in modern dress, is to revert to the delusions of Comte's positive politics.

It is perhaps well, at the close of this book, to dispel any possible misconception that the value of sociology culminates in its various applications to practical life which we have just been considering. To the question, "What is the use of sociology?" I would answer rather that it widens our sympathies and imagination, and increases our understanding of other human beings outside the narrow circle of our own time, locality, and social situation, than that it simply provides means to discover the remedies for present ills. But these purposes are not radically antithetical and they are perhaps of equal practical significance in the long run. Most sociologists would feel that in all spheres of their work they are making some contribution to the improvement of social life, by extending knowledge and engendering ideas which will help men to struggle more effectively for the kind of society they desire.

Notes on Reading for Part VI

Although the literature of applied sociology is still not abundant it has grown substantially during the past decade with the development of new social movements of criticism and protest. See:

Douglas, Jack D. (ed.) *The Impact of Sociology* (New York, Appleton-Century-Crofts, 1970).
The essays collected here deal in diverse ways with the relation of sociology to social practice.

Lynd, Robert S. *Knowledge for What*? (Princeton, Princeton University Press, 1939).
An earlier book which still provides an excellent guide to the uses and misuses of the social sciences.

A number of books and journals are concerned with a wide range of social problems:

Raab, E., and Selznick, G. J. *Major Social Problems* (2nd edn., New York, Harper and Row, 1964).
In spite of its textbook presentation, deals quite thoroughly with some important issues and includes a section on world social problems.

Merton, Robert K., and Nisbet, Robert A. (eds.). *Contemporary Social Problems* (2nd edn., New York, Harcourt, Brace and World, 1966).
Marks an advance in one important respect by including a chapter on war as a social problem.

See also R. M. Titmuss, *Essays on the 'Welfare State'* (London, Allen & Unwin, 1958); *Transactions of the Fourth World Congress of Sociology* (London, International Sociological Association, 1959), Vol. II; and the journals *Social Problems* and *Trans-action* mentioned in the text.

One of the most useful surveys of applied social research is Barbara Wootton, *Social Science and Social Pathology* (London, Allen & Unwin, 1959). There is still relatively little writing on the sociological aspects of planning, but the symposium on social planning in *Transactions of the Fourth World Congress of Sociology*, Vol. II, provides a useful introduction and the subject may be pursued further in the works by Gunnar Myrdal and others referred to in the text (page 328 above).

INDEX